Routing and Switching Essentials v6
Labs & Study Guide

Allan Johnson

Cisco Networking Academy

Cisco Press

800 East 96th Street

Indianapolis, Indiana 46240 USA

Routing and Switching Essentials v6 Labs & Study Guide

Allan Johnson
Cisco Networking Academy

Published by:
Cisco Press
800 East 96th Street
Indianapolis, IN 46240 USA

Printed in the United States of America

2   17

Library of Congress Control Number: 2016953794

ISBN-13: 978-1-58713-426-5
ISBN-10: 1-58713-426-8

Editor-in-Chief
Mark Taub

Product Line Manager
Brett Bartow

Business Operation Manager, Cisco Press
Ronald Fligge

Executive Editor
Mary Beth Ray

Managing Editor
Sandra Schroeder

Development Editor
Ellie Bru

Project Editor
Mandie Frank

Copy Editor
Paula Lowell

Technical Editor
Tony Chen

Editorial Assistant
Vanessa Evans

Designer
Chuti Prasertsith

Composition
Tricia Bronkella

Proofreader
Debbie Williams

Trademark Acknowledgments

All terms mentioned in this book that are known to be trademarks or service marks have been appropriately capitalized. Cisco Press or Cisco Systems, Inc., cannot attest to the accuracy of this information. Use of a term in this book should not be regarded as affecting the validity of any trademark or service mark.

Warning and Disclaimer

This book is designed to provide information about networking. Every effort has been made to make this book as complete and as accurate as possible, but no warranty or fitness is implied.

The information is provided on an "as is" basis. The author, Cisco Press, and Cisco Systems, Inc. shall have neither liability nor responsibility to any person or entity with respect to any loss or damages arising from the information contained in this book or from the use of the discs or programs that may accompany it.

The opinions expressed in this book belong to the author and are not necessarily those of Cisco Systems, Inc.

Special Sales

For government sales inquiries, please contact governmentsales@pearsoned.com.

For questions about sales outside the U.S., please contact intlcs@pearson.com.

Feedback Information

At Cisco Press, our goal is to create in-depth technical books of the highest quality and value. Each book is crafted with care and precision, undergoing rigorous development that involves the unique expertise of members from the professional technical community.

Readers' feedback is a natural continuation of this process. If you have any comments regarding how we could improve the quality of this book, or otherwise alter it to better suit your needs, you can contact us through email at feedback@ciscopress.com. Please make sure to include the book title and ISBN in your message.

We greatly appreciate your assistance.

Americas Headquarters	Asia Pacific Headquarters	Europe Headquarters
Cisco Systems, Inc.	Cisco Systems, Inc.	Cisco Systems International BV
170 West Tasman Drive	168 Robinson Road	Haarlerbergpark
San Jose, CA 95134-1706	#28-01 Capital Tower	Haarlerbergweg 13-19
USA	Singapore 068912	1101 CH Amsterdam
www.cisco.com	www.cisco.com	The Netherlands
Tel: 408 526-4000	Tel: +65 6317 7777	www-europe.cisco.com
800 553-NETS (6387)	Fax: +65 6317 7799	Tel: +31 0 800 020 0791
Fax: 408 527-0883		Fax: +31 0 20 357 1100

Cisco has more than 200 offices worldwide. Addresses, phone numbers, and fax numbers are listed on the Cisco Website at **www.cisco.com/go/offices.**

About the Author

Allan Johnson entered the academic world in 1999 after 10 years as a business owner/operator to dedicate his efforts to his passion for teaching. He holds both an MBA and an M.Ed in occupational training and development. He taught a variety of technology courses to high school students and is an adjunct instructor at Del Mar College in Corpus Christi, Texas. Since 2006, Allan has worked full time for Cisco Networking Academy in several roles. He is currently engaged as Curriculum Lead.

About the Technical Reviewer

Tony Chen is a Cisco Certified Academy Instructor (CCAI) and has taught at College of DuPage at Glen Ellyn, Illinois, for more than 15 years. He holds CCNA certification for Routing and Switching. His other certifications include MCSA for Microsoft Server 2012 and CompTIA A+ and Server+. Tony has an understanding wife, Joanne, and two children, Kylie and Ryan.

Dedication

For my wife, Becky. What a year! I couldn't ask for a better partner in life.

Acknowledgments

The Cisco Network Academy authors for the online curriculum and series of Companion Guides take the reader deeper, past the CCENT and CCNA exam topics, with the ultimate goal of not only preparing the student for certification, but also for more advanced college-level technology courses and degrees, as well. Thank you to the entire Curriculum and Assessment Engineering team.

Tony Chen, technical editor, did the arduous review work necessary to make sure that you get a book that is both technically accurate and unambiguous. I am grateful for his conscientious attention to detail.

Mary Beth Rey, executive editor, you amaze me with your ability to juggle multiple projects at once, steering each from beginning to end. I can always count on you to make the tough decisions.

As for development editor, Ellie Bru, her dedication to perfection pays dividends in countless, unseen ways. Thank you again, Ellie, for providing me with much-needed guidance and support. This book could not be a reality without your persistence.

Contents at a Glance

Contents

Command Syntax Conventions

The conventions used to present command syntax in this book are the same conventions used in the IOS Command Reference. The Command Reference describes these conventions as follows:

- **Boldface** indicates commands and keywords that are entered literally as shown. In actual configuration examples and output (not general command syntax), boldface indicates commands that are manually input by the user (such as a **show** command).

- *Italics* indicate arguments for which you supply actual values.

- Vertical bars (|) separate alternative, mutually exclusive elements.

- Square brackets [ ] indicate optional elements.

- Braces { } indicate a required choice.

- Braces within brackets [{ }] indicate a required choice within an optional element.

Introduction

This book supports instructors and students in Cisco Networking Academy, an IT skills and career building program for learning institutions and individuals worldwide. Cisco Networking Academy provides a variety of curricula choices including the very popular CCNA curriculum. It includes four courses oriented around the topics of the Cisco Certified Entry Networking Technician (CCENT) and Cisco Certified Network Associate (CCNA) certifications.

Routing and Switching Essentials v6, Labs & Study Guide is a supplement to your classroom and laboratory experience with the Cisco Networking Academy. To be successful on the exam and achieve your CCENT or CCNA certification, you should do everything in your power to arm yourself with a variety of tools and training materials to support your learning efforts. This *Labs & Study Guide* is just such a collection of tools. Used to its fullest extent, it will help you gain the knowledge as well as practice the skills associated with the content area of the Routing and Switching Essentials v6 course. Specifically, this book will help you work on these main areas:

- Configure and verify static routing and default routing.
- Configure and troubleshoot basic operations of a small switched network.
- Configure and troubleshoot basic operations of routers in a small routed network.
- Configure and troubleshoot VLANs and inter-VLAN routing.
- Configure, monitor, and troubleshoot ACLs for IPv4.
- Configure and verify DHCPv4 and DHCPv6.
- Configure and verify NAT for IPv4.
- Configure and monitor networks using device discovery, management, and maintenance tools.

Labs & Study Guides similar to this one are also available for the other three courses: *Introduction to Networks v6 Labs & Study Guide*; *Scaling Networks v6 Labs & Study Guide*; and *Connecting Networks v6 Labs & Study Guide*.

Goals and Methods

The most important goal of this book is to help you pass the 100-105 Interconnecting Cisco Networking Devices Part 1 (ICND1) exam, which is associated with the Cisco Certified Entry Network Technician (CCENT) certification. Passing the CCENT exam means that you have the knowledge and skills required to manage a small, enterprise network. You can view the detailed exam topics any time at http://learningnetwork.cisco.com. They are divided into five broad categories:

- Network Fundamentals
- LAN Switching Fundamentals
- Routing Fundamentals
- Infrastructure Services
- Infrastructure Maintenance

Each chapter of this book is divided into a Study Guide section followed by a Lab section.

The Study Guide section offers exercises that help you learn the concepts, configurations, and troubleshooting skills crucial to your success as a CCENT or CCNA exam candidate. Each chapter is slightly different and includes some or all of the following types of exercises:

- Vocabulary Matching Exercises
- Concept Questions Exercises
- Skill-Building Activities and Scenarios
- Configuration Scenarios
- Packet Tracer Exercises
- Troubleshooting Scenarios

The Labs & Activities section includes all the online course labs and Packet Tracer activity instructions. If applicable, this section begins with a Command Reference that you will complete to highlight all the commands introduced in the chapter.

Packet Tracer and Companion Website

This book includes the instructions for all the Packet Tracer activities in the online course. You will need to be enrolled in the *Routing and Switching Essentials v6* course to access the Packet Tracer files.

However, there are eight Packet Tracer activities created exclusively for this book. You can access these unique Packet Tracer files at this book's companion website.

To get your copy of Packet Tracer software and the eight unique files for this book, please go to the companion website for instructions. To access this companion website, follow these steps:

1. Go to www.ciscopress.com/register and log in or create a new account.
2. Enter the ISBN: 9781587134265
3. Answer the challenge question as proof of purchase.
4. Click on the Access Bonus Content link in the Registered Products section of your account page to be taken to the page where your downloadable content is available.

Audience for This Book

This book's main audience is anyone taking the Routing and Switching Essentials course of the Cisco Networking Academy curriculum. Many academies use this *Labs & Study Guide* as a required tool in the course, whereas other academies recommend the *Labs & Study Guide* as an additional resource to prepare for class exams and the CCENT certification.

The secondary audiences for this book include people taking CCENT- or CCNA-related classes from professional training organizations. This book can also be used for college- and university-level networking courses, as well as by anyone wanting to gain a detailed understanding of routing. However, the reader should know that the content of this book tightly aligns with the Cisco Networking Academy course. It may not be possible to complete some of the

Study Guide sections and Labs without access to the online course. Fortunately, you can purchase the *Routing and Switching Essentials v6 Companion Guide* (ISBN: 9781587134289).

How This Book Is Organized

Because the content of the *Routing and Switching Essentials v6 Labs & Study Guide* and the online curriculum is sequential, you should work through this *Labs & Study Guide* in order beginning with Chapter 1.

The book covers the major topic headings in the same sequence as the online curriculum. This book has 10 chapters, with the same names as the online course chapters.

- **Chapter 1, "Routing Concepts":** Introduces basic routing concepts including how to complete an initial router configuration and how routers make decisions. Routers use the routing table to determine the next hop for a packet. This chapter explores how the routing table is built with connected, statically learned, and dynamically learned routes.

- **Chapter 2, "Static Routing":** Focuses on the configuration, verification, and troubleshooting of static routes for IPv4 and IPv6, including default routes, floating static routes, and static host routes.

- **Chapter 3, "Dynamic Routing":** Introduces all the important IPv4 and IPv6 dynamic routing protocols. RIPv2 is used to demonstrate basic routing protocol configuration. The chapter concludes with an in-depth analysis of the IPv4 and IPv6 routing tables and the route lookup process

- **Chapter 4, "Switched Networks":** Introduces the concepts of converged networks, hierarchical network design, and the role of switches in the network. Switching operation including frame forwarding, broadcast domains, and collision domains is discussed.

- **Chapter 5, "Switch Configuration":** Focuses on the implementation of a basic switch configuration, verifying the configuration, and troubleshooting the configuration. Switch security is then discussed including configuring secure remote access with SSH and securing switch ports.

- **Chapter 6, "VLANs":** Introduces the concepts of VLANs, including how VLANs segment broadcast domains. VLAN implementation including configuration, verification, and troubleshooting is then covered. The chapter concludes with configuring router-on-a-stick inter-VLAN routing.

- **Chapter 7, "Access Control Lists":** Introduces the concept of using ACLs to filter traffic. Configuration, verification, and troubleshooting of standard IPv4 ACLs are covered. Securing remote access with an ACL is also discussed.

- **Chapter 8, "DHCP":** Dynamically assigning IP addressing to hosts is introduced. The operation of DHCPv4 and DHCPv6 is discussed. The configuration, verification, and troubleshooting of DHCPv4 and DHCPv6 implementations is covered.

- **Chapter 9, "NAT for IPv4":** Translating private IPv4 addresses to another IPv4 address using NAT for IPv4 is introduced. The configuration, verification, and troubleshooting of NAT for IPv4 is covered.

- **Chapter 10, "Device Discovery, Management, and Maintenance":** Introduces the concept of device discovery using CDP and LLDP. Device management topics include NTP and Syslog. The chapter concludes with a discussion of how to manage IOS and configuration files as well as IOS licenses.

CHAPTER 1

Routing Concepts

The router uses its routing table to determine the best path to use to forward a packet. It is the responsibility of the routers to deliver those packets in a timely manner. The effectiveness of internetwork communications depends, to a large degree, on the ability of routers to forward packets in the most efficient way possible. This chapter reviews router configurations, path determination, and routing table analysis.

The Study Guide portion of this chapter uses a combination of matching, fill-in-the-blank, multiple-choice, and open-ended question exercises to test your knowledge and skills of basic router concepts and configuration. The Labs and Activities portion of this chapter includes all the online curriculum labs and Packet Tracer activities to ensure that you have mastered the hands-on skills needed to understand basic IP addressing and router configuration.

As you work through this chapter, use Chapter 1 in *Routing and Switching Essentials v6 Companion Guide* or use the corresponding Chapter 1 in the Routing and Switching Essentials online curriculum for assistance.

Study Guide

Router Initial Configuration

Although there are many devices and technologies collaboratively working together to enable data transfer across networks, the primary device is the router. Stated simply, a router connects one network to another network.

Router Functions

A router is essentially a specialized computer. It requires a CPU and memory to temporarily and permanently store data to execute operating system instructions, such as system initialization, routing functions, and switching functions.

Routers store data using a variety of memory structures:

- _____: Provides temporary storage for various applications and processes, including the running IOS. Contents are lost when powered off.

- _____: Provides permanent storage for boot instructions, basic diagnostic software, and a limited IOS in case the router cannot load the full-featured IOS.

- _____: Provides permanent storage for the startup configuration file.

- _____: Provides permanent storage for the IOS and other system-related files.

In Table 1-1, indicate the memory type in the first column and whether the memory is volatile or nonvolatile in the second column.

Table 1-1   Types of Router Memory

Memory	Volatile or Nonvolatile?	Stores
NVRAM		Startup configuration file
ROM		Boot instructions
		Basic diagnostic software
		Limited IOS
Flash		IOS
		Other system files
RAM		Running IOS
		Running configuration file
		IP routing and ARP table
		Packet buffer

Each _____ that a router connects to usually requires a separate interface. These interfaces are used to connect a combination of both _____ and

_____ . _____ are commonly _____ networks that contain devices such as PCs, printers, and servers. _____ are used to connect networks over a large _____ area and are commonly used to connect a LAN to the _____ network.

What are the two primary functions of a router?

_____

_____

The router uses its _____ to determine the best path to forward the packet. When a match is found, the router _____ the IP packet into the data link frame of the outgoing or exit interface, and the packet is then forwarded toward its destination.

It is possible for a router to receive a packet _____ in one type of data link frame, such as an Ethernet frame, and to forward the packet out an interface that uses a different type of data link frame.

Routers use _____ routes and _____ protocols to learn about remote networks and build their routing tables.

Briefly describe the math analogy used to compare process switching, fast switching, and Cisco Express Forwarding (CEF).

_____

_____

_____

In Figure 1-1, draw the path that each packet will take through a router that is using process switching.

Figure 1-1   Process Switching Diagram

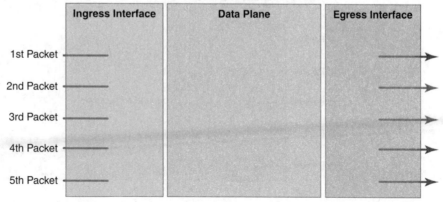
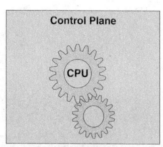

In Figure 1-2, draw the path that each packet will take through a router that is using fast switching.

Figure 1-2   Fast Switching Diagram

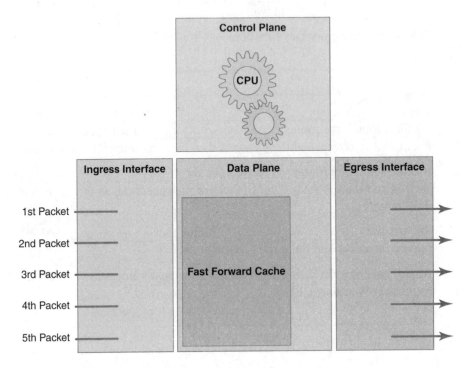

In Figure 1-3, draw the path that each packet will take through a router that is using CEF.

Figure 1-3   Cisco Express Forwarding Diagram

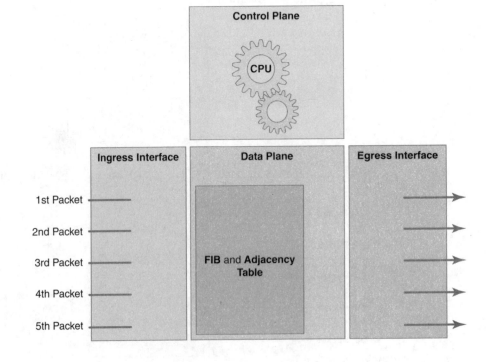

External Router Features

Figure 1-4 shows the backplane of a Cisco 1941 router. Match the letter in the figure with the backplane port or slot name.

Figure 1-4   Identify Router Components

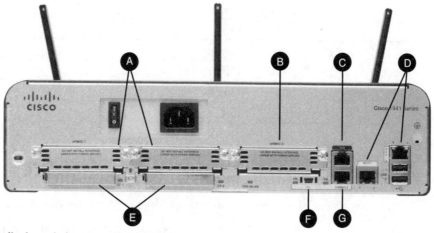

_____   4-GB flashcard slots

_____   Console RJ-45 port

_____   eWHIC 0 slot

_____   Console USB mini-B port

_____   LAN interfaces

_____   Double-wide eHWIC slots

_____   AUX port

In Figure 1-5, the LED lights are marked for each port type on the 1941 router. Complete Table 1-2 describing the meaning of each of the LED lights.

Figure 1-5   Zoom in View of Cisco 1941 LED Lights

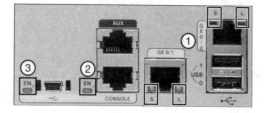

Table 1-2   LED Light Codes and Descriptions

No.	Port	LED	Code/Color	Description
1	GE0/0 and GE0/1	S (Speed)	1 blink + pause	
			2 blink + pause	
			3 blink + pause	
		L (Link)	Green	
			Off	
2	Console	EN	Green	
			Off	
3	USB	EN	Green	
			Off	

Topology and Addressing Documentation

What three pieces of addressing information does a device need to access the network?

- _____ : Identifies a unique host on a local network

- _____ : Identifies with which network subnet the host can communicate

- _____ : Identifies the router to send a packet to when the destination is not on the same local network subnet

The topology in Figure 1-6 is properly labeled with device names, connections, and addressing. Document the addressing scheme for Figure 1-6 in Table 1-3.

Figure 1-6   Topology Diagram

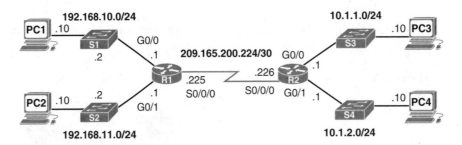

Table 1-3   Addressing Table for Figure 1-6

Device	Interface	IP Address	Subnet Mask	Default Gateway
R1	G0/0			N/A
	G0/1			N/A
	S0/0/0			N/A
R2	G0/0			N/A
	G0/1			N/A
	S0/0/0			N/A
S1	VLAN 1			
S2	VLAN 1			
S4	VLAN 1			

Device	Interface	IP Address	Subnet Mask	Default Gateway
S4	VLAN 1			
PC1	NIC			
PC2	NIC			
PC3	NIC			
PC4	NIC			

Record the commands necessary to configure S1 with appropriate IP addressing according to your documentation in Table 1-3.

_____

_____

_____

_____

_____

_____

_____

Configure and Verify Dual-Stack IPv4 and IPv6 Addressing

In this activity, you document the configuration for a router that is running both IPv4 and IPv6 (dual stack). Figure 1-7 shows the topology, and Table 1-4 documents the addressing scheme.

Figure 1-7   Dual-Stack Topology

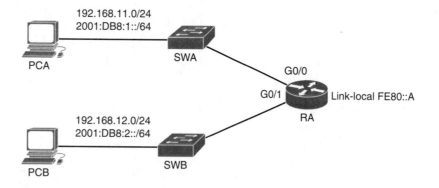

Table 1-4   Addressing Table for Figure 1-7

Device	Interface	IPv6 Address/Prefix		Default Gateway
		IP Address	Subnet Mask	
RA	G0/0	192.168.11.1	255.255.255.0	N/A
		2001:DB8:1::1/64		N/A
	G0/1	192.168.12.1	255.255.255.0	N/A
		2001:DB8:2::1/64		N/A
	Link local	FE80::A		N/A

Device	Interface	IPv6 Address/Prefix		Default Gateway
		IP Address	Subnet Mask	
PCA	NIC	192.168.11.10	255.255.255.0	192.168.11.1
		2001:DB8:1::3/64		FE80::A
PCA	NIC	192.168.12.10	255.255.255.0	192.168.12.1
		2001:DB8:2::3/64		FE80::A

In the space provided, document the script for configuring RA, including the following:

- Hostname
- Passwords
- Banner
- Interface addressing and descriptions

Packet Tracer Exercise 1-1: Dual Stack Addressing

Packet Tracer
☐ Activity

Now you are ready to use Packet Tracer to apply your documented configuration. Download and open the file LSG02-0101.pka found at the companion website for this book. Refer to the Introduction of this book for specifics on accessing files.

Note: The following instructions are also contained within the Packet Tracer exercise.

In this Packet Tracer activity, you will configure the RA router with basic configurations and dual stack addressing. You will then verify that PCA and PCB can ping each other using IPv4 and IPv6 addresses. Use the addressing table and the commands you documented in the section, "Configure and Verify Dual-Stack IPv4 and IPv6 Addressing."

Requirements

Configure RA with the following settings:

- The name of the router is **RA.**
- The privileged EXEC password is **class.**
- The line password is **cisco.**
- The message-of-the-day is **Authorized Access Only.**
- Configure and activate the **RA** interfaces according to Table 1-4.
- Save the configurations.
- Verify IPv4 and IPv6 connectivity between PCA and PCB.

Your completion percentage should be 100%. All the connectivity tests should show a status of "successful." If not, click **Check Results** to see which required components are not yet completed.

Verify Connectivity of Directly Connected Networks

After completing the Packet Tracer exercise, you can verify the configuration with a number of commands. Record the command that generated the following output:

```
RA# _____

Interface             IP-Address      OK? Method Status                Protocol
GigabitEthernet0/0    192.168.11.1    YES manual up                    up
GigabitEthernet0/1    192.168.12.1    YES manual up                    up
Serial0/0/0           unassigned      YES unset  administratively down down
Serial0/0/1           unassigned      YES unset  administratively down down
Vlan1                 unassigned      YES unset  administratively down down
```

```
RA# _____

Codes: L-local, C-connected, S-static, R-RIP, M-mobile, B-BGP
       D-EIGRP, EX-EIGRP external, O-OSPF, IA-OSPF inter area
       N1-OSPF NSSA external type 1, N2-OSPF NSSA external type 2
       E1-OSPF external type 1, E2-OSPF external type 2, E-EGP
```

```
           i-IS-IS, L1-IS-IS level-1, L2-IS-IS level-2, ia-IS-IS inter area
           *-candidate default, U-per-user static route, o-ODR
           P-periodic downloaded static route


Gateway of last resort is not set


      192.168.11.0/24 is variably subnetted, 2 subnets, 2 masks
C        192.168.11.0/24 is directly connected, GigabitEthernet0/0
L        192.168.11.1/32 is directly connected, GigabitEthernet0/0
      192.168.12.0/24 is variably subnetted, 2 subnets, 2 masks
C        192.168.12.0/24 is directly connected, GigabitEthernet0/1
L        192.168.12.1/32 is directly connected, GigabitEthernet0/1
```

RA# _____

```
GigabitEthernet0/0 is up, line protocol is up (connected)
  Hardware is CN Gigabit Ethernet, address is 0006.2a7b.b501 (bia 0006.2a7b.b501)
  Internet address is 192.168.11.1/24
  MTU 1500 bytes, BW 1000000 Kbit, DLY 10 usec,
     reliability 255/255, txload 1/255, rxload 1/255
  Encapsulation ARPA, loopback not set
  Keepalive set (10 sec)
  Full-duplex, 100Mbps, media type is RJ45
<output omitted>
```

RA# _____

```
GigabitEthernet0/0 is up, line protocol is up (connected)
  Internet address is 192.168.11.1/24
  Broadcast address is 255.255.255.255
  Address determined by setup command
  MTU is 1500 bytes
  Helper address is not set
  Directed broadcast forwarding is disabled
  Outgoing access list is not set
  Inbound  access list is not set
  Proxy ARP is enabled
  Security level is default
  Split horizon is enabled
  ICMP redirects are always sent
  ICMP unreachables are always sent
  ICMP mask replies are never sent
  IP fast switching is disabled
<output omitted>
```

```
RA# _____

GigabitEthernet0/0              [up/up]

    FE80::A

    2001:DB8:1::1

GigabitEthernet0/1              [up/up]

    FE80::A

    2001:DB8:2::1

Serial0/0/0                     [administratively down/down]

Serial0/0/1                     [administratively down/down]

Vlan1                           [administratively down/down]
```

```
RA# _____

GigabitEthernet0/0 is up, line protocol is up

  IPv6 is enabled, link-local address is FE80::A

  No Virtual link-local address(es):

  Global unicast address(es):

    2001:DB8:1::1, subnet is 2001:DB8:1::/64

  Joined group address(es):

    FF02::1

    FF02::2

    FF02::1:FF00:1

    FF02::1:FF00:A

  MTU is 1500 bytes

  ICMP error messages limited to one every 100 milliseconds

  ICMP redirects are enabled

  ICMP unreachables are sent

  ND DAD is enabled, number of DAD attempts: 1

  ND reachable time is 30000 milliseconds

  ND advertised reachable time is 0 milliseconds

  ND advertised retransmit interval is 0 milliseconds

  ND router advertisements are sent every 200 seconds

  ND router advertisements live for 1800 seconds

  ND advertised default router preference is Medium

  Hosts use stateless autoconfig for addresses.
```

```
RA# _____

IPv6 Routing Table-5 entries

Codes: C-Connected, L-Local, S-Static, R-RIP, B-BGP

        U-Per-user Static route, M-MIPv6

        I1-ISIS L1, I2-ISIS L2, IA-ISIS interarea, IS-ISIS summary

        O-OSPF intra, OI-OSPF inter, OE1-OSPF ext 1, OE2-OSPF ext 2

        ON1-OSPF NSSA ext 1, ON2-OSPF NSSA ext 2

        D-EIGRP, EX-EIGRP external
```

```
C    2001:DB8:1::/64 [0/0]
       via ::, GigabitEthernet0/0
L    2001:DB8:1::1/128 [0/0]
       via ::, GigabitEthernet0/0
C    2001:DB8:2::/64 [0/0]
       via ::, GigabitEthernet0/1
L    2001:DB8:2::1/128 [0/0]
       via ::, GigabitEthernet0/1
L    FF00::/8 [0/0]
       via ::, Null0
RA#
```

Routing Decisions

The activities in this section review the specifics of the two primary functions of a router: path determination and switching packets.

Switching Packets Between Networks

Refer to Figure 1-8 to answer the following questions.

Figure 1-8   Mapping Layer 2 and Layer 3 Addresses

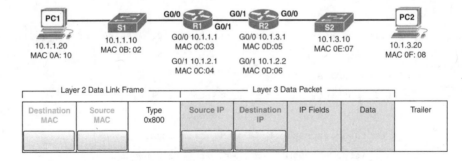

PC1 sends a ping to PC2. What are the Layer 2 and Layer 3 addresses that PC1 will use to encapsulate the packet and frame before sending it to R1?

- Destination MAC: _____

- Source MAC: _____

- Source IP: _____

- Destination IP: _____

R1 receives the ping from PC1. What are the Layer 2 and Layer 3 addresses that R1 will use to encapsulate the packet and frame before sending it to R2?

- Destination MAC: _____

- Source MAC: _____

- Source IP: _____

- Destination IP: _____

R2 receives the ping from R1. What are the Layer 2 and Layer 3 addresses that R2 will use to encapsulate the packet and frame before sending it to PC2?

- Destination MAC: _____

- Source MAC: _____

- Source IP: _____

- Destination IP: _____

PC2 receives the ping from R2. What are the Layer 2 and Layer 3 addresses that PC2 will use to encapsulate the reply packet and frame before sending it to R2?

- Destination MAC: _____

- Source MAC: _____

- Source IP: _____

- Destination IP: _____

What role do the switches have in relation to addressing in this scenario?

_____

_____

_____

What do you notice about the Layer 2 addressing?

_____

What do you notice about the Layer 3 addressing?

_____

Path Determination

Complete the flowchart in Figure 1-9 to indicate the path determination decisions that a router makes based on the destination address and the information in the routing table.

Figure 1-9   Path Determination Flowchart

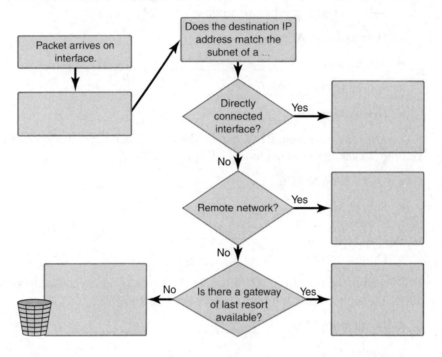

Match the path determination decision on the left with the scenario on the right. Some decisions may be used more than once.

Decision

   a. Drop the packet and send an ICMP message back to the source IP address.

   b. Encapsulate the frame and forward it out of the exit interface to the next hop.

   c. Check the ARP cache and forward to the host on the local subnet.

Scenario

_____ Your router has received a packet destined for an IP address of a local subnet. Your router has a recorded routing table entry for this subnet, and it is on a directly connected interface.

_____ Your router received a packet destined for an IP address on a remote network. Your router has a routing table entry for the remote network.

_____ Your router received a packet destined for an IP address on another network. The destination IP address is not on a local network and does not match anything in your routing table. There is no gateway of last resort available.

_____ Your router received a packet destined for an IP address on another network. The destination IP address is not on a local network and does not match anything in your routing table, but there is a gateway of last resort.

Administrative Distance Exercise

A router can learn about a route from multiple sources. If the type of source for two or more routes is different, the router must use administrative distance to help make the path determination decision.

Complete Table 1-5 for the default administrative distances used by a Cisco router.

Table 1-5   Default Administrative Distances

Route Source	AD
Connected	
EIGRP summary route	5
External BGP	20
Internal EIGRP	
IGRP	100
	110
IS-IS	115
External EIGRP	170
Internal BGP	200
Unknown	255

Router Operation

The routing table of a router stores information about directly connected routes learned when an interface is configured with an IP address and is activated. The routing table also stores information about remote networks connected to other routers. These routes are learned either from static configurations or dynamically through a configured routing protocol.

Analyze the Routing Table

Use the **show ip route** command to display the routing table for IPv4 routes, as shown in Example 1-1.

Example 1-1   IPv4 Routing Table

```
R1# show ip route
<output omitted>
Gateway of last resort is not set
     10.0.0.0/8 is variably subnetted, 2 subnets, 2 masks
D       10.1.1.0/24 [90/2170112] via 209.165.200.226, 00:00:05, Serial0/0/0
D       10.1.2.0/24 [90/2170112] via 209.165.200.226, 00:00:05, Serial0/0/0
     192.168.10.0/24 is variably subnetted, 2 subnets, 3 masks
C       192.168.10.0/24 is directly connected, GigabitEthernet0/0
L       192.168.10.1/32 is directly connected, GigabitEthernet0/0
     192.168.11.0/24 is variably subnetted, 2 subnets, 3 masks
```

```
C        192.168.11.0/24 is directly connected, GigabitEthernet0/1
L        192.168.11.1/32 is directly connected, GigabitEthernet0/1
      209.165.200.0/24 is variably subnetted, 2 subnets, 3 masks
C        209.165.200.224/30 is directly connected, Serial0/0/0
L        209.165.200.225/32 is directly connected, Serial0/0/0
R1#
```

The sources of the routing table entries are identified by a code. The code identifies how the route was learned. What does each of the following codes mean?

- L: _____

- C: _____

- S: _____

- D: _____

- O: _____

Refer to the topology in Figure 1-10. R1 has learned the route shown in the route entry below the topology. Label each part of the route entry with the letter shown in the legend.

Figure 1-10 Identify Parts of a Route Table Entry

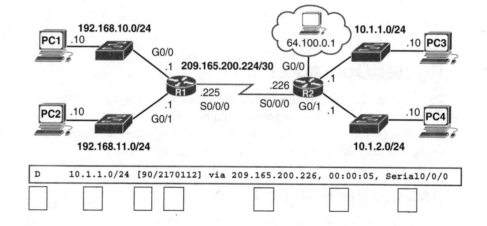

```
D     10.1.1.0/24 [90/2170112] via 209.165.200.226, 00:00:05, Serial0/0/0
```

Legend

A	Identifies the destination network
B	Identifies the amount of elapsed time since the network was discovered
C	Identifies the outgoing interface on the router to reach the destination network
D	Identifies the next hop IP address to reach the remote network
E	Identifies how the network was learned by the router
F	Identifies the administrative distance (trustworthiness) of the route source
G	Identifies the metric to reach the remote network

Directly Connected, Static, and Dynamic Routes

What three things must happen before the interface state on a router is considered up/up and added to the IPv4 routing table?

_____

_____

_____

In the following exercise, you configure three directly connected routers.

Enter the router prompt and commands to configure the GigabitEthernet 0/0 interface on R2 with the IP address 10.1.1.1 and subnet mask 255.255.255.0. Describe the link as Link to LAN 3 and activate the interface.

_____

_____

_____

_____

```
*Aug 11 15:08:34.139: %LINK-3-UPDOWN: Interface GigabitEthernet0/0, changed state to down

*Aug 11 15:08:36.951: %LINK-3-UPDOWN: Interface GigabitEthernet0/0, changed state to up

*Aug 11 15:08:37.951: %LINEPROTO-5-UPDOWN: Line protocol on Interface GigabitEthernet0/0,
changed state to up
```

Enter the router prompt and commands to configure the GigabitEthernet 0/1 interface on R2 with the IP address 10.1.2.1 and subnet mask 255.255.255.0. Describe the link as Link to LAN 4 and activate the interface.

_____

_____

_____

_____

```
*Aug 11 15:09:56.915: %LINK-3-UPDOWN: Interface GigabitEthernet0/1, changed state to down

*Aug 11 15:09:59.951: %LINK-3-UPDOWN: Interface GigabitEthernet0/1, changed state to up

*Aug 11 15:10:00.951: %LINEPROTO-5-UPDOWN: Line protocol on Interface GigabitEthernet0/1,
changed state to up
```

Enter the router prompt and commands to configure the Serial 0/0/0 interface with the IP address 209.165.200.226 and subnet mask 255.255.255.252. Describe the link as Link to R1 and activate the interface.

_____

_____

_____

```
*Aug 11 15:11:18.451: %LINK-3-UPDOWN: Interface Serial0/0/0, changed state to up

*Aug 11 15:11:19.451: %LINEPROTO-5-UPDOWN: Line protocol on Interface Serial0/0/0, changed
state to up
```

What are the two common types of static routes?

_____

_____

What is the command syntax to configure the two types of IPv4 static routes?

_____

_____

Enter the router prompt and commands to configure R2 with an IPv4 static route to the 192.168.10.0/24 network using the Serial 0/0/0 exit interface.

_____

Enter the router prompt and commands to configure R2 with an IPv4 default route using the Serial 0/0/0 exit interface.

_____

What is the command syntax to configure the two types of IPv6 static routes?

_____

_____

Enter the router prompt and commands to configure R2 with an IPv6 static route to the 2001:DB8:1:1::/64 network using the Serial 0/0/0 exit interface.

_____

Enter the router prompt and commands to configure R2 with an IPv6 default route using the Serial 0/0/0 exit interface.

_____

What are the four main routing protocols that are the focus of the CCNA certifications?

_____

Labs and Activities

Command Reference

In Table 1-6, record the command, including the correct router or switch prompt, that fits the description. Fill in any blanks with the appropriate missing information.

Table 1-6   Commands for Chapter 1, "Routing Concepts"

Command	Description
	Enter privileged EXEC mode.
	Exit privileged EXEC mode.
	Enter global configuration mode.
	Configure R1 as the hostname for the router.
	Enter line configuration mode for the console.
	Configure the console password to be "cisco123".
	Require a password for user EXEC mode.
	Configure "Authorized Access Only" as the message of the day. Use $ as the delimiting character.
	Enter interface configuration mode for g0/0.
	Configure the IPv4 address 172.16.1.1 255.255.255.0 on interface g0/0.
	Configure the IPv6 address 2001:DB8:1::1/64 on interface g0/0.
	Configure the IPv6 link-local address FE80::1 on interface g0/0.
	Activate the interface.
	Describe the interface as "R1 LAN1".
	Configure a static route to IPv4 network 192.168.1.0/24 using 172.16.1.2 as the next-hop IPv4 address.
	Configure a static route to the IPv6 network 2001:DB8:A::/64 using 2001:DB8:1::2 as the next-hop IPv6 address.
	Configure an IPv4 default route using Serial 0/0/0 as the exit interface.
	Configure an IPv6 default route using Serial 0/0/0 as the exit interface.
	View the configuration currently stored in RAM.
	Save the configuration to NVRAM.
	Erase the configuration stored in NVRAM.
	Reboot the switch.
	Test connectivity to another switch at IP address 192.168.2.1.
	Displays the routing table that the IOS is currently using to choose the best path to its destination networks.

Command	Description
	Displays all the interface configuration parameters and statistics.
	Displays abbreviated interface configuration information, including IP address and interface status.

1.0.1.2 Lab—Do We Really Need a Map?

Objectives

Describe the primary functions and features of a router.

Scenario

Using the Internet and Google Maps, located at http://maps.google.com, find a route between the capital city of your country and some other distant town, or between two places within your own city. Pay close attention to the driving or walking directions Google Maps suggests.

Notice that in many cases, Google Maps suggests more than one route between the two locations you chose. It also allows you to put additional constraints on the route, such as avoiding highways or tolls.

- Copy at least two route instructions supplied by Google Maps for this activity. Place your copies into a word processing document and save it to use with the next step.

- Open the .pdf accompanying this modeling activity and complete it with a fellow student. Discuss the reflection questions listed on the .pdf and record your answers.

Be prepared to present your answers to the class.

Resources

- Internet connection
- Web browser
- Google Maps, http://maps.google.com/

Reflection

1. What do the individual driving, or walking based on the criteria you input, and non-highway directions look like? What exact information do they contain? How do they relate to IP routing?

2. If Google Maps offered a set of different routes, what makes this route different from the first? Why would you choose one route over another?

3. What criteria can be used to evaluate the usefulness of a route?

4. Is it sensible to expect that a single route can be "the best one," i.e. meeting all various requirements? Justify your answer.

5. As a network administrator or developer, how could you use a network map, or routing table, in your daily network activities?

_____

1.1.1.8 Packet Tracer–Using Traceroute to Discover the Network

Topology

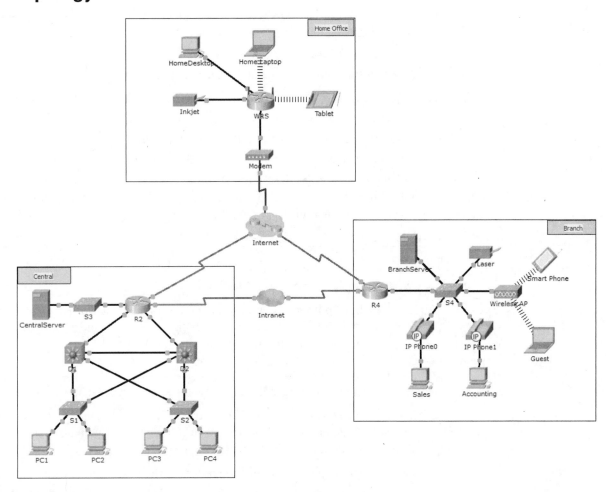

Scenario

The company you work for has acquired a new branch location. You asked for a topology map of the new location, but apparently one does not exist. However, you have username and password information for the new branch's networking devices and you know the web address for the new branch's server. Therefore, you will verify connectivity and use the **tracert** command to determine the path to the location. You will connect to the edge router of the new location to determine the devices and networks attached. As a part of this process, you will use various show commands to gather the necessary information to finish documenting the IP addressing scheme and create a diagram of the topology.

Note: The user EXEC password is **cisco**. The privileged EXEC password is **class**.

Trace and Document a Remote Location

Note: As you complete the following steps, copy command output into a text file for easy reference and record the missing information in the **Addressing Scheme Documentation** table.

Refer to the **Hints** page for a review of the commands used. In Packet Tracer, click the right arrow (>) on the bottom right side of the instruction window. If you have a printed version of the instructions, the **Hints** page is the last page.

a. Click **Sales** and the **Desktop** tab > **Command Prompt**. Use the **ipconfig** command to check the IP address configuration for **Sales**.

b. The new server web address is **b2server.pt.pka**. Enter the following **nslookup** command to discover the IP address for **b2server**:

```
PC> nslookup b2server.pt.pka
```

What address did the command return for **b2server**? _____

c. Enter the **tracert** command to determine the path from **Sales** to b2server.pt.pka.

```
PC> tracert b2server.pt.pka
```

d. Telnet to the first IP address in the **tracert** output and log in.

```
PC> telnet 172.16.0.1
```

e. You are connected to the **R4** router. Issue the **traceroute** command on the router using the address for b2server determined in step b. What is different about the **traceroute** command on the router compared to **tracert** on the PC? _____

_____

_____

What is the significance of **R4** to **Sales**? _____

f. Use the **show ip interface brief** command to display the status of the interfaces on **R4**. Based on the output of the command, which interface is used to reach the next device in the list output from the **tracert** command? _____

_____

Hint: Use **show running-config** to view the subnet mask values for the interfaces.

g. Telnet to the second IP address in the **tracert** list and log in. You can use the number in the far left column of the **tracert** output to track where you are in the list. What is the name of the device to which you are connected? _____

h. Issue the **show ip route** command and study the output. Referring to the list of codes at the beginning of the output, what are the different types of routes displayed in the routing table? _____

i. Based on the **show ip route** command output, which interface is the exit interface for the next IP address listed in your original **tracert** output?

_____

j. Telnet to the third IP address in the **tracert** list and log in. What is the hostname of the current device? _____

Issue the **show ip route connected** command. What networks are connected directly to this router? _____

Refer to the **Addressing Scheme Documentation** table. Which interfaces connect the devices between trace route 2 and trace route 3? _____

_____

k. Telnet to the fourth IP address in the **tracert** list and log in. What is the name of the device? _____

l. Issue a command to determine to what interface **b2server.pt.pka** is connected.

m. If you have used the **Addressing Scheme Documentation** table as you completed the previous steps, the table should now be complete. If not, finish the table now.

n. With a complete documentation of the addressing scheme and knowledge of the path from **Sales** to **branch2.pt.pka**, you should be able to now draw the new branch location in the **Topology Documentation** space below.

Addressing Scheme Documentation

Trace Route ID	Device	Interface	Address	Subnet Mask
-	Sales	NIC	172.16.0.x (DHCP)	255.255.255.0
1				
		S0/0/1.1	64.100.200.1	255.255.255.252
2				
		G0/1	64.104.223.1	255.255.255.252
		S0/0/0	64.100.100.2	
3				
		G0/2		255.255.255.0
		F0/1	128.107.46.1	
4		G0/0		
5	b2server.pt.pka	NIC	128.107.64.254	255.255.255.0

Topology Documentation

Use the space below to draw the topology for the new branch location.

Suggested Scoring Rubric

Activity Section	Possible Points	Earned Points
Questions (2 points each)	20	
Addressing Scheme Documentation	60	
Topology Documentation	20	
Total Points	**100**	

Hints–Command Summary Reference

DOS Commands

ipconfig–The output of the default command contains the IP address, network mask, and gateway for all physical and virtual network adapters.

ipconfig /all–This option displays the same IP addressing information for each adapter as the default option. Additionally, it displays DNS and WINS settings for each adapter.

Nslookup–Displays information that you can use to diagnose Domain Name System (DNS) infrastructure.

Syntax:

nslookup dns.name

Tracert–Determines the path taken to a destination by sending Internet Control Message Protocol (ICMP) Echo Request messages to the destination with incrementally increasing Time to Live (TTL) field values. The path displayed is the list of near-side router interfaces of the routers in the path between a source host and a destination. The near-side interface is the interface of the router that is closest to the sending host in the path. Used without parameters, tracert displays help.

Syntax:

tracert [TargetName/IP Address]

IOS Commands

show ip interface–Displays the IP interface status and configuration

show ip interface brief–Displays a brief summary of IP status and configuration

show ip route–Displays the full IP routing table

show ip route connected–Displays a list of active directly connected networks

show running-config–Displays the current operating configuration

traceroute–Trace route to destination

1.1.1.9 Lab–Mapping the Internet

Objectives

Part 1: Determine Network Connectivity to a Destination Host

Part 2: Trace a Route to a Remote Server Using Tracert

Background/Scenario

Route tracing computer software lists the networks that data traverses from the user's originating end device to a distant destination device.

This network tool is typically executed at the command line as:

`tracert <destination network name or end device address>`

(Microsoft Windows systems)

or

`traceroute <destination network name or end device address>`

(UNIX, Linux systems, and Cisco devices, such as switches and routers)

Both **tracert** and **traceroute** determine the route taken by packets across an IP network.

The **tracert** (or **traceroute**) tool is often used for network troubleshooting. By showing a list of routers traversed, the user can identify the path taken to reach a particular destination on the network or across internetworks. Each router represents a point where one network connects to another network and through which the data packet was forwarded. The number of routers is known as the number of hops the data traveled from source to destination.

The displayed list can help identify data flow problems when trying to access a service such as a website. It can also be useful when performing tasks, such as downloading data. If there are multiple websites (mirrors) available for the same data file, one can trace each mirror to get a good idea of which mirror would be the fastest to use.

Command-line based route tracing tools are usually embedded with the operating system of the end device. This activity should be performed on a computer that has Internet access and access to a command line.

Required Resources

PC with Internet access

Part 1: Determine Network Connectivity to a Destination Host

To trace the route to a distant network, the PC used must have a working connection to the Internet. Use the **ping** command to test whether a host is reachable. Packets of information are sent to the remote host with instructions to reply. Your local PC measures whether a response is received to each packet, and how long it takes for those packets to cross the network.

    a.   At the command-line prompt, type **ping www.cisco.com** to determine if it is reachable.

```
C:\>ping www.cisco.com

Pinging e144.dscb.akamaiedge.net [23.1.48.170] with 32 bytes of data:
Reply from 23.1.48.170: bytes=32 time=56ms TTL=57
Reply from 23.1.48.170: bytes=32 time=55ms TTL=57
Reply from 23.1.48.170: bytes=32 time=54ms TTL=57
Reply from 23.1.48.170: bytes=32 time=54ms TTL=57

Ping statistics for 23.1.48.170:
    Packets: Sent = 4, Received = 4, Lost = 0 (0% loss),
Approximate round trip times in milli-seconds:
    Minimum = 54ms, Maximum = 56ms, Average = 54ms
```

    b.   Now ping one of the Regional Internet Registry (RIR) websites located in different parts of the world to determine if it is reachable:

Africa:	**www.afrinic.net**
Australia:	**www.apnic.net**
South America:	**www.lacnic.net**
North America:	**www.arin.net**

Note: At the time of writing, the European RIR www.ripe.net does not reply to ICMP echo requests.

The website you selected will be used in Part 2 with the **tracert** command.

Part 2: Trace a Route to a Remote Server Using Tracert

After you determine if your chosen websites are reachable by using **ping**, you will use **tracert** to determine the path to reach the remote server. It is helpful to look more closely at each network segment that is crossed.

Each hop in the **tracert** results displays the routes that the packets take when traveling to the final destination. The PC sends three ICMP echo request packets to the remote host. Each router in the path decrements the time to live (TTL) value by 1 before passing it onto the next system. When the decremented TTL value reaches 0, the router sends an ICMP Time Exceeded message back to the source with its IP address and the current time. When the final destination is reached, an ICMP echo reply is sent to the source host.

For example, the source host sends three ICMP echo request packets to the first hop (192.168.1.1) with the TTL value of 1. When the router 192.168.1.1 receives the echo request packets, it decrements the TTL value to 0. The router sends an ICMP Time Exceeded message back to the source. This process continues until the source host sends the last three ICMP echo request packets with TTL values of 8 (hop number 8 in the output below), which is the final destination. After the ICMP echo request packets arrive at the final destination, the router responds to the source with ICMP echo replies.

For hops 2 and 3, these IP addresses are private addresses. These routers are the typical setup for point-of-presence (POP) of ISP. The POP devices connect users to an ISP network.

A web-based whois tool is found at http://whois.domaintools.com/. It is used to determine the domains traveled from the source to destination.

a. At the command-line prompt, trace the route to www.cisco.com. Save the **tracert** output in a text file. Alternatively, you can redirect the output to a text file by using **>** or **>>**.

```
C:\Users\User1> tracert www.cisco.com
```

or

```
C:\Users\User1> tracert www.cisco.com > tracert-cisco.txt
Tracing route to e144.dscb.akamaiedge.net [23.67.208.170]
over a maximum of 30 hops:

  1     1 ms    <1 ms    <1 ms   192.168.1.1
  2    14 ms     7 ms     7 ms   10.39.0.1
  3    10 ms     8 ms     7 ms   172.21.0.118
  4    11 ms    11 ms    11 ms   70.169.73.196
  5    10 ms     9 ms    11 ms   70.169.75.157
  6    60 ms    49 ms     *      68.1.2.109
  7    43 ms    39 ms    38 ms   Equinix-DFW2.netarch.akamai.com
       [206.223.118.102]
  8    33 ms    35 ms    33 ms   a23-67-208-170.deploy.akamaitechnologies.com
       [23.67.208.170]


Trace complete.
```

b. The web-based tool at http://whois.domaintools.com/ can be used to determine the owners of both the resulting IP address and domain names shown in the tracert tools output. Now perform a **tracert** to one of RIR websites from Part 1 and save the results.

Africa: **www.afrinic.net**

Australia: **www.apnic.net**

Europe: **www.ripe.net**

South America: **www.lacnic.net**

North America: **www.arin.net**

List the domains below from your tracert results using the web-based whois tool.

_____

_____

c. Compare the lists of domains crossed to reach the final destinations.

Reflection

What can affect **tracert** results?

_____

_____

1.1.2.9 Packet Tracer–Documenting the Network

Topology

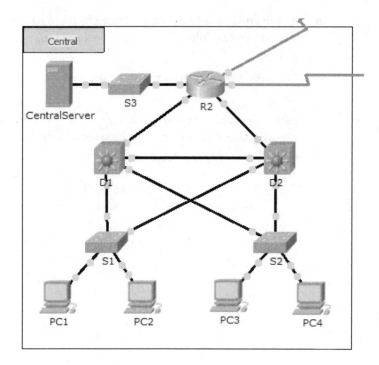

Background

In this activity, your job is to document the addressing scheme and connections used in the Central portion of the network. You must use a variety of commands to gather the required information.

Note: The user EXEC password is **cisco**. The privileged EXEC password is **class**.

Requirements

- Access the command line of the various devices in Central.
- Use commands to gather the information required in the **Addressing Scheme and Device Connection Documentation** table.
- If you do not remember the necessary commands, you can use the IOS built-in help system.
- If you still need additional hints, refer to the **Hints** page. In Packet Tracer, click the right arrow (>) on the bottom right side of the instruction window. If you have a printed version of the instructions, the **Hints** page is the last page.

Addressing Scheme and Device Connection Documentation

Device Name	Interface	Address	Subnet Mask	Connecting Device	
				Device Name	Interface
R2	G0/0				
	G0/1				
	G0/2				
	S0/0/0	64.100.100.1	255.255.255.252	Internet	N/A
	S0/0/1.1	64.100.200.2	255.255.255.252	Intranet	N/A
S3	VLAN 1	10.10.10.254	255.255.255.0	N/A	N/A
	F0/1	N/A	N/A	CentralServer	NIC
	G0/1	N/A	N/A		
CentralServer	NIC				
D1	VLAN2	10.2.0.1	255.255.255.0	N/A	N/A
	G0/1				
	G0/2				
	F0/23	N/A	N/A		
	F0/24	N/A	N/A		
S1	VLAN 2	10.2.0.2	255.255.255.0	N/A	N/A
	F0/23	N/A	N/A		
	G0/1	N/A	N/A		
D2	F0/23	N/A	N/A	S1	F0/23
	F0/24				
	G0/1				
	G0/2				
S2	VLAN 1	10.3.0.2	255.255.255.0	N/A	N/A
	F0/23	N/A	N/A		
	G0/1	N/A	N/A		

Hints

Use the following commands to gather the information you need to document the network:

```
show ip interface brief
```
```
show interfaces
```
```
show running-config
```
```
ipconfig
```

1.1.3.5 Packet Tracer–Configuring IPv4 and IPv6 Interfaces

Topology

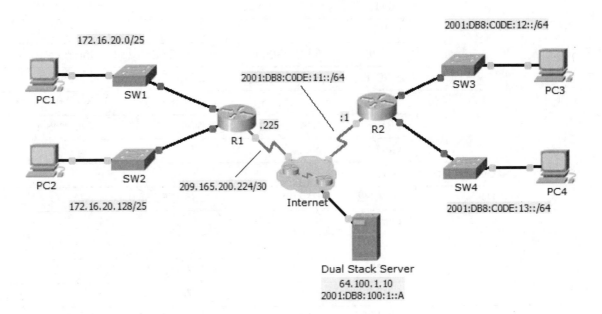

Addressing Table

Device	Interface	IPv4 Address	Subnet Mask	Default Gateway
		IPv6 Address/Prefix		
R1	G0/0	172.16.20.1	255.255.255.128	N/A
	G0/1	172.16.20.129	255.255.255.128	N/A
	S0/0/0	209.165.200.225	255.255.255.252	N/A
PC1	NIC	172.16.20.10	255.255.255.128	172.16.20.1
PC2	NIC	172.16.20.138	255.255.255.128	172.16.20.129
R2	G0/0	2001:DB8:C0DE:12::1/64		N/A
	G0/1	2001:DB8:C0DE:13::1/64		N/A
	S0/0/1	2001:DB8:C0DE:11::1/64		N/A
	Link-local	FE80::2		N/A
PC3	NIC	2001:DB8:C0DE:12::A/64		FE80::2
PC4	NIC	2001:DB8:C0DE:13::A/64		FE80::2

Objectives

Part 1: Configure IPv4 Addressing and Verify Connectivity

Part 2: Configure IPv6 Addressing and Verify Connectivity

Background

Routers R1 and R2 each have two LANs. Your task is to configure the appropriate addressing on each device and verify connectivity between the LANs.

Note: The user EXEC password is **cisco**. The privileged EXEC password is **class**.

Part 1: Configure IPv4 Addressing and Verify Connectivity

Step 1:   Assign IPv4 addresses to R1 and LAN devices.

Referring to the **Addressing Table**, configure IP addressing for **R1 LAN interfaces**, **PC1** and **PC2**. The serial interface is already configured.

Step 2:   Verify connectivity.

PC1 and PC2 should be able to ping each other and the **Dual Stack Server**.

Part 2: Configure IPv6 Addressing and Verify Connectivity

Step 1:   Assign IPv6 addresses to R2 and LAN devices.

Referring to the **Addressing Table**, configure IP addressing for **R2 LAN interfaces, PC3** and **PC4**. The serial interface is already configured.

Step 2:   Verify connectivity.

PC3 and **PC4** should be able to ping each other and the **Dual Stack Server**.

1.1.4.5 Packet Tracer–Configuring and Verifying a Small Network

Topology

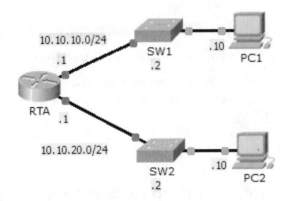

Addressing Table

Device	Interface	IP Address	Subnet Mask	Default Gateway
RTA	G0/0	10.10.10.1	255.255.255.0	N/A
	G0/1	10.10.20.1	255.255.255.0	N/A
SW1	VLAN1	10.10.10.2	255.255.255.0	10.10.10.1
SW2	VLAN1	10.10.20.2	255.255.255.0	10.10.20.1
PC1	NIC	10.10.10.10	255.255.255.0	10.10.10.1
PC2	NIC	10.10.20.10	255.255.255.0	10.10.20.1

Objectives

Part 1: Configure Devices and Verify Connectivity

Part 2: Gather Information with Show Commands

Background

In this activity, you will configure RTA with basic settings, including IP addressing. You will also configure SW1 for remote management and configure the PCs. Once you have successfully verified connectivity, you will use show commands to gather information about the network.

Note: The user EXEC password is cisco. The privileged EXEC password is class.

Part 1: Configure Devices and Verify Connectivity

Step 1: Apply basic configurations to RTA.

    a. Using the following information and the **Addressing Table**, configure RTA:

        ■ Hostname and banner

        ■ Line password set to **cisco**; encrypted password set to **class**

        ■ IP addressing and descriptions on LAN interfaces

    b. Save the configuration.

Step 2: Configure addressing on PC1 and PC2.

    a. Using the **Addressing Table**, configure IP addressing for PC1 and PC2.

    b. Test connectivity between **PC1** and **PC2**. Troubleshoot as necessary.

Step 3: Configure SW1 for remote management.

    a. Using the **Addressing Table**, configure the management interface for SW1.

    b. Configure the default gateway address.

    c. Save the configuration.

Part 2: Gather Information with Show Commands

Step 1: Gather information from show interface command output.

Issue each of the following commands and then answer the related questions:

```
show ip interface brief
show interfaces
show ip interface
```

Which commands display the status of the port?_____

_____

Which command shows only the IP address (no subnet mask or prefix)? _____

_____

Which command displays the description configured on the interface? _____

Which command displays the IP broadcast address? _____

Which command displays the MAC address of the interface? _____

Step 2: Gather information from show ip route command output.

Issue each of the following commands and then answer the related questions:

```
show ip route
show ip route connected
```

How many networks are known by the router based on the output of the **show ip route** command? _____ _____

What does the L at the beginning of the lines within the routing table represent?

_____

What does the /32 prefix listed in the route table indicate? _____

Step 3: Gather information after an interface state is changed.

    a. On **RTA**, shut down the Gigabit Ethernet 0/0 interface and issue the **show ip route** command. How many networks are displayed in the routing table now? _____

    b. Attempt to ping PC1. Was the ping successful? _____

    c. Issue the **show ip interface brief** command. What is the status of the Gigabit Ethernet 0/0 interface? _____

    d. Reactivate the Gigabit Ethernet 0/0 interface. Issue the **show ip route** command. Did the routing table repopulate? _____

What can be inferred about the interface status of routes that appear in the routing table? _____

Suggested Scoring Rubric

Activity Section	Question Location	Possible Points	Earned Points
Part 2: Gather Information with Show Commands	Step 1	15	
	Step 2	10	
	Step 3	15	
Part 2 Total		40	
Packet Tracer Score		60	
Total Score		100	

1.1.4.6 Lab–Configuring Basic Router Settings with IOS CLI

Topology

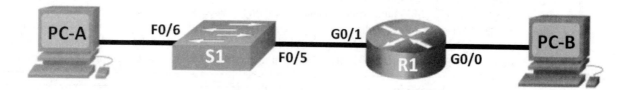

Addressing Table

Device	Interface	IP Address	Subnet Mask	Default Gateway
R1	G0/0	192.168.0.1	255.255.255.0	N/A
	G0/1	192.168.1.1	255.255.255.0	N/A
PC-A	NIC	192.168.1.3	255.255.255.0	192.168.1.1
PC-B	NIC	192.168.0.3	255.255.255.0	192.168.0.1

Objectives

Part 1: Set Up the Topology and Initialize Devices

- Cable equipment to match the network topology.

- Initialize and restart the router and switch.

Part 2: Configure Devices and Verify Connectivity

- Assign static IPv4 information to the PC interfaces.

- Configure basic router settings.

- Verify network connectivity.

- Configure the router for SSH.

Part 3: Display Router Information

- Retrieve hardware and software information from the router.

- Interpret the output from the startup configuration.

- Interpret the output from the routing table.

- Verify the status of the interfaces.

Part 4: Configure IPv6 and Verify Connectivity

Background/Scenario

This is a comprehensive lab to review previously covered IOS router commands. In Parts 1 and 2, you will cable the equipment and complete basic configurations and IPv4 interface settings on the router.

In Part 3, you will use SSH to connect to the router remotely and utilize IOS commands to retrieve information from the device to answer questions about the router. In Part 4, you will configure IPv6 on the router so that PC-B can acquire an IP address and then verify connectivity.

For review purposes, this lab provides the commands necessary for specific router configurations.

Note: The routers used with CCNA hands-on labs are Cisco 1941 Integrated Services Routers (ISRs) with Cisco IOS Release 15.2(4)M3 (universalk9 image). The switches used are Cisco Catalyst 2960 with Cisco IOS Release 15.0(2) (lanbasek9 image). Other routers, switches, and Cisco IOS versions can be used. Depending on the model and Cisco IOS version, the commands available and output produced might vary from what is shown in the labs. Refer to the Router Interface Summary Table at the end of this lab for the correct interface identifiers.

Note: Make sure that the router and switch have been erased and have no startup configurations. Refer to Appendix A for the procedures to initialize and reload devices.

Required Resources

- 1 Router (Cisco 1941 with Cisco IOS Release 15.2(4)M3 universal image or comparable)

- 1 Switch (Cisco 2960 with Cisco IOS Release 15.0(2) lanbasek9 image or comparable)

- 2 PCs (Windows 7, Vista, or XP with terminal emulation program, such as Tera Term)

- Console cables to configure the Cisco IOS devices via the console ports

- Ethernet cables as shown in the topology

Note: The Gigabit Ethernet interfaces on Cisco 1941 ISRs are autosensing and an Ethernet straight-through cable can be used between the router and PC-B. If using another model Cisco router, it may be necessary to use an Ethernet crossover cable.

Part 1: Set Up the Topology and Initialize Devices

Step 1:   Cable the network as shown in the topology.

    a.   Attach the devices as shown in the topology diagram, and cable as necessary.

    b.   Power on all the devices in the topology.

Step 2:   Initialize and reload the router and switch.

Note: Appendix A details the steps to initialize and reload the devices.

Part 2: Configure Devices and Verify Connectivity

Step 1:   Configure the PC interfaces.

    a.   Configure the IP address, subnet mask, and default gateway settings on PC-A.

    b.   Configure the IP address, subnet mask, and default gateway settings on PC-B.

Step 2:   Configure the router.

    a.   Console into the router and enable privileged EXEC mode.

```
Router> enable
Router#
```

b. Enter into global configuration mode.

```
Router# config terminal
Router(config)#
```

c. Assign a device name to the router.

```
Router(config)# hostname R1
```

d. Disable DNS lookup to prevent the router from attempting to translate incorrectly entered commands as though they were hostnames.

```
R1(config)# no ip domain-lookup
```

e. Require that a minimum of 10 characters be used for all passwords.

```
R1(config)# security passwords min-length 10
```

Besides setting a minimum length, list other ways to strengthen passwords.

---

f. Assign cisco12345 as the privileged EXEC encrypted password.

```
R1(config)# enable secret cisco12345
```

g. Assign ciscoconpass as the console password, establish a timeout, enable login, and add the **logging synchronous** command. The **logging synchronous** command synchronizes debug and Cisco IOS software output and prevents these messages from interrupting your keyboard input.

```
R1(config)# line con 0
R1(config-line)# password ciscoconpass
R1(config-line)# exec-timeout 5 0
R1(config-line)# login
R1(config-line)# logging synchronous
R1(config-line)# exit
R1(config)#
```

For the **exec-timeout** command, what do the **5** and **0** represent?

---

h. Assign ciscovtypass as the vty password, establish a timeout, enable login, and add the **logging synchronous** command.

```
R1(config)# line vty 0 4
R1(config-line)# password ciscovtypass
R1(config-line)# exec-timeout 5 0
R1(config-line)# login
R1(config-line)# logging synchronous
R1(config-line)# exit
R1(config)#
```

i. Encrypt the clear text passwords.

```
R1(config)# service password-encryption
```

j. Create a banner that warns anyone accessing the device that unauthorized access is prohibited.

```
R1(config)# banner motd #Unauthorized access prohibited!#
```

k. Configure an IP address and interface description. Activate both interfaces on the router.

```
R1(config)# int g0/0
R1(config-if)# description Connection to PC-B
R1(config-if)# ip address 192.168.0.1 255.255.255.0
R1(config-if)# no shutdown
R1(config-if)# int g0/1
R1(config-if)# description Connection to S1
R1(config-if)# ip address 192.168.1.1 255.255.255.0
R1(config-if)# no shutdown
R1(config-if)# exit
R1(config)# exit
R1#
```

l. Set the clock on the router; for example:

```
R1# clock set 17:00:00 18 Feb 2013
```

m. Save the running configuration to the startup configuration file.

```
R1# copy running-config startup-config
Destination filename [startup-config]?
R1#
```

What would be the result of reloading the router prior to completing the **copy running-config startup-config** command? _____

_____

Step 3: Verify network connectivity.

a. Ping PC-B from a command prompt on PC-A.

Note: It may be necessary to disable the PC's firewall.

Were the pings successful? ____

After completing this series of commands, what type of remote access could be used to access R1?

_____

b. Remotely access R1 from PC-A using the Tera Term Telnet client.

Open Tera Term and enter the G0/1 interface IP address of R1 in the Host: field of the Tera Term: New Connection window. Ensure that the **Telnet** radio button is selected and then click **OK** to connect to the router.

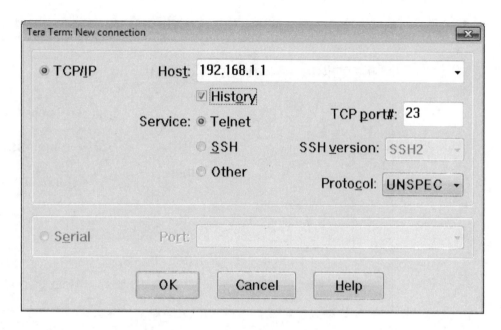

Was remote access successful? _____

Why is the Telnet protocol considered to be a security risk? _____

_____

Step 4:   Configure the router for SSH access.

a.   Enable SSH connections and create a user in the local database of the router.

```
R1# configure terminal
R1(config)# ip domain-name CCNA-lab.com
R1(config)# username admin privilege 15 secret adminpass1
R1(config)# line vty 0 4
R1(config-line)# transport input ssh
R1(config-line)# login local
R1(config-line)# exit
R1(config)# crypto key generate rsa modulus 1024
R1(config)# exit
```

b.   Remotely access R1 from PC-A using the Tera Term SSH client.

Open Tera Term and enter the G0/1 interface IP address of R1 in the Host: field of the Tera Term: New Connection window. Ensure that the **SSH** radio button is selected and then click **OK** to connect to the router.

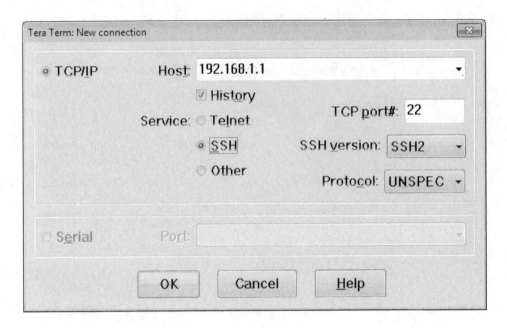

Was remote access successful? ____

Part 3: Display Router Information

In Part 3, you will use **show** commands from an SSH session to retrieve information from the router.

Step 1:   Establish an SSH session to R1.

Using Tera Term on PC-B, open an SSH session to R1 at IP address 192.168.0.1 and log in as **admin** with the password **adminpass1**.

Step 2:   Retrieve important hardware and software information.

    a.   Use the **show version** command to answer questions about the router.

        What is the name of the IOS image that the router is running?

        _____

        How much non-volatile random-access memory (NVRAM) does the router have?

        _____

        How much Flash memory does the router have?

        _____

        _____

    b.   The **show** commands often provide multiple screens of outputs. Filtering the output allows a user to display certain sections of the output. To enable the filtering command, enter a pipe (|) character after a **show** command, followed by a filtering parameter and a filtering expression. You can match the output to the filtering statement by using the **include** keyword to display all lines from the output that contain the filtering expression. Filter the **show version** command, using show version | include register to answer the following question.

        What is the boot process for the router on the next reload?

        _____

Step 3: Display the startup configuration.

Use the **show startup-config** command on the router to answer the following questions.

How are passwords presented in the output?

_____

_____

_____

Use the **show startup-config | begin vty** command.

What is the result of using this command?

_____

_____

Step 4: Display the routing table on the router.

Use the **show ip route** command on the router to answer the following questions.

What code is used in the routing table to indicate a directly connected network?

_____

_____

How many route entries are coded with a C code in the routing table? _____

Step 5: Display a summary list of the interfaces on the router.

Use the **show ip interface brief** command on the router to answer the following question.

What command changed the status of the Gigabit Ethernet ports from administratively down to up?

_____

Part 4: Configure IPv6 and Verify Connectivity

Step 1: Assign IPv6 addresses to R1 G0/0 and enable IPv6 routing.

Note: Assigning an IPv6 address in addition to an IPv4 address on an interface is known as dual stacking, because both the IPv4 and IPv6 protocol stacks are active. By enabling IPv6 unicast routing on R1, PC-B receives the R1 G0/0 IPv6 network prefix and can autoconfigure its IPv6 address and its default gateway.

    a. Assign an IPv6 global unicast address to interface G0/0, assign the link-local address in addition to the unicast address on the interface, and enable IPv6 routing.

```
R1# configure terminal
R1(config)# interface g0/0
R1(config-if)# ipv6 address 2001:db8:acad:a::1/64
R1(config-if)# ipv6 address fe80::1 link-local
R1(config-if)# no shutdown
R1(config-if)# exit
R1(config)# ipv6 unicast-routing
R1(config)# exit
```

b. Use the **show ipv6 int brief** command to verify IPv6 settings on R1.

If no IPv6 address is assigned to G0/1, why is it listed as [up/up]?

_____

_____

c. Issue the **ipconfig** command on PC-B to examine the IPv6 configuration.

What is the IPv6 address assigned to PC-B?

_____

What is the default gateway assigned to PC-B? _____

Issue a ping from PC-B to the R1 default gateway link local address. Was it successful?

_____

Issue a ping from PC-B to the R1 IPv6 unicast address 2001:db8:acad:a::1. Was it successful? _____

Reflection

1. In researching a network connectivity issue, a technician suspects that an interface was not enabled. What **show** command could the technician use to troubleshoot this issue?

_____

2. In researching a network connectivity issue, a technician suspects that an interface was assigned an incorrect subnet mask. What **show** command could the technician use to troubleshoot this issue?

_____

3. After configuring IPv6 on the R1 G0/0 PC-B LAN, if you were to ping from PC-A to the PC-B IPv6 address, would the ping succeed? Why or why not?

_____

Router Interface Summary Table

Router Interface Summary				
Router Model	Ethernet Interface #1	Ethernet Interface #2	Serial Interface #1	Serial Interface #2
1800	Fast Ethernet 0/0 (F0/0)	Fast Ethernet 0/1 (F0/1)	Serial 0/0/0 (S0/0/0)	Serial 0/0/1 (S0/0/1)
1900	Gigabit Ethernet 0/0 (G0/0)	Gigabit Ethernet 0/1 (G0/1)	Serial 0/0/0 (S0/0/0)	Serial 0/0/1 (S0/0/1)
2801	Fast Ethernet 0/0 (F0/0)	Fast Ethernet 0/1 (F0/1)	Serial 0/1/0 (S0/1/0)	Serial 0/1/1 (S0/1/1)
2811	Fast Ethernet 0/0 (F0/0)	Fast Ethernet 0/1 (F0/1)	Serial 0/0/0 (S0/0/0)	Serial 0/0/1 (S0/0/1)
2900	Gigabit Ethernet 0/0 (G0/0)	Gigabit Ethernet 0/1 (G0/1)	Serial 0/0/0 (S0/0/0)	Serial 0/0/1 (S0/0/1)

Note: To find out how the router is configured, look at the interfaces to identify the type of router and how many interfaces the router has. There is no way to effectively list all the combinations of configurations for each router class. This table includes identifiers for the possible combinations of Ethernet and Serial interfaces in the device. The table does not include any other type of interface, even though a specific router may contain one. An example of this might be an ISDN BRI interface. The string in parentheses is the legal abbreviation that can be used in Cisco IOS commands to represent the interface.

Appendix A: Initializing and Reloading a Router and Switch

Step 1: Initialize and reload the router.

a. Console into the router and enable privileged EXEC mode.

```
Router> enable
```

b. Type the **erase startup-config** command to remove the startup configuration from NVRAM.

```
Router# erase startup-config
Erasing the nvram filesystem will remove all configuration files! Continue?
[confirm]
[OK]
Erase of nvram: complete
Router#
```

c. Issue the **reload** command to remove an old configuration from memory. When prompted to **Proceed with reload**, press Enter to confirm the reload. (Pressing any other key aborts the reload.)

```
Router# reload
Proceed with reload? [confirm]
*Nov 29 18:28:09.923: %SYS-5-RELOAD: Reload requested by console. Reload
Reason: Reload Command.
```

Note: You may be prompted to save the running configuration prior to reloading the router. Type no and press Enter.

```
System configuration has been modified. Save? [yes/no]: no
```

d. After the router reloads, you are prompted to enter the initial configuration dialog. Enter **no** and press Enter.

```
Would you like to enter the initial configuration dialog? [yes/no]: no
```

e. You are prompted to terminate autoinstall. Type **yes** and then press Enter.

```
Would you like to terminate autoinstall? [yes]: yes
```

Step 2: Initialize and reload the switch.

a. Console into the switch and enter privileged EXEC mode.

```
Switch> enable
Switch#
```

b. Use the **show flash** command to determine if any VLANs have been created on the switch.

```
Switch# show flash
Directory of flash:/

    2  -rwx        1919   Mar 1 1993 00:06:33 +00:00  private-config.text
    3  -rwx        1632   Mar 1 1993 00:06:33 +00:00  config.text
    4  -rwx       13336   Mar 1 1993 00:06:33 +00:00  multiple-fs
    5  -rwx    11607161   Mar 1 1993 02:37:06 +00:00  c2960-lanbasek9-mz.150-2.
SE.bin
    6  -rwx         616   Mar 1 1993 00:07:13 +00:00  vlan.dat
32514048 bytes total (20886528 bytes free)
Switch#
```

c. If the **vlan.dat** file was found in flash, then delete this file.

```
Switch# delete vlan.dat
Delete filename [vlan.dat]?
```

d. You are prompted to verify the filename. At this point, you can change the filename or just press Enter if you have entered the name correctly.

e. You are prompted to confirm deleting this file. Press Enter to confirm deletion. (Pressing any other key aborts the deletion.)

```
Delete flash:/vlan.dat? [confirm]
Switch#
```

f. Use the **erase startup-config** command to erase the startup configuration file from NVRAM. You are prompted to confirm removing the configuration file. Press Enter to confirm to erase this file. (Pressing any other key aborts the operation.)

```
Switch# erase startup-config
Erasing the nvram filesystem will remove all configuration files! Continue?
[confirm]
[OK]
Erase of nvram: complete
Switch#
```

g. Reload the switch to remove any old configuration information from memory. You are prompted to confirm reloading the switch. Press Enter to proceed with the reload. (Pressing any other key aborts the reload.)

```
Switch# reload
Proceed with reload? [confirm]
```

Note: You may be prompted to save the running configuration prior to reloading the switch. Type no and press Enter.

```
System configuration has been modified. Save? [yes/no]: no
```

h. After the switch reloads, you should be prompted to enter the initial configuration dialog. Type **no** and press Enter.

```
Would you like to enter the initial configuration dialog? [yes/no]: no
Switch>
```

1.3.2.5 Packet Tracer–Investigating Directly Connected Routes

Topology

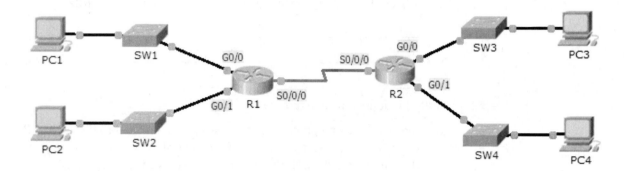

Objectives

Part 1: Investigate IPv4 Directly Connected Routes

Part 2: Investigate IPv6 Directly Connected Routes

Background

The network in the activity is already configured. You will log in to the routers and use **show** commands to discover and answer the questions below about the directly connected routes.

Note: The user EXEC password is **cisco** and the privileged exec password is **class.**

Part 1: Investigate IPv4 Directly Connected Routes

Step 1: Use **show** commands to gather information about the IPv4 directly connected networks.

Enter the following command on **R1:**

```
R1> show ip route ?
```

a. What option would be most beneficial in determining the networks assigned to the interfaces of the router? _____

b. Which networks are directly connected on **R1?** Hint: Use the option determined above.

_____

_____

_____

c. Which IP addresses are assigned to the LAN interfaces on **R1?**

_____

_____

_____

d. Which networks are directly connected on **R2**?

_____

_____

_____

e. Which IP addresses are assigned to the LAN interfaces on **R2**?

_____

_____

_____

Step 2:   Verify PC addressing and test connectivity.

a. Open a command prompt on **PC1**. Issue the command to display the IP settings. Based on the output, would you expect **PC1** to be able to communicate with all interfaces on the router? Provide a short answer describing your expectations.

_____

_____

b. Open a command prompt on **PC2**. Issue the command to display the IP settings. Based on the output, would you expect **PC2** to be able to communicate with **PC1**? Verify your expectations. _____

c. Determine the IP addresses of **PC3** and **PC4**. Record the results and determine if **PC3** and **PC4** are able to communicate.

_____

_____

d. Test connectivity from **PC1** to **PC3**. Was the test successful? _____

e. **Bonus:** Looking at the outputs of the routing tables on **R1** and **R2**, what might indicate a reason for the success or failure of communication between **PC1** and **PC3**?

_____

_____

Part 2: Investigate IPv6 Directly Connected Routes

Step 1:   Use **show** commands to gather information about the IPv6 directly connected networks.

a. Which IPv6 networks are available on **R1**?

_____

_____

_____

_____

_____

_____

_____

b. Which IPv6 unicast addresses are assigned to the LAN interfaces on **R1**?

_____

_____

_____

_____

c. Which IPv6 networks are available on R2?

_____

_____

_____

_____

_____

_____

_____

_____

_____

_____

d. Which IPv6 addresses are assigned to the LAN interfaces on **R2**?

_____

_____

_____

_____

Step 2: Verify PC settings and connectivity.

a. Open a command prompt on **PC1**. Issue the command to display the IPv6 settings. Based on the output, would you expect **PC1** to be able to communicate with all interfaces on the router? Provide a short answer describing your expectations.

_____

_____

b. Open a command prompt on **PC2**. Issue the command to display the IPv6 settings. Based on the output, would you expect **PC2** to be able to communicate with **PC1**? Verify your expectations. _____

c. Determine the IPv6 addresses of **PC3** and **PC4**. Record the results and determine if **PC3** and **PC4** are able to communicate.

_____

_____

    d. Test connectivity from **PC1** to **PC3**. Was the test successful? _____

    e. **Bonus:** What might indicate a reason for the success or failure of communication between **PC1** and **PC3** after looking at the outputs of the IPv6 routing tables on **R1** and **R2**? _____

_____

_____

Suggested Scoring Rubric

Activity Section	Question Location	Possible Points	Earned Points
Part 1: Investigate IPv4 Directly Connected Routes	Step 1	25	
	Step 2	25	
Part 2: Investigate IPv6 Directly Connected Routes	Step 1	25	
	Step 2	25	
Total Score		100	

1.4.1.1 Lab–We Really Could Use a Map!

Objectives

Describe the three types of routes that are populated in a routing table (to include: directly-connected, static, and dynamic).

Scenario

Use the Ashland and Richmond routing tables shown below. With the help of a classmate, draw a network topology using the information from the tables. To assist you with this activity, follow these guidelines:

- Start with the Ashland router–use its routing table to identify ports and IP addresses/networks.
- Add the Richmond router–use its routing table to identify ports and IP addresses/networks.
- Add any other intermediary and end devices, as specified by the tables.

In addition, record answers from your group to the reflection questions provided with this activity.

Be prepared to share your work with another group or the class.

Resources

```
Ashland> show ip route
Codes: L-local, C-connected, S-static, R-RIP, M-mobile, B-BGP
D-EIGRP, EX-EIGRP external, O-OSPF, IA-OSPF inter area
N1-OSPF NSSA external type 1, N2-OSPF NSSA external type 2
E1-OSPF external type 1, E2-OSPF external type 2, E-EGP
i-IS-IS, L1-IS-IS level-1, L2-IS-IS level-2, ia-IS-IS inter area
*-candidate default, U-per-user static route, o-ODR
P-periodic downloaded static route


Gateway of last resort is not set


      192.168.1.0/24 is variably subnetted, 2 subnets, 2 masks
C     192.168.1.0/24 is directly connected, GigabitEthernet0/1
L     192.168.1.1/32 is directly connected, GigabitEthernet0/1
      192.168.2.0/24 is variably subnetted, 2 subnets, 2 masks
C     192.168.2.0/24 is directly connected, Serial0/0/0
L     192.168.2.1/32 is directly connected, Serial0/0/0
D     192.168.3.0/24 [90/2170368] via 192.168.4.2, 01:53:50, GigabitEthernet0/0
      192.168.4.0/24 is variably subnetted, 2 subnets, 2 masks
C     192.168.4.0/24 is directly connected, GigabitEthernet0/0
L     192.168.4.1/32 is directly connected, GigabitEthernet0/0
D     192.168.5.0/24 [90/3072] via 192.168.4.2, 01:59:14, GigabitEthernet0/0
S     192.168.6.0/24 [1/0] via 192.168.2.2
Ashland>
```

```
Richmond> show ip route
Codes: L-local, C-connected, S-static, R-RIP, M-mobile, B-BGP
D-EIGRP, EX-EIGRP external, O-OSPF, IA-OSPF inter area
N1-OSPF NSSA external type 1, N2-OSPF NSSA external type 2
E1-OSPF external type 1, E2-OSPF external type 2, E-EGP
i-IS-IS, L1-IS-IS level-1, L2-IS-IS level-2, ia-IS-IS inter area
*-candidate default, U-per-user static route, o-ODR
P-periodic downloaded static route

Gateway of last resort is not set

S 192.168.1.0/24 [1/0] via 192.168.3.1
D 192.168.2.0/24 [90/2170368] via 192.168.5.2, 01:55:09, GigabitEthernet0/1
  192.168.3.0/24 is variably subnetted, 2 subnets, 2 masks
C 192.168.3.0/24 is directly connected, Serial0/0/0
L 192.168.3.2/32 is directly connected, Serial0/0/0
D 192.168.4.0/24 [90/3072] via 192.168.5.2, 01:55:09, GigabitEthernet0/1
  192.168.5.0/24 is variably subnetted, 2 subnets, 2 masks
C 192.168.5.0/24 is directly connected, GigabitEthernet0/1
L 192.168.5.1/32 is directly connected, GigabitEthernet0/1
  192.168.6.0/24 is variably subnetted, 2 subnets, 2 masks
C 192.168.6.0/24 is directly connected, GigabitEthernet0/0
L 192.168.6.1/32 is directly connected, GigabitEthernet0/0
Richmond>
```

Reflection

1. How many directly connected routes are listed on the Ashland router? What letter represents a direct connection to a network on a routing table?

    _____

2. Find the route to the 192.168.6.0/24 network. What kind of route is this? Was it dynamically discovered by the Ashland router or manually configured by a network administrator on the Ashland router?

    _____

3. If you were configuring a default (static route) to any network from the Ashland router and wanted to send all data to 192.168.2.2 (the next hop) for routing purposes, how would you write it?

    _____

4. If you were configuring a default (static route) to any network from the Ashland router and wanted to send all data through your exit interface, how would you write it?

    _____

5. When would you choose to use static routing, instead of letting dynamic routing take care of the routing paths for you?

    _____

6. What is the significance of the L on the left side of the routing table?

    _____

CHAPTER 2

Static Routing

Routers learn about remote networks using one of the following methods:

- Dynamically, using routing protocols
- Manually, using static routes

This chapter covers static routing, including default routes and summary routes, for both IPv4 and IPv6 networks.

The Study Guide portion of this chapter uses a combination of matching, fill-in-the-blank, multiple-choice, and open-ended question exercises to test your knowledge and skills of basic router concepts and configuration. The Labs and Activities portion of this chapter includes all the online curriculum labs and Packet Tracer activities to ensure that you have mastered the hands-on skills needed to understand basic IP addressing and router configuration.

As you work through this chapter, use Chapter 2 in *Routing and Switching Essentials v6 Companion Guide* or use the corresponding Chapter 2 in the Routing and Switching Essentials online curriculum for assistance.

Study Guide

Implement Static Routes

Unlike a dynamic routing protocol, static routes are not automatically updated and must be manually reconfigured any time the network topology changes. A static route does not change until the administrator manually reconfigures it.

Static Routing

In Table 2-1, indicate the type of routing for each characteristic.

Table 2-1   Dynamic vs. Static Routing

Characteristic	Dynamic Routing	Static Routing
This type of routing is more secure.		
The route to the destination depends on the current topology.		
Administrator intervention is required when there is a topology change.		
Uses no extra router resources.		
Suitable for simple and complex topologies.		
This type of routing is less secure.		
Configuration complexity increases with network size.		
Configuration complexity is generally independent of the network size.		
Uses more CPU, memory, and link bandwidth.		
The route to the destination is always the same.		
Suitable for simple topologies.		
Automatically adapts to topology changes.		

Briefly describe three reasons to use static routing:

_____

_____

_____

_____

_____

_____

_____

Types of Static Routes

Briefly describe each of the following types of static routes:

- Standard static route: _____

  _____

- Default static route: _____

  _____

  _____

- Summary static route: _____

  _____

  _____

- Floating static route: _____

  _____

  _____

  _____

In Table 2-2, indicate what type of route is described.

Table 2-2   Identify Types of Static Routes

Static Routing Descriptor	Standard	Default	Summary	Floating
Uses a single network address to send multiple static routes to one destination address				
Backs up a route already discovered by a dynamic routing protocol				
Configured with a higher administrative distance than the original dynamic routing protocol				
Useful when connecting to stub networks				
Matches all packets and sends them to a specific default gateway				
Commonly used with edge routers to connect to the ISP network				

Configure Static and Default Routes

We briefly covered static and default route configurations in Chapter 1, "Routing Concepts." In this chapter, we use a master topology to guide your configuration of both IPv4 and IPv6 static routes.

Configuring IPv4 Static and Default Routes

Figure 2-1 shows the topology for IPv4 routes, and Table 2-3 shows the addressing scheme.

Note: The topology uses loopback interfaces to simulate directly connected LANs. By using loopback interfaces, you can build rather complex scenarios without the need for a physical interface for every network.

Figure 2-1   Topology for IPv4 Static Routes

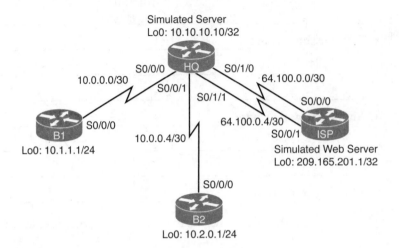

Table 2-3   Addressing Table for IPv4 Static Routes Topology

Device	Interface	IP Address	Subnet Mask
ISP	S0/0/0	64.100.0.1	255.255.255.252
	S0/0/1	64.100.0.5	255.255.255.252
	Lo0	209.165.201.1	255.255.255.252
HQ	S0/0/0	10.0.0.1	255.255.255.252
	S0/0/1	10.0.0.5	255.255.255.252
	S0/1/0	64.100.0.2	255.255.255.252
	S0/1/1	64.100.0.6	255.255.255.252
	Lo0	10.10.10.10	255.255.255.255
B1	S0/0/0	10.0.0.2	255.255.255.252
	Lo0	10.1.1.1	255.255.255.0
B2	S0/0/0	10.0.0.6	255.255.255.252
	Lo0	10.2.0.1	255.255.255.0

B1 and B2 Routing Strategy

Because B1 and B2 are both stub routers, what type of static route would you configure on these routers?

_____

Record the commands to configure the appropriate type of static route on B1 using the next-hop IP address argument.

B1# _____

_____

Record the commands to configure the appropriate type of static route on B2 using the exit interface argument.

B2# _____

_____

HQ Routing Strategy

HQ operates as a hub router for B1 and B2 and provides access to the Internet through ISP. What type of static routes would you configure on HQ?

_____

Record the commands to configure the appropriate type of static routes on HQ. Assume that HQ will use both links to ISP. Configure the routes to B1 and B2 with the next-hop IP address argument. Configure the routes to ISP with the exit interface argument.

_____

_____

_____

_____

_____

Briefly explain a fully specified static route and when it might be used.

_____

_____

_____

_____

_____

Configuring IPv6 Static and Default Routes

Figure 2-2 shows the topology for IPv6 routes and Table 2-4 shows the addressing scheme.

Figure 2-2   Topology for IPv6 Static Routes

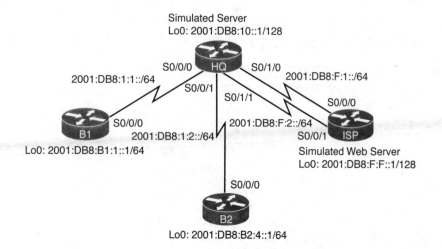

Table 2-4   Addressing Table for IPv6 Static Routes Topology

Device	Interface	IPv6 Address/Prefix
ISP	S0/0/0	2001:DB8:F:1::1/64
	S0/0/1	2001:DB8:F:2::1/64
	Lo0	2001:DB8:F:F::1/128
	Link local	FE80::F
HQ	S0/0/0	2001:DB8:1:1::1/64
	S0/0/1	2001:DB8:1:2::1/64
	S0/1/0	2001:DB8:F:1::2/64
	S0/1/1	2001:DB8:F:2::2/64
	Lo0	2001:DB8:10::1/128
	Link local	FE80::A
B1	S0/0/0	2001:DB8:1:1::2/64
	Lo0	2001:DB8:B1:1::1/64
	Link local	FE80::1
B2	S0/0/0	2001:DB8:1:2::2/64
	Lo0	2001:DB8:B2:4::1/64
	Link local	FE80::2

B1 and B2 Routing Strategy

Because B1 and B2 are both stub routers, what type of static route would you configure on these routers?

_____

Record the commands to configure the appropriate type of static route on B1 using the next-hop IP address argument.

B1# _____

_____

Record the commands to configure the appropriate type of static route on B2 using the exit interface argument.

B2# _____

_____

HQ Routing Strategy

HQ operates as a hub router for B1 and B2 and provides access to the Internet through an ISP. What type of static routes would you configure on HQ?

_____

Record the commands to configure the appropriate type of static routes on HQ. Assume that HQ will use both links to ISP. Configure the routes to B1 and B2 with the next-hop IP address argument. Configure the routes to ISP with the exit interface argument.

_____

_____

_____

_____

_____

In what situation must you use a fully specified IPv6 static route?

_____

_____

Record the commands to configure a fully specified IPv6 default route from B1 to HQ using the link-local address.

B1# _____

_____

Configure Floating Static Routes

As you recall from Chapter 1, administrative distance is used by the router to choose a route when more than one route exists for a given destination. We can leverage this route decision process to create a floating static route that will not be installed in the routing table unless the primary static route fails.

For example, refer to the topologies in Figures 2-1 and 2-2. HQ has two connections to ISP. Let's assume that the link attached to Serial 0/1/0 is a high-speed primary route that HQ uses as the primary route to send traffic to ISP. The other link attached to Serial 0/1/1 is a much slower connection and is used only as a backup route in case the primary route fails.

To configure this backup route as a floating static route, we must manually set the administrative distance to be higher than the default administrative distance of a static route. Because a static route's default administrative distance is 1, anything higher than 1 will suffice to create the floating static route. The command syntax for both IPv4 and IPv6 static and default routes with the administrative distance option follows:

```
Router(config)# ip route network mask {next-hop-ip | exit-intf} [admin-dist]

Router(config)# ip route 0.0.0.0 0.0.0.0 {exit-intf | next-hop-ip} [admin-dist]

Router(config)# ipv6 route ::/0 {ipv6-address | interface-type interface-number} [admin-dist]

Router(config)# ipv6 route ipv6-prefix/prefix-length {ipv6-address|interface-type interface-number}  [admin-dist]
```

Refer to Figure 2-1. Record the command to configure HQ with an IPv4 floating static default route to ISP.

HQ(config)# _____

Refer to Figure 2-2. Record the command to configure HQ with an IPv6 floating static default route to ISP.

HQ(config)# _____

Configure Static Host Routes

A host route is an IPv4 address with a 32-bit mask or an IPv6 address with a 128-bit mask. A host route can be added to the routing table three ways:

- Automatically installed when an IP address is configured on the router

- Configured as a static host route

- Host route automatically obtained through other methods (discussed in later chapters)

In routing tables in Example 2-1, indicate which route entries are host routes.

Example 2-1   Identify the Host Routes

```
R1# show ip route
Codes: L-local, C-connected, S-static, R-RIP, M-mobile, B-BGP
       D-EIGRP, EX-EIGRP external, O-OSPF, IA-OSPF inter area
       N1-OSPF NSSA external type 1, N2-OSPF NSSA external type 2
       E1-OSPF external type 1, E2-OSPF external type 2, E-EGP
       i-IS-IS, L1-IS-IS level-1, L2-IS-IS level-2, ia-IS-IS inter area
       *-candidate default, U-per-user static route, o-ODR
       P-periodic downloaded static route


Gateway of last resort is not set


      192.168.11.0/24 is variably subnetted, 2 subnets, 2 masks
C        192.168.11.0/24 is directly connected, GigabitEthernet0/0
L        192.168.11.1/32 is directly connected, GigabitEthernet0/0
      192.168.12.0/24 is variably subnetted, 2 subnets, 2 masks
C        192.168.12.0/24 is directly connected, GigabitEthernet0/1
L        192.168.12.1/32 is directly connected, GigabitEthernet0/1
R1# show ipv6 route
IPv6 Routing Table-5 entries
Codes: C-Connected, L-Local, S-Static, R-RIP, B-BGP
       U-Per-user Static route, M-MIPv6
       I1-ISIS L1, I2-ISIS L2, IA-ISIS interarea, IS-ISIS summary
       O-OSPF intra, OI-OSPF inter, OE1-OSPF ext 1, OE2-OSPF ext 2
       ON1-OSPF NSSA ext 1, ON2-OSPF NSSA ext 2
       D-EIGRP, EX-EIGRP external
C   2001:DB8:1::/64 [0/0]
     via ::, GigabitEthernet0/0
L   2001:DB8:1::1/128 [0/0]
     via ::, GigabitEthernet0/0
C   2001:DB8:2::/64 [0/0]
     via ::, GigabitEthernet0/1
L   2001:DB8:2::1/128 [0/0]
     via ::, GigabitEthernet0/1
```

```
L   FF00::/8 [0/0]
       via ::, Null0


R1#
```

To configure a static host route, use a destination IP address and a 255.255.255.255 (/32) mask for IPv4 host routes and a /128 prefix length for IPv6 host routes.

Record the static host routes to configure B1 to access the server on HQ. Both routes should use the next-hop IP address. For the IPv6 static host route, use the link-local address as the next hop and record to the command to fully specify the route.

B1# _____

_____

_____

Packet Tracer Exercise 2-1: Configuring Static and Default Routes

Now you are ready to use Packet Tracer to apply your knowledge about static and default routing. Download and open the file LSG02-0201.pka found at the companion website for this book. Refer to the Introduction of this book for specifics on accessing files.

Note: The following instructions are also contained within the Packet Tracer Exercise.

In this Packet Tracer activity, you will configure B1, B2, and HQ with a variety of static routes.

Requirements

Configure B1 using the following requirements:

- Next-hop IPv4 static default route to HQ

- Fully specified IPv6 static default route to HQ

- Next-hop IPv4 static host route to the HQ Simulated Server

- Next-hop IPv6 static host route to the HQ Simulated Server

Configure B2 using the following requirements:

- Next-hop IPv4 static default route to HQ

- Exit interface IPv6 static default route to HQ

Configure HQ using the following requirements:

- Next-hop IPv4 static route to the B1 LAN

- Next-hop IPv4 static route to the B2 LAN

- Next-hop IPv6 static route to the B1 LAN

- Next-hop IPv6 static route to the B2 LAN

- Exit interface (Serial 0/1/0) IPv4 static default route to ISP

- Exit interface (Serial 0/1/1) IPv4 floating static default route to ISP with AD of 5

- Exit interface (Serial 0/1/0) IPv6 static default route to ISP

- Exit interface (Serial 0/1/1) IPv6 floating static default route to ISP with AD of 5

Test your floating static route configurations by disabling one of the interfaces on HQ. All routers should still be able to ping ISP's Simulated Web Server. Your completion percentage should be 100%. If not, click **Check Results** to see which required components are not yet completed.

Troubleshoot Static and Default Route Issues

When there is a change in the network, connectivity may be lost. Network administrators are responsible for pinpointing and solving the problem. To find and solve these issues, a network administrator must be familiar with the tools to help isolate routing problems quickly.

Common IOS troubleshooting commands include the following:

```
ping
traceroute
show ip route
show ip interface brief
show cdp neighbors detail
```

IPv4 Static and Default Route Implementation

One of the best ways to learn how to troubleshoot a given technology is to practice. Implement the IPv4 scenario in Figure 2-1 and Table 2-3 in a simulator or with lab equipment. Verify your configurations by testing for full connectivity. From B1 and B2, you should be able to ping the loopback interface on ISP. After you have a complete implementation, ask a fellow student or lab partner to break your configuration. Use your troubleshooting skills to locate and solve the problem.

IPv6 Static and Default Route Implementation

Now practice implementing IPv6 static and default routes. For an extra challenge, implement IPv6 in a dual-stack configuration with your IPv4 implementation. Verify connectivity, and then have your lab partner break your configuration. Use your troubleshooting skills to locate and solve the problem.

Labs and Activities

Command Reference

In Table 2-5, record the command, including the correct router or switch prompt, that fits the description. Fill in any blanks with the appropriate missing information.

Table 2-5 Commands for Chapter 2, "Static Routing"

Command	Description
	Configure a static route to IPv4 network 192.168.1.0/24 using 172.16.1.2 as the next-hop IPv4 address.
	Configure a static route to the IPv6 network 2001:DB8:A::/64 using 2001:DB8:1::2 as the next-hop IPv6 address.
	Configure an IPv4 default route using Serial 0/0/0 as the exit interface.
	Configure an IPv6 default route using Serial 0/0/0 as the exit interface.
	Configure an IPv4 floating static route to network 10.0.0.0/24 using Serial 0/0/0 as the exit interface and an AD of 10.
	Configure an IPv6 fully specified floating static default route using Serial 0/0/0 as the exit, fe80::1 as the next-hop address, and an AD of 10.

2.0.1.2 Lab–Which Way Should We Go?

Objectives

Explain the benefits of using static routes.

Scenario

A huge sporting event is about to take place in your city. To attend the event, you make concise plans to arrive at the sports arena on time to see the entire game.

There are two routes you can take to drive to the event:

- Highway route—It is easy to follow and fast driving speeds are allowed.

- Alternative, direct route—You found this route using a city map. Depending on conditions, such as the amount of traffic or congestion, this just may be the way to get to the arena on time!

With a partner, discuss these options. Choose a preferred route to arrive at the arena in time to see every second of the huge sporting event.

Compare your optional preferences to network traffic; which route would you choose to deliver data communications for your small- to medium-sized business? Would it be the fastest, easiest route or the alternative, direct route? Justify your choice.

Complete the modeling activity .pdf and be prepared to justify your answers to the class or with another group.

Required Resources

None

Reflection

1. Which route did you choose as your first preference? On what criteria did you base your decision?

   _____

2. If traffic congestion were to occur on either route, would this change the path you would take to the arena? Explain your answer.

   _____

3. A popular phrase that can be argued is "the shortest distance between two points is a straight line." Is this always true with delivery of network data? How do you compare your answer to this modeling activity scenario?

   _____

2.2.2.4 Packet Tracer–Configuring IPv4 Static and Default Routes

Topology

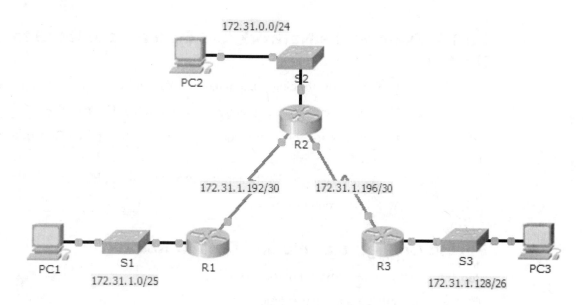

Addressing Table

Device	Interface	IPv4 Address	Subnet Mask	Default Gateway
R1	G0/0	172.31.1.1	255.255.255.128	N/A
	S0/0/0	172.31.1.194	255.255.255.252	N/A
R2	G0/0	172.31.0.1	255.255.255.0	N/A
	S0/0/0	172.31.1.193	255.255.255.252	N/A
	S0/0/1	172.31.1.197	255.255.255.252	N/A
R3	G0/0	172.31.1.129	255.255.255.192	N/A
	S0/0/1	172.31.1.198	255.255.255.252	N/A
PC1	NIC	172.31.1.126	255.255.255.128	172.31.1.1
PC2	NIC	172.31.0.254	255.255.255.0	172.31.0.1
PC3	NIC	172.31.1.190	255.255.255.192	172.31.1.129

Objectives

Part 1: Examine the Network and Evaluate the Need for Static Routing

Part 2: Configure Static and Default Routes

Part 3: Verify Connectivity

Background

In this activity, you will configure static and default routes. A static route is a route that is entered manually by the network administrator to create a reliable and safe route. There are four different static routes that are used in this activity: a recursive static route, a directly attached static route, a fully specified static route, and a default route.

Part 1: Examine the Network and Evaluate the Need for Static Routing

a. Looking at the topology diagram, how many networks are there in total? _____

b. How many networks are directly connected to R1, R2, and R3? _____

c. How many static routes are required by each router to reach networks that are not directly connected? _____

d. Test connectivity to the R2 and R3 LANs by pinging PC2 and PC3 from PC1.

Why were you unsuccessful? _____

Part 2: Configure Static and Default Routes

Step 1:   Configure recursive static routes on R1.

a. What is a recursive static route? _____

_____

_____

b. Why does a recursive static route require two routing table lookups? _____

_____

_____

c. Configure a recursive static route to every network not directly connected to R1, including the WAN link between R2 and R3.

_____

_____

_____

d. Test connectivity to the R2 LAN and ping the IP addresses of PC2 and PC3.

Why were you unsuccessful? _____

_____

Step 2:   Configure directly attached static routes on R2.

a. How does a directly attached static route differ from a recursive static route? _____

_____

_____

b. Configure a directly attached static route from R2 to every network not directly connected.

_____

_____

c. Which command only displays directly connected networks? _____

d. Which command only displays the static routes listed in the routing table? _____

_____

e. When viewing the entire routing table, how can you distinguish between a directly attached static route and a directly connected network? _____

_____

Step 3: Configure a default route on R3.

a. How does a default route differ from a regular static route? _____

_____

_____

_____

b. Configure a default route on R3 so that every network not directly connected is reachable.

_____

c. How is a static route displayed in the routing table? _____

Step 4: Document the commands for fully specified routes.

Note: Packet Tracer does not currently support configuring fully specified static routes. Therefore, in this step, document the configuration for fully specified routes.

a. Explain a fully specified route. _____

_____

b. Which command provides a fully specified static route from R3 to the R2 LAN?

_____

c. Write a fully specified route from R3 to the network between R2 and R1. Do not configure the route; just calculate it.

_____

d. Write a fully specified static route from R3 to the R1 LAN. Do not configure the route; just calculate it.

_____

Step 5: Verify static route configurations.

Use the appropriate **show** commands to verify correct configurations.

Which **show** commands can you use to verify that the static routes are configured correctly?

_____

Part 3: Verify Connectivity

Every device should now be able to ping every other device. If not, review your static and default route configurations.

Suggested Scoring Rubric

Activity Section	Question Location	Possible Points	Earned Points
Part 1: Examine the Network and Evaluate the Need for Static Routing	a-d	10	
	Part 1 Total	10	
Part 2: Configure Static and Default Routes	Step 1	7	
	Step 2	7	
	Step 3	3	
	Step 4	10	
	Step 5	3	
	Part 2 Total	30	
	Packet Tracer Score	60	
	Total Score	100	

2.2.2.5 Lab–Configuring IPv4 Static and Default Routes

Topology

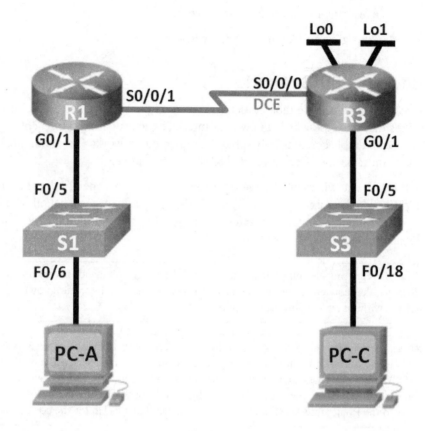

Addressing Table

Device	Interface	IP Address	Subnet Mask	Default Gateway
R1	G0/1	192.168.0.1	255.255.255.0	N/A
	S0/0/1	10.1.1.1	255.255.255.252	N/A
R3	G0/1	192.168.1.1	255.255.255.0	N/A
	S0/0/0 (DCE)	10.1.1.2	255.255.255.252	N/A
	Lo0	209.165.200.225	255.255.255.224	N/A
	Lo1	198.133.219.1	255.255.255.0	N/A
PC-A	NIC	192.168.0.10	255.255.255.0	192.168.0.1
PC-C	NIC	192.168.1.10	255.255.255.0	192.168.1.1

Objectives

Part 1: Set Up the Topology and Initialize Devices

Part 2: Configure Basic Device Settings and Verify Connectivity

Part 3: Configure Static Routes

- Configure a recursive static route.

- Configure a directly connected static route.

- Configure and remove static routes.

Part 4: Configure and Verify a Default Route

Background/Scenario

A router uses a routing table to determine where to send packets. The routing table contains a set of routes that describe which gateway or interface the router uses to reach a specified network. Initially, the routing table contains only directly connected networks. To communicate with distant networks, routes must be specified and added to the routing table.

In this lab, you will manually configure a static route to a specified distant network based on a next-hop IP address or exit interface. You will also configure a static default route. A default route is a type of static route that specifies a gateway to use when the routing table does not contain a path for the destination network.

Note: This lab provides minimal assistance with the actual commands necessary to configure static routing. However, the required commands are provided in Appendix A. Test your knowledge by trying to configure the devices without referring to the appendix.

Note: The routers used with CCNA hands-on labs are Cisco 1941 Integrated Services Routers (ISRs) with Cisco IOS Release 15.2(4)M3 (universalk9 image). The switches used are Cisco Catalyst 2960s with Cisco IOS Release 15.0(2) (lanbasek9 image). Other routers, switches, and Cisco IOS versions can be used. Depending on the model and Cisco IOS version, the commands available and output produced might vary from what is shown in the labs. Refer to the Router Interface Summary Table at the end of this lab for the correct interface identifiers.

Note: Make sure that the routers and switches have been erased and have no startup configurations. If you are unsure, contact your instructor.

Required Resources

- 2 Routers (Cisco 1941 with Cisco IOS Release 15.2(4)M3 universal image or comparable)

- 2 Switches (Cisco 2960 with Cisco IOS Release 15.0(2) lanbasek9 image or comparable)

- 2 PCs (Windows 7, Vista, or XP with terminal emulation program, such as Tera Term)

- Console cables to configure the Cisco IOS devices via the console ports

- Ethernet and serial cables as shown in the topology

Part 1: Set Up the Topology and Initialize Devices

Step 1:   Cable the network as shown in the topology.

Step 2:   Initialize and reload the router and switch.

Part 2: Configure Basic Device Settings and Verify Connectivity

In Part 2, you will configure basic settings, such as the interface IP addresses, device access, and passwords. You will verify LAN connectivity and identify routes listed in the routing tables for R1 and R3.

Step 1:   Configure the PC interfaces.

Step 2:   Configure basic settings on the routers.

    a.   Configure device names, as shown in the Topology and Addressing Table.

    b.   Disable DNS lookup.

    c.   Assign **class** as the enable password and assign **cisco** as the console and vty password.

    d.   Save the running configuration to the startup configuration file.

Step 3:   Configure IP settings on the routers.

    a.   Configure the R1 and R3 interfaces with IP addresses according to the Addressing Table.

    b.   The S0/0/0 connection is the DCE connection and requires the **clock rate** command. The R3 S0/0/0 configuration is displayed below.

```
R3(config)# interface s0/0/0
R3(config-if)# ip address 10.1.1.2 255.255.255.252
R3(config-if)# clock rate 128000
R3(config-if)# no shutdown
```

Step 4:   Verify connectivity of the LANs.

    a.   Test connectivity by pinging from each PC to the default gateway that has been configured for that host.

       From PC-A, is it possible to ping the default gateway? _____

       From PC-C, is it possible to ping the default gateway? _____

    b.   Test connectivity by pinging between the directly connected routers.

       From R1, is it possible to ping the S0/0/0 interface of R3? _____

       If the answer is **no** to any of these questions, troubleshoot the configurations and correct the error.

    c.   Test connectivity between devices that are not directly connected.

       From PC-A, is it possible to ping PC-C? _____

       From PC-A, is it possible to ping Lo0? _____

       From PC-A, is it possible to ping Lo1? _____

       Were these pings successful? Why or why not?

       _____

       _____

Note: It may be necessary to disable the PC firewall to ping between PCs.

Step 5:   Gather information.

a.   Check the status of the interfaces on R1 with the **show ip interface brief** command.

How many interfaces are activated on R1? _____

b.   Check the status of the interfaces on R3.

How many interfaces are activated on R3? _____

c.   View the routing table information for R1 using the **show ip route** command.

What networks are present in the Addressing Table of this lab, but not in the routing table for R1?

_____

d.   View the routing table information for R3.

What networks are present in the Addressing Table in this lab, but not in the routing table for R3?

_____

Why are all the networks not in the routing tables for each of the routers?

_____

_____

Part 3: Configure Static Routes

In Part 3, you will employ multiple ways to implement static and default routes, you will confirm that the routes have been added to the routing tables of R1 and R3, and you will verify connectivity based on the introduced routes.

Note: This lab provides minimal assistance with the actual commands necessary to configure static routing. However, the required commands are provided in Appendix A. Test your knowledge by trying to configure the devices without referring to the appendix.

Step 1:   Configure a recursive static route.

With a recursive static route, the next-hop IP address is specified. Because only the next-hop IP is specified, the router must perform multiple lookups in the routing table before forwarding packets. To configure recursive static routes, use the following syntax:

```
Router(config)# ip route network-address subnet-mask ip-address
```

a.   On the R1 router, configure a static route to the 192.168.1.0 network using the IP address of the Serial 0/0/0 interface of R3 as the next-hop address. Write the command you used in the space provided.

_____

b.   View the routing table to verify the new static route entry.

How is this new route listed in the routing table?

_____

From host PC-A, is it possible to ping the host PC-C? _____

These pings should fail. If the recursive static route is correctly configured, the ping arrives at PC-C. PC-C sends a ping reply back to PC-A. However, the ping reply is discarded at R3 because R3 does not have a return route to the 192.168.0.0 network in the routing table.

Step 2:   Configure a directly connected static route.

With a directly connected static route, the *exit-interface* parameter is specified, which allows the router to resolve a forwarding decision in one lookup. A directly connected static route is typically used with a point-to-point serial interface. To configure directly connected static routes with an exit interface specified, use the following syntax:

```
Router(config)# ip route network-address subnet-mask exit-intf
```

a.   On the R3 router, configure a static route to the 192.168.0.0 network using S0/0/0 as the exit interface. Write the command you used in the space provided.

_____

b.   View the routing table to verify the new static route entry.

How is this new route listed in the routing table?

_____

c.   From host PC-A, is it possible to ping the host PC-C? _____

This ping should be successful.

_____

Note: It may be necessary to disable the PC firewall to ping between PCs.

_____

Step 3:   Configure a static route.

a.   On the R1 router, configure a static route to the 198.133.219.0 network using one of the static route configuration options from the previous steps. Write the command you used in the space provided.

_____

b.   On the R1 router, configure a static route to the 209.165.200.224 network on R3 using the other static route configuration option from the previous steps. Write the command you used in the space provided.

_____

c.   View the routing table to verify the new static route entry.

How is this new route listed in the routing table?

_____

d.   From host PC-A, is it possible to ping the R1 address 198.133.219.1? _____

This ping should be successful.

Step 4:   Remove static routes for loopback addresses.

a.   On R1, use the **no** command to remove the static routes for the two loopback addresses from the routing table. Write the commands you used in the space provided.

_____

b. View the routing table to verify the routes have been removed.

How many network routes are listed in the routing table on R1? _____

Is the Gateway of last resort set? _____

Part 4: Configure and Verify a Default Route

In Part 4, you will implement a default route, confirm that the route has been added to the routing table, and verify connectivity based on the introduced route.

A default route identifies the gateway to which the router sends all IP packets for which it does not have a learned or static route. A default static route is a static route with 0.0.0.0 as the destination IP address and subnet mask. This is commonly referred to as a "quad zero" route.

In a default route, either the next-hop IP address or exit interface can be specified. To configure a default static route, use the following syntax:

```
Router(config)# ip route 0.0.0.0 0.0.0.0 {ip-address or exit-intf}
```

a. Configure the R1 router with a default route using the exit interface of S0/0/1. Write the command you used in the space provided.

_____

b. View the routing table to verify the new static route entry.

How is this new route listed in the routing table?

_____

What is the Gateway of last resort?

_____

c. From host PC-A, is it possible to ping the 209.165.200.225? _____

d. From host PC-A, is it possible to ping the 198.133.219.1? _____

These pings should be successful.

Reflection

1. A new network 192.168.3.0/24 is connected to interface G0/0 on R1. What commands could be used to configure a static route to that network from R3?

_____

_____

2. Is there a benefit to configuring a directly connected static route instead of a recursive static route?

_____

_____

3. Why is it important to configure a default route on a router?

_____

Router Interface Summary Table

	Router Interface Summary			
Router Model	Ethernet Interface #1	Ethernet Interface #2	Serial Interface #1	Serial Interface #2
1800	Fast Ethernet 0/0 (F0/0)	Fast Ethernet 0/1 (F0/1)	Serial 0/0/0 (S0/0/0)	Serial 0/0/1 (S0/0/1)
1900	Gigabit Ethernet 0/0 (G0/0)	Gigabit Ethernet 0/1 (G0/1)	Serial 0/0/0 (S0/0/0)	Serial 0/0/1 (S0/0/1)
2801	Fast Ethernet 0/0 (F0/0)	Fast Ethernet 0/1 (F0/1)	Serial 0/1/0 (S0/1/0)	Serial 0/1/1 (S0/1/1)
2811	Fast Ethernet 0/0 (F0/0)	Fast Ethernet 0/1 (F0/1)	Serial 0/0/0 (S0/0/0)	Serial 0/0/1 (S0/0/1)
2900	Gigabit Ethernet 0/0 (G0/0)	Gigabit Ethernet 0/1 (G0/1)	Serial 0/0/0 (S0/0/0)	Serial 0/0/1 (S0/0/1)

Note: To find out how the router is configured, look at the interfaces to identify the type of router and how many interfaces the router has. There is no way to effectively list all the combinations of configurations for each router class. This table includes identifiers for the possible combinations of Ethernet and Serial interfaces in the device. The table does not include any other type of interface, even though a specific router may contain one. An example of this might be an ISDN BRI interface. The string in parentheses is the legal abbreviation that can be used in Cisco IOS commands to represent the interface.

Appendix A: Configuration Commands for Parts 2, 3, and 4

The commands listed in Appendix A are for reference only. This appendix does not include all the specific commands necessary to complete this lab.

Basic Device Settings

Configure IP settings on the router.

```
R3(config)# interface s0/0/0
R3(config-if)# ip address 10.1.1.2 255.255.255.252
R3(config-if)# clock rate 128000
R3(config-if)# no shutdown
```

Static Route Configurations

Configure a recursive static route.

```
R1(config)# ip route 192.168.1.0 255.255.255.0 10.1.1.2
```

Configure a directly connected static route.

```
R3(config)# ip route 192.168.0.0 255.255.255.0 s0/0/0
```

Remove static routes.

```
R1(config)# no ip route 209.165.200.224 255.255.255.224 serial0/0/1
```

or

```
R1(config)# no ip route 209.165.200.224 255.255.255.224 10.1.1.2
```

or

```
R1(config)# no ip route 209.165.200.224 255.255.255.224
```

Default Route Configuration

```
R1(config)# ip route 0.0.0.0 0.0.0.0 s0/0/1
```

2.2.4.4 Packet Tracer–Configuring IPv6 Static and Default Routes

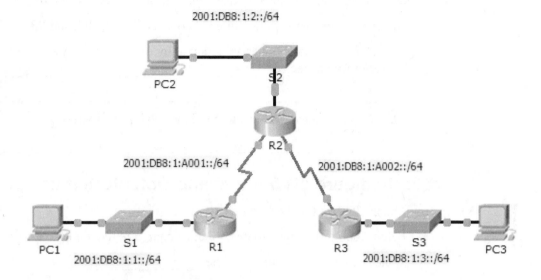

IPv6 Addressing Table

Device	Interface	IPv6 Address/Prefix	Default Gateway
R1	G0/0	2001:DB8:1:1::1/64	N/A
	S0/0/0	2001:DB8:1:A001::1/64	N/A
R2	G0/0	2001:DB8:1:2::1/64	N/A
	S0/0/0	2001:DB8:1:A001::2/64	N/A
	S0/0/1	2001:DB8:1:A002::1/64	N/A
R3	G0/0	2001:DB8:1:3::1/64	N/A
	S0/0/1	2001:DB8:1:A002::2/64	N/A
PC1	NIC	2001:DB8:1:1::F/64	FE80::1
PC2	NIC	2001:DB8:1:2::F/64	FE80::2
PC3	NIC	2001:DB8:1:3::F/64	FE80::3

Objectives

Part 1: Examine the Network and Evaluate the Need for Static Routing

Part 2: Configure IPv6 Static and Default Routes

Part 3: Verify Connectivity

Background

In this activity, you will configure IPv6 static and default routes. A static route is a route that is entered manually by the network administrator in order to create a route that is reliable and safe. There are four different static routes used in this activity: a recursive static route; a directly attached static route; a fully specified static route; and a default route.

Part 1: Examine the Network and Evaluate the Need for Static Routing

a. Looking at the topology diagram, how many networks are there in total? _____

b. How many networks are directly connected to R1, R2, and R3? _____

c. How many static routes are required by each router to reach networks that are not directly connected? _____

_____

d. Which command is used to configure IPv6 static routes? _____

_____

Part 2: Configure IPv6 Static and Default Routes

Step 1: Enable IPv6 routing on all routers.

Before configuring static routes, we must configure the router to forward IPv6 packets

Which command accomplishes this?_____

Enter this command on each router.

Step 2: Configure recursive static routes on R1.

Configure an IPv6 recursive static route to every network not directly connected to R1.

_____

_____

_____

Step 3: Configure a directly attached and a fully specified static route on R2.

a. Configure a directly attached static route from R2 to the R1 LAN.

_____

b. Configure a fully specific route from R2 to the R3 LAN.

_____

Note: Packet Tracer v6.0.1 only checks for directly attached and recursive static routes. Your instructor may ask to review your configuration of a fully specified IPv6 static route.

Step 4: Configure a default route on R3.

Configure a recursive default route on R3 to reach all networks not directly connected.

_____

Step 5: Verify static route configurations.

a. Which command is used in Packet Tracer to verify the IPv6 configuration of a PC from the command prompt? _____

b. Which command displays the IPv6 addresses configured on a router's interface? _____

_____

c. Which command displays the contents of the IPv6 routing table? _____

Part 3: Verify Network Connectivity

Every device should now be able to ping every other device. If not, review your static and default route configurations.

Suggested Scoring Rubric

Activity Section	Question Location	Possible Points	Earned Points
Part 1: Exam the Network and Evaluate the Need for Static Routing	a-d	20	
	Part 1 Total	20	
Part 2: Configure IPv6 Static and Default Routes	Step 1	5	
	Step 5	15	
	Part 2 Total	20	
	Packet Tracer Score	60	
	Total Score	100	

2.2.4.5 Lab–Configuring IPv6 Static and Default Routes

Topology

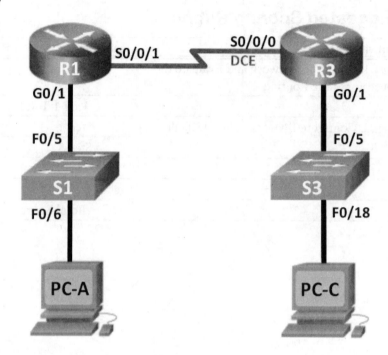

Addressing Table

Device	Interface	IPv6 Address/Prefix Length	Default Gateway
R1	G0/1	2001:DB8:ACAD:A::/64 eui-64	N/A
	S0/0/1	FC00::1/64	N/A
R3	G0/1	2001:DB8:ACAD:B::/64 eui-64	N/A
	S0/0/0	FC00::2/64	N/A
PC-A	NIC	SLAAC	SLAAC
PC-C	NIC	SLAAC	SLAAC

Objectives

Part 1: Build the Network and Configure Basic Device Settings

- Enable IPv6 unicast routing and configure IPv6 addressing on the routers.
- Disable IPv4 addressing and enable IPv6 SLAAC for the PC network interfaces.
- Use **ipconfig** and **ping** to verify LAN connectivity.
- Use **show** commands to verify IPv6 settings.

Part 2: Configure IPv6 Static and Default Routes

- Configure a directly attached IPv6 static route.

- Configure a recursive IPv6 static route.

- Configure a default IPv6 static route.

Background/Scenario

In this lab, you will configure the entire network to communicate using only IPv6 addressing, including configuring the routers and PCs. You will use stateless address auto-configuration (SLAAC) for configuring the IPv6 addresses for the hosts. You will also configure IPv6 static and default routes on the routers to enable communication to remote networks that are not directly connected.

Note: The routers used with CCNA hands-on labs are Cisco 1941 Integrated Services Routers (ISRs) with Cisco IOS Release 15.2(4)M3 (universalk9 image). The switches used are Cisco Catalyst 2960s with Cisco IOS Release 15.0(2) (lanbasek9 image). Other routers, switches, and Cisco IOS versions can be used. Depending on the model and Cisco IOS version, the commands available and output produced might vary from what is shown in the labs. Refer to the Router Interface Summary Table at the end of this lab for the correct interface identifiers.

Note: Make sure that the routers and switches have been erased and have no startup configurations. If you are unsure, contact your instructor.

Required Resources

- 2 Routers (Cisco 1941 with Cisco IOS Release 15.2(4)M3 universal image or comparable)

- 2 Switches (Cisco 2960 with Cisco IOS Release 15.0(2) lanbasek9 image or comparable)

- 2 PCs (Windows 7, Vista, or XP with terminal emulation program, such as Tera Term)

- Console cables to configure the Cisco IOS devices via the console ports

- Ethernet and serial cables as shown in the topology

Part 1: Build the Network and Configure Basic Device Settings

In Part 1, you will cable and configure the network to communicate using IPv6 addressing.

Step 1: Cable the network as shown in the topology diagram.

Step 2: Initialize and reload the routers and switches.

Step 3: Enable IPv6 unicast routing and configure IPv6 addressing on the routers.

    a. Using Tera Term, console into the router labeled R1 in the topology diagram and assign the router the name R1.

    b. Within global configuration mode, enable IPv6 routing on R1.

```
R1(config)# ipv6 unicast-routing
```

    c. Configure the network interfaces on R1 with IPv6 addresses. Notice that IPv6 is enabled on each interface. The G0/1 interface has a globally routable unicast address and EUI-64 is used to create the interface identifier portion of the address. The S0/0/1 interface has a privately routable, unique-local address, which is recommended for point-to-point serial connections.

```
R1(config)# interface g0/1
R1(config-if)# ipv6 address 2001:DB8:ACAD:A::/64 eui-64
R1(config-if)# no shutdown
R1(config-if)# interface serial 0/0/1
R1(config-if)# ipv6 address FC00::1/64
R1(config-if)# no shutdown
R1(config-if)# exit
```

    d. Assign a device name to router R3.

    e. Within global configuration mode, enable IPv6 routing on R3.

```
R3(config)# ipv6 unicast-routing
```

    f. Configure the network interfaces on R3 with IPv6 addresses. Notice that IPv6 is enabled on each interface. The G0/1 interface has a globally routable unicast address and EUI-64 is used to create the interface identifier portion of the address. The S0/0/0 interface has a privately routable, unique-local address, which is recommended for point-to-point serial connections. The clock rate is set because it is the DCE end of the serial cable.

```
R3(config)# interface gigabit 0/1
R3(config-if)# ipv6 address 2001:DB8:ACAD:B::/64 eui-64
R3(config-if)# no shutdown
R3(config-if)# interface serial 0/0/0
R3(config-if)# ipv6 address FC00::2/64
R3(config-if)# clock rate 128000
R3(config-if)# no shutdown
R3(config-if)# exit
```

Step 4:   Disable IPv4 addressing and enable IPv6 SLAAC for the PC network interfaces.

    a. On both PC-A and PC-C, navigate to the **Start** menu > **Control Panel**. Click the **Network and Sharing Center** link while viewing with icons. In the Network and Sharing Center window, click the **Change adapter settings** link on the left side of the window to open the Network Connections window.

    b. In the Network Connections window, you see the icons for your network interface adapters. Double-click the Local Area Connection icon for the PC network interface that is connected to the switch. Click the **Properties** to open the Local Area Connection Properties dialog window.

    c. With the Local Area Connection Properties window open, scroll down through the items and uncheck the item **Internet Protocol Version 4 (TCP/IPv4)** check box to disable the IPv4 protocol on the network interface.

    d. With the Local Area Connection Properties window still open, click the **Internet Protocol Version 6 (TCP/IPv6)** check box, and then click **Properties**.

    e. With the Internet Protocol Version 6 (TCP/IPv6) Properties window open, check to see if the radio buttons for **Obtain an IPv6 address automatically** and **Obtain DNS server address automatically** are selected. If not, select them.

    f. With the PCs configured to obtain an IPv6 address automatically, they will contact the routers to obtain the network subnet and gateway information, and auto-configure their IPv6 address information. In the next step, you will verify the settings.

Step 5:   Use ipconfig and ping to verify LAN connectivity.

    a.   From PC-A, open a command prompt, type **ipconfig /all** and press Enter. The output should look similar to that shown below. In the output, you should see that the PC now has an IPv6 global unicast address, a link-local IPv6 address, and a link-local IPv6 default gateway address. You may also see a temporary IPv6 address and under the DNS server addresses, three site-local addresses that start with FEC0. Site-local addresses are private addresses that were meant to be backwards compatible with NAT. However, they are not supported in IPv6 and are replaced by unique-local addresses.

```
C:\Users\User1> ipconfig /all
Windows IP Configuration

<Output omitted>

Ethernet adapter Local Area Connection:

   Connection-specific DNS Suffix  . :
   Description . . . . . . . . . . . : Intel(R) 82577LC Gigabit Network
Connection
   Physical Address. . . . . . . . . : 1C-C1-DE-91-C3-5D
   DHCP Enabled. . . . . . . . . . . : No
   Autoconfiguration Enabled . . . . : Yes
   IPv6 Address. . . . . . . . . . . : 2001:db8:acad:a:7c0c:7493:218d:2f6c
(Preferred)
   Temporary IPv6 Address. . . . . . : 2001:db8:acad:a:bc40:133a:54e7:d497
(Preferred)
   Link-local IPv6 Address . . . . . : fe80::7c0c:7493:218d:2f6c%13(Preferred)
   Default Gateway . . . . . . . . . : fe80::6273:5cff:fe0d:1a61%13
   DNS Servers . . . . . . . . . . . : fec0:0:0:ffff::1%1
                                       fec0:0:0:ffff::2%1
                                       fec0:0:0:ffff::3%1
   NetBIOS over Tcpip. . . . . . . . : Disabled
```

    Based on your network implementation and the output of the **ipconfig /all** command, did PC-A receive IPv6 addressing information from R1?

    _____

    _____

    _____

    b.   What is the PC-A global unicast IPv6 address?

    _____

    c.   What is the PC-A link-local IPv6 address?

    _____

    d.   What is the PC-A default gateway IPv6 address?

    _____

    e.   From PC-A, use the **ping -6** command to issue an IPv6 ping to the link-local default gateway address. You should see replies from the R1 router.

```
C:\Users\User1> ping -6 <default-gateway-address>
```

Did PC-A receive replies to the ping from PC-A to R1?

_____

f.   Repeat Step 5a from PC-C.

Did PC-C receive IPv6 addressing information from R3?

_____

g.   What is the PC-C global unicast IPv6 address?

_____

h.   What is the PC-C link-local IPv6 address?

_____

i.   What is the PC-C default gateway IPv6 address?

_____

j.   From PC-C, use the **ping -6** command to ping the PC-C default gateway.

Did PC-C receive replies to the pings from PC-C to R3?

_____

k.   Attempt an IPv6 **ping -6** from PC-A to the PC-C IPv6 address.

```
C:\Users\User1> ping -6 PC-C-IPv6-address
```

Was the ping successful? Why or why not?

_____

_____

_____

_____

Step 6:   Use show commands to verify IPv6 settings.

a.   Check the status of the interfaces on R1 with the **show ipv6 interface brief** command.

What are the two IPv6 addresses for the G0/1 interface and what kind of IPv6 addresses are they?

_____

What are the two IPv6 addresses for the S0/0/1 interface and what kind of IPv6 addresses are they?

_____

b.   To see more detailed information on the IPv6 interfaces, type a **show ipv6 interface** command on R1 and press Enter.

What are the multicast group addresses for the Gigabit Ethernet 0/1 interface?

_____

What are the multicast group addresses for the S0/0/1 interface?

_____

What is an FF02::1 multicast address used for?

_____

What is an FF02::2 multicast address used for?

_____

What kind of multicast addresses are FF02::1:FF00:1 and FF02::1:FF0D:1A60, and what are they used for?

_____

c. View the IPv6 routing table information for R1 using the **show ipv6 route** command. The IPv6 routing table should have two connected routes, one for each interface, and three local routes, one for each interface and one for multicast traffic to a Null0 interface.

In what way does the routing table output of R1 reveal why you were unable to ping PC-C from PC-A?

_____

_____

_____

Part 2: Configure IPv6 Static and Default Routes

In Part 2, you will configure IPv6 static and default routes three different ways. You will confirm that the routes have been added to the routing tables, and you will verify successful connectivity between PC-A and PC-C.

You will configure three types of IPv6 static routes:

- **Directly Connected IPv6 Static Route**–A directly connected static route is created when specifying the outgoing interface.

- **Recursive IPv6 Static Route**–A recursive static route is created when specifying the next-hop IP address. This method requires the router to execute a recursive lookup in the routing table in order to identify the outgoing interface.

- **Default IPv6 Static Route**–Similar to a quad zero IPv4 route, a default IPv6 static route is created by making the destination IPv6 prefix and prefix length all zeros, ::/0.

Step 1: Configure a directly connected IPv6 static route.

In a directly connected IPv6 static route, the route entry specifies the router outgoing interface. A directly connected static route is typically used with a point-to-point serial interface. To configure a directly attached IPv6 static route, use the following command format:

```
Router(config)# ipv6 route <ipv6-prefix/prefix-length> <outgoing-interface-type>
<outgoing-interface-number>
```

a. On router R1, configure an IPv6 static route to the 2001:DB8:ACAD:B::/64 network on R3, using the R1 outgoing S0/0/1 interface.

```
R1(config)# ipv6 route 2001:DB8:ACAD:B::/64 serial 0/0/1
R1(config)#
```

b. View the IPv6 routing table to verify the new static route entry.

What is the code letter and routing table entry for the newly added route in the routing table?

_____

_____

c. Now that the static route has been configured on R1, is it now possible to ping the host PC-C from PC-A?

_____

These pings should fail. If the recursive static route is correctly configured, the ping arrives at PC-C. PC-C sends a ping reply back to PC-A. However, the ping reply is discarded at R3 because R3 does not have a return route to the 2001:DB8:ACAD:A::/64 network in the routing table. To successfully ping across the network, you must also create a static route on R3.

d. On router R3, configure an IPv6 static route to the 2001:DB8:ACAD:A::/64 network, using the R3 outgoing S0/0/0 interface.

```
R3(config)# ipv6 route 2001:DB8:ACAD:A::/64 serial 0/0/0
R3(config)#
```

e. Now that both routers have static routes, attempt an IPv6 **ping -6** from PC-A to the PC-C global unicast IPv6 address.

Was the ping successful? Why?

_____

Step 2:   Configure a recursive IPv6 static route.

In a recursive IPv6 static route, the route entry has the next-hop router IPv6 address. To configure a recursive IPv6 static route, use the following command format:

```
Router(config)# ipv6 route <ipv6-prefix/prefix-length> <next-hop-ipv6-address>
```

a. On router R1, delete the directly attached static route and add a recursive static route.

```
R1(config)# no ipv6 route 2001:DB8:ACAD:B::/64 serial 0/0/1
R1(config)# ipv6 route 2001:DB8:ACAD:B::/64 FC00::2
R1(config)# exit
```

b. On router R3, delete the directly attached static route and add a recursive static route.

```
R3(config)# no ipv6 route 2001:DB8:ACAD:A::/64 serial 0/0/0
R3(config)# ipv6 route 2001:DB8:ACAD:A::/64 FC00::1
R3(config)# exit
```

c. View the IPv6 routing table on R1 to verify the new static route entry.

What is the code letter and routing table entry for the newly added route in the routing table?

_____

d. Verify connectivity by issuing a **ping -6** command from PC-A to PC-C.

Was the ping successful? _____

Note: It may be necessary to disable the PC firewall to ping between PCs.

Step 3:   Configure a default IPv6 static route.

In a default static route, the destination IPv6 prefix and prefix length are all zeros.

```
Router(config)# ipv6 route ::/0 <outgoing-interface-type> <outgoing-interface-number> {and/or} <next-hop-ipv6-address>
```

a. On router R1, delete the recursive static route and add a default static route.

```
R1(config)# no ipv6 route 2001:DB8:ACAD:B::/64 FC00::2
R1(config)# ipv6 route ::/0 serial 0/0/1
R1(config)#
```

b. Delete the recursive static route and add a default static route on R3.

c. View the IPv6 routing table on R1 to verify the new static route entry.

What is the code letter and routing table entry for the newly added default route in the routing table?

_____

d. Verify connectivity by issuing a **ping -6** command from PC-A to PC-C.

Was the ping successful? _____

Note: It may be necessary to disable the PC firewall to ping between PCs.

Reflection

1. This lab focuses on configuring IPv6 static and default routes. Can you think of a situation where you would need to configure both IPv6 and IPv4 static and default routes on a router?

_____

_____

_____

_____

2. In practice, configuring an IPv6 static and default route is very similar to configuring an IPv4 static and default route. Aside from the obvious differences between the IPv6 and IPv4 addressing, what are some other differences when configuring and verifying an IPv6 static route as compared to an IPv4 static route?

_____

_____

_____

_____

Router Interface Summary Table

Router Interface Summary				
Router Model	Ethernet Interface #1	Ethernet Interface #2	Serial Interface #1	Serial Interface #2
1800	Fast Ethernet 0/0 (F0/0)	Fast Ethernet 0/1 (F0/1)	Serial 0/0/0 (S0/0/0)	Serial 0/0/1 (S0/0/1)
1900	Gigabit Ethernet 0/0 (G0/0)	Gigabit Ethernet 0/1 (G0/1)	Serial 0/0/0 (S0/0/0)	Serial 0/0/1 (S0/0/1)
2801	Fast Ethernet 0/0 (F0/0)	Fast Ethernet 0/1 (F0/1)	Serial 0/1/0 (S0/1/0)	Serial 0/1/1 (S0/1/1)
2811	Fast Ethernet 0/0 (F0/0)	Fast Ethernet 0/1 (F0/1)	Serial 0/0/0 (S0/0/0)	Serial 0/0/1 (S0/0/1)
2900	Gigabit Ethernet 0/0 (G0/0)	Gigabit Ethernet 0/1 (G0/1)	Serial 0/0/0 (S0/0/0)	Serial 0/0/1 (S0/0/1)

Note: To find out how the router is configured, look at the interfaces to identify the type of router and how many interfaces the router has. There is no way to effectively list all the combinations of configurations for each router class. This table includes identifiers for the possible combinations of Ethernet and Serial interfaces in the device. The table does not include any other type of interface, even though a specific router may contain one. An example of this might be an ISDN BRI interface. The string in parentheses is the legal abbreviation that can be used in Cisco IOS commands to represent the interface.

2.2.5.5 Packet Tracer–Configuring Floating Static Routes

Topology

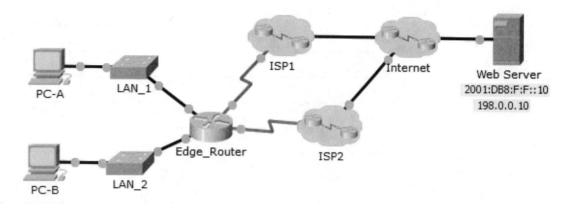

Objectives

Part 1: Configure an IPv4 Floating Static Route

Part 2: Test Failover to the IPv4 Floating Static Route

Part 3: Configure and Test Failover for an IPv6 Floating Static Route

Background

In this activity, you will configure IPv4 and IPv6 floating static routes. These routes are manually configured with an administrative distance greater than that of the primary route and, therefore, would not be in the routing table until the primary route fails. You will test failover to the backup routes, and then restore connectivity to the primary route.

Part 1: Configure an IPv4 Floating Static Route

Step 1:   Configure an IPv4 static default route.

    a.   Configure a directly connected static default route from **Edge_Router** to the Internet. The primary default route should be through **ISP1**.

---

    b.   Display the contents of the routing table. Verify that the default route is visible in the routing table.

---

c. What command is used to trace a path from a PC to a destination? _____

From **PC-A**, trace the route to the **Web Server**. The route should start at the default gateway 192.168.10.1 and go through the 10.10.10.1 address. If not, check your static default route configuration.

_____

_____

_____

_____

_____

_____

_____

_____

Step 2:   Configure an IPv4 floating static route.

    a. What is the administrative distance of a static route? _____

_____

    b. Configure a directly connected floating static default route with an administrative distance of 5. The route should point to **ISP2**.

_____

    c. View the running configuration and verify that the IPv4 floating static default route is there, as well as the IPv4 static default route.

_____

_____

_____

_____

_____

_____

    d. Display the contents of the routing table. Is the IPv4 floating static route visible in the routing table? Explain. _____

_____

_____

Part 2: Test Failover to the IPv4 Floating Static Route

    a. On **Edge_Router**, administratively disable the exit interface of the primary route.

_____

_____

b. Verify that the IPv4 floating static route is now in the routing table.

_____

_____

_____

_____

c. Trace the route from **PC-A** to the **Web Server**.

_____

_____

_____

_____

_____

_____

_____

Did the backup route work? If not, wait a few more seconds for convergence and then re-test. If the backup route is still not working, investigate your floating static route configuration.

d. Restore connectivity to the primary route.

_____

_____

e. Trace the route from **PC-A** to the **Web Server** to verify that the primary route is restored.

_____

_____

_____

_____

_____

_____

_____

_____

Part 3: Configure and Test Failover to an IPv6 Floating Static Route

Step 1: Configure an IPv6 floating static route.

a. The IPv6 static default route to ISP1 is already configured. Configure an IPv6 floating static default route with an administrative distance of 5. The route should point to IPv6 address (**2001:DB8:A:2::1**) of **ISP2**.

_____

b. View the running configuration to verify that the IPv6 floating static default route is now listed under the IPv6 static default route.

_____

_____

_____

_____

_____

_____

_____

Step 2: Test failover to the IPv6 floating static route.

a. On **Edge_Router**, administratively disable the exit interface of the primary route.

_____

b. Verify that the IPv6 floating static route is now in the routing table.

_____

_____

_____

_____

_____

c. Trace the route from **PC-A** to the **Web Server**.

_____

_____

_____

_____

_____

_____

_____

Did the backup route work? If not, wait a few more seconds for convergence and then re-test. If the backup route is still not working, investigate your floating static route configuration.

d. Restore connectivity to the primary route.

_____

_____

e. Trace the route from **PC-A** to the **Web Server** to verify that the primary route is restored.

_____

_____

_____

_____

_____

_____

_____

_____

_____

Suggested Scoring Rubric

Activity Section	Question Location	Possible Points	Earned Points
Part 1: Configuring a Floating Static Route	Step 1c	2	
	Step 2a	3	
	Step 2d	5	
	Part 1 Total	10	
	Packet Tracer Score	90	
	Total Score	100	

Packet Tracer
☐ Activity

2.3.2.3 Packet Tracer–Troubleshooting Static Routes

Topology

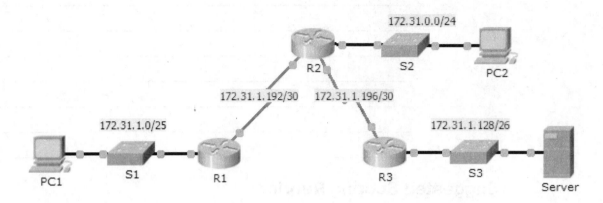

Addressing Table

Device	Interface	IPv4 Address	Subnet Mask	Default Gateway
R1	G0/0	172.31.1.1	255.255.255.128	N/A
	S0/0/0	172.31.1.194	255.255.255.252	N/A
R2	G0/0	172.31.0.1	255.255.255.0	N/A
	S0/0/0	172.31.1.193	255.255.255.252	N/A
	S0/0/1	172.31.1.197	255.255.255.252	N/A
R3	G0/0	172.31.1.129	255.255.255.192	N/A
	S0/0/1	172.31.1.198	255.255.255.252	N/A
PC1	NIC	172.31.1.126	255.255.255.128	172.31.1.1
PC2	NIC	172.31.0.254	255.255.255.0	172.31.0.1
Server	NIC	172.31.1.190	255.255.255.192	172.31.1.129

Objectives

Part 1: Locate the Problem

Part 2: Determine the Solution

Part 3: Implement the Solution

Part 4: Verify That the Issue Is Resolved

Background

In this activity, PC1 reports that they cannot access resources on the server. Locate the problem, decide on an appropriate solution and resolve the issue.

Part 1: Locate the Problem

PC1 cannot access files on the server. Locate the problem using the appropriate **show** commands on all routers and any troubleshooting commands on the PCs that you have learned from previous chapters.

What are some of the troubleshooting commands on routers and PCs that can be used to identify the source of the problem? _____

Part 2: Determine the Solution

After you have located the problem that is preventing PC1 from accessing files on the server, fill in the table below.

Problem	Solution

Part 3: Implement the Solution

a. If there are any misconfigured static routes, you must remove them before the correct ones can be added to the configuration.

_____

_____

_____

_____

b. Add any missing static routes by configuring directly attached routes.

_____

Part 4: Verify That the Issue Is Resolved

a. Ping from PC1 to the server.

b. Open a web connection to the server. After you correctly identify and implement the correct solution to the problem, you will receive a message in the web browser when you connect to the server.

Suggested Scoring Rubric

Activity Section	Possible Points	Earned Points
Part 1: Locate the Problem	2	
Part 2: Determine the Solution	8	
Packet Tracer Score	90	
Total Score	100	

2.3.2.4 Lab–Troubleshooting IPv4 and IPv6 Static Routes

Topology

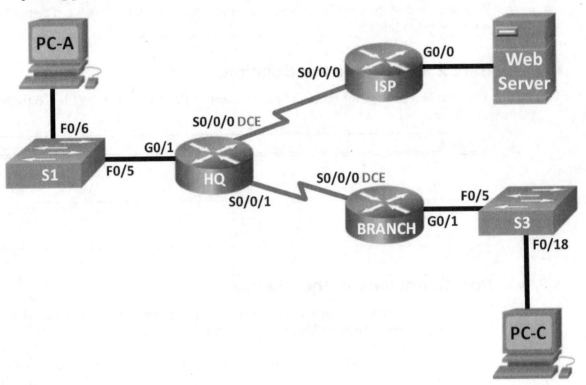

Addressing Table

Device	Interface	IP Address	Default Gateway
HQ	G0/1	192.168.0.1/25	N/A
		2001:DB8:ACAD::1/64	
		FE80::1 link-local	
	S0/0/0 (DCE)	10.1.1.2/30	N/A
		2001:DB8:ACAD::20:2/64	
	S0/0/1	192.168.0.253/30	N/A
		2001:DB8:ACAD:2::1/30	
ISP	G0/0	172.16.3.1/24	N/A
		2001:DB8:ACAD:30::1/64	
		FE80::1 link-local	
	S0/0/0	10.1.1.1/30	N/A
		2001:DB8:ACAD:20::1/64	

Device	Interface	IP Address	Default Gateway
BRANCH	G0/1	192.168.1.1/24	N/A
		2001:DB8:ACAD:1::1/64	
		FE80::1 link-local	
	S0/0/0 (DCE)	192.168.0.254/30	N/A
		2001:DB8:ACAD:2::2/64	
S1	VLAN 1	N/A	N/A
S3	VLAN 1	N/A	N/A
PC-A	NIC	192.168.0.3/25	192.168.0.1
		2001:DB8:ACAD::3/64	FE80::1
Web Server	NIC	172.16.3.3/24	172.16.3.1
		2001:DB8:ACAD:30::3/64	FE80::1
PC-C	NIC	192.168.1.3/24	192.168.1.1
		2001:DB8:ACAD:1::3/64	FE80::1

Objectives

Part 1: Build the Network and Configure Basic Device Settings

Part 2: Troubleshoot Static Routes in an IPv4 Network

Part 3: Troubleshoot Static Routes in an IPv6 Network

Background/Scenario

As a network administrator, you must be able to configure routing of traffic using static routes. Understanding how to configure and troubleshoot static routing is a requirement. Static routes are commonly used for stub networks and default routes. Your company's ISP has hired you to troubleshoot connectivity issues on the network. You will have access to the HQ, BRANCH, and the ISP routers.

In this lab, you will begin by loading configuration scripts on each of the routers. These scripts contain errors that will prevent end-to-end communication across the network. You will need to troubleshoot each router to determine the configuration errors, and then use the appropriate commands to correct the configurations. When you have corrected all of the configuration errors, the hosts on the network should be able to communicate with each other.

Note: The routers used with CCNA hands-on labs are Cisco 1941 Integrated Services Routers (ISRs) with Cisco IOS Release 15.2(4)M3 (universalk9 image). The switches used are Cisco Catalyst 2960s with Cisco IOS Release 15.0(2) (lanbasek9 image). Other routers, switches, and Cisco IOS versions can be used. Depending on the model and Cisco IOS version, the commands available and output produced might vary from what is shown in the labs. Refer to the Router Interface Summary Table at the end of this lab for the correct interface identifiers.

Note: Make sure that the routers and switches have been erased and have no startup configurations. If you are unsure, contact your instructor.

Required Resources

- 3 Routers (Cisco 1941 with Cisco IOS Release 15.2(4)M3 universal image or comparable)

- 2 Switches (Cisco 2960 with Cisco IOS Release 15.0(2) lanbasek9 image or comparable)

- 3 PCs (Windows 7, Vista, or XP with terminal emulation program, such as Tera Term)

- Console cables to configure the Cisco IOS devices via the console ports

- Ethernet and serial cables as shown in the topology

Part 1: Build the Network and Configure Basic Device Settings

In Part 1, you will set up the network topology and configure the routers and switches with some basic settings, such as passwords and IP addresses. Preset configurations are also provided for you for the initial router configurations. You will also configure the IP settings for the PCs in the topology.

Step 1: Cable the network as shown in the topology.

Attach the devices as shown in the topology diagram and cable, as necessary.

Step 2: Initialize and reload the routers and switches.

Step 3: Configure basic settings for each router.

    a. Disable DNS lookup.

    b. Configure device name as shown in the topology.

    c. Assign **class** as the privileged EXEC mode password.

    d. Assign **cisco** as the console and vty passwords.

    e. Configure **logging synchronous** to prevent console messages from interrupting command entry.

Step 4: Configure hosts and Web Server.

    a. Configure IP addresses for IPv4 and IPv6.

    b. Configure IPv4 default gateway.

Step 5: Load router configurations.

Router HQ

```
hostname HQ
ipv6 unicast-routing
interface GigabitEthernet0/1
 ipv6 address 2001:DB8:ACAD::1/64
 ip address 192.168.0.1 255.255.255.128
 ipv6 address FE80::1 link-local
interface Serial0/0/0
 ipv6 address 2001:DB8:ACAD:20::2/64
 ip address 10.1.1.2 255.255.255.252
 clock rate 800000
 no shutdown
```

```
interface Serial0/0/1
  ipv6 address 2001:DB8:ACAD:2::3/64
  ip address 192.168.0.253 255.255.255.252
  no shutdown
ip route 172.16.3.0 255.255.255.0 10.1.1.1
ip route 192.168.1.0 255.255.255.0 192.16.0.254
ipv6 route 2001:DB8:ACAD:1::/64 2001:DB8:ACAD:2::2
ipv6 route 2001:DB8:ACAD:30::/64 2001:DB8:ACAD::20:1
```

Router ISP

```
hostname ISP
ipv6 unicast-routing
interface GigabitEthernet0/0
  ipv6 address 2001:DB8:ACAD:30::1/64
  ip address 172.16.3.11 255.255.255.0
  ipv6 address FE80::1 link-local
  no shutdown
interface Serial0/0/0
  ipv6 address 2001:DB8::ACAD:20:1/64
  ip address 10.1.1.1 255.255.255.252
  no shutdown
ip route 192.168.1.0 255.255.255.0 10.1.1.2
ipv6 route 2001:DB8:ACAD::/62 2001:DB8:ACAD:20::2
```

Router BRANCH

```
hostname BRANCH
ipv6 unicast-routing
interface GigabitEthernet0/1
  ipv6 address 2001:DB8:ACAD:1::1/64
  ip address 192.168.1.1 255.255.255.0
  ipv6 address FE80::1 link-local
  no shutdown
interface Serial0/0/0
  ipv6 address 2001:DB8:ACAD:2::2/64
  clock rate 128000
  ip address 192.168.0.249 255.255.255.252
  clock rate 128000
  no shutdown
ip route 0.0.0.0 0.0.0.0 10.1.1.2
ipv6 route ::/0 2001:DB8:ACAD::1
```

Part 2: Troubleshoot Static Routes in an IPv4 Network

IPv4 Addressing Table

Device	Interface	IP Address	Subnet Mask	Default Gateway
HQ	G0/1	192.168.0.1	255.255.255.0	N/A
	S0/0/0 (DCE)	10.1.1.2	255.255.255.252	N/A
	S0/0/1	192.168.0.253	255.255.255.252	N/A
ISP	G0/0	172.16.3.1	255.255.255.0	N/A
	S0/0/0	10.1.1.1	255.255.255.252	N/A
BRANCH	G0/1	192.168.1.1	255.255.255.0	N/A
	S0/0/0 (DCE)	192.168.0.254	255.255.255.252	N/A
S1	VLAN 1	192.168.0.11	255.255.255.128	192.168.0.1
S3	VLAN 1	192.168.1.11	255.255.255.0	192.168.1.1
PC-A	NIC	192.168.0.3	255.255.255.128	192.168.0.1
Web Server	NIC	172.16.3.3	255.255.255.0	172.16.3.1
PC-C	NIC	192.168.1.3	255.255.255.0	192.168.1.1

Step 1:   Troubleshoot the HQ router.

The HQ router is the link between the ISP router and the BRANCH router. The ISP router represents the outside network while the BRANCH router represents the corporate network. The HQ router is configured with static routes to ISP and BRANCH networks.

a.   Display the status of the interfaces on HQ. Enter **show ip interface brief**. Record and resolve any issues as necessary.

_____

_____

b.   Ping from HQ router to BRANCH router (192.168.0.254). Were the pings successful?

_____

c.   Ping from HQ router to ISP router (10.1.1.1). Were the pings successful? _____

d.   Ping from PC-A to the default gateway. Were the pings successful? _____

e.   Ping from PC-A to PC-C. Were the pings successful? _____

f.   Ping from PC-A to Web Server. Were the pings successful? _____

g.   Display the routing table on HQ. What non-directly connected routes are shown in the routing table?

_____

_____

h.   Based on the results of the pings, routing table output, and static routes in the running configuration, what can you conclude about network connectivity?

_____

_____

i. What commands (if any) need to be entered to resolve routing issues? Record the command(s).

_____

_____

_____

j. Repeat any of the steps from b to f to verify whether the problems have been resolved. Record your observations and possible next steps in troubleshooting connectivity.

_____

_____

_____

Step 2:   Troubleshoot the ISP router.

For the ISP router, there should be a route to HQ and BRANCH routers. One static route is configured on the ISP router to reach the 192.168.1.0/24, 192.168.0.0/25, and 192.168.0.252/30 networks.

a. Display the status of interfaces on ISP. Enter **show ip interface brief**. Record and resolve any issues as necessary.

_____

_____

_____

b. Ping from the ISP router to the HQ router (10.1.1.2). Were the pings successful?

_____

c. Ping from Web Server to the default gateway. Were the pings successful? _____

d. Ping from Web Server to PC-A. Were the pings successful? _____

e. Ping from Web Server to PC-C. Were the pings successful? _____

f. Display the routing table on ISP. What non-directly connected routes are shown in the routing table?

_____

_____

g. Based on the results of the pings, routing table output, and static routes in the running configuration, what can you conclude about network connectivity?

_____

_____

_____

h. What commands (if any) need to be entered to resolve routing issues? Record the command(s).

(Hint: ISP only requires one summarized route to the company's networks 192.168.1.0/24, 192.168.0.0/25, and 192.168.0.252/32.)

_____

_____

_____

i. Repeat any of the steps from b to e to verify whether the problems have been resolved. Record your observations and possible next steps in troubleshooting connectivity.

_____

_____

_____

Step 3: Troubleshoot the BRANCH router.

For the BRANCH router, a default route is set to reach the rest of the network and ISP.

a. Display the status of the interfaces on BRANCH. Enter **show ip interface brief**. Record and resolve any issues, as necessary.

_____

_____

b. Ping from the BRANCH router to the HQ router (192.168.0.253). Were the pings successful? _____

c. Ping from PC-C to the default gateway. Were the pings successful? _____

d. Ping from PC-C to PC-A. Were the pings successful? _____

e. Ping from PC-C to Web Server. Were the pings successful? _____

f. Display the routing table on BRANCH. What non-directly connected routes are shown in the routing table?

_____

_____

g. Based on the results of the pings, routing table output, and static routes in the running configuration, what can you conclude about network connectivity?

_____

_____

_____

h. What commands (if any) need to be entered to resolve routing issues? Record the command(s).

_____

_____

_____

i. Repeat any of the steps from b to e to verify whether the problems have been resolved. Record your observations and possible next steps in troubleshooting connectivity.

_____

_____

_____

Part 3: Troubleshoot Static Routes in an IPv6 Network

Device	Interface	IPv6 Address	Prefix Length	Default Gateway
HQ	G0/1	2001:DB8:ACAD::1	64	N/A
	S0/0/0 (DCE)	2001:DB8:ACAD::20:2	64	N/A
	S0/0/1	2001:DB8:ACAD:2::1	64	N/A
ISP	G0/0	2001:DB8:ACAD:30::1	64	N/A
	S0/0/0	2001:DB8:ACAD:20::1	64	N/A
BRANCH	G0/1	2001:DB8:ACAD:1::1	64	N/A
	S0/0/0 (DCE)	2001:DB8:ACAD:2::2	64	N/A
PC-A	NIC	2001:DB8:ACAD::3	64	FE80::1
Web Server	NIC	2001:DB8:ACAD:30::3	64	FE80::1
PC-C	NIC	2001:DB8:ACAD:1::3	64	FE80::1

Step 1: Troubleshoot the HQ router.

The HQ router is the link between the ISP router and the BRANCH router. The ISP router represents the outside network while the BRANCH router represents the corporate network. The HQ router is configured with static routes to both the ISP and the BRANCH networks.

a. Display the status of the interfaces on HQ. Enter **show ipv6 interface brief**. Record and resolve any issues, as necessary.

_____

_____

b. Ping from the HQ router to the BRANCH router (2001:DB8:ACAD:2::2). Were the pings successful? _____

c. Ping from the HQ router to the ISP router (2001:DB8:ACAD:20::1). Were the pings successful? _____

d. Ping from PC-A to the default gateway. Were the pings successful? _____

e. Ping from PC-A to Web Server. Were the pings successful? _____

f. Ping from PC-A to PC-C. Were the pings successful? _____

g. Display the routing table by issuing a **show ipv6 route** command. What non-directly connected routes are shown in the routing table?

_____

_____

_____

h. Based on the results of the pings, routing table output, and static routes in the running configuration, what can you conclude about network connectivity?

_____

_____

_____

i. What commands (if any) need to be entered to resolve routing issues? Record the command(s).

_____

_____

_____

j. Repeat any of the steps from b to f to verify whether the problems have been resolved. Record your observations and possible next steps in troubleshooting connectivity.

_____

_____

_____

Step 2: Troubleshoot the ISP router.

On the ISP router, one static route is configured to reach all the networks on HQ and BRANCH routers.

a. Display the status of the interfaces on ISP. Enter **show ipv6 interface brief**. Record and resolve any issues, as necessary.

_____

_____

b. Ping from the ISP router to the HQ router (2001:DB8:ACAD:20::2). Were the pings successful? _____

c. Ping from Web Server to the default gateway. Were the pings successful? _____

d. Ping from Web Server to PC-A. Were the pings successful? _____

e. Ping from Web Server to PC-C. Were the pings successful? _____

f. Display the routing table. What non-directly connected routes are shown in the routing table?

_____

_____

g. Based on the results of the pings, routing table output, and static routes in the running configuration, what can you conclude about network connectivity?

_____

_____

_____

h. What commands (if any) need to be entered to resolve routing issues? Record the command(s).

_____

_____

i. Repeat any of the steps from b to e to verify whether the problems have been resolved. Record your observations and possible next steps in troubleshooting connectivity.

_____

_____

_____

Step 3: Troubleshoot the BRANCH router.

For the BRANCH routers, there is a default route to the HQ router. This default route allows the BRANCH network to the ISP router and Web Server.

a. Display the status of the interfaces on BRANCH. Enter **show ipv6 interface brief**. Record and resolve any issues, as necessary.

_____

_____

b. Ping from the BRANCH router to the HQ router (2001:DB8:ACAD:2::1). Were the pings successful? _____

c. Ping from the BRANCH router to the ISP router (2001:DB8:ACAD:20::1). Were the pings successful? _____

d. Ping from PC-C to the default gateway. Were the pings successful? _____

e. Ping from PC-C to PC-A. Were the pings successful? _____

f. Ping from PC-C to Web Server. Were the pings successful? _____

g. Display the routing table. What non-directly connected routes are shown in the routing table?

_____

_____

h. Based on the results of the pings, routing table output, and static routes in the running configuration, what can you conclude about network connectivity?

_____

_____

_____

i. What commands (if any) need to be entered to resolve routing issues? Record the command(s).

_____

_____

j. Repeat any of the steps from b to f to verify whether the problems have been resolved. Record your observations and possible next steps in troubleshooting connectivity.

_____

_____

_____

Router Interface Summary Table

Router Interface Summary				
Router Model	Ethernet Interface #1	Ethernet Interface #2	Serial Interface #1	Serial Interface #2
1800	Fast Ethernet 0/0 (F0/0)	Fast Ethernet 0/1 (F0/1)	Serial 0/0/0 (S0/0/0)	Serial 0/0/1 (S0/0/1)
1900	Gigabit Ethernet 0/0 (G0/0)	Gigabit Ethernet 0/1 (G0/1)	Serial 0/0/0 (S0/0/0)	Serial 0/0/1 (S0/0/1)
2801	Fast Ethernet 0/0 (F0/0)	Fast Ethernet 0/1 (F0/1)	Serial 0/1/0 (S0/1/0)	Serial 0/1/1 (S0/1/1)
2811	Fast Ethernet 0/0 (F0/0)	Fast Ethernet 0/1 (F0/1)	Serial 0/0/0 (S0/0/0)	Serial 0/0/1 (S0/0/1)
2900	Gigabit Ethernet 0/0 (G0/0)	Gigabit Ethernet 0/1 (G0/1)	Serial 0/0/0 (S0/0/0)	Serial 0/0/1 (S0/0/1)

Note: To find out how the router is configured, look at the interfaces to identify the type of router and how many interfaces the router has. There is no way to effectively list all the combinations of configurations for each router class. This table includes identifiers for the possible combinations of Ethernet and Serial interfaces in the device. The table does not include any other type of interface, even though a specific router may contain one. An example of this might be an ISDN BRI interface. The string in parentheses is the legal abbreviation that can be used in Cisco IOS commands to represent the interface.

2.4.1.1 Class Activity–Make It Static!

Objectives

Configure a static route.

As the use of IPv6 addressing becomes more prevalent, it is important for network administrators to be able to direct network traffic between routers.

To prove that you are able to direct IPv6 traffic correctly and review the IPv6 default static route curriculum concepts, use the topology as shown in the .pdf file provide, specifically for this activity. Work with a partner to write an IPv6 statement for each of the three scenarios. Try to write the route statements without the assistance of completed labs, Packet Tracer files, etc.

- Scenario 1

  IPv6 default static route from R2 directing all data through your S0/0/0 interface to the next hop address on R1.

- Scenario 2

  IPv6 default static route from R3 directing all data through your S0/0/1 interface to the next hop address on R2.

- Scenario 3

  IPv6 default static route from R2 directing all data through your S0/0/1 interface to the next hop address on R3.

When complete, get together with another group and compare your written answers. Discuss any differences found in your comparisons.

Resources

Topology Diagram

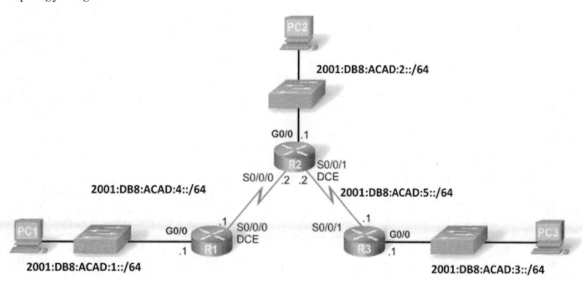

- Scenario 1

IPv6 default static route from R2 directing all data to the next hop address on R1.

Configuration Command	IPv6 Network to Route	Next Hop IPv6 Address
R2(config)# ipv6 route		

- Scenario 2

IPv6 default static route from R3 directing all data to the next hop address on R2.

Configuration Command	IPv6 Network to Route	Next Hop IPv6 Address
R3(config)# ipv6 route		

- Scenario 3

IPv6 default static route from R2 directing all data to the next hop address on R3.

Configuration Command	IPv6 Network to Route	Next Hop IPv6 Address
R2(config)# ipv6 route		

CHAPTER 3

Dynamic Routing

Routers forward packets by using information in the routing table. Routes to remote networks can be learned by the router in two ways: static routes and dynamic routes. In a large network with numerous networks and subnets, configuring and maintaining static routes between these networks requires a great deal of administrative and operational overhead. Implementing dynamic routing protocols can ease the burden of configuration and maintenance tasks and give the network scalability.

The Study Guide portion of this chapter uses a combination of matching, fill-in-the-blank, multiple-choice, and open-ended question exercises to test your knowledge and skills of basic router concepts and configuration. The Labs and Activities portion of this chapter includes all the online curriculum labs and Packet Tracer activities to ensure that you have mastered the hands-on skills needed to understand basic IP addressing and router configuration.

As you work through this chapter, use Chapter 3 in *Routing and Switching Essentials v6 Companion Guide* or use the corresponding Chapter 3 in the Routing and Switching Essentials online curriculum for assistance.

Study Guide

Dynamic Routing Protocols

Dynamic routing protocols have been used in networks since the late 1980s. As networks evolved and became more complex, new routing protocols emerged. To support the communication based on IPv6, newer versions of the IP routing protocols have been developed.

Dynamic Routing Protocol Overview

List at least three purposes of a dynamic routing protocol.

_____

_____

_____

_____

Briefly describe the three main components of dynamic routing protocols.

- Data structures: _____

  _____

- Routing protocol messages: _____

  _____

  _____

- Algorithm: _____

  _____

Compare Static and Dynamic Routing

In Table 3-1, indicate whether the characteristic applies to static routing or dynamic routing.

Table 3-1   Static and Dynamic Routing Characteristics

Characteristic	Static Routing	Dynamic Routing
Suitable for multiple router topologies.		
If possible, adapts topology to reroute traffic.		
Easy to implement in a small network.		
Requires more CPU, RAM, and link bandwidth.		
Route to the destination is always the same.		
More secure because route information is not advertised.		

RIPv2

Although RIP is rarely used in modern networks, it is useful as a foundation for understanding basic network routing. For this reason, this section provides practice for configuring RIPv2 and RIPng.

Configuring the RIP Protocol

Refer to the topology in Figure 3-1 and the addressing scheme in Table 3-2. Label the topology with interface designations and network addresses.

Figure 3-1   RIPv2 Topology

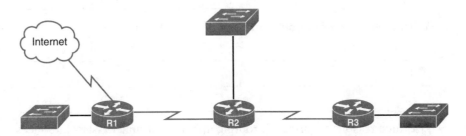

Table 3-2   RIPv2 Addressing Scheme

Device	Interface	IPv4 Address	Subnet Mask
R1	G0/0	172.16.1.1	255.255.255.0
	S0/0/0	172.16.2.1	255.255.255.0
	S0/0/1	209.165.201.2	255.255.255.252
R2	G0/0	172.16.3.1	255.255.255.0
	S0/0/0	172.16.2.2	255.255.255.0
	S0/0/1	172.16.4.2	255.255.255.0
R3	G0/0	172.16.5.1	255.255.255.0
	S0/0/1	172.16.4.1	255.255.255.0

Record the commands to configure each router with RIPv2, disable automatic summarization, and stop routing updates from propagating out unnecessary interfaces.

R1# _____

_____

_____

_____

_____

_____

_____

R2# _____

_____

_____

_____

_____

_____

_____

R3# _____

_____

_____

_____

_____

What is the effect of disabling automatic summarization?

_____

_____

_____

List three reasons for disabling routing updates out unnecessary interfaces.

_____

_____

_____

_____

_____

R1 is connected to the Internet out of Serial 0/0/1, as shown in Figure 3-1. Record the commands to configure a default route and advertise the default route to R2.

R1(config)# _____

_____

_____

Packet Tracer Exercise 3-1: Configuring RIPv2

Now you are ready to use Packet Tracer to apply your knowledge about RIPv2 routing. Download and open the file LSG02-0301.pka found at the companion website for this book. Refer to the Introduction of this book for specifics on accessing files.

Note: The following instructions are also contained in the Packet Tracer exercise.

In this Packet Tracer activity, you will configure the routers to use RIPv2 to advertise networks. Use the addressing table and the commands you documented in the section "Configuring the RIP Protocols."

Requirements

Configure the routers with the following requirements:

- Configure routers to advertise directly connected networks with RIPv2.

- Disable routing updates on unnecessary interfaces.

- Do not allow the routers to summarize networks.

- On R1, configure and propagate a default route to the Internet. Use the next-hop IPv4 address 209.165.201.1.

All routers should now have converged routing tables and be able to ping the Internet at 209.165.201.1. Your completion percentage should be 100%. If not, click **Check Results** to see which required components are not yet completed.

The Routing Table

The structure or format of the routing table might seem obvious until you take a closer look. Understanding the structure of the routing table will help you verify and troubleshoot routing issues because you will understand the routing table lookup process. You will know exactly what the Cisco IOS does when it searches for a route.

Parts of an IPv4 Route Entry

The purpose of this exercise is to practice how to correctly identify the route source, administrative distance, and metric for a given route based on output from the **show ip route** command.

The output is not common for most routing tables. Running more than one routing protocol on the same router is rare. Running three, as shown here, is more of an academic exercise and has value in that it will help you learn to interpret the routing table output.

Using the **show ip route** information in Example 3-1, fill in the missing spaces in Table 3-3.

Note: The output is from IOS 12 so local routes are not shown.

Example 3-1   Multiple Routing Sources in the Routing Table

```
R2# show ip route
Codes: C - connected, S - static, I - IGRP, R - RIP, M - mobile, B - BGP
       D - EIGRP, EX - EIGRP external, O - OSPF, IA - OSPF inter area
       N1 - OSPF NSSA external type 1, N2 - OSPF NSSA external type 2
       E1 - OSPF external type 1, E2 - OSPF external type 2, E - EGP
       i - IS-IS, L1 - IS-IS level-1, L2 - IS-IS level-2, ia - IS-IS inter area
       * - candidate default, U - per-user static route, o - ODR
       P - periodic downloaded static route


Gateway of last resort is not set

     10.0.0.0/16 is subnetted, 1 subnets
S       10.4.0.0 is directly connected, Serial0/0
     172.16.0.0/24 is subnetted, 3 subnets
C       172.16.1.0 is directly connected, FastEthernet0/0
C       172.16.2.0 is directly connected, Serial0/0
D       172.16.3.0 [90/2172416] via 172.16.2.1, 00:00:18, Serial0/0
C    192.168.1.0/24 is directly connected, Serial0/1
O    192.168.100.0/24 [110/65] via 172.16.2.1, 00:00:03, Serial0/0
O    192.168.110.0/24 [110/65] via 172.16.2.1, 00:00:03, Serial0/0
R    192.168.120.0/24 [120/1] via 172.16.2.1, 00:00:18, Serial0/0
```

Table 3-3   Route Sources, AD Values, and Metrics

Route	Route Source	AD	Metric
10.4.0.0/16			
172.16.1.0/24			
172.16.2.0/24			
172.16.3.0/24			
192.168.1.0/24			
192.168.100.0/24			
192.168.110.0/24			
192.168.120.0/24			

Dynamically Learned IPv4 Routes

The Cisco IP routing table is not a flat database, but a _____ structure that is used to speed up the lookup process when locating routes and forwarding packets. This structure includes several levels. For simplicity, we will discuss all routes as one of two levels: level 1 or level 2.

Briefly describe an ultimate route.

_____

_____

Briefly describe a level 1 route.

_____

List the three types of level 1 routes.

_____

List the three sources of level 1 routes.

_____

The level 1 route can be further defined as an ultimate route.

Indicate which of the following routes are level 1 routes by writing **yes** or **no** in the blank in front of the route:

_____   192.168.1.0/24

_____   192.168.1.32/27

_____   192.168.4.0/22

_____   172.16.0.0/14

_____   172.16.0.0/16

_____   172.16.1.0/24

_____   10.1.0.0/16

_____   10.0.0.0/8

What is the main difference between a parent route and an ultimate route?

_____

_____

What is the relationship between parent and child routes?

_____

_____

In the partial output of the routing table in Example 3-2, indicate whether each route is a parent route or a child route by checking the appropriate column.

Example 3-2   Parent and Child Routes: Classful

```
        172.16.0.0/16 is subnetted, 2 subnets
C          172.16.1.0/24 is directly connected, GigabitEthernet0/0
L          172.16.1.1/32 is directly connected, GigabitEthernet0/0
R          172.16.2.0/24 [120/1] via 209.165.200.226, 00:00:12, Serial0/0/0
```

Route	Parent	Child
172.16.0.0		
172.16.1.0		
172.16.1.1		
172.16.2.0		

In Example 3-2, notice that our child routes do not share the same subnet mask, as was the case in the classful example. In this case, we are implementing a network addressing scheme with VLSM.

In the partial output of the routing table in Example 3-3, indicate whether each route is a parent route or a child route by checking the appropriate column.

Example 3-3   Parent and Child Routes: Classless

```
        172.16.0.0/16 is variably subnetted, 5 subnets, 3 masks
C          172.16.1.0/24 is directly connected, GigabitEthernet0/0
L          172.16.1.1/32 is directly connected, GigabitEthernet0/0
R          172.16.2.0/24 [120/1] via 209.165.200.226, 00:00:12, Serial0/0/0
R          172.16.3.0/24 [120/2] via 209.165.200.226, 00:00:12, Serial0/0/0
R          172.16.4.0/28 [120/2] via 209.165.200.226, 00:00:12, Serial0/0/0
```

Route	Parent	Child
172.16.0.0		
172.16.1.0		
172.16.1.1		
172.16.2.0		
172.16.3.0		
172.16.4.0		

The IPv4 Route Lookup Process

When a router receives a packet on one of its interfaces, the routing table lookup process compares the destination IP address of the packet with the entries in the routing table. The best match between the packet's destination IP address and the route in the routing table is used to determine which interface to forward the packet.

Routing Table Lookup Chart

Figure 3-2 shows an incomplete version of the chart used to explain the routing table lookup process. Write in the correct labels for the chart.

Figure 3-2   Routing Table: Parent/Child Relationship

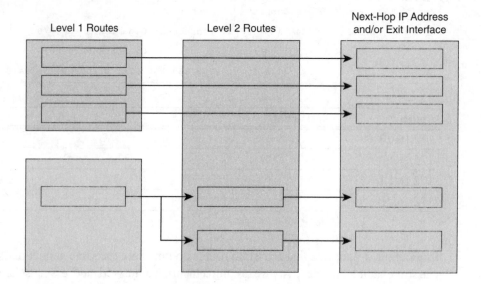

Routing Table Lookup Exercise

Use the routing table shown in Example 3-4 for this exercise.

Note: The output is from IOS 12 so local routes are not shown.

Example 3-4   Routing Table for B2

```
B2# show ip route
Codes: C - connected, S - static, I - IGRP, R - RIP, M - mobile, B - BGP
<output omitted>


Gateway of last resort is not set

     10.0.0.0/30 is subnetted, 3 subnets
R       10.10.10.0 [120/1] via 10.10.10.5, 00:00:21, Serial0/0/0
C       10.10.10.4 is directly connected, Serial0/0/0
R       10.10.10.8 [120/1] via 10.10.10.5, 00:00:21, Serial0/0/0
     172.16.0.0/16 is variably subnetted, 8 subnets, 6 masks
```

```
R        172.16.0.0/18 [120/1] via 10.10.10.5, 00:00:21, Serial0/0/0
C        172.16.68.0/22 is directly connected, FastEthernet0/0
C        172.16.72.0/23 is directly connected, FastEthernet0/1
R        172.16.128.0/20 [120/1] via 10.10.10.5, 00:00:21, Serial0/0/0
R        172.16.160.0/21 [120/2] via 10.10.10.5, 00:00:21, Serial0/0/0
R        172.16.176.0/22 [120/2] via 10.10.10.5, 00:00:21, Serial0/0/0
R        172.16.188.0/23 [120/2] via 10.10.10.5, 00:00:21, Serial0/0/0
R        172.16.190.0/24 [120/2] via 10.10.10.5, 00:00:21, Serial0/0/0
```

The router, B2, receives a packet from 172.16.68.10 destined for 172.16.142.10. Use binary to prove which route in Example 3-4 is the longest match. Make sure that you designate the bits that must match between the IP address and the longest match route. If no route matches, simply state "No Match."

_____

_____

_____

The router, B2, receives a packet from 172.16.72.10 destined for 172.16.179.10. Use binary to prove which route in Example 3-4 is the longest match. Make sure that you designate the bits that must match between the IP address and the longest match route. If no route matches, simply state "No Match."

_____

_____

_____

The router, B2, receives a packet from 172.16.69.10 destined for 172.16.65.10. Use binary to prove which route in Example 3-4 is the longest match. Make sure that you designate the bits that must match between the IP address and the longest match route. If no route matches, simply state "No Match."

_____

_____

_____

Analyze an IPv6 Routing Table

Refer to the output in Example 3-5 and analyze the IPv6 routing table. In Table 3-4, fill in the missing information.

Example 3-5   IPv6 Routing Table for R1

```
R1# show ipv6 route
<Output omitted>
C   2001:DB8:CAFE:1::/64 [0/0]
     via GigabitEthernet0/0, directly connected
L   2001:DB8:CAFE:1::1/128 [0/0]
     via GigabitEthernet0/0, receive
D   2001:DB8:CAFE:2::/64 [90/3524096]
     via FE80::3, Serial0/0/1
```

```
D   2001:DB8:CAFE:3::/64 [90/2170112]
      via FE80::3, Serial0/0/1
C   2001:DB8:CAFE:A001::/64 [0/0]
      via Serial0/0/0, directly connected
L   2001:DB8:CAFE:A001::1/128 [0/0]
      via Serial0/0/0, receive
D   2001:DB8:CAFE:A002::/64 [90/3523840]
      via FE80::3, Serial0/0/1
C   2001:DB8:CAFE:A003::/64 [0/0]
      via Serial0/0/1, directly connected
L   2001:DB8:CAFE:A003::1/128 [0/0]
      via Serial0/0/1, receive
L   FF00::/8 [0/0]
      via Null0, receive
```

Table 3-4   IPv6 Route Sources, AD Values, and Metrics

Route	Route Source	AD	Metric
2001:DB8:CAFE:A001::/64			
2001:DB8:CAFE:1::1/128			
2001:DB8:CAFE:A002::/64			

Labs and Activities

Command Reference

In Table 3-5, record the command, including the correct router or switch prompt, that fits the description. Fill in any blanks with the appropriate missing information.

Table 3-5   Commands for Chapter 3, "Dynamic Routing"

Command	Description
	Configure RIP as the routing protocol
	Configure RIP to advertise the 192.168.1.0 network
	Configure RIP to send subnet mask information in routing updates
	Configure RIP to not automatically summarize networks at the classful boundary
	Disable RIP updates on the GigabitEthernet 0/0 interface

3.0.1.2 Lab–How Much Does This Cost?

Objectives

Explain the operation of dynamic routing protocols.

Scenario

This modeling activity illustrates the network concept of routing cost.

You will be a member of a team of five students who travel routes to complete the activity scenarios. One digital camera or bring your own device (BYOD) with camera, a stopwatch, and the student file for this activity will be required per group. One person will function as the photographer and event recorder, as selected by each group. The remaining four team members will actively participate in the scenarios below.

A school or university classroom, hallway, outdoor track area, school parking lot, or any other location can serve as the venue for these activities.

Activity 1

The tallest person in the group establishes a start and finish line by marking 15 steps from start to finish, indicating the distance of the team route. Each student will take 15 steps from the start line toward the finish line and then stop on the 15th step—no further steps are allowed.

Note: Not all of the students may reach the same distance from the start line due to their height and stride differences. The photographer will take a group picture of the entire team's final location after taking the 15 steps required.

Activity 2

A new start and finish line will be established; however, this time, a longer distance for the route will be established than the distance specified in Activity 1. No maximum steps are to be used as a basis for creating this particular route. One at a time, students will "walk the new route from beginning to end twice."

Each team member will count the steps taken to complete the route. The recorder will time each student and at the end of each team member's route, record the time that it took to complete the full route and how many steps were taken, as recounted by each team member and recorded on the team's student file.

Once both activities have been completed, teams will use the digital picture taken for Activity 1 and their recorded data from Activity 2 file to answer the reflection questions.

Group answers can be discussed as a class, time permitting.

Required Resources

- Digital or BYOD camera to record Activity 1's team results. Activity 2's data is based solely upon number of steps taken and the time it took to complete the route and no camera is necessary for Activity 2.

- Stopwatch
- Student file accompanying this modeling activity so that Activity 2 results can be recorded as each student finishes the route.

Scenario–Part 2 Recording Matrix

Student Team Member Name	Time Used to Finish the Route	Number of Steps Taken to Finish the Route

Reflection Questions

1. The photographer took a picture of the team's progress after taking 15 steps for Activity 1. Most likely, some team members did not reach the finish line on their 15th step due to height and stride differences. What do you think would happen if network data did not reach the finish line, or destination, in the allowed number of hops or steps?

2. What could be done to help team members reach the finish line if they did not reach it in Activity 1?

3. Which person would best be selected to deliver data using the network route completed in Activity 2? Justify your answer.

4. Using the data recorded in Activity 2 and a limit of 255 steps, or hops, did all members of the team take more than 255 steps to finish their route? What would happen if they had to stop on the 254th step, or hop?

5. Use the data that was recorded in Activity 2. Would you say the parameters for the route were enough to finish it successfully if all team members reached the finish line with 255 or less steps, or hops? Justify your answer.

6. In network routing, different parameters are set for routing protocols. Use the data recorded for Activity 2. Would you select time, or number of steps, or hops, or a combination of both as your preferred routing type? List at least three reasons for your answers.

3.2.1.8 Packet Tracer–Configuring RIPv2

Topology

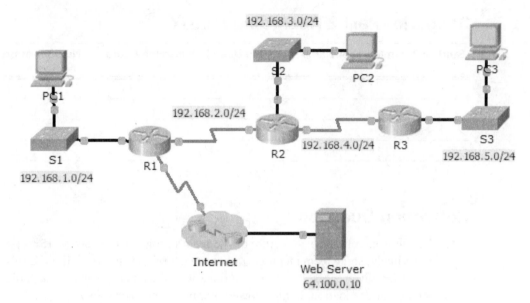

Objectives

Part 1: Configure RIPv2

Part 2: Verify Configurations

Background

Although RIP is rarely used in modern networks, it is useful as a foundation for understanding basic network routing. In this activity, you will configure a default route, RIP version 2, with appropriate network statements and passive interfaces, and verify full connectivity.

Part 1: Configure RIPv2

Step 1:   Configure RIPv2 on R1.

  a. Use the appropriate command to create a default route on **R1** for all Internet traffic to exit the network through S0/0/1.

  _____

  b. Enter RIP protocol configuration mode.

  _____

  c. Use version 2 of the RIP protocol and disable the summarization of networks.

  _____

  _____

d. Configure RIP for the networks that connect to **R1**.

_____

_____

e. Configure the LAN port that contains no routers so that it does not send out any routing information.

_____

f. Advertise the default route configured in step 1a with other RIP routers.

_____

g. Save the configuration.

Step 2:   Configure RIPv2 on R2.

a. Enter RIP protocol configuration mode.

_____

b. Use version 2 of the RIP protocol and disable the summarization of networks.

_____

_____

c. Configure RIP for the networks directly connected to **R2**.

_____

_____

_____

d. Configure the interface that contains no routers so that it does not send out routing information.

_____

e. Save the configuration.

Step 3:   Configure RIPv2 on R3

Repeat Step 2 on **R3**.

_____

_____

_____

_____

_____

_____

Part 2: Verify Configurations

Step 1:   View routing tables of R1, R2, and R3.

    a.   Use the appropriate command to show the routing table of **R1**. RIP (R) now appears with connected (C) and local (L) routes in the routing table. All networks have an entry. You also see a default route listed.

    b.   View the routing tables for **R2** and **R3**. Notice that each router has a full listing of all the 192.168.x.0 networks and a default route.

Step 2:   Verify full connectivity to all destinations.

Every device should now be able to ping every other device inside the network. In addition, all devices should be able to ping the **Web Server**.

3.2.1.9 Lab–Configuring Basic RIPv2

Topology

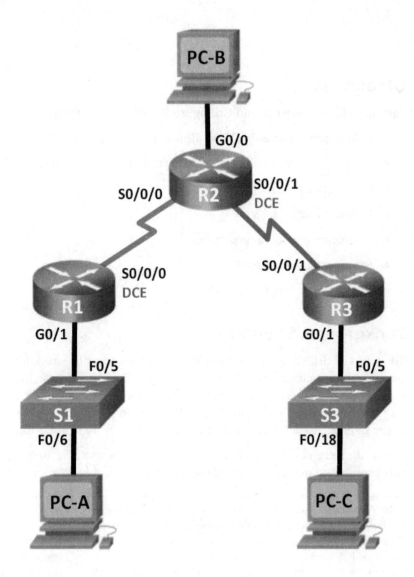

Addressing Table

Device	Interface	IP Address	Subnet Mask	Default Gateway
R1	G0/1	172.30.10.1	255.255.255.0	N/A
	S0/0/0 (DCE)	10.1.1.1	255.255.255.252	N/A
R2	G0/0	209.165.201.1	255.255.255.0	N/A
	S0/0/0	10.1.1.2	255.255.255.252	N/A
	S0/0/1 (DCE)	10.2.2.2	255.255.255.252	N/A
R3	G0/1	172.30.30.1	255.255.255.0	N/A
	S0/0/1	10.2.2.1	255.255.255.252	N/A
S1	N/A	VLAN 1	N/A	N/A
S3	N/A	VLAN 1	N/A	N/A

Device	Interface	IP Address	Subnet Mask	Default Gateway
PC-A	NIC	172.30.10.3	255.255.255.0	172.30.10.1
PC-B	NIC	209.165.201.2	255.255.255.0	209.165.201.1
PC-C	NIC	172.30.30.3	255.255.255.0	172.30.30.1

Objectives

Part 1: Build the Network and Configure Basic Device Settings

Part 2: Configure and Verify RIPv2 Routing

- Configure RIPv2 on the routers and verify that it is running.

- Configure a passive interface.

- Examine routing tables.

- Disable automatic summarization.

- Configure a default route.

- Verify end-to-end connectivity.

Background/Scenario

RIP version 2 (RIPv2) is used for routing of IPv4 addresses in small networks. RIPv2 is a classless, distance-vector routing protocol, as defined by RFC 1723. Because RIPv2 is a classless routing protocol, subnet masks are included in the routing updates. By default, RIPv2 automatically summarizes networks at major network boundaries. When automatic summarization has been disabled, RIPv2 no longer summarizes networks to their classful address at boundary routers.

In this lab, you will configure the network topology with RIPv2 routing, disable automatic summarization, propagate a default route, and use CLI commands to display and verify RIP routing information.

Note: The routers used with CCNA hands-on labs are Cisco 1941 Integrated Services Routers (ISRs) with Cisco IOS Release 15.2(4)M3 (universalk9 image). The switches used are Cisco Catalyst 2960s with Cisco IOS Release 15.0(2) (lanbasek9 image). Other routers, switches, and Cisco IOS versions can be used. Depending on the model and Cisco IOS version, the commands available and output produced might vary from what is shown in this lab. Refer to the Router Interface Summary Table at the end of the lab for the correct interface identifiers.

Note: Make sure that the routers and switches have been erased and have no startup configurations. If you are unsure, contact your instructor.

Required Resources

- 3 Routers (Cisco 1941 with Cisco IOS Release 15.2(4)M3 universal image or comparable)

- 2 Switches (Cisco 2960 with Cisco IOS Release 15.0(2) lanbasek9 image or comparable)

- 3 PCs (Windows 7, Vista, or XP with terminal emulation program, such as Tera Term)

- Console cables to configure the Cisco IOS devices via the console ports

- Ethernet and Serial cables as shown in the topology

Part 1: Build the Network and Configure Basic Device Settings

In Part 1, you will set up the network topology and configure basic settings.

Step 1:   Cable the network as shown in the topology.

Step 2:   Initialize and reload the router and switch.

Step 3:   Configure basic settings for each router and switch.

    a.   Disable DNS lookup.

    b.   Configure device names as shown in the topology.

    c.   Configure password encryption.

    d.   Assign **class** as the privileged EXEC password.

    e.   Assign **cisco** as the console and vty passwords.

    f.   Configure a MOTD banner to warn users that unauthorized access is prohibited.

    g.   Configure **logging synchronous** for the console line.

    h.   Configure the IP addresses listed in the Addressing Table for all interfaces.

    i.   Configure a description for each interface with an IP address.

    j.   Configure the clock rate, if applicable, to the DCE serial interface.

    k.   Copy the running-configuration to the startup-configuration.

Step 4:   Configure PC IP Addressing.

    Refer to the Addressing Table for IP address information of the PCs.

Step 5:   Test connectivity.

    At this point, the PCs are unable to ping each other.

    a.   Each workstation should be able to ping the attached router. Verify and troubleshoot if necessary.

    b.   The routers should be able to ping one another. Verify and troubleshoot if necessary.

Part 2: Configure and Verify RIPv2 Routing

In Part 2, you will configure RIPv2 routing on all routers in the network and then verify that the routing tables are updated correctly. After RIPv2 has been verified, you will disable automatic summarization, configure a default route, and verify end-to-end connectivity.

Step 1:   Configure RIPv2 routing.

    a.   Configure RIPv2 on R1 as the routing protocol and advertise the appropriate connected networks.

```
R1# config t
R1(config)# router rip
R1(config-router)# version 2
R1(config-router)# passive-interface g0/1
R1(config-router)# network 172.30.0.0
R1(config-router)# network 10.0.0.0
```

The **passive-interface** command stops routing updates out the specified interface. This process prevents unnecessary routing traffic on the LAN. However, the network that the specified interface belongs to is still advertised in routing updates that are sent out across other interfaces.

   b. Configure RIPv2 on R3 and use the **network** statement to add the appropriate connected networks and prevent routing updates on the LAN interface.

   c. Configure RIPv2 on R2 and use the network statements to add the appropriate connected networks. Do not advertise the 209.165.201.0 network.

Note: It is not necessary to make the G0/0 interface passive on R2 because the network associated with this interface is not being advertised.

Step 2:   Examine the current state of the network.

   a. The status of the two serial links can quickly be verified using the **show ip interface brief** command on R2.

```
R2# show ip interface brief
Interface                     IP-Address     OK? Method Status                 Protocol
Embedded-Service-Engine0/0    unassigned     YES unset  administratively down down
GigabitEthernet0/0            209.165.201.1  YES manual up                          up
GigabitEthernet0/1            unassigned     YES unset  administratively down down
Serial0/0/0                   10.1.1.2       YES manual up                          up
Serial0/0/1                   10.2.2.2       YES manual up                          up
```

   b. Check connectivity between PCs.

From PC-A, is it possible to ping PC-B? _____ Why?

_____

From PC-A, is it possible to ping PC-C? _____ Why?

_____

From PC-C, is it possible to ping PC-B? _____ Why?

_____

From PC-C, is it possible to ping PC-A? _____ Why?

_____

   c. Verify that RIPv2 is running on the routers.

You can use the **debug ip rip**, **show ip protocols**, and **show run** commands to confirm that RIPv2 is running. The **show ip protocols** command output for R1 is shown below.

```
R1# show ip protocols
Routing Protocol is "rip"
Outgoing update filter list for all interfaces is not set
Incoming update filter list for all interfaces is not set
Sending updates every 30 seconds, next due in 7 seconds
Invalid after 180 seconds, hold down 180, flushed after 240
Redistributing: rip
Default version control: send version 2, receive 2
  Interface           Send  Recv  Triggered RIP  Key-chain
  Serial0/0/0          2     2
```

```
Automatic network summarization is in effect
Maximum path: 4
Routing for Networks:
  10.0.0.0
  172.30.0.0
Passive Interface(s):
    GigabitEthernet0/1
Routing Information Sources:
  Gateway          Distance      Last Update
  10.1.1.2              120
Distance: (default is 120)
```

When issuing the **debug ip rip** command on R2, what information is provided that confirms RIPv2 is running?

When you are finished observing the debugging outputs, issue the **undebug all** command at the privileged EXEC prompt.

When issuing the **show run** command on R3, what information is provided that confirms RIPv2 is running?

```
router rip
 version 2
```

d. Examine the automatic summarization of routes.

The LANs connected to R1 and R3 are composed of discontiguous networks. R2 displays two equal-cost paths to the 172.30.0.0/16 network in the routing table. R2 displays only the major classful network address of 172.30.0.0 and does not display any of the subnets for this network.

```
R2# show ip route
<Output omitted>
      10.0.0.0/8 is variably subnetted, 4 subnets, 2 masks
C        10.1.1.0/30 is directly connected, Serial0/0/0
L        10.1.1.2/32 is directly connected, Serial0/0/0
C        10.2.2.0/30 is directly connected, Serial0/0/1
L        10.2.2.2/32 is directly connected, Serial0/0/1
R     172.30.0.0/16 [120/1] via 10.2.2.1, 00:00:23, Serial0/0/1
                    [120/1] via 10.1.1.1, 00:00:09, Serial0/0/0
      209.165.201.0/24 is variably subnetted, 2 subnets, 2 masks
C        209.165.201.0/24 is directly connected, GigabitEthernet0/0
L        209.165.201.1/32 is directly connected, GigabitEthernet0/0
```

R1 displays only its own subnet for the 172.30.10.0/24 network. R1 does not have a route for the 172.30.30.0/24 subnet on R3.

```
R1# show ip route
<Output omitted>
      10.0.0.0/8 is variably subnetted, 3 subnets, 2 masks
C        10.1.1.0/30 is directly connected, Serial0/0/0
L        10.1.1.1/32 is directly connected, Serial0/0/0
```

```
R          10.2.2.0/30 [120/1] via 10.1.1.2, 00:00:21, Serial0/0/0
          172.30.0.0/16 is variably subnetted, 2 subnets, 2 masks
C          172.30.10.0/24 is directly connected, GigabitEthernet0/1
L          172.30.10.1/32 is directly connected, GigabitEthernet0/1
```

R3 only displays its own subnet for the 172.30.30.0/24 network. R3 does not have a route for the 172.30.10.0/24 subnets on R1.

```
R3# show ip route
<Output omitted>
          10.0.0.0/8 is variably subnetted, 3 subnets, 2 masks
C          10.2.2.0/30 is directly connected, Serial0/0/1
L          10.2.2.1/32 is directly connected, Serial0/0/1
R          10.1.1.0/30 [120/1] via 10.2.2.2, 00:00:23, Serial0/0/1
          172.30.0.0/16 is variably subnetted, 2 subnets, 2 masks
C          172.30.30.0/24 is directly connected, GigabitEthernet0/1
L          172.30.30.1/32 is directly connected, GigabitEthernet0/1
```

Use the **debug ip rip** command on R2 to determine the routes received in the RIP updates from R3 and list them here.

_____

R3 is not sending any of the 172.30.0.0 subnets, only the summarized route of 172.30.0.0/16, including the subnet mask. Therefore, the routing tables on R1 and R2 do not display the 172.30.0.0 subnets on R3.

Step 3:   Disable automatic summarization.

  a.   The **no auto-summary** command is used to turn off automatic summarization in RIPv2. Disable auto summarization on all routers. The routers will no longer summarize routes at major classful network boundaries. R1 is shown here as an example.

```
R1(config)# router rip
R1(config-router)# no auto-summary
```

  b.   Issue the **clear ip route** * command to clear the routing table.

```
R1(config-router)# end
R1# clear ip route *
```

  c.   Examine the routing tables. Remember that it will take some time to converge the routing tables after clearing them.

The LAN subnets connected to R1 and R3 should now be included in all three routing tables.

```
R2# show ip route
<Output omitted>
Gateway of last resort is not set

          10.0.0.0/8 is variably subnetted, 4 subnets, 2 masks
C          10.1.1.0/30 is directly connected, Serial0/0/0
L          10.1.1.2/32 is directly connected, Serial0/0/0
C          10.2.2.0/30 is directly connected, Serial0/0/1
L          10.2.2.2/32 is directly connected, Serial0/0/1
          172.30.0.0/16 is variably subnetted, 3 subnets, 2 masks
R          172.30.0.0/16 [120/1] via 10.2.2.1, 00:01:01, Serial0/0/1
                        [120/1] via 10.1.1.1, 00:01:15, Serial0/0/0
```

```
R           172.30.10.0/24 [120/1] via 10.1.1.1, 00:00:21, Serial0/0/0
R           172.30.30.0/24 [120/1] via 10.2.2.1, 00:00:04, Serial0/0/1
        209.165.201.0/24 is variably subnetted, 2 subnets, 2 masks
C           209.165.201.0/24 is directly connected, GigabitEthernet0/0
L           209.165.201.1/32 is directly connected, GigabitEthernet0/0
R1# show ip route
<Output omitted>
Gateway of last resort is not set

        10.0.0.0/8 is variably subnetted, 3 subnets, 2 masks
C           10.1.1.0/30 is directly connected, Serial0/0/0
L           10.1.1.1/32 is directly connected, Serial0/0/0
R           10.2.2.0/30 [120/1] via 10.1.1.2, 00:00:12, Serial0/0/0
        172.30.0.0/16 is variably subnetted, 3 subnets, 2 masks
C           172.30.10.0/24 is directly connected, GigabitEthernet0/1
L           172.30.10.1/32 is directly connected, GigabitEthernet0/1
R           172.30.30.0/24 [120/2] via 10.1.1.2, 00:00:12, Serial0/0/0
R3# show ip route
<Output omitted>
        10.0.0.0/8 is variably subnetted, 3 subnets, 2 masks
C           10.2.2.0/30 is directly connected, Serial0/0/1
L           10.2.2.1/32 is directly connected, Serial0/0/1
R           10.1.1.0/30 [120/1] via 10.2.2.2, 00:00:23, Serial0/0/1
        172.30.0.0/16 is variably subnetted, 2 subnets, 2 masks
C           172.30.30.0/24 is directly connected, GigabitEthernet0/1
L           172.30.30.1/32 is directly connected, GigabitEthernet0/1
R           172.30.10.0 [120/2] via 10.2.2.2, 00:00:16, Serial0/0/1
```

d. Use the **debug ip rip** command on R2 to examine the RIP updates.

```
R2# debug ip rip
```

After 60 seconds, issue the **no debug ip rip** command.

What routes are in the RIP updates that are received from R3?

_____

Are the subnet masks included in the routing updates? _____

Step 4: Configure and redistribute a default route for Internet access.

a. From R2, create a static route to network 0.0.0.0 0.0.0.0, using the **ip route** command. This forwards any traffic with an unknown destination address to PC-B at 209.165.201.2, simulating the Internet by setting a Gateway of Last Resort on router R2.

```
R2(config)# ip route 0.0.0.0 0.0.0.0 209.165.201.2
```

b. R2 will advertise a route to the other routers if the **default-information originate** command is added to its RIP configuration.

```
R2(config)# router rip
R2(config-router)# default-information originate
```

Step 5:   Verify the routing configuration.

    a.   View the routing table on R1.

```
R1# show ip route
<Output omitted>
Gateway of last resort is 10.1.1.2 to network 0.0.0.0

R*     0.0.0.0/0 [120/1] via 10.1.1.2, 00:00:13, Serial0/0/0
       10.0.0.0/8 is variably subnetted, 3 subnets, 2 masks
C         10.1.1.0/30 is directly connected, Serial0/0/0
L         10.1.1.1/32 is directly connected, Serial0/0/0
R         10.2.2.0/30 [120/1] via 10.1.1.2, 00:00:13, Serial0/0/0
       172.30.0.0/16 is variably subnetted, 3 subnets, 2 masks
C         172.30.10.0/24 is directly connected, GigabitEthernet0/1
L         172.30.10.1/32 is directly connected, GigabitEthernet0/1
R         172.30.30.0/24 [120/2] via 10.1.1.2, 00:00:13, Serial0/0/0
```

How can you tell from the routing table that the subnetted network shared by R1 and R3 has a pathway for Internet traffic?

_____

_____

    b.   View the routing table on R2.

How is the pathway for Internet traffic provided in its routing table?

_____

_____

Step 6:   Verify connectivity.

    a.   Simulate sending traffic to the Internet by pinging from PC-A and PC-C to 209.165.201.2.

Were the pings successful? _____

    b.   Verify that hosts within the subnetted network can reach each other by pinging between PC-A and PC-C.

Were the pings successful? _____

Note: It may be necessary to disable the PC's firewall.

Reflection

1.   Why would you turn off automatic summarization for RIPv2?

_____

2.   How did R1 and R3 learn the pathway to the Internet?

_____

Router Interface Summary Table

Router Interface Summary

Router Model	Ethernet Interface #1	Ethernet Interface #2	Serial Interface #1	Serial Interface #2
1800	Fast Ethernet 0/0 (F0/0)	Fast Ethernet 0/1 (F0/1)	Serial 0/0/0 (S0/0/0)	Serial 0/0/1 (S0/0/1)
1900	Gigabit Ethernet 0/0 (G0/0)	Gigabit Ethernet 0/1 (G0/1)	Serial 0/0/0 (S0/0/0)	Serial 0/0/1 (S0/0/1)
2801	Fast Ethernet 0/0 (F0/0)	Fast Ethernet 0/1 (F0/1)	Serial 0/1/0 (S0/1/0)	Serial 0/1/1 (S0/1/1)
2811	Fast Ethernet 0/0 (F0/0)	Fast Ethernet 0/1 (F0/1)	Serial 0/0/0 (S0/0/0)	Serial 0/0/1 (S0/0/1)
2900	Gigabit Ethernet 0/0 (G0/0)	Gigabit Ethernet 0/1 (G0/1)	Serial 0/0/0 (S0/0/0)	Serial 0/0/1 (S0/0/1)

Note: To find out how the router is configured, look at the interfaces to identify the type of router and how many interfaces the router has. There is no way to effectively list all the combinations of configurations for each router class. This table includes identifiers for the possible combinations of Ethernet and Serial interfaces in the device. The table does not include any other type of interface, even though a specific router may contain one. An example of this might be an ISDN BRI interface. The string in parentheses is the legal abbreviation that can be used in Cisco IOS commands to represent the interface.

3.4.1.1 Class Activity–IPv6 - Details, Details...

Objectives

Analyze a routing table to determine the route source, administrative distance, and metric for a given route to include IPv4/IPv6.

Scenario

After studying the concepts presented in this chapter concerning IPv6, you should be able to read a routing table easily and interpret the IPv6 routing information listed within it.

With a partner, use the IPv6 routing table diagram shown below. Record your answers to the Reflection questions. Then compare your answers with, at least, one other group from the class.

Required Resources

- Routing Table Diagram (as shown below)
- Two PCs or bring your own devices (BYODs): one PC or BYOD will display the Routing Table Diagram for your group to access while recording answers to the Reflection questions on the other PC or BYOD.

Routing Table Diagram

```
R3# show ipv6 route
IPv6 Routing Table - default - 8 entries
Codes: C - Connected, L - Local, S - Static, U - Per-user Static route
       B - BGP, R - RIP, I1 - ISIS L1, I2 - ISIS L2
       IA - ISIS interarea, IS - ISIS summary, D - EIGRP, EX - EIGRP external
       ND - ND Default, NDp - ND Prefix, DCE - Destination, NDr - Redirect
       O - OSPF Intra, OI - OSPF Inter, OE1 - OSPF ext 1, OE2 - OSPF ext 2
       ON1 - OSPF NSSA ext 1, ON2 - OSPF NSSA ext 2
R    2001:DB8:CAFE:1::/64 [120/3]
      via FE80::FE99:47FF:FE71:78A0, Serial0/0/1
R    2001:DB8:CAFE:2::/64 [120/2]
      via FE80::FE99:47FF:FE71:78A0, Serial0/0/1
C    2001:DB8:CAFE:3::/64 [0/0]
      via GigabitEthernet0/0, directly connected
L    2001:DB8:CAFE:3::1/128 [0/0]
      via GigabitEthernet0/0, receive
(output omitted)
```

Reflection

1. How many different IPv6 networks are shown on the routing table diagram? List them in the following table.

Routing Table IPv6 Networks

_____

_____

_____

_____

_____

2. The 2001:DB8:CAFE:3:: route is listed twice on the routing table, once with a /64 and once with a /128. What is the significance of this dual network entry?

_____

3. How many routes in this table are RIP routes? What types of RIP routes are listed: RIP, RIPv2, or RIPng?

_____

4. Use the first RIP route, as listed on the routing table, as a reference. What is the administrative distance of this route? What is the cost? What is the significance of these two values?

_____

5. Use the second RIP route, as referenced by the routing table diagram. How many hops would it take to get to the 2001:DB8:CAFE:2::/64 network? What would happen to this routing table entry if the cost for this route exceeded 15 hops?

_____

6. You are designing an IPv6 addressing scheme to add another router to your network's physical topology. Use the /64 prefix for this addressing scheme and an IPv6 network base of 2001:DB8:CAFF:2::/64,. What would be the next, numerical network assignment you could use if the first three hextets remained the same? Justify your answer.

_____

CHAPTER 4

Switched Networks

Modern networks continue to evolve to keep pace with the changing way organizations carry out their daily business. Different devices must seamlessly work together to provide a fast, secure, and reliable connection between hosts. LAN switches provide the connection point for end users into the enterprise network and are also primarily responsible for the control of information within the LAN environment. In this chapter, we review current network design models and the way LAN switches build forwarding tables to switch data efficiently.

The Study Guide portion of this chapter uses a combination of matching, fill-in-the-blank, multiple-choice, and open-ended question exercises to test your knowledge and skills of basic router concepts and configuration. The Labs and Activities portion of this chapter includes all the online curriculum labs and Packet Tracer activities to ensure that you have mastered the hands-on skills needed to understand basic IP addressing and router configuration.

As you work through this chapter, use Chapter 4 in *Routing and Switching Essentials v6 Companion Guide* or use the corresponding Chapter 4 in the Routing and Switching Essentials online curriculum for assistance.

Study Guide

LAN Design

In today's globalized workplace, employees can access resources from anywhere in the world and information must be available at any time, and on any device. To encourage collaboration, business networks not only support traditional data access, but employ converged solutions to support voice and video as well. In this section, we review some basic design principles relating to LANs.

LAN Design Principles

Watch this Cisco video on YouTube:

http://youtu.be/lCg2HctgvJE or search YouTube for "Evolution of Borderless Networks."

Then briefly describe the Cisco Borderless Network.

_____

_____

_____

_____

Indicate which borderless switched network design principle is best described by the characteristic in Table 4-1.

Table 4-1   Identify the Borderless Switched Network Design Principle

Characteristic	Hierarchical	Modularity	Resiliency	Flexibility
Allows networks to grow and provide on-demand services				
Uses all network resources available to provide data traffic load sharing				
Helps every device on every tier to employ a specific role				
Provides a way for the network to always be accessible				

In Table 4-2, identify which layer for each of the switch functions is described.

Table 4-2   Identify the Hierarchical Layer

Switch Function	Core	Distribution	Access
Can be combined with the Distribution layer to provide for a collapsed design			
Allows data to flow on equal-cost switching paths to the backbone			
Supports Layer 2 broadcast domains and Layer 3 routing boundaries			
The network backbone area for switching			
Includes redundancy as an important feature for switched network access			

Switch Function	Core	Distribution	Access
Helps applications to operate on the switched network more safely and securely			
Provides direct, switched network connectivity to the user			
Interfaces with the backbone and users to provide intelligent switching, routing, and security			
Provides fault isolation and high-speed backbone switch connectivity			

Selecting Switch Hardware

Match the switch selection criteria on the left with the switch category names on the right.

Switch Selection Criteria

  a. How fast the interfaces will process network data

  b. Ability to adjust to growth of network users

  c. Switches with preset features or options

  d. Continuous access to the network

  e. Availability through PoE

  f. Daisy-chain switches with high-bandwidth throughput

  g. Includes number/speed of interfaces, features, and expandability

  h. The capacity to store frames in the cache

  i. Affected by the number of network devices to support

  j. Switches with insertable switching line/port cards

Switch Category Name

_____ cost

_____ modular

_____ frame buffers

_____ scalability

_____ port speed

_____ stackable

_____ power

_____ fixed configuration

_____ port density

_____ reliability

The Switched Environment

In a LAN switch, a master switching table describes a strict association between addresses and ports. Cisco LAN switches use this table to forward traffic based on the ingress port and the destination MAC address. LAN switches also segment collision domains so that devices that share the same logical network do not have to share bandwidth (as with hubs). In this section, we look at frame forwarding methods and how switches alleviate congestion on the network.

Frame Forwarding Methods and Terminology

Switches use basically two methods to forward frames: store-and-forward and cut-through. In store-and-forward switching, when the switch receives the frame, it stores the data in _____ until the complete frame has been received. During the storage process, the switch performs an error check using the _____ trailer portion of the Ethernet frame. After confirming the integrity of the frame, the frame is _____. If an error is detected, the frame is _____.

In cut-through switching, the switch buffers just enough of the frame to read the _____ MAC address so that it can determine to which port to forward the data.

In Table 4-3, indicate which method matches the descriptions.

Table 4-3   Identify the Frame Forwarding Method

Description	Store-and-Forward	Cut-Through
Checks the frame for errors before releasing it out of its switch ports. If the full frame was not received, the switch discards it.		
Low-latency switch method used by high-performance computing (HPC) applications requiring process-to-process latencies of 10 microseconds or less.		
No error checking on frames is performed by the switch before releasing the frame out of its ports.		
Buffers frames until the full frame has been received by the switch.		
ASICs-capable switch function; allows frames to be filtered and forwarded after the first 14 bytes and an additional 40 bytes in the frame header have been received.		

Building the MAC Address Table

Assume that the switch in Figure 4-1 was just installed and powered on. The MAC address table is empty. Answer the following questions and complete Table 4-4 as the switch would build it.

Figure 4-1   Building the MAC Address Table

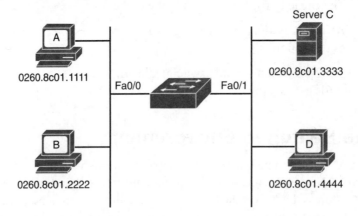

Table 4-4   MAC Address Table

Port	MAC Address

1. Host A sends a unicast frame to Host B. What entry, if any, will the switch enter in its MAC address table?

_____

_____

What will the switch do with the frame?

_____

_____

2. Host B responds to Host A with a unicast frame. What entry, if any, will the switch enter in its MAC address table?

_____

_____

What will the switch do with the frame?

_____

_____

3. Host D attempts to log in to Server C. What entry, if any, will the switch enter in its MAC address table?

_____

_____

What will the switch do with the frame?

_____

_____

4. Server C responds to the login attempt by Host D. What entry, if any, will the switch enter in its MAC address table?

_____

_____

What will the switch do with the frame?

_____

_____

5. Server C sends out a broadcast frame announcing its services to all potential clients. What entry, if any, will the switch enter in its MAC address table?

_____

What will the switch do with the frame?

_____

_____

Collision and Broadcast Domains

Using Figure 4-2, circle all the collision domains with a solid line and all the broadcast domains with a dashed line.

Figure 4-2   Collision and Broadcast Domains: Topology 1

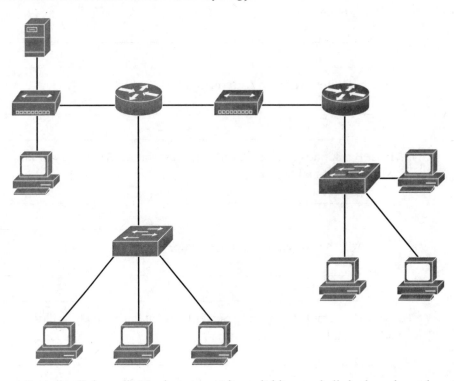

Using Figure 4-3, circle all the collision domains with a solid line and all the broadcast domains with a dashed line.

Figure 4-3   Collision and Broadcast Domains: Topology 2

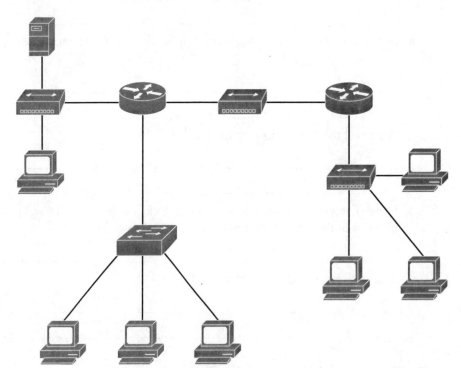

Using Figure 4-4, circle all the collision domains with a solid line and all the broadcast domains with a dashed line.

Figure 4-4   Collision and Broadcast Domains: Topology 3

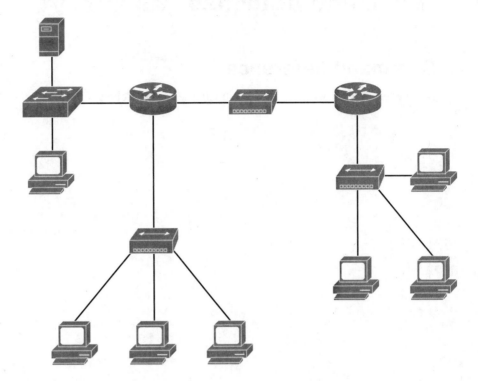

Labs and Activities

Command Reference

No new commands were introduced in Chapter 4, "Switched Networks."

4.0.1.2 Lab Sent or Received

Objectives

Describe convergence of data, voice, and video in the context of switched networks.

Scenario

Individually, or in groups (per the instructor's decision), discuss various ways hosts send and receive data, voice, and streaming video.

- Develop a matrix (table) listing network data types that can be sent and received. Provide five examples.

Your matrix table might look something like this:

Sent	Received
Client requests a web page from a web server.	Web server sends web page to requesting client.

Save your work in either hard- or soft-copy format. Be prepared to discuss your matrix and statements in a class discussion.

Resources

Internet connectivity

Reflection

1. If you are receiving data, how do you think a switch assists in that process?

2. If you are sending network data, how do you think a switch assists in that process?

4.3.1.1 Lab–It's Network Access Time

Objectives

Describe features available for switches to support requirements of a small- to medium-sized business network.

_____

_____

Scenario

Use Packet Tracer for this activity. Work with a classmate to create two network designs to accommodate the following scenarios:

Scenario 1 – Classroom Design (LAN)

- 15 student end devices represented by 1 or 2 PCs.

- 1 instructor end device; a server is preferred.

- Device capability to stream video presentations over LAN connection. Internet connectivity is not required in this design.

Scenario 2 – Administrative Design (WAN)

- All requirements as listed in Scenario 1.

- Add access to and from a remote administrative server for video presentations and pushed updates for network application software.

Both the LAN and WAN designs should fit on to one Packet Tracer file screen. All intermediary devices should be labeled with the switch model (or name) and the router model (or name).

Save your work and be ready to justify your device decisions and layout to your instructor and the class.

Reflection

1. What are some problems that may be encountered if you receive streaming video from your instructor's server through a low-end switch?

   _____

2. How would the traffic flow be determined: multicast or broadcast – in transmission?

   _____

3. What would influence your decision on the type of switch to use for voice, streaming video, and regular data transmissions?

   _____

4. As you learned in the first course of the Academy, video and voice use a special TCP/IP model, transport layer protocol. What protocol is used in this layer and why is it important to voice and video streaming?

   _____

CHAPTER 5

Switch Configuration

Although Cisco LAN switches are ready to go "out of the box," they also require certain configurations for them to boot and carry out their functionality in a reliable, secure manner. Although they normally operate at the network access layer of the TCP/IP model and base their forwarding decisions on MAC addresses, they are routinely configured with an IP address to allow remote management. This chapter reviews some of the basic switch configuration settings required to maintain a secure, available, switched LAN environment.

The Study Guide portion of this chapter uses a combination of matching, fill-in-the-blank, multiple-choice, and open-ended question exercises to test your knowledge and skills of basic router concepts and configuration. The Labs and Activities portion of this chapter includes all the online curriculum labs and Packet Tracer activities to ensure that you have mastered the hands-on skills needed to understand basic IP addressing and router configuration.

As you work through this chapter, use Chapter 5 in *Routing and Switching Essentials v6 Companion Guide* or use the corresponding Chapter 5 in the Routing and Switching Essentials online curriculum for assistance.

Study Guide

Basic Switch Configuration

After the switch is powered on and goes through its boot sequence, it is ready to be configured. To prepare a switch for remote management access, the switch must be configured with an IP address, a subnet mask, and a default gateway. In this section, we review the boot sequence and configuring a switch's initial settings.

Switch Boot Sequence

Briefly explain the steps in the switch boot sequence.

After a Cisco switch is powered on, it goes through the following boot sequence:

Step 1. _____

Step 2. _____

Step 3. _____

Step 4. _____

Step 5. _____

Half-Duplex, Full-Duplex, and Auto-MDIX

_____ communication relies on unidirectional data flow, where sending and receiving data are not performed at the same time. This is similar to how walkie-talkies or two-way radios communicate.

_____ communication is the most common today. Data flow is bidirectional, so data can be sent and received at the same time. The collision detect circuit is

_____.

The Cisco Catalyst switches have three settings:

- The _____ option sets autonegotiation of duplex mode. With autonegotiation enabled, the two ports communicate to decide the best mode of operation.

- The _____ option sets full-duplex mode.

- The _____ option sets half-duplex mode.

For Fast Ethernet and 10/100/1000 ports, the default is _____. For 100BASE-FX ports, the default is _____.

In addition, you can now use the _____ interface configuration command in the CLI to enable the automatic medium-dependent interface crossover (auto-MDIX) feature, which detects the required cable type for copper Ethernet connections and configures the interfaces accordingly.

Configure a Switch with Initial Settings

In this exercise, use Figure 5-1 and Table 5-1 to answer the following questions. Some of these questions are review from previous chapters.

Figure 5-1 Basic Switch Configuration Topology

10.1.1.0/24

Table 5-1 Addressing Table for Chapter 5 Topology

Device	Interface	IP Address	Subnet Mask	Default Gateway
R1	G0/0	10.1.1.1	255.255.255.0	N/A
S1	VLAN 99	10.1.1.11	255.255.255.0	10.1.1.1
PC1	NIC	10.1.1.21	255.255.255.0	10.1.1.1

When configuring a switch, certain basic tasks are performed, including the following:

- Naming the switch

- Setting passwords

- Configuring a banner

- Configuring the VLAN interface

- Saving changes on a switch

- Verifying basic configuration

The first prompt is at _____ EXEC mode and allows you to view the state of the switch. What major limitation does this mode have?

_____

What is the switch prompt for this mode?

_____

The _____ command is used to enter _____ EXEC mode. What is the major difference between this mode and the previous mode?

_____

What is the switch prompt for this mode?

_____

Basic Configuration Tasks

Table 5-2 lists the basic switch configuration tasks in the left column. Fill in the right column with the correct command syntax for each of the tasks. Do not enter the actual values for command parameters at this point. Only record the syntax. The first one is done for you as an example.

Table 5-2 Basic Switch Configuration Command Syntax

Configuration Task	Command Syntax
Naming the switch	`Switch(config)# hostname name`
Setting the privileged mode encrypted password	
Encrypting all clear-text passwords	
Entering console line configuration	
Setting the console password	
Requiring users to log in	
Entering vty line configuration mode	
Setting the vty passwords	
Requiring users to log in	
Configuring a message-of-the-day banner	
Configuring the VLAN interface	
Configuring addressing on an interface	
Activating an interface	
Configuring the default gateway	
Setting the port speed to 100 Mbps	
Setting the duplex mode to full	
Setting the port speed to autoconfigure	
Setting the duplex mode to autoconfigure	
Setting the port to automatically detect the cable connection type	
Saving changes on a router	

Applying a Basic Configuration

The following exercise walks you through a basic configuration.

First, enter global configuration mode for the switch:

```
Switch# _____
```

Next, apply a unique hostname to the switch. Use S1 for this example:

```
Switch(config)# _____
```

Now, configure the password that is to be used to enter privileged EXEC mode. Use **class** as the password:

```
S1(config)# _____
```

Next, configure the console and Telnet lines with the password **cisco**. The console commands follow:

```
S1(config)# _____
S1(config-line)# _____
S1(config-line)# _____
```

The Telnet lines use similar commands. You do not need to exit line configuration mode to switch to the Telnet lines:

```
S1(config-line)# _____
```

```
S1(config-line)# _____
```

```
S1(config-line)# _____
```

Return to global configuration mode:

```
S1(config-line)# _____
```

From global configuration mode, configure the message-of-the-day banner. Use the following text: Authorized Access Only. A delimiting character such as a # is used at the beginning and at the end of the message.

```
S1(config)# _____
```

Refer to Table 5-1 for the VLAN interface configuration information. What is the command to enter VLAN interface configuration mode for S1?

```
S1(config)# _____
```

Enter the command to configure the IP address using the address specified in Table 5-1.

```
S1(config-if)# _____
```

Enter the command to activate the VLAN interface:

```
S1(config-if)# _____
```

Enter interface configuration mode for the Fa0/5 interface connected to PC1:

```
S1(config)# _____
```

Enter the command to set the interface to 100 Mbps:

```
S1(config-if)# _____
```

Enter the command to force full-duplex operation:

```
S1(config-if)# _____
```

Return to global configuration mode:

```
S1(config-if)# _____
```

Use the address in Table 5-1 to configure S1 with a default gateway:

```
S1(config)# _____
```

Return to the privileged EXEC prompt:

```
S1(config)# _____
```

What command will save the current configuration?

```
S1# _____
```

Verifying Basic Switch Configuration

You can verify basic configurations using the four basic **show** commands in Table 5-3. The second four basic **show** commands in the table do not necessarily verify the configuration but might also be helpful. List the command in the left column that fits the description in the right column.

Table 5-3   Basic Router Configuration Verification Commands

Command	Description
	Displays interface status and configuration for a single interface or all interfaces available on the switch
	Displays the startup configuration file stored in NVRAM
	Displays the current running configuration that is stored in RAM
	Displays abbreviated interface configuration information, including IP address and interface status
	Displays information about the flash file system
	Displays system hardware and software status
	Displays the session command history
	Displays the MAC forwarding table

Switch Security

In modern networks, security is integral to implementing any device, protocol, or technology. You should already have strong skills in configuring passwords on a switch. The exercises in this section review configuring Secure Shell (SSH), common security attacks, and configuring port security.

Secure Remote Access with SSH

Older switches may not support secure communication with _____ (SSH). However, Packet Tracer and the more recent 2960 IOS images do support SSH. Why is Telnet an unsecure way of accessing a network device?

_____

_____

_____

To implement SSH, you need to generate RSA keys. RSA involves a public key, kept on a public RSA server, and a private key, kept only by the sender and receiver.

To configure a Catalyst 2960 switch as an SSH server, fill in the blanks in the following steps:

Step 1.   Configure a host domain for S1. Use the domain mydomain.com.

```
S1(config)# _____
```

Step 2.   Enter the command to generate an encrypted RSA key pair. Use 1024 as the modulus size.

```
S1(config)# _____
The name for the keys will be: S1.mydomain.com
Choose the size of the key modulus in the range of 360 to 2048 for your
   General Purpose Keys. Choosing a key modulus greater than 512 may take
   a few minutes.

How many bits in the modulus [512]: _____
% Generating 1024 bit RSA keys, keys will be non-exportable...[OK]
      %SSH-5-ENABLED: SSH 1.99 has been enabled
```

Step 3.   Enter the command to verify the current SSH configuration:

```
S1# _____
SSH Enabled - version 1.99
      Authentication timeout: 120 secs; Authentication retries: 3
```

Step 4.   Enter the commands to configure SSH version 2, change the timeout to 30 seconds, and change the authentication retries to 5:

```
S1(config)# _____
S1(config)# _____
S1(config)# _____
```

Step 5.   Enter the command to configure all vty lines to allow only SSH access:

```
S1(config)# _____
S1(config-line)# _____
```

Switch Port Security

A switch that does not provide port security allows an attacker to attach a system to an unused, enabled port and to perform information gathering or to launch attacks.

All switch ports or interfaces should be secured before the switch is deployed. Port security can limit the number of valid MAC addresses allowed on a port to one and automatically shut down a port if a security violation occurs. In addition, all unused ports should be administratively shut down.

List the three ways a switch can learn the MAC addresses allowed on a port.

_____

_____

_____

_____

_____

List and explain the three violation modes you can configure.

_____

_____

_____

_____

_____

_____

_____

_____

_____

_____

_____

_____

_____

In Table 5-4, list the violation mode and answer yes or no to each of the different effects listed.

Table 5-4   Port Security Violation Modes

Violation Mode	Forwards Traffic	Sends SNMP Trap	Sends Syslog Message	Displays Error Message	Increases Violation Counter	Shuts Down Port

In Table 5-5, list the default security settings for ports.

Table 5-5   Port Security Default Settings

Feature	Default Setting
Port security	
Maximum number of secure MAC addresses	
Violation mode	
Sticky address learning	

Reference Figure 5-2 when answering the port security questions that follow.

Figure 5-2   Configuring Port Security Topology

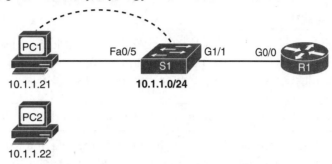

10.1.1.21

10.1.1.0/24

10.1.1.22

Enter the commands to enable port security on interface FastEthernet 0/5:

```
S1(config)#_____
```

```
S1(config-if)#_____
```

Although 1 is the default setting, enter the command to explicitly configure the maximum number of secure MAC addresses to 1:

```
S1(config-if)#_____
```

Enter the command to enable dynamically learned MAC addresses to be added to the running configuration:

```
S1(config-if)#_____
```

Enter the command to set the violation mode to shutdown:

```
S1(config-if)#_____
```

What command can you use to verify port security on the entire switch?

```
S1#_____
```

What command do you use to verify port security on interface FastEthernet 0/5?

```
S1#_____
```

Assume PC2 in Figure 5-2 is attached to FastEthernet 0/5 after the MAC address for PC1 has already been learned. Port security disables the interface. Further assume that PC2 is replacing PC1. What steps must you take to enable PC2 to gain access to the network?

Step 1.   Remove the "stuck" MAC address from the running configuration using the **no switchport port-security mac-address sticky mac_address** command.

Step 2.   Reactivate the shutdown interface with the **no shutdown** command. On some switches, you must administratively shut down the interface before entering the **no shutdown** command. However, on 2960 switches this is not necessary.

Packet Tracer Exercise 5-1: Configuring Secure Access and Port Security

Now you are ready to use Packet Tracer to apply your knowledge about SSH and port security. Download and open the file LSG02-0501.pka found at the companion website for this book. Refer to the Introduction of this book for specifics on accessing files.

Note: The following instructions are also contained within the Packet Tracer Exercise.

In this Packet Tracer activity, you will configure the switch for secure remote access using SSH and port security. Use the commands you documented in this chapter to help you complete the activity.

Requirements

Access Sw1 with the privileged EXEC password **class**. Configure Sw1 with the following requirements:

- Configure Sw1 to use mydomain.com.
- Secure remote access with SSHv2:
- Use a 2048 modulus.
- SSH sessions should timeout after idle for 30 seconds.
- Allow up to five failed authentication attempts.
- Configure port security on Fa0/1 and Fa0/2:
- Maximum number of MACs is 2.
- Learned MAC addresses should be applied to the running configuration.
- Port security violations should not shut down the port, but packets are dropped from any violating MAC addresses.
- Ping between the Admin PC and the Employee PC to make sure the MAC addresses are applied to the running configuration.

Your completion percentage should be 100%. If not, click **Check Results** to see which required components are not yet completed.

Labs and Activities

Command Reference

In Table 5-6, record the command, including the correct router or switch prompt, that fits the description. Fill in any blanks with the appropriate missing information.

Table 5-6   Commands for Chapter 5, "Switch Configuration"

Command	Description
	Set the switch's domain to example.com.
	Generate an encrypted RSA key pair.
	Configure SSH to use version 2.
	Configure SSH to timeout after 60 seconds.
	Configure SSH to allow three authentication attempts.
	Configure the VTY lines to only use SSH for remote access.
	Enter the command to verify the SSH configuration.
	Enable port security on a switch port.
	Configure 3 as the maximum number of MACs that the port can learn.
	Configure the port record learned MAC address in the running configuration.
	Configure the port to report a security violation but allow the port to remain operational for the secure MACs.
	Enter the command to verify port security on the entire switch
	Enter the command to verify port security on FastEthernet0/10.

5.0.1.2 Lab–Stand By Me

Objective

Describe the role of unicast, broadcast, and multicast in a switched network.

Scenario

When you arrived to class today, you were given a number by your instructor to use for this introductory class activity.

Once class begins, your instructor will ask certain students with specific numbers to stand. Your job is to record the standing students' numbers for each scenario.

Scenario 1

Students with numbers _____ with the number _____ should stand. Record the numbers of the standing students.

Scenario 2

Students with numbers _____ in _____ should stand. Record the numbers of the standing students.

Scenario 3

Students with the number _____ should stand. Record the number of the standing student.

At the end of this activity, divide into small groups and record answers to the Reflection questions on the PDF for this activity.

Reflection

1. Why do you think you were asked to record the students' numbers when and as requested?

   _____

2. What is the significance of the number 5 in this activity? How many people were identified with this number?

   _____

3. What is the significance of the letter C in this activity? How many people were identified with this number?

   _____

4. Why did only one person stand for 504C?

   _____

5. How do you think this activity represents data travelling on local area networks?

   _____

Save your work and be prepared to share it with another student or the entire class.

5.1.1.6 Lab–Configuring Basic Switch Settings

Topology

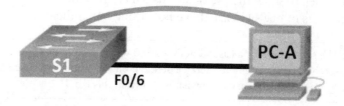

Addressing Table

Device	Interface	IP Address	Subnet Mask	Default Gateway
S1	VLAN 99	192.168.1.2	255.255.255.0	192.168.1.1
PC-A	NIC	192.168.1.10	255.255.255.0	192.168.1.1

Objectives

Part 1: Cable the Network and Verify the Default Switch Configuration

Part 2: Configure Basic Network Device Settings

- Configure basic switch settings.
- Configure the PC IP address.

Part 3: Verify and Test Network Connectivity

- Display device configuration.
- Test end-to-end connectivity with ping.
- Test remote management capabilities with Telnet.
- Save the switch running configuration file.

Part 4: Manage the MAC Address Table

- Record the MAC address of the host.
- Determine the MAC addresses that the switch has learned.
- List the **show mac address-table** command options.
- Set up a static MAC address.

Background/Scenario

Cisco switches can be configured with a special IP address known as the switch virtual interface (SVI). The SVI, or management address, can be used for remote access to the switch to display or configure settings. If the VLAN 1 SVI is assigned an IP address, by default all ports in VLAN 1 have access to the SVI IP address.

In this lab, you will build a simple topology using Ethernet LAN cabling and access a Cisco switch using the console and remote access methods. You will examine default switch configurations before configuring basic switch settings. These basic switch settings include device name, interface description, local passwords, message of the day (MOTD) banner, IP addressing, and static MAC address. You will also demonstrate the use of a management IP address for remote switch management. The topology consists of one switch and one host using only Ethernet and console ports.

Note: The switch used is a Cisco Catalyst 2960 with Cisco IOS Release 15.0(2) (lanbasek9 image). Other switches and Cisco IOS versions can be used. Depending on the model and Cisco IOS version, the commands available and output produced might vary from what is shown in this lab.

Note: Make sure that the switch has been erased and has no startup configuration. Refer to Appendix A for the procedures to initialize and reload a switch.

Required Resources

- 1 Switch (Cisco 2960 with Cisco IOS Release 15.0(2) lanbasek9 image or comparable)
- 1 PC (Windows 7, Vista, or XP with terminal emulation program, such as Tera Term, and Telnet capability)
- 1 Console cable to configure the Cisco IOS device via the console port
- 1 Ethernet cable as shown in the topology

Part 1: Cable the Network and Verify the Default Switch Configuration

In Part 1, you will set up the network topology and verify default switch settings.

Step 1:   Cable the network as shown in the topology.

   a.   Connect the console cable as shown in the topology. Do not connect the PC-A Ethernet cable at this time.

Note: If you are using Netlab, shut down F0/6 on S1. This has the same effect as not connecting PC-A to S1.

---

   b.   Connect to the switch from PC-A using Tera Term or other terminal emulation program.

   Why must you use a console connection to initially configure the switch? Why is it not possible to connect to the switch via Telnet or SSH?

Step 2:   Verify the default switch configuration.

   In this step, you will examine the default switch settings, such as current switch configuration, IOS information, interface properties, VLAN information, and flash memory.

   You can access all the switch IOS commands in privileged EXEC mode. Access to privileged EXEC mode should be restricted by password protection to prevent unauthorized use because it provides direct access to global configuration mode and commands used to configure operating parameters. You will set passwords later in this lab.

The privileged EXEC mode command set includes those commands contained in user EXEC mode, as well as the **configure** command through which access to the remaining command modes is gained. Use the **enable** command to enter privileged EXEC mode.

a. Assuming the switch had no configuration file stored in nonvolatile random-access memory (NVRAM), a console connection using Tera Term or other terminal emulation program will place you at the user EXEC mode prompt on the switch with a prompt of Switch>. Use the **enable** command to enter privileged EXEC mode.

```
Switch> enable
Switch#
```

Notice that the prompt changed in the configuration to reflect privileged EXEC mode.

Verify that there is a clean default configuration file on the switch by issuing the **show running-config** privileged EXEC mode command. If a configuration file was previously saved, it must be removed. Depending on the switch model and IOS version, your configuration may look slightly different. However, there should be no configured passwords or IP address. If your switch does not have a default configuration, erase and reload the switch.

Note: Appendix A details the steps to initialize and reload a switch.

---

b. Examine the current running configuration file.

```
Switch# show running-config
```

How many FastEthernet interfaces does a 2960 switch have? _____

How many Gigabit Ethernet interfaces does a 2960 switch have? _____

What is the range of values shown for the vty lines? _____

c. Examine the startup configuration file in NVRAM.

```
Switch# show startup-config
startup-config is not present
```

Why does this message appear?

_____

d. Examine the characteristics of the SVI for VLAN 1.

```
Switch# show interface vlan1
```

Is there an IP address assigned to VLAN 1? _____

What is the MAC address of this SVI? Answers will vary.

_____

Is this interface up?

_____

e. Examine the IP properties of the SVI VLAN 1.

```
Switch# show ip interface vlan1
```

What output do you see?

_____

_____

    f. Connect an Ethernet cable from PC-A to port 6 on the switch and examine the IP properties of the SVI VLAN 1. Allow time for the switch and PC to negotiate duplex and speed parameters.

Note: If you are using Netlab, enable interface F0/6 on S1.

```
Switch# show ip interface vlan1
```
What output do you see?

_____

_____

    g. Examine the Cisco IOS version information of the switch.

```
Switch# show version
```
What is the Cisco IOS version that the switch is running?

_____

What is the system image filename?

_____

What is the base MAC address of this switch? Answers will vary.

_____

    h. Examine the default properties of the FastEthernet interface used by PC-A.

```
Switch# show interface f0/6
```
Is the interface up or down? _____

What event would make an interface go up?

_____

What is the MAC address of the interface? _____

What is the speed and duplex setting of the interface? _____

    i. Examine the default VLAN settings of the switch.

```
Switch# show vlan
```
What is the default name of VLAN 1? _____

Which ports are in VLAN 1?

_____

Is VLAN 1 active? _____

What type of VLAN is the default VLAN? _____

    j. Examine flash memory.

Issue one of the following commands to examine the contents of the flash directory.

```
Switch# show flash
Switch# dir flash:
```
Files have a file extension, such as .bin, at the end of the filename. Directories do not have a file extension.

What is the filename of the Cisco IOS image?

_____

Part 2: Configure Basic Network Device Settings

In Part 2, you will configure basic settings for the switch and PC.

Step 1:   Configure basic switch settings.

    a. Copy the following basic configuration and paste it into S1 while in global configuration mode.

```
no ip domain-lookup
hostname S1
service password-encryption
enable secret class
banner motd #
Unauthorized access is strictly prohibited. #
Line con 0
password cisco
login
logging synchronous
line vty 0 15
password cisco
login
exit
```

    b. Set the SVI IP address of the switch. This allows remote management of the switch.

Before you can manage S1 remotely from PC-A, you must assign the switch an IP address. The default configuration on the switch is to have the management of the switch controlled through VLAN 1. However, a best practice for basic switch configuration is to change the management VLAN to a VLAN other than VLAN 1.

For management purposes, use VLAN 99. The selection of VLAN 99 is arbitrary and in no way implies that you should always use VLAN 99.

First, create the new VLAN 99 on the switch. Then set the IP address of the switch to 192.168.1.2 with a subnet mask of 255.255.255.0 on the internal virtual interface VLAN 99.

```
S1# configure terminal
S1(config)# vlan 99
S1(config-vlan)# exit
S1(config)# interface vlan99
%LINEPROTO-5-UPDOWN: Line protocol on Interface Vlan99, changed state to down
S1(config-if)# ip address 192.168.1.2 255.255.255.0
S1(config-if)# no shutdown
S1(config-if)# exit
S1(config)#
```

Notice that the VLAN 99 interface is in the down state even though you entered the **no shutdown** command. The interface is currently down because no switch ports are assigned to VLAN 99.

    c. Assign all user ports to VLAN 99.

```
S1(config)# interface range f0/1-24,g0/1 - 2
S1(config-if-range)# switchport access vlan 99
S1(config-if-range)# exit
S1(config)#
```

```
%LINEPROTO-5-UPDOWN: Line protocol on Interface Vlan1, changed state to down
%LINEPROTO-5-UPDOWN: Line protocol on Interface Vlan99, changed state to up
```

To establish connectivity between the host and the switch, the ports used by the host must be in the same VLAN as the switch. Notice in the above output that the VLAN 1 interface goes down because none of the ports are assigned to VLAN 1. After a few seconds, VLAN 99 comes up because at least one active port (F0/6 with PC-A attached) is now assigned to VLAN 99.

d. Issue the **show vlan brief** command to verify that all ports are in VLAN 99.

```
S1# show vlan brief

VLAN Name                             Status    Ports
---- -------------------------------- --------- -------------------------------
1    default                          active
99   VLAN0099                         active    Fa0/1, Fa0/2, Fa0/3, Fa0/4
                                                Fa0/5, Fa0/6, Fa0/7, Fa0/8
                                                Fa0/9, Fa0/10, Fa0/11, Fa0/12
                                                Fa0/13, Fa0/14, Fa0/15, Fa0/16
                                                Fa0/17, Fa0/18, Fa0/19, Fa0/20
                                                Fa0/21, Fa0/22, Fa0/23, Fa0/24
                                                Gi0/1, Gi0/2
1002 fddi-default                     act/unsup
1003 token-ring-default               act/unsup
1004 fddinet-default                  act/unsup
1005 trnet-default                    act/unsup
```

e. Configure the default gateway for S1. If no default gateway is set, the switch cannot be managed from a remote network that is more than one router away. Although this activity does not include an external IP gateway, assume that you will eventually connect the LAN to a router for external access. Assuming that the LAN interface on the router is 192.168.1.1, set the default gateway for the switch.

```
S1(config)# ip default-gateway 192.168.1.1
S1(config)#
```

f. Console port access should also be restricted. The default configuration is to allow all console connections with no password needed. To prevent console messages from interrupting commands, use the **logging synchronous** option.

```
S1(config)# line con 0
S1(config-line)# password cisco
S1(config-line)# login
S1(config-line)# logging synchronous
S1(config-line)# exit
S1(config)#
```

g. Configure the virtual terminal (vty) lines for the switch to allow Telnet access. If you do not configure a vty password, you will not be able to Telnet to the switch.

```
S1(config)# line vty 0 15
S1(config-line)# password cisco
S1(config-line)# login
S1(config-line)# end
S1#
*Mar  1 00:06:11.590: %SYS-5-CONFIG_I: Configured from console by console
```

Why is the **login** command required? _____

Step 2:   Configure an IP address on PC-A.

Assign the IP address and subnet mask to the PC as shown in the Addressing Table. An abbreviated version of the procedure is described here. A default gateway is not required for this topology; however, you can enter **192.168.1.1** to simulate a router attached to S1.

1) Click the Windows **Start** icon > **Control Panel**.

2) Click **View By:** and choose **Small icons.**

3) Choose **Network and Sharing Center** > **Change adapter settings.**

4) Select **Local Area Network Connection,** right click and choose **Properties.**

5) Choose **Internet Protocol Version 4 (TCP/IPv4)** > **Properties.**

6) Click the **Use the following IP address** radio button and enter the IP address and subnet mask.

Part 3: Verify and Test Network Connectivity

In Part 3, you will verify and document the switch configuration, test end-to-end connectivity between PC-A and S1, and test the switch's remote management capability.

Step 1:   Display the switch configuration.

Use the console connection on PC-A to display and verify the switch configuration. The **show run** command displays the entire running configuration, one page at a time. Use the spacebar to advance paging.

a.   A sample configuration is shown here. The settings you configured are highlighted in gray. The other configuration settings are IOS defaults.

```
S1# show run
Building configuration...

Current configuration : 2206 bytes
!
version 15.0
no service pad
service timestamps debug datetime msec
service timestamps log datetime msec
service password-encryption
!
hostname S1
!
boot-start-marker
boot-end-marker
!
enable secret 4 06YFDUHH61wAE/kLkDq9BGho1QM5EnRtoyr8cHAUg.2
!
no aaa new-model
system mtu routing 1500
!
!
no ip domain-lookup
!
```

```
<output omitted>
!
interface FastEthernet0/24
 switchport access vlan 99
!
interface GigabitEthernet0/1
 switchport access vlan 99
!
interface GigabitEthernet0/2
 switchport access vlan 99
!
interface Vlan1
 no ip address
 no ip route-cache
!
interface Vlan99
 ip address 192.168.1.2 255.255.255.0
 no ip route-cache
!
ip default-gateway 192.168.1.1
ip http server
ip http secure-server
!
banner motd ^C
Unauthorized access is strictly prohibited. ^C
!
line con 0
 password 7 104D000A0618
 logging synchronous
 login
line vty 0 4
 password 7 14141B180F0B
 login
line vty 5 15
 password 7 14141B180F0B
 login
!
end

S1#
```

b. Verify the management VLAN 99 settings.

```
S1# show interface vlan 99
Vlan99 is up, line protocol is up
  Hardware is EtherSVI, address is 0cd9.96e2.3d41 (bia 0cd9.96e2.3d41)
  Internet address is 192.168.1.2/24
  MTU 1500 bytes, BW 1000000 Kbit, DLY 10 usec,
     reliability 255/255, txload 1/255, rxload 1/255
  Encapsulation ARPA, loopback not set
  ARP type: ARPA, ARP Timeout 04:00:00
  Last input 00:00:06, output 00:08:45, output hang never
```

```
Last clearing of "show interface" counters never
Input queue: 0/75/0/0 (size/max/drops/flushes); Total output drops: 0
Queueing strategy: fifo
Output queue: 0/40 (size/max)
5 minute input rate 0 bits/sec, 0 packets/sec
5 minute output rate 0 bits/sec, 0 packets/sec
    175 packets input, 22989 bytes, 0 no buffer
    Received 0 broadcasts (0 IP multicast)
    0 runts, 0 giants, 0 throttles
    0 input errors, 0 CRC, 0 frame, 0 overrun, 0 ignored
    1 packets output, 64 bytes, 0 underruns
    0 output errors, 0 interface resets
    0 output buffer failures, 0 output buffers swapped out
```

What is the bandwidth on this interface? _____

What is the VLAN 99 state? _____

What is the line protocol state? _____

Step 2:   Test end-to-end connectivity with ping.

    a.   From the command prompt on PC-A, ping the address of PC-A first.

        `C:\Users\User1> ping 192.168.1.10`

    b.   From the command prompt on PC-A, ping the SVI management address of S1.

        `C:\Users\User1> ping 192.168.1.2`

    Because PC-A needs to resolve the MAC address of S1 through ARP, the first packet may time out. If ping results continue to be unsuccessful, troubleshoot the basic device configurations. Check both the physical cabling and logical addressing.

Step 3:   Test and verify remote management of S1.

You will now use Telnet to remotely access the switch. In this lab, PC-A and S1 reside side by side. In a production network, the switch could be in a wiring closet on the top floor while your management PC is located on the ground floor. In this step, you will use Telnet to remotely access switch S1 using its SVI management address. Telnet is not a secure protocol; however, you will use it to test remote access. With Telnet, all information, including passwords and commands, is sent across the session in plain text. In subsequent labs, you will use SSH to remotely access network devices.

Note: If you are using Windows 7, the administrator may need to enable the Telnet protocol. To install the Telnet client, open a command window and type **pkgmgr /iu:"TelnetClient"**. An example is shown below.
`C:\Users\User1> pkgmgr /iu:"TelnetClient"`

    a.   With the command window still open on PC-A, issue a Telnet command to connect to S1 via the SVI management address. The password is **cisco**.

        `C:\Users\User1> telnet 192.168.1.2`

    b.   After entering the password **cisco**, you will be at the user EXEC mode prompt. Access privileged EXEC mode using the **enable** command and providing the secret password **class**.

    c.   Type **exit** to end the Telnet session.

Step 4: Save the switch running configuration file.

Save the configuration.

```
S1# copy running-config startup-config
Destination filename [startup-config]? [Enter]
Building configuration...
[OK]
S1#
```

Part 4: Manage the MAC Address Table

In Part 4, you will determine the MAC addresses that the switch has learned, set up a static MAC address on one interface of the switch, and then remove the static MAC address from that interface.

Step 1: Record the MAC address of the host.

Open a command prompt on PC-A and issue the **ipconfig /all** command to determine and record the Layer 2 (physical) addresses of the NIC.

_____

Step 2: Determine the MAC addresses that the switch has learned.

Display the MAC addresses using the **show mac address-table** command.

```
S1# show mac address-table
```

How many dynamic addresses are there? _____

How many MAC addresses are there in total? _____

Does the dynamic MAC address match the MAC address of PC-A? _____

Step 3: List the **show mac address-table** options.

a. Display the MAC address table options.

```
S1# show mac address-table ?
```

How many options are available for the **show mac address-table** command?

_____

b. Issue the **show mac address-table dynamic** command to display only the MAC addresses that were learned dynamically.

```
S1# show mac address-table dynamic
```

How many dynamic addresses are there? _____

c. View the MAC address entry for PC-A. The MAC address formatting for the command is xxxx.xxxx.xxxx.

```
S1# show mac address-table address <PC-A MAC here>
```

Step 4: Set up a static MAC address.

a. Clear the MAC address table.

To remove the existing MAC addresses, use the **clear mac address-table dynamic** command in privileged EXEC mode.

```
S1# clear mac address-table dynamic
```

b. Verify that the MAC address table was cleared.

```
S1# show mac address-table
```

How many static MAC addresses are there?

_____

How many dynamic addresses are there?

_____

c. Examine the MAC table again.

More than likely, an application running on your PC has already sent a frame out the NIC to S1. Look at the MAC address table again in privileged EXEC mode to see if S1 has relearned the MAC address of PC-A.

```
S1# show mac address-table
```

How many dynamic addresses are there? _____

Why did this change from the last display?

_____

If S1 has not yet relearned the MAC address for PC-A, ping the VLAN 99 IP address of the switch from PC-A, and then repeat the **show mac address-table** command.

d. Set up a static MAC address.

To specify which ports a host can connect to, one option is to create a static mapping of the host MAC address to a port.

Set up a static MAC address on F0/6 using the address that was recorded for PC-A in Part 4, Step 1. The MAC address 0050.56BE.6C89 is used as an example only. You must use the MAC address of PC-A, which is different than the one given here as an example.

```
S1(config)# mac address-table static 0050.56BE.6C89 vlan 99 interface
fastethernet 0/6
```

e. Verify the MAC address table entries.

```
S1# show mac address-table
```

How many total MAC addresses are there? _____

How many static addresses are there? _____

f. Remove the static MAC entry. Enter global configuration mode and remove the command by putting a **no** in front of the command string.

Note: The MAC address 0050.56BE.6C89 is used in the example only. Use the MAC address for PC-A.

```
S1(config)# no mac address-table static 0050.56BE.6C89 vlan 99 interface
fastethernet 0/6
```

g. Verify that the static MAC address has been cleared.

```
S1# show mac address-table
```

How many total static MAC addresses are there? _____

Reflection

1. Why should you configure the vty password for the switch?

_____

2. Why change the default VLAN 1 to a different VLAN number?

_____

3. How can you prevent passwords from being sent in plain text?

_____

4. Why configure a static MAC address on a port interface?

_____

Appendix A: Initializing and Reloading a Switch

a. Console into the switch and enter privileged EXEC mode.

```
Switch> enable
Switch#
```

b. Use the **show flash** command to determine if any VLANs have been created on the switch.

```
Switch# show flash
Directory of flash:/

    2  -rwx        1919   Mar 1 1993 00:06:33 +00:00  private-config.text
    3  -rwx        1632   Mar 1 1993 00:06:33 +00:00  config.text
    4  -rwx       13336   Mar 1 1993 00:06:33 +00:00  multiple-fs
    5  -rwx    11607161   Mar 1 1993 02:37:06 +00:00  c2960-lanbasek9-mz.150-2.
SE.bin
    6  -rwx         616   Mar 1 1993 00:07:13 +00:00  vlan.dat

32514048 bytes total (20886528 bytes free)
Switch#
```

c. If the **vlan.dat** file was found in flash, then delete this file.

```
Switch# delete vlan.dat
Delete filename [vlan.dat]?
```

d. You are prompted to verify the filename. If you have entered the name correctly, press Enter; otherwise, you can change the filename.

e. You are prompted to confirm deletion of this file. Press Enter to confirm.

```
Delete flash:/vlan.dat? [confirm]
Switch#
```

f. Use the **erase startup-config** command to erase the startup configuration file from NVRAM. You are prompted to remove the configuration file. Press Enter to confirm.

```
Switch# erase startup-config
Erasing the nvram filesystem will remove all configuration files! Continue?
[confirm]
[OK]
Erase of nvram: complete
Switch#
```

g. Reload the switch to remove any old configuration information from memory. You will then receive a prompt to confirm reloading of the switch. Press Enter to proceed.

```
Switch# reload
Proceed with reload? [confirm]
```

Note: You may receive a prompt to save the running configuration prior to reloading the switch. Respond by typing **no** and press Enter.

```
System configuration has been modified. Save? [yes/no]: no
```

h. After the switch reloads, you should see a prompt to enter the initial configuration dialog. Respond by entering **no** at the prompt and press Enter.

```
Would you like to enter the initial configuration dialog? [yes/no]: no
Switch>
```

5.2.1.4 Packet Tracer–Configuring SSH

Topology

PC1   S1

Addressing Table

Device	Interface	IP Address	Subnet Mask
S1	VLAN 1	10.10.10.2	255.255.255.0
PC1	NIC	10.10.10.10	255.255.255.0

Objectives

Part 1: Secure Passwords

Part 2: Encrypt Communications

Part 3: Verify SSH Implementation

Background

SSH should replace Telnet for management connections. Telnet uses insecure plain text communications. SSH provides security for remote connections by providing strong encryption of all transmitted data between devices. In this activity, you will secure a remote switch with password encryption and SSH.

Part 1: Secure Passwords

    a. Using the command prompt on **PC1**, Telnet to **S1**. The user EXEC and privileged EXEC password is **cisco**.

    b. Save the current configuration so that any mistakes you might make can be reversed by toggling the power for **S1**.

    c. Show the current configuration and note that the passwords are in plain text. Enter the command that encrypts plain text passwords:

    _____

    d. Verify that the passwords are encrypted.

Part 2: Encrypt Communications

Step 1:   Set the IP domain name and generate secure keys.

It is generally not safe to use Telnet, because data is transferred in plain text. Therefore, use SSH whenever it is available.

      a.   Configure the domain name to be **netacad.pka**.

      b.   Secure keys are needed to encrypt the data. Generate the RSA keys using a 1024 key length.

Step 2:   Create an SSH user and reconfigure the VTY lines for SSH-only access.

      a.   Create an **administrator** user with **cisco** as the secret password.

      b.   Configure the VTY lines to check the local username database for login credentials and to only allow SSH for remote access. Remove the existing vty line password.

Part 3: Verify SSH Implementation

      a.   Exit the Telnet session and attempt to log back in using Telnet. The attempt should fail.

      b.   Attempt to log in using SSH. Type **ssh** and press **Enter** without any parameters to reveal the command usage instructions. Hint: The -**1** option is the letter "L", not the number 1.

      c.   Upon successful login, enter privileged EXEC mode and save the configuration. If you were unable to successfully access **S1**, toggle the power and begin again at Part 1.

5.2.2.7 Packet Tracer–Configuring Switch Port Security

Topology

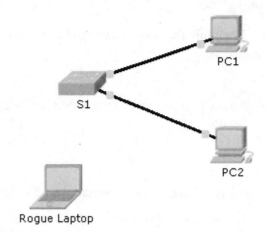

Addressing Table

Device	Interface	IP Address	Subnet Mask
S1	VLAN 1	10.10.10.2	255.255.255.0
PC1	NIC	10.10.10.10	255.255.255.0
PC2	NIC	10.10.10.11	255.255.255.0
Rogue Laptop	NIC	10.10.10.12	255.255.255.0

Objective

Part 1: Configure Port Security

Part 2: Verify Port Security

Background

In this activity, you will configure and verify port security on a switch. Port security allows you to restrict a port's ingress traffic by limiting the MAC addresses that are allowed to send traffic into the port.

Part 1: Configure Port Security

    a.   Access the command line for **S1** and enable port security on Fast Ethernet ports 0/1 and 0/2.

    b.   Set the maximum so that only one device can access the Fast Ethernet ports 0/1 and 0/2.

    c. Secure the ports so that the MAC address of a device is dynamically learned and added to the running configuration.

    _____

    d. Set the violation so that the Fast Ethernet ports 0/1 and 0/2 are not disabled when a violation occurs, but packets are dropped from an unknown source.

    _____

    e. Disable all the remaining unused ports. Hint: Use the **range** keyword to apply this configuration to all the ports simultaneously.

    _____

    _____

Part 2: Verify Port Security

    a. From **PC1**, ping **PC2**.

    b. Verify port security is enabled and the MAC addresses of **PC1** and **PC2** were added to the running configuration.

    c. Attach **Rogue Laptop** to any unused switch port and notice that the link lights are red.

    d. Enable the port and verify that **Rogue Laptop** can ping **PC1** and **PC2**. After verification, shut down the port connected to **Rogue Laptop.**

    e. Disconnect **PC2** and connect **Rogue Laptop** to **PC2**'s port. Verify that **Rogue Laptop** is unable to ping **PC1**.

    f. Display the port security violations for the port **Rogue Laptop** is connected to.

    _____

    g. Disconnect **Rogue Laptop** and reconnect **PC2**. Verify **PC2** can ping **PC1**.

    h. Why is **PC2** able to ping **PC1**, but the **Rogue Laptop** is not?

    _____

    _____

Packet Tracer
☐ Activity

5.2.2.8 Packet Tracer–Troubleshooting Switch Port Security

Topology

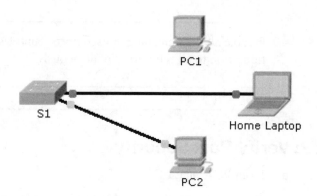

Scenario

The employee who normally uses PC1 brought his laptop from home, disconnected PC1 and connected the laptop to the telecommunication outlet. After reminding him of the security policy that does not allow personal devices on the network, you now must reconnect PC1 and re-enable the port.

Requirements

- Disconnect **Home Laptop** and reconnect **PC1** to the appropriate port.
    - When **PC1** was reconnected to the switch port, did the port status change? _____
    - Enter the command to view the port status. What is the state of the port?

      _____

      _____

    - Which port security command enabled this feature?

      _____

- Enable the port using the necessary command.

  _____

  _____

- Verify connectivity. PC1 should now be able to ping **PC2**.

Suggested Scoring Rubric

Packet Tracer scores 90 points. Answers to the questions are worth 10 points.

5.2.2.9 Lab–Configuring Switch Security Features

Topology

Addressing Table

Device	Interface	IP Address	Subnet Mask	Default Gateway
R1	G0/1	172.16.99.1	255.255.255.0	N/A
S1	VLAN 99	172.16.99.11	255.255.255.0	172.16.99.1
PC-A	NIC	172.16.99.3	255.255.255.0	172.16.99.1

Objectives

Part 1: Set up the Topology and Initialize Devices

Part 2: Configure Basic Device Settings and Verify Connectivity

Part 3: Configure and Verify SSH Access on S1

- Configure SSH access.

- Modify SSH parameters.

- Verify the SSH configuration.

Part 4: Configure and Verify Security Features on S1

- Configure and verify general security features.

- Configure and verify port security.

Background/Scenario

It is quite common to lock down access and install strong security features on PCs and servers. It is important that your network infrastructure devices, such as switches and routers, are also configured with security features.

In this lab, you will follow some best practices for configuring security features on LAN switches. You will only allow SSH and secure HTTPS sessions. You will also configure and verify port security to lock out any device with a MAC address not recognized by the switch.

Note: The router used with CCNA hands-on labs is a Cisco 1941 Integrated Services Router (ISR) with Cisco IOS Release 15.2(4)M3 (universalk9 image). The switch used is a Cisco Catalyst 2960 with Cisco IOS Release 15.0(2) (lanbasek9 image). Other routers, switches, and Cisco IOS versions can be used. Depending on the model and Cisco IOS version, the commands available and output produced might vary from what is shown in this lab. Refer to the Router Interface Summary Table at the end of this lab for the correct interface identifiers.

Note: Make sure that the router and switch have been erased and have no startup configurations. If you are unsure, contact your instructor or refer to the previous lab for the procedures to initialize and reload devices.

Required Resources

- 1 Router (Cisco 1941 with Cisco IOS Release 15.2(4)M3 universal image or comparable)
- 1 Switch (Cisco 2960 with Cisco IOS Release 15.0(2) lanbasek9 image or comparable)
- 1 PC (Windows 7, Vista, or XP with terminal emulation program, such as Tera Term)
- 1 Console cable to configure the Cisco IOS devices via the console ports
- 2 Ethernet cables as shown in the topology

Part 1: Set Up the Topology and Initialize Devices

In Part 1, you will set up the network topology and clear any configurations if necessary.

Step 1: Cable the network as shown in the topology.

Step 2: Initialize and reload the router and switch.

If configuration files were previously saved on the router or switch, initialize and reload these devices back to their default configurations.

Part 2: Configure Basic Device Settings and Verify Connectivity

In Part 2, you will configure basic settings on the router, switch, and PC. Refer to the Topology and Addressing Table at the beginning of this lab for device names and address information.

Step 1: Configure an IP address on PC-A.

Refer to the Addressing Table for the IP address information.

Step 2: Configure basic settings on R1.

    a. Console into R1 and enter global configuration mode.

    b. Copy the following basic configuration and paste it to running-configuration on R1.

```
no ip domain-lookup
hostname R1
service password-encryption
enable secret class
banner motd #
Unauthorized access is strictly prohibited. #
line con 0
password cisco
login
logging synchronous
line vty 0 4
password cisco
login
```

```
interface g0/1
 ip address 172.16.99.1 255.255.255.0
 no shutdown
end
```

c. Save the running configuration to startup configuration.

Step 3: Configure basic settings on S1.

a. Console into S1 and enter global configuration mode.

b. Copy the following basic configuration and paste it to running-configuration on S1.

```
no ip domain-lookup
hostname S1
service password-encryption
enable secret class
banner motd #
Unauthorized access is strictly prohibited. #
line con 0
password cisco
login
logging synchronous
line vty 0 15
password cisco
login
exit
```

c. Create VLAN 99 on the switch and name it **Management**.

```
S1(config)# vlan 99
S1(config-vlan)# name Management
S1(config-vlan)# exit
S1(config)#
```

d. Configure the VLAN 99 management interface IP address, as shown in the Addressing Table, and enable the interface.

```
S1(config)# interface vlan 99
S1(config-if)# ip address 172.16.99.11 255.255.255.0
S1(config-if)# no shutdown
S1(config-if)# end
S1#
```

e. Issue the **show vlan** command on S1. What is the status of VLAN 99?

_____

f. Issue the **show ip interface brief** command on S1. What is the status and protocol for management interface VLAN 99?

_____

Why is the protocol down, even though you issued the **no shutdown** command for interface VLAN 99?

_____

g. Assign ports F0/5 and F0/6 to VLAN 99 on the switch.

```
S1# config t
S1(config)# interface f0/5
S1(config-if)# switchport mode access
S1(config-if)# switchport access vlan 99
S1(config-if)# interface f0/6
S1(config-if)# switchport mode access
S1(config-if)# switchport access vlan 99
S1(config-if)# end
```

h. Save the running configuration to startup configuration.

i. Issue the **show ip interface brief** command on S1. What is the status and protocol showing for interface VLAN 99? _____

Note: There may be a delay while the port states converge.

Step 4: Verify connectivity between devices.

a. From PC-A, ping the default gateway address on R1. Were your pings successful?

_____

b. From PC-A, ping the management address of S1. Were your pings successful?

_____

c. From S1, ping the default gateway address on R1. Were your pings successful?

_____

d. From PC-A, open a web browser and go to http://172.16.99.11. If you are prompted for a username and password, leave the username blank and use **class** for the password. If you are prompted for a secured connection, answer **No**. Were you able to access the web interface on S1? _____

e. Close the browser.

Note: The non-secure web interface (HTTP server) on a Cisco 2960 switch is enabled by default. A common security measure is to disable this service, as described in Part 4.

Part 3: Configure and Verify SSH Access on S1

Step 1: Configure SSH access on S1.

a. Enable SSH on S1. From global configuration mode, create a domain name of **CCNA-Lab.com**.

```
S1(config)# ip domain-name CCNA-Lab.com
```

b. Create a local user database entry for use when connecting to the switch via SSH. The user should have administrative level access.

Note: The password used here is NOT a strong password. It is merely being used for lab purposes.

```
S1(config)# username admin privilege 15 secret sshadmin
```

c. Configure the transport input for the vty lines to allow SSH connections only, and use the local database for authentication.

```
S1(config)# line vty 0 15
S1(config-line)# transport input ssh
S1(config-line)# login local
S1(config-line)# exit
```

d. Generate an RSA crypto key using a modulus of 1024 bits.

```
S1(config)# crypto key generate rsa modulus 1024
The name for the keys will be: S1.CCNA-Lab.com

% The key modulus size is 1024 bits
% Generating 1024 bit RSA keys, keys will be non-exportable...
[OK] (elapsed time was 3 seconds)

S1(config)#
S1(config)# end
```

e. Verify the SSH configuration.

```
S1# show ip ssh
```

What version of SSH is the switch using? _____

How many authentication attempts does SSH allow? _____

What is the default timeout setting for SSH? _____

Step 2:   Modify the SSH configuration on S1.

Modify the default SSH configuration.

```
S1# config t
S1(config)# ip ssh time-out 75
S1(config)# ip ssh authentication-retries 2
```

How many authentication attempts does SSH allow? _____

What is the timeout setting for SSH? _____

Step 3:   Verify the SSH configuration on S1.

a. Using the SSH client software on PC-A (such as Tera Term), open an SSH connection to S1. If you receive a message on your SSH client regarding the host key, accept it. Log in with **admin** for username and **sshadmin** for the password.

Was the connection successful? _____

What prompt was displayed on S1? Why?

_____

_____

_____

b. Type **exit** to end the SSH session on S1.

Part 4: Configure and Verify Security Features on S1

In Part 4, you will shut down unused ports, turn off certain services running on the switch, and configure port security based on MAC addresses. Switches can be subject to MAC address table overflow attacks, MAC spoofing attacks, and unauthorized connections to switch ports. You will configure port security to limit the number of MAC addresses that can be learned on a switch port and disable the port if that number is exceeded.

Step 1:   Configure general security features on S1.

    a.   Change the message of the day (MOTD) banner on S1 to, "Unauthorized access is strictly prohibited. Violators will be prosecuted to the full extent of the law."

    b.   Issue a **show ip interface brief** command on S1. What physical ports are up?

_____

    c.   Shut down all unused physical ports on the switch. Use the **interface range** command.

```
S1(config)# interface range f0/1-4
S1(config-if-range)# shutdown
S1(config-if-range)# interface range f0/7-24
S1(config-if-range)# shutdown
S1(config-if-range)# interface range g0/1-2
S1(config-if-range)# shutdown
S1(config-if-range)# end
S1#
```

    d.   Issue the **show ip interface brief** command on S1. What is the status of ports F0/1 to F0/4?

_____

    e.   Issue the **show ip http server status** command.

        What is the HTTP server status? _____

        What server port is it using? _____

        What is the HTTP secure server status? _____

        What secure server port is it using? _____

    f.   HTTP sessions send everything in plain text. You will disable the HTTP service running on S1.

```
S1(config)# no ip http server
```

    g.   From PC-A, open a web browser and go to http://172.16.99.11. What was your result?

_____

    h.   From PC-A, open a web browser and go to https://172.16.99.11. Accept the certificate. Log in with no username and a password of **class**. What was your result?

_____

    i.   Close the web browser.

Step 2: Configure and verify port security on S1.

a. Record the R1 G0/1 MAC address. From the R1 CLI, use the **show interface g0/1** command and record the MAC address of the interface.

```
R1# show interface g0/1
GigabitEthernet0/1 is up, line protocol is up
  Hardware is CN Gigabit Ethernet, address is 30f7.0da3.1821 (bia
3047.0da3.1821)
```

What is the MAC address of the R1 G0/1 interface?

_____

b. From the S1 CLI, issue a **show mac address-table** command from privileged EXEC mode. Find the dynamic entries for ports F0/5 and F0/6. Record them below.

F0/5 MAC address: _____

F0/6 MAC address: _____

c. Configure basic port security.

Note: This procedure would normally be performed on all access ports on the switch. F0/5 is shown here as an example.

1) From the S1 CLI, enter interface configuration mode for the port that connects to R1.

```
S1(config)# interface f0/5
```

2) Shut down the port.

```
S1(config-if)# shutdown
```

3) Enable port security on F0/5.

```
S1(config-if)# switchport port-security
```

Note: Entering the **switchport port-security** command sets the maximum MAC addresses to 1 and the violation action to shutdown. The **switchport port-security maximum** and **switchport port-security violation** commands can be used to change the default behavior.

4) Configure a static entry for the MAC address of R1 G0/1 interface recorded in Step 2a.

```
S1(config-if)# switchport port-security mac-address xxxx.xxxx.xxxx
```

(xxxx.xxxx.xxxx is the actual MAC address of the router G0/1 interface)

Note: Optionally, you can use the `switchport port-security mac-address sticky` command to add all the secure MAC addresses that are dynamically learned on a port (up to the maximum set) to the switch running configuration.

5) Enable the switch port.

```
S1(config-if)# no shutdown
S1(config-if)# end
```

d. Verify port security on S1 F0/5 by issuing a **show port-security interface** command.

```
S1# show port-security interface f0/5
Port Security            : Enabled
Port Status              : Secure-up
Violation Mode           : Shutdown
Aging Time               : 0 mins
```

```
Aging Type                  : Absolute
SecureStatic Address Aging  : Disabled
Maximum MAC Addresses       : 1
Total MAC Addresses         : 1
Configured MAC Addresses    : 1
Sticky MAC Addresses        : 0
Last Source Address:Vlan    : 0000.0000.0000:0
Security Violation Count    : 0
```

What is the port status of F0/5?

_____

e. From R1 command prompt, ping PC-A to verify connectivity.

```
R1# ping 172.16.99.3
```

f. You will now violate security by changing the MAC address on the router interface. Enter interface configuration mode for G0/1 and shut it down.

```
R1# config t
R1(config)# interface g0/1
R1(config-if)# shutdown
```

g. Configure a new MAC address for the interface, using **aaaa.bbbb.cccc** as the address.

```
R1(config-if)# mac-address aaaa.bbbb.cccc
```

h. If possible, have a console connection open on S1 at the same time that you do the next two steps. You will eventually see messages displayed on the console connection to S1 indicating a security violation. Enable the G0/1 interface on R1.

```
R1(config-if)# no shutdown
```

i. From R1 privileged EXEC mode, ping PC-A. Was the ping successful? Why or why not?

_____

j. On the switch, verify port security with the following commands.

```
S1# show port-security
Secure Port MaxSecureAddr CurrentAddr SecurityViolation Security Action
                (Count)      (Count)       (Count)
-----------------------------------------------------------------
      Fa0/5          1            1             1          Shutdown
-----------------------------------------------------------------
Total Addresses in System (excluding one mac per port)     :0
Max Addresses limit in System (excluding one mac per port) :8192


S1# show port-security interface f0/5
Port Security               : Enabled
Port Status                 : Secure-shutdown
Violation Mode              : Shutdown
Aging Time                  : 0 mins
Aging Type                  : Absolute
SecureStatic Address Aging  : Disabled
Maximum MAC Addresses       : 1
Total MAC Addresses         : 1
Configured MAC Addresses    : 1
Sticky MAC Addresses        : 0
```

```
Last Source Address:Vlan   : aaaa.bbbb.cccc:99
Security Violation Count    : 1


S1# show interface f0/5
FastEthernet0/5 is down, line protocol is down (err-disabled)
  Hardware is Fast Ethernet, address is 0cd9.96e2.3d05 (bia 0cd9.96e2.3d05)
  MTU 1500 bytes, BW 10000 Kbit/sec, DLY 1000 usec,
      reliability 255/255, txload 1/255, rxload 1/255
<output omitted>


S1# show port-security address
                Secure Mac Address Table
-------------------------------------------------------------------

Vlan    Mac Address        Type           ·Ports    Remaining Age
                                                    (mins)

----    -----------        ----           -----    -------------

 99     30f7.0da3.1821     SecureConfigured   Fa0/5      -

-------------------------------------------------------------------
Total Addresses in System (excluding one mac per port)   :0
Max Addresses limit in System (excluding one mac per port) :8192
```

k. On the router, shut down the G0/1 interface, remove the hard-coded MAC address from the router, and re-enable the G0/1 interface.

```
R1(config-if)# shutdown
R1(config-if)# no mac-address aaaa.bbbb.cccc
R1(config-if)# no shutdown
R1(config-if)# end
```

l. From R1, ping PC-A again at 172.16.99.3. Was the ping successful? _____

m. On the switch, issue the **show interface f0/5** command to determine the cause of ping failure. Record your findings.

_____

n. Clear the S1 F0/5 error disabled status.

```
S1# config t
S1(config)# interface f0/5
S1(config-if)# shutdown
S1(config-if)# no shutdown
```

Note: There may be a delay while the port states converge.

---

o. Issue the **show interface f0/5** command on S1 to verify F0/5 is no longer in error disabled mode.

```
S1# show interface f0/5
FastEthernet0/5 is up, line protocol is up (connected)
  Hardware is Fast Ethernet, address is 0023.5d59.9185 (bia 0023.5d59.9185)
  MTU 1500 bytes, BW 100000 Kbit/sec, DLY 100 usec,
      reliability 255/255, txload 1/255, rxload 1/255
```

p. From the R1 command prompt, ping PC-A again. The ping should be successful.

Reflection

1. Why would you enable port security on a switch?

_____

_____

2. Why should unused ports on a switch be disabled?

_____

_____

Router Interface Summary Table

	Router Interface Summary			
Router Model	Ethernet Interface #1	Ethernet Interface #2	Serial Interface #1	Serial Interface #2
1800	Fast Ethernet 0/0 (F0/0)	Fast Ethernet 0/1 (F0/1)	Serial 0/0/0 (S0/0/0)	Serial 0/0/1 (S0/0/1)
1900	Gigabit Ethernet 0/0 (G0/0)	Gigabit Ethernet 0/1 (G0/1)	Serial 0/0/0 (S0/0/0)	Serial 0/0/1 (S0/0/1)
2801	Fast Ethernet 0/0 (F0/0)	Fast Ethernet 0/1 (F0/1)	Serial 0/1/0 (S0/1/0)	Serial 0/1/1 (S0/1/1)
2811	Fast Ethernet 0/0 (F0/0)	Fast Ethernet 0/1 (F0/1)	Serial 0/0/0 (S0/0/0)	Serial 0/0/1 (S0/0/1)
2900	Gigabit Ethernet 0/0 (G0/0)	Gigabit Ethernet 0/1 (G0/1)	Serial 0/0/0 (S0/0/0)	Serial 0/0/1 (S0/0/1)

Note: To find out how the router is configured, look at the interfaces to identify the type of router and how many interfaces the router has. There is no way to effectively list all the combinations of configurations for each router class. This table includes identifiers for the possible combinations of Ethernet and Serial interfaces in the device. The table does not include any other type of interface, even though a specific router may contain one. An example of this might be an ISDN BRI interface. The string in parentheses is the legal abbreviation that can be used in Cisco IOS commands to represent the interface.

5.3.1.1 Lab–Switch Trio

Objective

Verify the Layer 2 configuration of a switch port connected to an end station.

Scenario

You are the network administrator for a small- to medium-sized business. Corporate headquarters for your business has mandated that on all switches in all offices, security must be implemented. The memorandum delivered to you this morning states:

"By Monday, April 18, 20xx, the first three ports of all configurable switches located in all offices must be secured with MAC addresses — one address will be reserved for the PC, one address will be reserved for the laptop in the office, and one address will be reserved for the office server.

If a port's security is breached, we ask you to shut it down until the reason for the breach can be certified.

Please implement this policy no later than the date stated in this memorandum. For questions, call 1.800.555.1212. Thank you. The Network Management Team"

Work with a partner in the class and create a Packet Tracer example to test this new security policy. Once you have created your file, test it with, at least, one device to ensure it is operational or validated.

Save your work and be prepared to share it with the entire class.

Reflection

1. Why would one port on a switch be secured on a switch using these scenario parameters (and not all the ports on the same switch)?

   _____

2. Why would a network administrator use a network simulator to create, configure, and validate a security plan, instead of using the small- to medium-sized business' actual, physical equipment?

   _____

5.3.1.2 Packet Tracer–Skills Integration Challenge

Topology

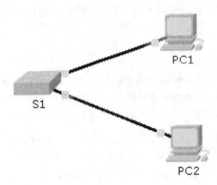

Addressing Table

Device	Interface	IP Address	Subnet Mask
S1	VLAN 1	10.10.10.2	255.255.255.0
PC1	NIC	10.10.10.10	255.255.255.0
PC2	NIC	10.10.10.11	255.255.255.0

Scenario

The network administrator asked you to configure a new switch. In this activity, you will use a list of requirements to configure the new switch with initial settings, SSH, and port security.

Requirements

- Configure **S1** with the following initial settings:
    - Hostname
    - Banner that includes the word **warning**
    - Console port login and password **cisco**
    - Encrypted enable password of **class**
    - Encrypt plain text passwords
    - Management interface addressing
- Configure SSH to secure remote access with the following settings:
    - Domain name of **cisco.com**
    - RSA key-pair parameters to support SSH version 2
    - Set SSH version 2

- User **admin** with secret password **ccna**
- VTY lines only accept SSH connections and use local login for authentication
- Configure the port security feature to restrict network access:
  - Disable all unused ports.
  - Set the interface mode to access.
  - Enable port security to allow only two hosts per port.
  - Record the MAC address in the running configuration.
  - Ensure that port violations disable ports.

CHAPTER 6

VLANs

One of the contributing technologies to excellent network performance is the separation of large broadcast domains into smaller ones with virtual local area networks (VLANs). Smaller broadcast domains limit the number of devices participating in broadcasts and allow devices to be separated into functional groups. This chapter offers exercises to help you review how to configure, manage, and troubleshoot VLANs and Ethernet trunk links. It also reviews security considerations and strategies relating to VLANs and trunks and best practices for VLAN design.

The Study Guide portion of this chapter uses a combination of matching, fill-in-the-blank, multiple-choice, and open-ended question exercises to test your knowledge and skills of basic router concepts and configuration. The Labs and Activities portion of this chapter includes all the online curriculum labs and Packet Tracer activities to ensure that you have mastered the hands-on skills needed to understand basic IP addressing and router configuration.

As you work through this chapter, use Chapter 6 in *Routing and Switching Essentials v6 Companion Guide* or use the corresponding Chapter 6 in the Routing and Switching Essentials online curriculum for assistance.

Study Guide

VLAN Segmentation

VLANs give network administrators flexibility in LAN design. VLANs extend the traditional router-bounded broadcast domain to a VLAN-bounded broadcast domain; VLANs make it possible to sculpt a broadcast domain into any shape that can be defined and bounded by the switches within the network.

Overview of VLANs

A VLAN creates a _____ broadcast domain that can span multiple physical LAN segments. VLANs enable the implementation of access and security policies according to specific groupings of users. Each switch port can be assigned to only one VLAN. What are two exceptions to this rule?

_____

Briefly describe each of the following primary benefits of using VLANs:

- Security: _____

  _____

- Cost reduction: _____

  _____

- Better performance: _____
- Shrink broadcast domains: _____

  _____

- Improved IT staff efficiency: _____

  _____

  _____

- Simpler project and application management: _____

  _____

  _____

How does a VLAN implementation affect your addressing scheme?

_____

_____

A number of distinct types of VLANs are used in modern networks. Some VLAN types are defined by traffic classes. Other types of VLANs are defined by the specific function that they serve.

_____ VLAN

A _____ VLAN is a VLAN that is configured to carry user-generated traffic. A VLAN carrying voice or management traffic would not be part of a _____ VLAN. Separating voice and management traffic from _____ traffic is common practice.

_____ VLAN

All switch ports become a part of the _____ VLAN after the initial boot of a switch loading the default configuration. The _____ VLAN for Cisco switches is VLAN _____.

What is the primary reason for having this VLAN?

_____

_____

What are three unique features about VLAN 1?

_____

_____

_____

Native VLAN

Briefly explain the purpose for the native VLAN.

_____

_____

Management VLAN

Briefly explain the purpose for the management VLAN.

_____

_____

_____

Voice VLAN

A separate VLAN is needed to support Voice over IP (VoIP). List four requirements of VoIP traffic:

_____

_____

_____

_____

VLANs in a Multiswitched Environment

Briefly define a VLAN trunk.

_____

_____

Explain what a switch does with a frame received on an access port assigned to one VLAN before placing the frame on a trunk link for all VLANs:

_____

_____

_____

The VLAN tag field consists of the following fields:

- _____ : A 2-byte value called the tag protocol ID (TPID) value. For Ethernet, it is set to hexadecimal _____ .

- _____ : A 3-bit value that supports level or service implementation.

- _____ (CFI): A 1-bit identifier that enables Token Ring frames to be carried across Ethernet links.

- _____ (VID): A 12-bit VLAN identification number that supports up to _____ .

What does the switch do after tagging the frame, but before it switches it to the outbound port?

_____

_____

The native VLAN is used for control traffic, which is not tagged. What does an 802.1Q trunk do if it receives a frame tagged with the native VLAN ID?

_____

VLAN Implementations

In this section, we review VLAN implementations, including configuring and verifying VLANs, trunking VLANS, and troubleshooting VLAN and trunking issues.

VLAN Configuration Exercise

Use the information in Figure 6-1 and Table 6-1 to answer the following questions related to configuring VLANs and trunks.

Figure 6-1   VLAN Configuration Topology

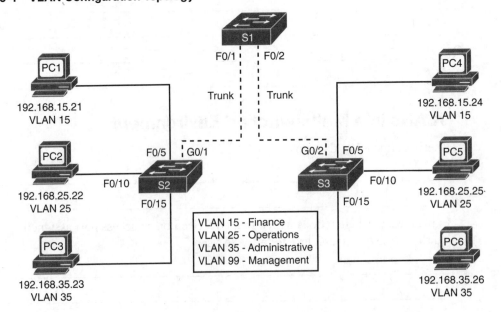

PC1
192.168.15.21
VLAN 15

PC2
192.168.25.22
VLAN 25

PC3
192.168.35.23
VLAN 35

S1
F0/1   F0/2
Trunk   Trunk

F0/5   G0/1

F0/10   S2

F0/15

G0/2   F0/5

S3   F0/10

F0/15

VLAN 15 - Finance
VLAN 25 - Operations
VLAN 35 - Administrative
VLAN 99 - Management

PC4
192.168.15.24
VLAN 15

PC5
192.168.25.25
VLAN 25

PC6
192.168.35.26
VLAN 35

Table 6-1   VLAN Configuration Addressing Table

Device	Interface	IP Address	Subnet Mask	Default Gateway
S1	VLAN 99	192.168.99.11	255.255.255.0	N/A
S2	VLAN 99	192.168.99.12	255.255.255.0	N/A
S3	VLAN 99	192.168.99.13	255.255.255.0	N/A
PC1	NIC	192.168.15.21	255.255.255.0	192.168.15.1
PC2	NIC	192.168.25.22	255.255.255.0	192.168.25.1
PC3	NIC	192.168.35.23	255.255.255.0	192.168.35.1
PC4	NIC	192.168.15.24	255.255.255.0	192.168.15.1
PC5	NIC	192.168.25.25	255.255.255.0	192.168.25.1
PC6	NIC	192.168.35.26	255.255.255.0	192.168.35.1

Enter the commands, including the switch prompts, to configure the management interface on each switch.

Enter the commands, including the switch prompts, to configure the VLANs on each switch. (The commands are the same on each switch, so you only need to enter the commands for S1 here.)

Enter the commands, including the switch prompts, to configure access ports and assign VLANs for the PCs that are attached to S2 and S3. (Because the commands are the same on both switches, you only need to record them once.)

_____

_____

_____

_____

_____

_____

_____

After you configure a VLAN, you can validate the VLAN configurations using Cisco IOS **show** commands. Enter the command used to display the following output:

S1# _____

```
VLAN Name                             Status    Ports
---- -------------------------------- --------- ------------------------------
1    default                          active    Fa0/1, Fa0/2, Fa0/3, Fa0/4
                                                Fa0/5, Fa0/6, Fa0/7, Fa0/8
                                                Fa0/9, Fa0/10, Fa0/11, Fa0/12
                                                Fa0/13, Fa0/14, Fa0/15, Fa0/16
                                                Fa0/17, Fa0/18, Fa0/19, Fa0/20
                                                Fa0/21, Fa0/22, Fa0/23, Fa0/24
15   Finance                          active
25   Operations                       active
35   Administrative                   active
99   Management                       active
1002 fddi-default                     active
1003 token-ring-default               active
1004 fddinet-default                  active
1005 trnet-default                    active
S1#
```

Enter the command used to display the information for only one VLAN, specifying the VLAN number:

S1# _____

```
VLAN Name                             Status    Ports
---- -------------------------------- --------- ------------------------------
15   Finance                          active
```

```
VLAN Type  SAID       MTU   Parent RingNo BridgeNo Stp  BrdgMode Trans1 Trans2
---- ----- ---------- ----- ------ ------ -------- ---- -------- ------ ------
15   enet  100015     1500  -      -      -        -    -        0      0
```

S1#

Enter the command used to display the information for only one VLAN, specifying the VLAN name:

S1# _____

```
VLAN Name                             Status    Ports
---- -------------------------------- --------- ------------------------------
25   Operations                       active
```

```
VLAN Type  SAID       MTU   Parent RingNo BridgeNo Stp  BrdgMode Trans1 Trans2
---- ----- ---------- ----- ------ ------ -------- ---- -------- ------ ------
25   enet  100025     1500  -      -      -        -    -        0      0
```

S1#

Enter the command that will display the following output:

S1# _____

```
Number of existing VLANs         : 9
Number of existing VTP VLANs     : 9
Number of existing extended VLANs : 0
```

Enter the command that will display the following output:

S2# _____

```
Name: Fa0/5
Switchport: Enabled
Administrative Mode: static access
Operational Mode: static access
Administrative Trunking Encapsulation: dot1q
Operational Trunking Encapsulation: native
Negotiation of Trunking: On
Access Mode VLAN: 15 (Finance)
Trunking Native Mode VLAN: 1 (default)
Voice VLAN: none
Administrative private-vlan host-association: none
Administrative private-vlan mapping: none
Administrative private-vlan trunk native VLAN: none
Administrative private-vlan trunk encapsulation: dot1q
Administrative private-vlan trunk normal VLANs: none
Administrative private-vlan trunk private VLANs: none
Operational private-vlan: none
Trunking VLANs Enabled: ALL
Pruning VLANs Enabled: 2-1001
```

```
Capture Mode Disabled

Capture VLANs Allowed: ALL

Protected: false

Appliance trust: none
```

Practice VLAN Configuration

Now you are ready to use Packet Tracer, another simulator, or lab equipment to apply your VLAN configurations.

VLAN Trunk Configuration Exercise

In Table 6-2, enter the syntax for each of the trunk configuration commands.

Table 6-2   Trunk Configuration Commands

Description	Syntax
Force the link to be a trunk link.	S1(config-if)#
Specify a native VLAN for untagged 802.1Q trunks.	S1(config-if)#
Specify the list of VLANs to be allowed on the trunk link.	S1(config-if)#

On S1, enter the commands to configure GigabitEthernet 0/1 to be an 802.1Q trunk. Use VLAN 99 as the native VLAN.

```
S1(config)# _____

S1(config-if)# _____

S1(config-if)# _____
```

What command will display the switch port status of the new trunk port shown in Example 6-1?

Example 6-1   Verifying a Trunk Configuration

```
S1# _____

Name: Gig0/1

Switchport: Enabled

Administrative Mode: trunk

Operational Mode: trunk

Administrative Trunking Encapsulation: dot1q

Operational Trunking Encapsulation: dot1q

Negotiation of Trunking: On

Access Mode VLAN: 1 (default)

Trunking Native Mode VLAN: 99 (Management)

Administrative Native VLAN tagging: enabled

Voice VLAN: none

Administrative private-vlan host-association: none

Administrative private-vlan mapping: none

Administrative private-vlan trunk native VLAN: none
```

```
Administrative private-vlan trunk Native VLAN tagging: enabled
Administrative private-vlan trunk encapsulation: dot1q
Administrative private-vlan trunk normal VLANs: none
Administrative private-vlan trunk associations: none
Administrative private-vlan trunk mappings: none
Operational private-vlan: none
Trunking VLANs Enabled: ALL
Pruning VLANs Enabled: 2-1001
Capture Mode Disabled
Capture VLANs Allowed: ALL

Protected: false
Unknown unicast blocked: disabled
Unknown multicast blocked: disabled
Appliance trust: none
S1#
```

Packet Tracer Exercise 6-1: Configuring VLANs and Trunking

Now you are ready to use Packet Tracer to apply your knowledge about VLAN configuration. Download and open the file LSG02-0601.pka found at the companion website for this book. Refer to the Introduction of this book for specifics on accessing files.

Note: The following instructions are also contained within the Packet Tracer exercise.

In this Packet Tracer activity, you will configure and verify VLANs and trunking. Use the commands you documented in the "VLAN Implementations" section to help you complete the activity.

Requirements

- Configure interface VLAN 99 on each switch.
- Create and name VLANs on each switch. Names are case sensitive.
- Assign ports to the correct VLANs.
- Configure trunking between the switches assigning VLAN 99 as the native VLAN.
- Verify that PCs on the same VLAN can ping each other.
- Verify the switches can ping each other.

Your completion percentage should be 100%. If not, click **Check Results** to see which required components are not yet completed.

Troubleshoot VLANs and Trunks

Given the information shown in Figure 6-2 and assuming all subnets are /24, locate and explain the issue.

Figure 6-2 Troubleshooting VLANs and Trunks: IP Addressing

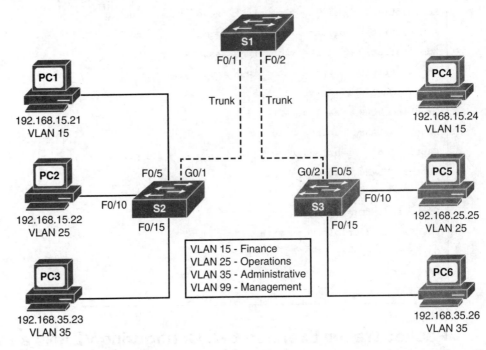

Each VLAN must correspond to a unique IP subnet. If two devices in the same VLAN have different subnet addresses, they cannot communicate. PC2 cannot communicate with P5 because even though they are in the same VLAN, they are on different subnets.

If IP addressing issues are resolved but there is still no connection between the devices, you will need to troubleshoot VLAN configurations and assignments. Complete the flowchart in Figure 6-3, which can be used to resolve a VLAN configuration issue.

Figure 6-3 Troubleshooting VLANs and Trunks: Missing VLAN

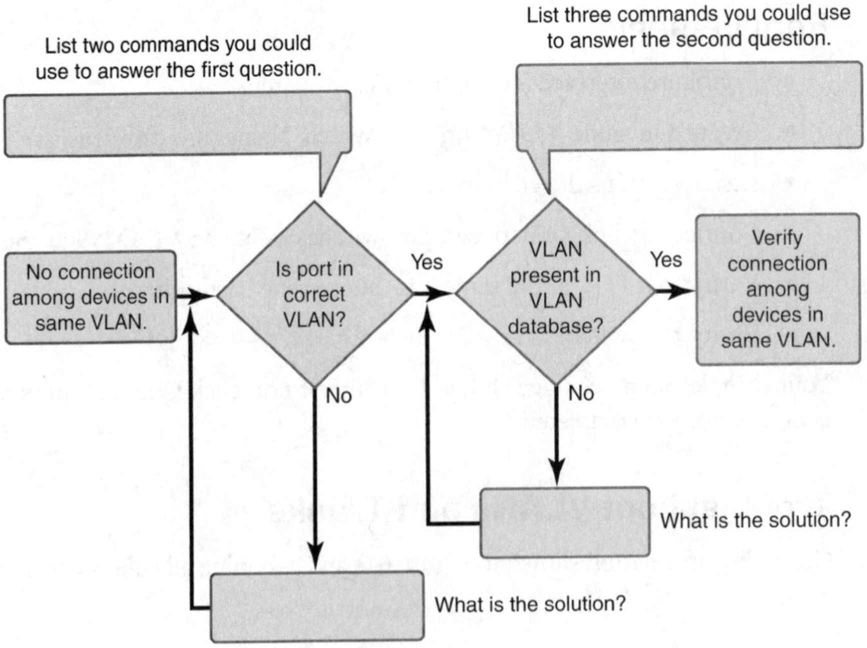

Sometimes a switch port may behave like a trunk port even if it is not configured as a trunk port. For example, an access port might accept frames from VLANs different from the VLAN to which it is assigned. This is called VLAN _____.

In Table 6-3, indicate which trunking problem is associated with each example.

Table 6-3   Troubleshooting VLANs and Trunks: Trunk Issues

Problem	Result	Example
	Causes unexpected traffic or no traffic to be sent over the trunk	The list of allowed VLANs does not support current VLAN trunking requirements.
	Poses a security risk and creates unintended results	For example, one port is in VLAN 99; the other is in VLAN 1.
	Causes loss of network connectivity	For example, one side of the trunk is configured as an access port.

What command can you use to quickly check on the status of all the trunk ports on the switch?

S1# _____

What commands can you use to correct the list of VLANs for a trunk?

S1(config-if)# _____

S1(config-if)# _____

S1(config-if)# _____

Inter-VLAN Routing Configuration

Remember that a VLAN is a broadcast domain, so computers on separate VLANs are unable to communicate without the intervention of a routing device. Any device that supports Layer 3 routing, such as a router or a multilayer switch, can be used to perform the necessary routing functionality.

Types of Inter-VLAN Routing

Briefly describe each of the types of inter-VLAN routing.

_____

_____

_____

_____

_____

_____

_____

_____

_____

_____

In Figure 6-4, identify the type of inter-VLAN routing shown in each of the topologies.

Figure 6-4   Topology Examples of Types of Inter-VLAN Routing

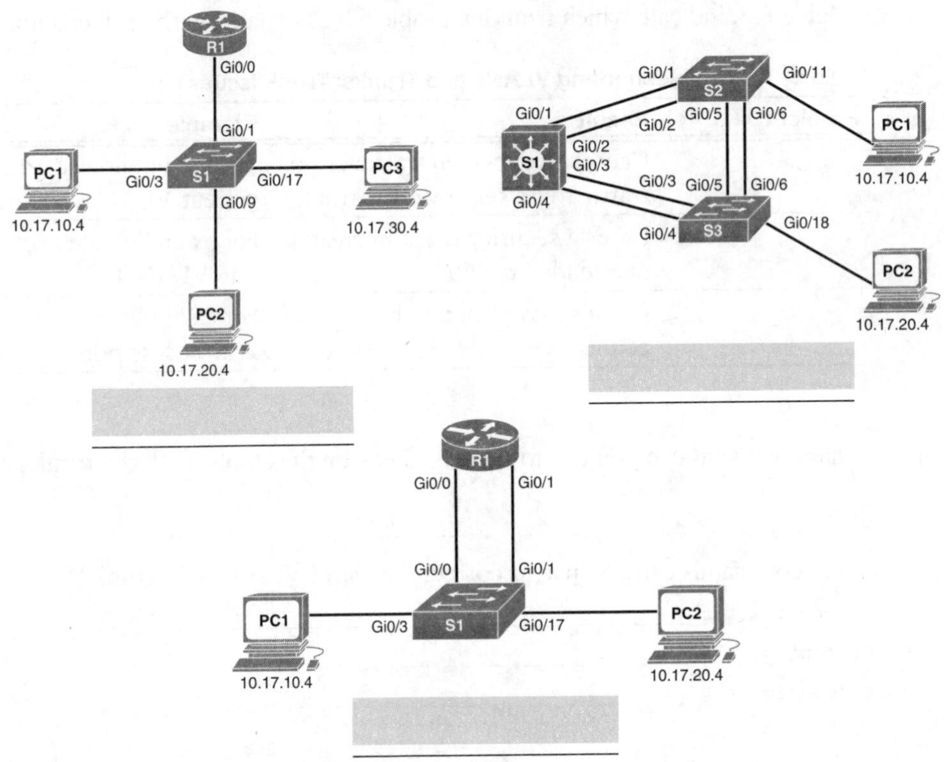

Configuring Inter-VLAN Routing

Legacy inter-VLAN routing (or per-interface inter-VLAN routing) requires multiple physical interfaces between the router and the switch. The switch interfaces are set to access mode and assigned one VLAN. The router needs nothing special to route the VLAN traffic other than addressing for the VLAN's subnet. Because this is legacy inter-VLAN routing, we will not review it any further. You just need to be aware of what it is and how it is configured.

An alternative in larger networks is to use VLAN trunking and subinterfaces. VLAN trunking allows a single physical router interface to route traffic for multiple VLANs. This technique is termed *router-on-a-stick* and uses virtual subinterfaces on the router to overcome the hardware limitations based on physical router interfaces.

List the commands including command syntax and prompt to configure a router for router-on-a-stick inter-VLAN routing:

_____

_____

_____

_____

_____

_____

_____

List the commands including syntax and prompt to configure a switch to support inter-VLAN routing:

_____

_____

_____

_____

What commands cannot be used on the router? Why?

_____

_____

Refer to Figure 6-5 and enter the commands for both R1 and S1 to enable inter-VLAN routing.

Figure 6-5   Inter-VLAN Routing Topology

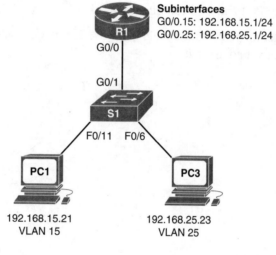

```
R1(config)#
```

_____

_____

_____

_____

_____

_____

_____

_____

```
S1(config)#
```

_____

_____

Packet Tracer Exercise 6-2: Configuring Inter-VLAN Routing

Now you are ready to use Packet Tracer to apply your knowledge about inter-VLAN routing configuration. Download and open the file LSG02-0602.pka found at the companion website for this book. Refer to the Introduction of this book for specifics on accessing files.

Note: The following instructions are also contained within the Packet Tracer exercise.

In this Packet Tracer activity, you will configure and verify VLANs and trunking. Use the commands you documented in the "Configuring Inter-VLAN Routing" section to help you complete the activity.

Requirements

- Configure R1 for inter-VLAN routing.
- Configure the S1 link to R1 as a trunk.
- Verify PC1 and PC3 can ping each other.

Your completion percentage should be 100%. If not, click **Check Results** to see which required components are not yet completed.

Labs and Activities

Command Reference

In Table 6-4, record the command, including the correct router or switch prompt, that fits the description. Fill in any blanks with the appropriate missing information.

Table 6-4   Commands for Chapter 6, "VLANs"

Command	Description
	Create VLAN 75.
	Assign the name Admin to a VLAN.
	Assign a switch interface to use VLAN 75.
	Display an abbreviated output of configured VLANs.
	Display information for VLAN 75.
	Display information for VLAN Admin.
	Display a summary of VLAN information.
	Verify the VLAN configurations on Fa0/10.
	Configure a port to trunk.
	Configure VLAN 86 as the native trunking VLAN.
	Configure a trunk to allow VLANs 75 and 86.
	Display the status of all trunk ports.
	Create subinterface 100 on a router G0/1 interface.
	Configure a subinterface to use 801.Q encapsulation for VLAN 75.

Lab 6.0.1.2–Vacation Station

Objective

Explain the purpose of VLANs in a switched network.

Scenario

You have purchased a vacation home at the beach for rental purposes. There are three identical floors in the home. Each floor offers one digital television for renters to use.

According to the local Internet service provider, only three stations may be offered within a television package. It is your job to decide which television packages you offer your guests.

- Divide the class into groups of three students per group.

- Choose three different stations to make one subscription package for each floor of your rental home.

- Complete the PDF for this activity.

Share your completed group reflection answers with the class.

Television Station Subscription Package–Floor 1

Local News	Sports	Weather
❑	❑	❑
Home Improvement	Movies	History
❑	❑	❑

Television Station Subscription Package–Floor 2

Local News	Sports	Weather
❑	❑	❑
Home Improvement	Movies	History
❑	❑	❑

Television Station Subscription Package–Floor 3

Local News	Sports	Weather
❑	❑	❑
Home Improvement	Movies	History
❑	❑	❑

Reflection

1. What were some of the criteria you used to select the final three stations?

   _____

2. Why do you think this Internet service provider offers different television station options to subscribers? Why not offer all stations to all subscribers?

   _____

3. Compare this scenario to data communications and networks for small- to medium-sized businesses. Why would it be a good idea to divide your small- to medium-sized business networks into logical and physical groups?

   _____

6.1.1.5 Packet Tracer–Who Hears the Broadcast?

Topology

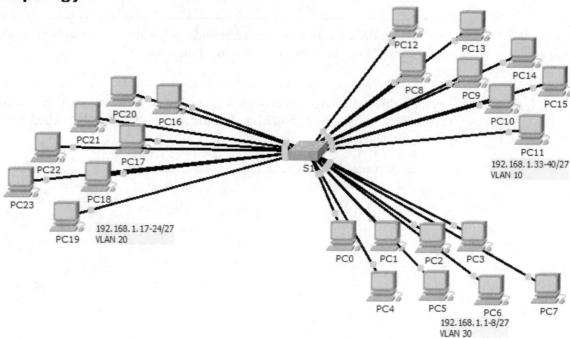

Objectives

Part 1: Observe Broadcast Traffic in a VLAN Implementation

Part 2: Complete Review Questions

Scenario

In this activity, a 24-port Catalyst 2960 switch is fully populated. All ports are in use. You will observe broadcast traffic in a VLAN implementation and answer some reflection questions.

Part 1: Observe Broadcast Traffic in a VLAN Implementation

Step 1:   Use ping to generate traffic.

    a.   Click **PC0** and click the **Desktop** tab> **Command Prompt**.

    b.   Enter the **ping 192.168.1.8** command. The ping should succeed.

    Unlike a LAN, a VLAN is a broadcast domain created by switches. Using Packet Tracer Simulation mode, ping the end devices within their own VLAN. Based on your observation, answer the questions in Step 2.

Step 2:   Generate and examine broadcast traffic.

    a.   Switch to **Simulation** mode.

    b.   Click **Edit Filters** in the Simulation Panel. Uncheck the **Show All/None** checkbox. Check the **ICMP** checkbox.

    c.   Click the **Add Complex PDU** tool; this is the open envelope icon on the right toolbar.

    d.   Float the mouse cursor over the topology and the pointer changes to an envelope with a plus (+) sign.

e. Click **PC0** to serve as the source for this test message and the **Create Complex PDU** dialog window opens. Enter the following values:

- Destination IP Address: 255.255.255.255 (broadcast address)

- Sequence Number: 1

- One Shot Time: 0

Within the PDU settings, the default for **Select Application:** is PING. What are at least three other applications available for use?

_____

_____

f. Click **Create PDU.** This test broadcast packet now appears in the **Simulation Panel Event List.** It also appears in the PDU List window. It is the first PDU for Scenario 0.

g. Click **Capture/Forward** twice. What happened to the packet?

_____

_____

h. Repeat this process for **PC8** and **PC16.**

Part 2: Complete Review Questions

1. If a PC in VLAN 10 sends a broadcast message, which devices receive it?

_____

2. If a PC in VLAN 20 sends a broadcast message, which devices receive it?

_____

3. If a PC in VLAN 30 sends a broadcast message, which devices receive it?

_____

4. What happens to a frame sent from a PC in VLAN 10 to a PC in VLAN 30?

_____

5. Which ports on the switch light up if a PC connected to port 11 sends a unicast message to a PC connected to port 13?

_____

6. Which ports on the switch light up if a PC connected to port 2 sends a unicast message to a PC connected to port 23?

_____

7. In terms of ports, what are the collision domains on the switch?

_____

8. In terms of ports, what are the broadcast domains on the switch?

_____

Suggested Scoring Rubric

There are 10 questions worth 10 points each.

6.1.2.7 Packet Tracer–Investigating a VLAN Implementation

Topology

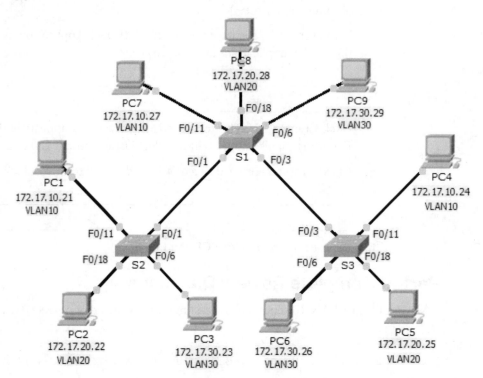

Addressing Table

Device	Interface	IP Address	Subnet Mask	Default Gateway
S1	VLAN 99	172.17.99.31	255.255.255.0	N/A
S2	VLAN 99	172.17.99.32	255.255.255.0	N/A
S3	VLAN 99	172.17.99.33	255.255.255.0	N/A
PC1	NIC	172.17.10.21	255.255.255.0	172.17.10.1
PC2	NIC	172.17.20.22	255.255.255.0	172.17.20.1
PC3	NIC	172.17.30.23	255.255.255.0	172.17.30.1
PC4	NIC	172.17.10.24	255.255.255.0	172.17.10.1
PC5	NIC	172.17.20.25	255.255.255.0	172.17.20.1
PC6	NIC	172.17.30.26	255.255.255.0	172.17.30.1
PC7	NIC	172.17.10.27	255.255.255.0	172.17.10.1
PC8	NIC	172.17.20.28	255.255.255.0	172.17.20.1
PC9	NIC	172.17.30.29	255.255.255.0	172.17.30.1

Objectives

Part 1: Observe Broadcast Traffic in a VLAN Implementation

Part 2: Observe Broadcast Traffic without VLANs

Part 3: Complete Reflection Questions

Background

In this activity, you will observe how broadcast traffic is forwarded by the switches when VLANs are configured and when VLANs are not configured.

Part 1: Observe Broadcast Traffic in a VLAN Implementation

Step 1:   Ping from **PC1** to **PC6**.

    a.   Wait for all the link lights to turn to green. To accelerate this process, click **Fast Forward Time** located in the bottom yellow tool bar.

    b.   Click the **Simulation** tab and use the **Add Simple PDU** tool. Click on **PC1**, and then click on **PC6**.

    c.   Click the **Capture/Forward** button to step through the process. Observe the ARP requests as they traverse the network. When the Buffer Full window appears, click the **View Previous Events** button.

    d.   Were the pings successful? Why?

    _____

    _____

    e.   Look at the Simulation Panel; where did **S3** send the packet after receiving it?

    _____

In normal operation, when a switch receives a broadcast frame on one of its ports, it forwards the frame out all other ports. Notice that **S2** only sends the ARP request out Fa0/1 to **S1**. Also notice that **S3** only sends the ARP request out F0/11 to **PC4**. **PC1** and **PC4** both belong to VLAN 10. **PC6** belongs to VLAN 30. Because broadcast traffic is contained within the VLAN, **PC6** never receives the ARP request from **PC1**. Because **PC4** is not the destination, it discards the ARP request. The ping from **PC1** fails because **PC1** never receives an ARP reply.

Step 2:   Ping from **PC1** to **PC4**.

    a.   Click the **New** button under the Scenario 0 dropdown tab. Now click on the **Add Simple PDU** icon on the right side of Packet Tracer and ping from **PC1** to **PC4**.

    b.   Click the **Capture/Forward** button to step through the process. Observe the ARP requests as they traverse the network. When the Buffer Full window appears, click the **View Previous Events** button.

    c.   Were the pings successful? Why?

    _____

    _____

    d. Examine the Simulation Panel. When the packet reached **S1**, why does it also forward the packet to **PC7**?

_____

_____

Part 2: Observe Broadcast Traffic without VLANs

Step 1: Clear the configurations on all three switches and delete the VLAN database.

    a. Return to **Realtime** mode.

    b. Delete the startup configuration on all 3 switches. What command is used to delete the startup configuration of the switches? _____

    c. Where is the VLAN file stored in the switches? _____

    d. Delete the VLAN file on all 3 switches. What command deletes the VLAN file stored in the switches? _____

Step 2: Reload the switches.

Use the **reload** command in privileged EXEC mode to reset all the switches. Wait for the entire link to turn green. To accelerate this process, click **Fast Forward Time** located in the bottom yellow tool bar.

Step 3: Click **Capture/Forward** to send ARP requests and pings.

    a. After the switches reload and the link lights return to green, the network is ready to forward your ARP and ping traffic.

    b. Select **Scenario 0** from the drop-down tab to return to Scenario 0.

    c. From **Simulation** mode, click the **Capture/Forward** button to step through the process. Notice that the switches now forward the ARP requests out all ports, except the port on which the ARP request was received. This default action of switches is why VLANs can improve network performance. Broadcast traffic is contained within each VLAN. When the **Buffer Full** window appears, click the **View Previous Events** button.

Part 3: Complete Reflection Questions

  1. If a PC in VLAN 10 sends a broadcast message, which devices receive it?

_____

  2. If a PC in VLAN 20 sends a broadcast message, which devices receive it?

_____

  3. If a PC in VLAN 30 sends a broadcast message, which devices receive it?

_____

  4. What happens to a frame sent from a PC in VLAN 10 to a PC in VLAN 30?

_____

  5. In terms of ports, what are the collision domains on the switch?

_____

6. In terms of ports, what are the broadcast domains on the switch?

Suggested Scoring Rubric

Activity Section	Question Location	Possible Points	Earned Points
Part 1: Observe Broadcast Traffic in a VLAN Implementation	Step 1d	6	
	Step 1e	5	
	Step 2c	6	
	Step 2d	5	
	Part 1 Total	22	
Part 2: Observe Broadcast Traffic without VLANs	Step 1b	6	
	Step 1c	6	
	Step 1d	6	
	Part 2 Total	18	
Part 3: Complete Reflection Questions	1	10	
	2	10	
	3	10	
	4	10	
	5	10	
	6	10	
	Part 3 Total	60	
	Total Score	100	

Packet Tracer
☐ Activity

6.2.1.7 Packet Tracer–Configuring VLANs

Topology

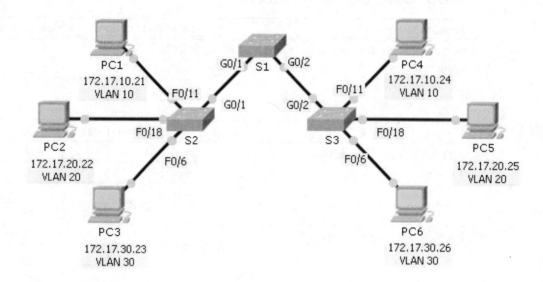

Addressing Table

Device	Interface	IP Address	Subnet Mask	VLAN
PC1	NIC	172.17.10.21	255.255.255.0	10
PC2	NIC	172.17.20.22	255.255.255.0	20
PC3	NIC	172.17.30.23	255.255.255.0	30
PC4	NIC	172.17.10.24	255.255.255.0	10
PC5	NIC	172.17.20.25	255.255.255.0	20
PC6	NIC	172.17.30.26	255.255.255.0	30

Objectives

Part 1: Verify the Default VLAN Configuration

Part 2: Configure VLANs

Part 3: Assign VLANs to Ports

Background

VLANs are helpful in the administration of logical groups, allowing members of a group to be easily moved, changed, or added. This activity focuses on creating and naming VLANs, and assigning access ports to specific VLANs.

Part 1: View the Default VLAN Configuration

Step 1:   Display the current VLANs.

On S1, issue the command that displays all VLANs configured. By default, all interfaces are assigned to VLAN 1.

Step 2:   Verify connectivity between PCs on the same network.

Notice that each PC can ping the other PC that shares the same network.

- PC1 can ping PC4
- PC2 can ping PC5
- PC3 can ping PC6

Pings to PCs in other networks fail.

What benefit will configuring VLANs provide to the current configuration?

_____

_____

_____

Part 2: Configure VLANs

Step 1:   Create and name VLANs on S1.

Create the following VLANs. Names are case-sensitive:

- VLAN 10: Faculty/Staff
- VLAN 20: Students
- VLAN 30: Guest(Default)
- VLAN 99: Management&Native

_____

_____

_____

_____

_____

_____

_____

Step 2:   Verify the VLAN configuration.

Which command will only display the VLAN name, status, and associated ports on a switch?

_____

Step 3:   Create the VLANs on S2 and S3.

Using the same commands from Step 1, create and name the same VLANs on S2 and S3.

Step 4:   Verify the VLAN configuration.

Part 3: Assign VLANs to Ports

Step 1:   Assign VLANs to the active ports on S2.

Assign the VLANs to the following ports:

- VLAN 10: Fast Ethernet 0/11

- VLAN 20: Fast Ethernet 0/18

- VLAN 30: Fast Ethernet 0/6

_____

_____

_____

_____

_____

Step 2:   Assign VLANs to the active ports on S3.

S3 uses the same VLAN access port assignments as S2.

Step 3:   Verify loss of connectivity.

Previously, PCs that shared the same network could ping each other successfully. Try pinging between PC1 and PC4. Although the access ports are assigned to the appropriate VLANs, were the pings successful? Why?

_____

_____

What could be done to resolve this issue?

_____

Suggested Scoring Rubric

Activity Section	Question Location	Possible Points	Earned Points
Part 1: Verify the Default VLAN Configuration	Step 2	4	
Part 2: Configure VLANs	Step 2	2	
Part 3: Assign VLANs to Ports	Step 3	4	
	Packet Tracer Score	90	
	Total Score	100	

6.2.2.4 Packet Tracer–Configuring Trunks

Topology

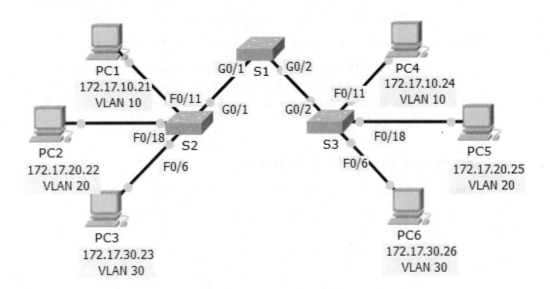

Addressing Table

Device	Interface	IP Address	Subnet Mask	Switch Port	VLAN
PC1	NIC	172.17.10.21	255.255.255.0	S2 F0/11	10
PC2	NIC	172.17.20.22	255.255.255.0	S2 F0/18	20
PC3	NIC	172.17.30.23	255.255.255.0	S2 F0/6	30
PC4	NIC	172.17.10.24	255.255.255.0	S3 F0/11	10
PC5	NIC	172.17.20.25	255.255.255.0	S3 F0/18	20
PC6	NIC	172.17.30.26	255.255.255.0	S3 F0/6	30

Objectives

Part 1: Verify VLANs

Part 2: Configure Trunks

Background

Trunks are required to pass VLAN information between switches. A port on a switch is either an access port or a trunk port. Access ports carry traffic from a specific VLAN assigned to the port. A trunk port by default is a member of all VLANs; therefore, it carries traffic for all VLANs. This activity focuses on creating trunk ports, and assigning them to a native VLAN other than the default.

Part 1: Verify VLANs

Step 1:   Display the current VLANs.

    a.   On **S1**, issue the command that will display all VLANs configured. There should be ten VLANs in total. Notice how all 24 access ports on the switch are assigned to VLAN 1.

    b.   On **S2** and **S3**, display and verify all the VLANs are configured and assigned to the correct switch ports according to the **Addressing Table**.

Step 2:   Verify loss of connectivity between PCs on the same network.

Although **PC1** and **PC4** are on the same network, they cannot ping one another. This is because the ports connecting the switches are assigned to VLAN 1 by default. In order to provide connectivity between the PCs on the same network and VLAN, trunks must be configured.

Part 2: Configure Trunks

Step 1:   Configure trunking on S1 and use VLAN 99 as the native VLAN.

    a.   Configure G0/1 and G0/2 interfaces on S1 for trunking.

_____

_____

    b.   Configure VLAN 99 as the native VLAN for G0/1 and G0/2 interfaces on **S1**.

_____

The trunk port takes about a minute to become active due to Spanning Tree. Click **Fast Forward Time** to speed the process. After the ports become active, you will periodically receive the following syslog messages:

```
%CDP-4-NATIVE_VLAN_MISMATCH: Native VLAN mismatch discovered on
GigabitEthernet0/2 (99), with S3 GigabitEthernet0/2 (1).

%CDP-4-NATIVE_VLAN_MISMATCH: Native VLAN mismatch discovered on
GigabitEthernet0/1 (99), with S2 GigabitEthernet0/1 (1).
```

You configured VLAN 99 as the native VLAN on S1. However, S2 and S3 are using VLAN 1 as the default native VLAN as indicated by the syslog message.

Although you have a native VLAN mismatch, pings between PCs on the same VLAN are now successful. Why?

_____

_____

_____

Step 2:   Verify trunking is enabled on S2 and S3.

On **S2** and **S3**, issue the **show interface trunk** command to confirm that DTP has successfully negotiated trunking with S1 on S2 and S3. The output also displays information about the trunk interfaces on S2 and S3.

Which active VLANs are allowed to cross the trunk?   _____

Step 3:   Correct the native VLAN mismatch on S2 and S3.

    a.   Configure VLAN 99 as the native VLAN for the appropriate interfaces on S2 and S3.

    b.   Issue the **show interface trunk** command to verify the correct native VLAN configuration.

Step 4:   Verify configurations on S2 and S3.

    a.   Issue the **show interface** *interface* **switchport** command to verify that the native VLAN is now 99.

    b.   Use the **show vlan** command to display information regarding configured VLANs. Why is port G0/1 on S2 no longer assigned to VLAN 1?

Suggested Scoring Rubric

Packet Tracer scores 80 points. The three questions in Step 1, 2, and 4 are worth 20 points.

6.2.2.5 Lab–Configuring VLANs and Trunking

Topology

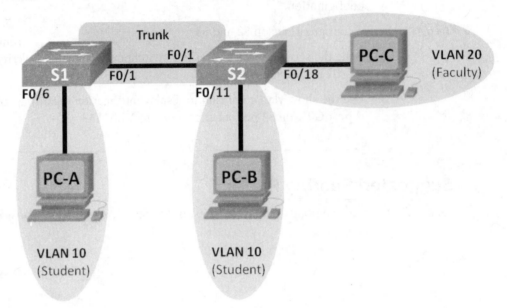

Addressing Table

Device	Interface	IP Address	Subnet Mask	Default Gateway
S1	VLAN 1	192.168.1.11	255.255.255.0	N/A
S2	VLAN 1	192.168.1.12	255.255.255.0	N/A
PC-A	NIC	192.168.10.3	255.255.255.0	192.168.10.1
PC-B	NIC	192.168.10.4	255.255.255.0	192.168.10.1
PC-C	NIC	192.168.20.3	255.255.255.0	192.168.20.1

Objectives

Part 1: Build the Network and Configure Basic Device Settings

Part 2: Create VLANs and Assign Switch Ports

Part 3: Maintain VLAN Port Assignments and the VLAN Database

Part 4: Configure an 802.1Q Trunk between the Switches

Part 5: Delete the VLAN Database

Background/Scenario

Modern switches use virtual local area networks (VLANs) to improve network performance by separating large Layer 2 broadcast domains into smaller ones. VLANs can also be used as a security measure by controlling which hosts can communicate. In general, VLANs make it easier to design a network to support the goals of an organization.

VLAN trunks are used to span VLANs across multiple devices. Trunks allow the traffic from multiple VLANS to travel over a single link, while keeping the VLAN identification and segmentation intact.

In this lab, you will create VLANs on both switches in the topology, assign VLANs to switch access ports, verify that VLANs are working as expected, and then create a VLAN trunk between the two switches to allow hosts in the same VLAN to communicate through the trunk, regardless of which switch the host is actually attached to.

Note: The switches used are Cisco Catalyst 2960s with Cisco IOS Release 15.0(2) (lanbasek9 image). Other switches and Cisco IOS versions can be used. Depending on the model and Cisco IOS version, the commands available and output produced might vary from what is shown in the labs.

Note: Ensure that the switches have been erased and have no startup configurations. If you are unsure contact your instructor.

Required Resources

- 2 Switches (Cisco 2960 with Cisco IOS Release 15.0(2) lanbasek9 image or comparable)
- 3 PCs (Windows 7, Vista, or XP with terminal emulation program, such as Tera Term)
- Console cables to configure the Cisco IOS devices via the console ports
- Ethernet cables as shown in the topology

Part 1: Build the Network and Configure Basic Device Settings

In Part 1, you will set up the network topology and configure basic settings on the PC hosts and switches.

Step 1: Cable the network as shown in the topology.

Attach the devices as shown in the topology diagram, and cable as necessary.

Step 2: Initialize and reload the switches as necessary.

Step 3: Configure basic settings for each switch.

    a. Console into the switch and enter global configuration mode.

    b. Copy the following basic configuration and paste it to the running-configuration on the switch.

```
no ip domain-lookup
service password-encryption
enable secret class
banner motd #
Unauthorized access is strictly prohibited. #
line con 0
password cisco
login
logging synchronous
line vty 0 15
password cisco
```

```
logging synchronous
login
exit
```

c. Configure the host name as shown in the topology.

d. Configure the IP address listed in the Addressing Table for VLAN 1 on the switch.

e. Administratively deactivate all unused ports on the switch.

f. Copy the running configuration to the startup configuration.

Step 4: Configure PC hosts.

Refer to the Addressing Table for PC host address information.

Step 5: Test connectivity.

Verify that the PC hosts can ping one another.

Note: It may be necessary to disable the PC's firewall to ping between PCs.

Can PC-A ping PC-B? _____

Can PC-A ping PC-C? _____

Can PC-A ping S1? _____

Can PC-B ping PC-C? _____

Can PC-B ping S2? _____

Can PC-C ping S2? _____

Can S1 ping S2? _____

If you answered no to any of the above questions, why were the pings unsuccessful?

_____

_____

Part 2: Create VLANs and Assign Switch Ports

In Part 2, you will create student, faculty, and management VLANs on both switches. You will then assign the VLANs to the appropriate interface. The **show vlan** command is used to verify your configuration settings.

Step 1: Create VLANs on the switches.

a. Create the VLANs on S1.

```
S1(config)# vlan 10
S1(config-vlan)# name Student
S1(config-vlan)# vlan 20
S1(config-vlan)# name Faculty
S1(config-vlan)# vlan 99
S1(config-vlan)# name Management
S1(config-vlan)# end
```

b. Create the same VLANs on S2.

c. Issue the **show vlan** command to view the list of VLANs on S1.

```
S1# show vlan
```

VLAN	Name	Status	Ports
1	default	active	Fa0/1, Fa0/2, Fa0/3, Fa0/4
			Fa0/5, Fa0/6, Fa0/7, Fa0/8
			Fa0/9, Fa0/10, Fa0/11, Fa0/12
			Fa0/13, Fa0/14, Fa0/15, Fa0/16
			Fa0/17, Fa0/18, Fa0/19, Fa0/20
			Fa0/21, Fa0/22, Fa0/23, Fa0/24
			Gi0/1, Gi0/2
10	Student	active	
20	Faculty	active	
99	Management	active	
1002	fddi-default	act/unsup	
1003	token-ring-default	act/unsup	
1004	fddinet-default	act/unsup	
1005	trnet-default	act/unsup	

VLAN	Type	SAID	MTU	Parent	RingNo	BridgeNo	Stp	BrdgMode	Trans1	Trans2
1	enet	100001	1500	-	-	-	-	-	0	0
10	enet	100010	1500	-	-	-	-	-	0	0
20	enet	100020	1500	-	-	-	-	-	0	0
99	enet	100099	1500	-	-	-	-	-	0	0

VLAN	Type	SAID	MTU	Parent	RingNo	BridgeNo	Stp	BrdgMode	Trans1	Trans2
1002	fddi	101002	1500	-	-	-	-	-	0	0
1003	tr	101003	1500	-	-	-	-	-	0	0
1004	fdnet	101004	1500	-	-	-	ieee	-	0	0
1005	trnet	101005	1500	-	-	-	ibm	-	0	0

```
Remote SPAN VLANs
------------------------------------------------------------------------------


Primary Secondary Type            Ports
------- --------- ---------------- ------------------------------------------
```

What is the default VLAN? _____

What ports are assigned to the default VLAN?

Step 2:   Assign VLANs to the correct switch interfaces.

  a. Assign VLANs to the interfaces on S1.

  1) Assign PC-A to the Student VLAN.

```
S1(config)# interface f0/6
S1(config-if)# switchport mode access
S1(config-if)# switchport access vlan 10
```

  2) Move the switch IP address VLAN 99.

```
S1(config)# interface vlan 1
S1(config-if)# no ip address
S1(config-if)# interface vlan 99
S1(config-if)# ip address 192.168.1.11 255.255.255.0
S1(config-if)# end
```

  b. Issue the **show vlan brief** command and verify that the VLANs are assigned to the correct interfaces.

```
S1# show vlan brief

VLAN Name                             Status    Ports
---- -------------------------------- --------- -------------------------------
1    default                          active    Fa0/1, Fa0/2, Fa0/3, Fa0/4
                                                Fa0/5, Fa0/7, Fa0/8, Fa0/9
                                                Fa0/10, Fa0/11, Fa0/12, Fa0/13
                                                Fa0/14, Fa0/15, Fa0/16, Fa0/17
                                                Fa0/18, Fa0/19, Fa0/20, Fa0/21
                                                Fa0/22, Fa0/23, Fa0/24, Gi0/1
                                                Gi0/2
10   Student                          active    Fa0/6
20   Faculty                          active
99   Management                       active
1002 fddi-default                     act/unsup
1003 token-ring-default               act/unsup
1004 fddinet-default                  act/unsup
1005 trnet-default                    act/unsup
```

  c. Issue the **show ip interface brief** command.

  What is the status of VLAN 99? Why?

  _____

  d. Use the topology to assign VLANs to the appropriate ports on S2.

  e. Remove the IP address for VLAN 1 on S2.

  f. Configure an IP address for VLAN 99 on S2 according to the Addressing Table.

g. Use the **show vlan brief** command to verify that the VLANs are assigned to the correct interfaces.

```
S2# show vlan brief
```

```
VLAN Name                             Status    Ports
---- -------------------------------- --------- -------------------------------
1    default                          active    Fa0/1, Fa0/2, Fa0/3, Fa0/4
                                                Fa0/5, Fa0/6, Fa0/7, Fa0/8
                                                Fa0/9, Fa0/10, Fa0/12, Fa0/13
                                                Fa0/14, Fa0/15, Fa0/16, Fa0/17
                                                Fa0/19, Fa0/20, Fa0/21, Fa0/22
                                                Fa0/23, Fa0/24, Gi0/1, Gi0/2
10   Student                          active    Fa0/11
20   Faculty                          active    Fa0/18
99   Management                       active
1002 fddi-default                     act/unsup
1003 token-ring-default               act/unsup
1004 fddinet-default                  act/unsup
1005 trnet-default                    act/unsup
```

Is PC-A able to ping PC-B? Why?

_____

Is S1 able to ping S2? Why?

_____

Part 3: Maintain VLAN Port Assignments and the VLAN Database

In Part 3, you will change VLAN assignments to ports and remove VLANs from the VLAN database.

Step 1: Assign a VLAN to multiple interfaces.

a. On S1, assign interfaces F0/11–24 to VLAN 10.

```
S1(config)# interface range f0/11-24
S1(config-if-range)# switchport mode access
S1(config-if-range)# switchport access vlan 10
S1(config-if-range)# end
```

b. Issue the **show vlan brief** command to verify VLAN assignments.

c. Reassign F0/11 and F0/21 to VLAN 20.

d. Verify that VLAN assignments are correct.

Step 2: Remove a VLAN assignment from an interface.

a. Use the **no switchport access vlan** command to remove the VLAN 10 assignment to F0/24.

```
S1(config)# interface f0/24
S1(config-if)# no switchport access vlan
S1(config-if)# end
```

b. Verify that the VLAN change was made.

Which VLAN is F0/24 now associated with?

_____

Step 3: Remove a VLAN ID from the VLAN database.

a. Add VLAN 30 to interface F0/24 without issuing the VLAN command.

```
S1(config)# interface f0/24
S1(config-if)# switchport access vlan 30
% Access VLAN does not exist. Creating vlan 30
```

Note: Current switch technology no longer requires that the **vlan** command be issued to add a VLAN to the database. By assigning an unknown VLAN to a port, the VLAN adds to the VLAN database.

b. Verify that the new VLAN is displayed in the VLAN table.

```
S1# show vlan brief

VLAN Name                             Status    Ports
---- -------------------------------- --------- -------------------------------
1    default                          active    Fa0/1, Fa0/2, Fa0/3, Fa0/4
                                                Fa0/5, Fa0/6, Fa0/7, Fa0/8
                                                Fa0/9, Fa0/10, Gi0/1, Gi0/2
10   Student                          active    Fa0/12, Fa0/13, Fa0/14, Fa0/15
                                                Fa0/16, Fa0/17, Fa0/18, Fa0/19
                                                Fa0/20, Fa0/22, Fa0/23
20   Faculty                          active    Fa0/11, Fa0/21
30   VLAN0030                         active    Fa0/24
99   Management                       active
1002 fddi-default                     act/unsup
1003 token-ring-default               act/unsup
1004 fddinet-default                  act/unsup
1005 trnet-default                    act/unsup
```

What is the default name of VLAN 30?

_____

c. Use the **no vlan 30** command to remove VLAN 30 from the VLAN database.

```
S1(config)# no vlan 30
S1(config)# end
```

d. Issue the **show vlan brief** command. F0/24 was assigned to VLAN 30.

After deleting VLAN 30, what VLAN is port F0/24 assigned to? What happens to the traffic destined to the host attached to F0/24?

_____

```
S1# show vlan brief

VLAN Name                             Status    Ports
---- -------------------------------- --------- -------------------------------
1    default                          active    Fa0/1, Fa0/2, Fa0/3, Fa0/4
                                                Fa0/5, Fa0/6, Fa0/7, Fa0/8
                                                Fa0/9, Fa0/10, Gi0/1, Gi0/2
```

```
10    Student                         active    Fa0/12, Fa0/13, Fa0/14, Fa0/15
                                                Fa0/16, Fa0/17, Fa0/18, Fa0/19
                                                Fa0/20, Fa0/22, Fa0/23
20    Faculty                         active    Fa0/11, Fa0/21
99    Management                      active
1002  fddi-default                    act/unsup
1003  token-ring-default              act/unsup
1004  fddinet-default                 act/unsup
1005  trnet-default                   act/unsup
```

e. Issue the **no switchport access vlan** command on interface F0/24.

_____

_____

_____

f. Issue the **show vlan brief** command to determine the VLAN assignment for F0/24. To which VLAN is F0/24 assigned?

_____

_____

Note: Before removing a VLAN from the database, it is recommended that you reassign all the ports assigned to that VLAN.

Why should you reassign a port to another VLAN before removing the VLAN from the VLAN database?

_____

_____

_____

Part 4: Configure an 802.1Q Trunk Between the Switches

In Part 4, you will configure interface F0/1 to use the Dynamic Trunking Protocol (DTP) to allow it to negotiate the trunk mode. After this has been accomplished and verified, you will disable DTP on interface F0/1 and manually configure it as a trunk.

Step 1: Use DTP to initiate trunking on F0/1.

The default DTP mode of a 2960 switch port is dynamic auto. This allows the interface to convert the link to a trunk if the neighboring interface is set to trunk or dynamic desirable mode.

a. Set F0/1 on S1 to negotiate trunk mode.

```
S1(config)# interface f0/1
S1(config-if)# switchport mode dynamic desirable
*Mar  1 05:07:28.746: %LINEPROTO-5-UPDOWN: Line protocol on Interface Vlan1,
changed state to down
*Mar  1 05:07:29.744: %LINEPROTO-5-UPDOWN: Line protocol on Interface
FastEthernet0/1, changed state to down
S1(config-if)#
*Mar  1 05:07:32.772: %LINEPROTO-5-UPDOWN: Line protocol on Interface
FastEthernet0/1, changed state to up
S1(config-if)#
```

```
*Mar  1 05:08:01.789: %LINEPROTO-5-UPDOWN: Line protocol on Interface Vlan99,
changed state to up
*Mar  1 05:08:01.797: %LINEPROTO-5-UPDOWN: Line protocol on Interface Vlan1,
changed state to up
```

You should also receive link status messages on S2.

```
S2#
*Mar  1 05:07:29.794: %LINEPROTO-5-UPDOWN: Line protocol on Interface
FastEthernet0/1, changed state to down
S2#
*Mar  1 05:07:32.823: %LINEPROTO-5-UPDOWN: Line protocol on Interface
FastEthernet0/1, changed state to up
S2#
*Mar  1 05:08:01.839: %LINEPROTO-5-UPDOWN: Line protocol on Interface Vlan99,
changed state to up
*Mar  1 05:08:01.850: %LINEPROTO-5-UPDOWN: Line protocol on Interface Vlan1,
changed state to up
```

b. Issue the **show vlan brief** command on S1 and S2. Interface F0/1 is no longer assigned to VLAN 1. Trunked interfaces are not listed in the VLAN table.

```
S1# show vlan brief

VLAN Name                             Status    Ports
---- -------------------------------- --------- -------------------------------
1    default                          active    Fa0/2, Fa0/3, Fa0/4, Fa0/5
                                                Fa0/7, Fa0/8, Fa0/9, Fa0/10
                                                Fa0/24, Gi0/1, Gi0/2
10   Student                          active    Fa0/6, Fa0/12, Fa0/13, Fa0/14
                                                Fa0/15, Fa0/16, Fa0/17, Fa0/18
                                                Fa0/19, Fa0/20, Fa0/22, Fa0/23
20   Faculty                          active    Fa0/11, Fa0/21
99   Management                       active
1002 fddi-default                     act/unsup
1003 token-ring-default               act/unsup
1004 fddinet-default                  act/unsup
1005 trnet-default                    act/unsup
```

c. Issue the **show interfaces trunk** command to view trunked interfaces. Notice that the mode on S1 is set to desirable, and the mode on S2 is set to auto.

```
S1# show interfaces trunk

Port      Mode         Encapsulation  Status        Native vlan
Fa0/1     desirable    802.1q         trunking      1

Port      Vlans allowed on trunk
Fa0/1     1-4094

Port      Vlans allowed and active in management domain
Fa0/1     1,10,20,99

Port      Vlans in spanning tree forwarding state and not pruned
Fa0/1     1,10,20,99
```

```
S2# show interfaces trunk

Port            Mode                 Encapsulation  Status       Native vlan
Fa0/1           auto                 802.1q         trunking     1


Port            Vlans allowed on trunk
Fa0/1           1-4094


Port            Vlans allowed and active in management domain
Fa0/1           1,10,20,99


Port            Vlans in spanning tree forwarding state and not pruned
Fa0/1           1,10,20,99
```

Note: By default, all VLANs are allowed on a trunk. The **switchport trunk** command allows you to control what VLANs have access to the trunk. For this lab, keep the default settings, which allows all VLANs to traverse F0/1.

    d. Verify that VLAN traffic is traveling over trunk interface F0/1.

        Can S1 ping S2? _____

        Can PC-A ping PC-B? _____

        Can PC-A ping PC-C? _____

        Can PC-B ping PC-C? _____

        Can PC-A ping S1? _____

        Can PC-B ping S2? _____

        Can PC-C ping S2? _____

        If you answered no to any of the above questions, explain below.

        _____

        _____

Step 2: Manually configure trunk interface F0/1.

    The **switchport mode trunk** command is used to manually configure a port as a trunk. This command should be issued on both ends of the link.

    a. Change the switchport mode on interface F0/1 to force trunking. Make sure to do this on both switches.

```
S1(config)# interface f0/1
S1(config-if)# switchport mode trunk
```

    b. Issue the **show interfaces trunk** command to view the trunk mode. Notice that the mode changed from **desirable** to **on**.

```
S2# show interfaces trunk

Port            Mode                 Encapsulation  Status       Native vlan
Fa0/1           on                   802.1q         trunking     99


Port            Vlans allowed on trunk
Fa0/1           1-4094
```

```
Port        Vlans allowed and active in management domain
Fa0/1       1,10,20,99


Port        Vlans in spanning tree forwarding state and not pruned
Fa0/1       1,10,20,99
```

Why might you want to manually configure an interface to trunk mode instead of using DTP?

_____

_____

Part 5: Delete the VLAN Database

In Part 5, you will delete the VLAN database from the switch. It is necessary to do this when initializing a switch back to its default settings.

Step 1:   Determine if the VLAN database exists.

Issue the **show flash** command to determine if a **vlan.dat** file exists in flash.

```
S1# show flash


Directory of flash:/

    2   -rwx        1285   Mar 1 1993 00:01:24 +00:00  config.text
    3   -rwx       43032   Mar 1 1993 00:01:24 +00:00  multiple-fs
    4   -rwx           5   Mar 1 1993 00:01:24 +00:00  private-config.text
    5   -rwx    11607161   Mar 1 1993 02:37:06 +00:00  c2960-lanbasek9-mz.150-2.
SE.bin
    6   -rwx         736   Mar 1 1993 00:19:41 +00:00  vlan.dat


32514048 bytes total (20858880 bytes free)
```

Note: If there is a **vlan.dat** file located in flash, then the VLAN database does not contain its default settings.

Step 2:   Delete the VLAN database.

a.   Issue the **delete vlan.dat** command to delete the vlan.dat file from flash and reset the VLAN database back to its default settings. You will be prompted twice to confirm that you want to delete the vlan.dat file. Press Enter both times.

```
S1# delete vlan.dat
Delete filename [vlan.dat]?
Delete flash:/vlan.dat? [confirm]
S1#
```

b.   Issue the **show flash** command to verify that the vlan.dat file has been deleted.

```
S1# show flash


Directory of flash:/

    2   -rwx        1285   Mar 1 1993 00:01:24 +00:00  config.text
    3   -rwx       43032   Mar 1 1993 00:01:24 +00:00  multiple-fs
```

```
    4  -rwx           5   Mar 1 1993 00:01:24 +00:00  private-config.text
    5  -rwx    11607161   Mar 1 1993 02:37:06 +00:00  c2960-lanbasek9-mz.150-2.
SE.bin

32514048 bytes total (20859904 bytes free)
```
To initialize a switch back to its default settings, what other commands are needed?

_____

_____

Reflection

1. What is needed to allow hosts on VLAN 10 to communicate to hosts on VLAN 20?

_____

_____

2. What are some primary benefits that an organization can receive through effective use of VLANs?

_____

_____

_____

_____

6.2.3.7 Packet Tracer–Troubleshooting a VLAN Implementation Scenario 1

Topology

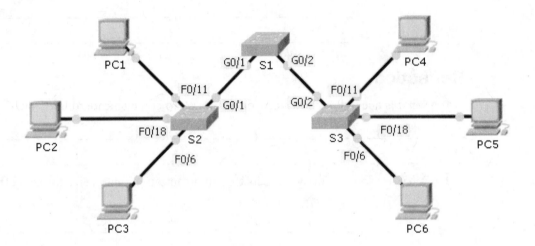

Addressing Table

Device	Interface	IPv4 Address	Subnet Mask	Switch Port	VLAN
PC1	NIC	172.17.10.21	255.255.255.0	S1 F0/11	10
PC2	NIC	172.17.20.22	255.255.255.0	S1 F0/18	20
PC3	NIC	172.17.30.23	255.255.255.0	S1 F0/6	30
PC4	NIC	172.17.10.24	255.255.255.0	S2 F0/11	10
PC5	NIC	172.17.20.25	255.255.255.0	S2 F0/18	20
PC6	NIC	172.17.30.26	255.255.255.0	S2 F0/6	30

Objectives

Part 1: Test Connectivity Between PCs on the Same VLAN

Part 2: Investigate Connectivity Problems by Gathering Data

Part 3: Implement the Solution and Test Connectivity

Scenario

In this activity, you will troubleshoot connectivity problems between PCs on the same VLAN. The activity is complete when PCs on the same VLAN can ping each other. Any solution you implement must conform to the Addressing Table.

Part 1: Test Connectivity Between PCs on the Same VLAN

From the command prompt on each PC, ping between PCs on the same VLAN.

    a. Can PC1 ping PC4? _____

    b. Can PC2 ping PC5? _____

    c. Can PC3 ping PC6? _____

Part 2: Investigate Connectivity Problems by Gathering Data

Step 1:   Verify configuration on the PCs.

Based on your knowledge, verify if the following configurations for each PC are correct.

- IP address
- Subnet mask

Step 2:   Verify the configuration on the switches.

Based on your knowledge, verify if the following configurations on the switches are correct.

- Ports assigned to the correct VLANs.
- Ports configured for the correct mode.
- Ports connected to the correct devices.

Step 3:   Document the problem and the solutions.

List the problems and the solutions that will allow these PCs to ping each other. Keep in mind that there could be more than one problem or more than one solution.

PC1 to PC4

    a. Explain the connectivity issues between PC1 and PC4.

       _____

       _____

    b. Record the necessary actions to correct the issues.

       _____

       _____

PC2 to PC5

    c. Explain the connectivity issues between PC2 and PC5.

       _____

       _____

    d. Record the necessary actions to correct the issues.

       _____

       _____

PC3 to PC6

e. What are the reasons why connectivity failed between the PCs?

_____

_____

f. Record the necessary actions to correct the issues.

_____

_____

Part 3: Implement the Solution and Test Connectivity

Verify PCs on the same VLAN can now ping each other. If not, continue to troubleshoot.

Suggested Scoring Rubric

Packet Tracer scores 70 points. Documentation in Part 2, Step 3 is worth 30 points.

6.2.3.8 Packet Tracer–Troubleshooting a VLAN Implementation Scenario 2

Topology

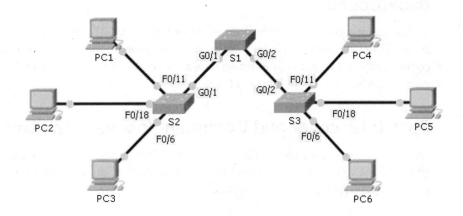

Addressing Table

Device	Interface	IPv4 Address	Subnet Mask	Default Gateway
S1	VLAN 56	192.168.56.11	255.255.255.0	N/A
S2	VLAN 56	192.168.56.12	255.255.255.0	N/A
S3	VLAN 56	192.168.56.13	255.255.255.0	N/A
PC1	NIC	192.168.10.21	255.255.255.0	192.168.10.1
PC2	NIC	192.168.20.22	255.255.255.0	192.168.20.1
PC3	NIC	192.168.30.23	255.255.255.0	192.168.30.1
PC4	NIC	192.168.10.24	255.255.255.0	192.168.10.1
PC5	NIC	192.168.20.25	255.255.255.0	192.168.20.1
PC6	NIC	192.168.30.26	255.255.255.0	192.168.30.1

VLAN and Port Assignments

Ports	VLAN Number - Name	Network
F0/1–F0/5	VLAN 56–Management&Native	192.168.56.0/24
F0/6–F0/10	VLAN 30–Guest(Default)	192.168.30.0/24
F0/11–F0/17	VLAN 10–Faculty/Staff	192.168.10.0/24
F0/18–F0/24	VLAN 20–Students	192.168.20.0/24

Objectives

Part 1: Discover and Document Issues in the Network

Part 2: Implement the Solution and Test Connectivity

Background

In this activity, you will troubleshoot a misconfigured VLAN environment. The initial network has errors. Your objective is to locate and correct the errors in the configurations and establish end-to-end connectivity. Your final configuration should match the Topology diagram and Addressing Table. The native VLAN for this topology is VLAN 56.

Part 1: Discover and Document Issues in the Network

Use the Topology, Addressing Table, VLAN and Port Assignments table and your knowledge of VLANs and trunking to discover issues in the network. Complete the **Documentation** table listing the problems you discovered and potential solutions.

Documentation

Problems	Solutions

Part 2: Implement the Solution and Test Connectivity

Verify PCs on the same VLAN can now ping each other. If not, continue to troubleshoot.

Suggested Scoring Rubric

Packet Tracer scores 70 points. Documentation in Part 1 is worth 30 points.

6.2.3.9 Lab–Troubleshooting VLAN Configurations

Topology

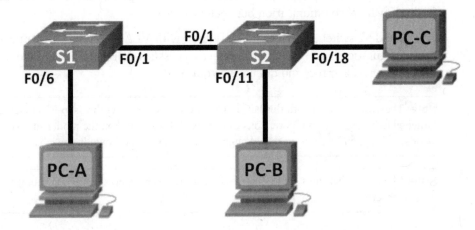

Addressing Table

Device	Interface	IP Address	Subnet Mask	Default Gateway
S1	VLAN 1	192.168.1.2	255.255.255.0	N/A
S2	VLAN 1	192.168.1.3	255.255.255.0	N/A
PC-A	NIC	192.168.10.2	255.255.255.0	192.168.10.1
PC-B	NIC	192.168.10.3	255.255.255.0	192.168.10.1
PC-C	NIC	192.168.20.3	255.255.255.0	192.168.20.1

Switch Port Assignment Specifications

Ports	Assignment	Network
F0/1	802.1Q Trunk	N/A
F0/6-12	VLAN 10–Students	192.168.10.0/24
F0/13-18	VLAN 20–Faculty	192.168.20.0/24
F0/19-24	VLAN 30–Guest	192.168.30.0/24

Objectives

Part 1: Build the Network and Configure Basic Device Settings

Part 2: Troubleshoot VLAN 10

Part 3: Troubleshoot VLAN 20

Background/Scenario

VLANs provide logical segmentation within an internetwork and improve network performance by separating large broadcast domains into smaller ones. By separating hosts into different networks, VLANs can be used to control which hosts can communicate. In this lab, a school has decided to implement VLANs in order to separate traffic from different end users. The school is using 802.1Q trunking to facilitate VLAN communication between switches.

The S1 and S2 switches have been configured with VLAN and trunking information. Several errors in the configuration have resulted in connectivity issues. You have been asked to troubleshoot and correct the configuration errors and document your work.

Note: The switches used with this lab are Cisco Catalyst 2960s with Cisco IOS Release 15.0(2) (lanbasek9 image). Other switches and Cisco IOS versions can be used. Depending on the model and Cisco IOS version, the commands available and output produced might vary from what is shown in the labs.

Note: Make sure that the switches have been erased and have no startup configurations. If you are unsure, contact your instructor.

Required Resources

- 2 Switches (Cisco 2960 with Cisco IOS Release 15.0(2) lanbasek9 image or comparable)
- 3 PCs (Windows 7, Vista, or XP with terminal emulation program, such as Tera Term)
- Console cables to configure the Cisco IOS devices via the console ports
- Ethernet cables as shown in the topology

Part 1: Build the Network and Configure Basic Device Settings

In Part 1, you will set up the network topology and configure the switches with some basic settings, such as passwords and IP addresses. Preset VLAN-related configurations, which contain errors, are provided for you for the initial switch configurations. You will also configure the IP settings for the PCs in the topology.

Step 1: Cable the network as shown in the topology.

Step 2: Configure PC hosts.

Step 3: Initialize and reload the switches as necessary.

Step 4: Configure basic settings for each switch.

  a. Disable DNS lookup.

  b. Configure the IP address according to the Addressing Table.

  c. Assign **cisco** as the console and vty passwords and enable login for console and vty lines.

  d. Assign **class** as the privileged EXEC password.

  e. Configure **logging synchronous** to prevent console messages from interrupting command entry.

Step 5:   Load switch configurations.

The configurations for the switches S1 and S2 are provided for you. There are errors within these configurations, and it is your job to determine the incorrect configurations and correct them.

Switch S1 Configuration:

```
hostname S1
vlan 10
 name Students
vlan 2

name Faculty
vlan 30
 name Guest
interface range f0/1-24
 switchport mode access
 shutdown




interface range f0/7-12


 switchport access vlan 10
interface range f0/13-18
 switchport access vlan 2


interface range f0/19-24
 switchport access vlan 30
end
```

Switch S2 Configuration:

```
hostname S2
vlan 10
 name Students
vlan 20
 name Faculty
vlan 30
 name Guest
interface f0/1
 switchport mode trunk
 switchport trunk allowed vlan 1,10,2,30

interface range f0/2-24
 switchport mode access
```

```
        shutdown


interface range f0/13-18
 switchport access vlan 20
interface range f0/19-24
 switchport access vlan 30
 shutdown
end
```

Step 6:   Copy the running configuration to the startup configuration.

Part 2: Troubleshoot VLAN 10

In Part 2, you must examine VLAN 10 on S1 and S2 to determine if it is configured correctly. You will troubleshoot the scenario until connectivity is established.

Step 1:   Troubleshoot VLAN 10 on S1.

    a.   Can PC-A ping PC-B? _____

    b.   After verifying that PC-A was configured correctly, examine the S1 switch to find possible configuration errors by viewing a summary of the VLAN information. Enter the **show vlan brief** command.

    c.   Are there any problems with the VLAN configuration?

    _____

    d.   Examine the switch for trunk configurations using the **show interfaces trunk** and the **show interfaces f0/1 switchport** commands.

    e.   Are there any problems with the trunking configuration?

    _____

    f.   Examine the running configuration of the switch to find possible configuration errors.

    Are there any problems with the current configuration?

    _____

    g.   Correct the errors found regarding F0/1 and VLAN 10 on S1. Record the commands used in the space below.

    _____

    _____

    _____

    _____

    h.   Verify the commands had the desired effects by issuing the appropriate **show** commands.

    i.   Can PC-A ping PC-B? _____

Step 2: Troubleshoot VLAN 10 on S2.

    a. Using the previous commands, examine the S2 switch to find possible configuration errors.

    Are there any problems with the current configuration?

    _____

    b. Correct the errors found regarding interfaces and VLAN 10 on S2. Record the commands below.

    _____

    _____

    _____

    _____

    _____

    _____

    c. Can PC-A ping PC-B? _____

Part 3: Troubleshoot VLAN 20

In Part 3, you must examine VLAN 20 on S1 and S2 to determine if it is configured correctly. To verify functionality, you will reassign PC-A into VLAN 20, and then troubleshoot the scenario until connectivity is established.

Step 1: Assign PC-A to VLAN 20.

    a. On PC-A, change the IP address to 192.168.20.2/24 with a default gateway of 192.168.20.1.

    b. On S1, assign the port for PC-A to VLAN 20. Write the commands needed to complete the configuration.

    _____

    _____

    c. Verify that the port for PC-A has been assigned to VLAN 20.

    d. Can PC-A ping PC-C? _____

Step 2: Troubleshoot VLAN 20 on S1.

    a. Using the previous commands, examine the S1 switch to find possible configuration errors.

    Are there any problems with the current configuration?

    _____

    _____

    b. Correct the errors found regarding VLAN 20.

    c. Can PC-A ping PC-C? _____

Step 3:   Troubleshoot VLAN 20 on S2.

   a.   Using the previous commands, examine the S2 switch to find possible configuration errors.

   Are there any problems with the current configuration?

   _____

   b.   Correct the errors found regarding VLAN 20. Record the commands used below.

   _____

   _____

   _____

   _____

   _____

   c.   Can PC-A ping PC-C? _____

   Note: It may be necessary to disable the PC firewall to ping between PCs.

Reflection

   1.   Why is a correctly configured trunk port critical in a multi-VLAN environment?

   _____

   _____

   2.   Why would a network administrator limit traffic for specific VLANs on a trunk port?

   _____

   _____

6.3.2.4 Lab–Configuring Per-Interface Inter-VLAN Routing

Topology

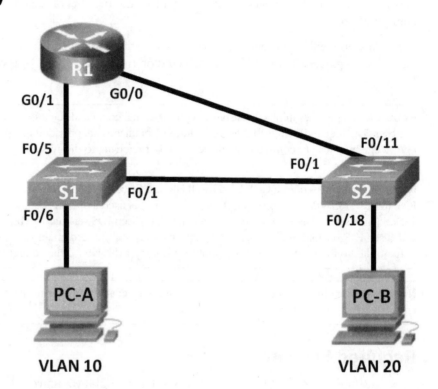

Addressing Table

Device	Interface	IP Address	Subnet Mask	Default Gateway
R1	G0/0	192.168.20.1	255.255.255.0	N/A
	G0/1	192.168.10.1	255.255.255.0	N/A
S1	VLAN 10	192.168.10.11	255.255.255.0	192.168.10.1
S2	VLAN 10	192.168.10.12	255.255.255.0	192.168.10.1
PC-A	NIC	192.168.10.3	255.255.255.0	192.168.10.1
PC-B	NIC	192.168.20.3	255.255.255.0	192.168.20.1

Objectives

Part 1: Build the Network and Configure Basic Device Settings

Part 2: Configure Switches with VLANs and Trunking

Part 3: Verify Trunking, VLANs, Routing, and Connectivity

Background/Scenario

Legacy inter-VLAN routing is seldom used in today's networks; however, it is helpful to configure and understand this type of routing before moving on to router-on-a-stick (trunk-based) inter-VLAN routing or configuring Layer-3 switching. Also, you may encounter per-interface inter-VLAN routing in organizations with very small networks. One of the benefits of legacy inter-VLAN routing is ease of configuration.

In this lab, you will set up one router with two switches attached via the router Gigabit Ethernet interfaces. Two separate VLANs will be configured on the switches, and you will set up routing between the VLANs.

Note: This lab provides minimal assistance with the actual commands necessary to configure the router and switches. The required switch VLAN configuration commands are provided in Appendix A of this lab. Test your knowledge by trying to configure the devices without referring to the appendix.

Note: The routers used with CCNA hands-on labs are Cisco 1941 Integrated Services Routers (ISRs) with Cisco IOS, Release 15.2(4)M3 (universalk9 image). The switches used are Cisco Catalyst 2960s with Cisco IOS, Release 15.0(2) (lanbasek9 image). Other routers, switches and Cisco IOS versions can be used. Depending on the model and Cisco IOS version, the commands available and output produced might vary from what is shown in the labs. Refer to the Router Interface Summary Table at the end of this lab for the correct interface identifiers.

Note: Make sure that the routers and switches have been erased and have no startup configurations. If you are unsure, contact your instructor.

Required Resources

- 1 Router (Cisco 1941 with Cisco IOS Release 15.2(4)M3 universal image or comparable)
- 2 Switches (Cisco 2960 with Cisco IOS Release 15.0(2) lanbasek9 image or comparable)
- 2 PCs (Windows 7, Vista, or XP with terminal emulation program, such as Tera Term)
- Console cables to configure the Cisco IOS devices via the console ports
- Ethernet cables as shown in the topology

Part 1: Build the Network and Configure Basic Device Settings

In Part 1, you will set up the network topology and clear any configurations, if necessary.

Step 1:   Cable the network as shown in the topology.

Step 2:   Initialize and reload the router and switches.

Step 3:   Configure basic settings for R1.

    a.   Console into R1 and enter global configuration mode.

    b.   Copy the following basic configuration and paste it to the running-configuration on R1.

```
no ip domain-lookup
hostname R1
service password-encryption
enable secret class
banner motd #
```

```
Unauthorized access is strictly prohibited. #
line con 0
password cisco
login
logging synchronous
line vty 0 4
password cisco
login
```

   c. Configure addressing on G0/0 and G0/1 and enable both interfaces.

   d. Copy the running configuration to the startup configuration.

Step 4: Configure basic settings on both switches.

   a. Console into the switch and enter global configuration mode.

   b. Copy the following basic configuration and paste it to running-configuration on the switch.

```
no ip domain-lookup
service password-encryption
enable secret class
banner motd #
Unauthorized access is strictly prohibited. #
Line con 0
password cisco
login
logging synchronous
line vty 0 15
password cisco
login
exit
```

   c. Configure the host name as shown in the topology.

   d. Copy the running configuration to the startup configuration.

Step 5: Configure basic settings on PC-A and PC-B.

Configure PC-A and PC-B with IP addresses and a default gateway address according to the Addressing Table.

Part 2: Configure Switches with VLANs and Trunking

In Part 2, you will configure the switches with VLANs and trunking.

Step 1: Configure VLANs on S1.

   a. On S1, create VLAN 10. Assign **Student** as the VLAN name.

   b. Create VLAN 20. Assign **Faculty-Admin** as the VLAN name.

   c. Configure F0/1 as a trunk port.

   d. Assign ports F0/5 and F0/6 to VLAN 10 and configure both F0/5 and F0/6 as access ports.

  e. Assign an IP address to VLAN 10 and enable it. Refer to the Addressing Table.

  f. Configure the default gateway according to the Addressing Table.

Step 2: Configure VLANs on S2.

  a. On S2, create VLAN 10. Assign **Student** as the VLAN name.

  b. Create VLAN 20. Assign **Faculty-Admin** as the VLAN name.

  c. Configure F0/1 as a trunk port.

  d. Assign ports F0/11 and F0/18 to VLAN 20 and configure both F0/11 and F0/18 as access ports.

  e. Assign an IP address to VLAN 10 and enable it. Refer to the Addressing Table.

  f. Configure the default gateway according to the Addressing Table.

Part 3: Verify Trunking, VLANs, Routing, and Connectivity

Step 1: Verify the R1 routing table.

  a. On R1, issue the **show ip route** command. What routes are listed on R1?

  _____

  _____

  b. On both S1 and S2, issue the **show interface trunk** command. Is the F0/1 port on both switches set to trunk? _____

  c. Issue a **show vlan brief** command on both S1 and S2. Verify that VLANs 10 and 20 are active and that the proper ports on the switches are in the correct VLANs. Why is F0/1 not listed in any of the active VLANs?

  _____

  d. Ping from PC-A in VLAN 10 to PC-B in VLAN 20. If Inter-VLAN routing is functioning correctly, the pings between the 192.168.10.0 network and the 192.168.20.0 should be successful.

  Note: It may be necessary to disable the PC firewall to ping between PCs.

---

  e. Verify connectivity between devices. You should be able to ping between all devices. Troubleshoot if you are not successful.

Reflection

What is an advantage of using legacy inter-VLAN routing?

_____

_____

_____

Router Interface Summary Table

Router Interface Summary				
Router Model	Ethernet Interface #1	Ethernet Interface #2	Serial Interface #1	Serial Interface #2
1800	Fast Ethernet 0/0 (F0/0)	Fast Ethernet 0/1 (F0/1)	Serial 0/0/0 (S0/0/0)	Serial 0/0/1 (S0/0/1)
1900	Gigabit Ethernet 0/0 (G0/0)	Gigabit Ethernet 0/1 (G0/1)	Serial 0/0/0 (S0/0/0)	Serial 0/0/1 (S0/0/1)
2801	Fast Ethernet 0/0 (F0/0)	Fast Ethernet 0/1 (F0/1)	Serial 0/1/0 (S0/1/0)	Serial 0/1/1 (S0/1/1)
2811	Fast Ethernet 0/0 (F0/0)	Fast Ethernet 0/1 (F0/1)	Serial 0/0/0 (S0/0/0)	Serial 0/0/1 (S0/0/1)
2900	Gigabit Ethernet 0/0 (G0/0)	Gigabit Ethernet 0/1 (G0/1)	Serial 0/0/0 (S0/0/0)	Serial 0/0/1 (S0/0/1)

Note: To find out how the router is configured, look at the interfaces to identify the type of router and how many interfaces the router has. There is no way to effectively list all the combinations of configurations for each router class. This table includes identifiers for the possible combinations of Ethernet and Serial interfaces in the device. The table does not include any other type of interface, even though a specific router may contain one. An example of this might be an ISDN BRI interface. The string in parentheses is the legal abbreviation that can be used in Cisco IOS commands to represent the interface.

Appendix A: Configuration Commands

Switch S1

```
S1(config)# vlan 10
S1(config-vlan)# name Student
S1(config-vlan)# exit
S1(config)# vlan 20
S1(config-vlan)# name Faculty-Admin
S1(config-vlan)# exit
S1(config)# interface f0/1
S1(config-if)# switchport mode trunk
S1(config-if)# interface range f0/5-6
S1(config-if-range)# switchport mode access
S1(config-if-range)# switchport access vlan 10
S1(config-if-range)# interface vlan 10
S1(config-if)# ip address 192.168.10.11 255.255.255.0
S1(config-if)# no shut
S1(config-if)# exit
S1(config)# ip default-gateway 192.168.10.1
```

Switch S2

```
S2(config)# vlan 10
S2(config-vlan)# name Student
S2(config-vlan)# exit
S2(config)# vlan 20
S2(config-vlan)# name Faculty-Admin
S2(config-vlan)# exit
S2(config)# interface f0/1
S2(config-if)# switchport mode trunk
S2(config-if)# interface f0/11
S2(config-if)# switchport mode access
S2(config-if)# switchport access vlan 20
S2(config-if)# interface f0/18
S2(config-if)# switchport mode access
S2(config-if)# switchport access vlan 20
S2(config-if-range)# interface vlan 10
S2(config-if)#ip address 192.168.10.12 255.255.255.0
S2(config-if)# no shut
S2(config-if)# exit
S2(config)# ip default-gateway 192.168.10.1
```

Packet Tracer
☐ Activity

6.3.3.6 Packet Tracer–Configuring Router-on-a-Stick Inter-VLAN Routing

Topology

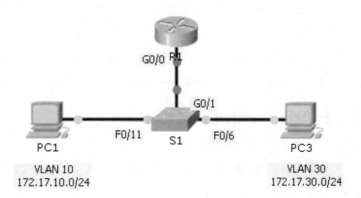

Addressing Table

Device	Interface	IPv4 Address	Subnet Mask	Default Gateway
R1	G0/0.10	172.17.10.1	255.255.255.0	N/A
	G0/0.30	172.17.30.1	255.255.255.0	N/A
PC1	NIC	172.17.10.10	255.255.255.0	172.17.10.1
PC2	NIC	172.17.30.10	255.255.255.0	172.17.30.1

Objectives

Part 1: Test Connectivity without Inter-VLAN Routing

Part 2: Add VLANs to a Switch

Part 3: Configure Subinterfaces

Part 4: Test Connectivity with Inter-VLAN Routing

Scenario

In this activity, you will check for connectivity prior to implementing inter-VLAN routing. You will then configure VLANs and inter-VLAN routing. Finally, you will enable trunking and verify connectivity between VLANs.

Part 1: Test Connectivity Without Inter-VLAN Routing

Step 1:   Ping between **PC1** and **PC3**.

Wait for switch convergence or click **Fast Forward Time** a few times. When the link lights are green for **PC1** and **PC3**, ping between **PC1** and **PC3**. Because the two PCs are on separate networks and **R1** is not configured, the ping fails.

Step 2:   Switch to Simulation mode to monitor pings.

    a.   Switch to Simulation mode by clicking the **Simulation** tab or pressing **Shift+S**.

    b.   Click **Capture/Forward** to see the steps the ping takes between **PC1** and **PC3**. Notice how the ping never leaves **PC1**. What process failed and why?

_____

_____

_____

_____

Part 2: Add VLANs to a Switch

Step 1:   Create VLANs on S1.

Return to **Realtime** mode and create VLAN 10 and VLAN 30 on **S1**.

Step 2:   Assign VLANs to ports.

    a.   Configure interface F0/6 and F0/11 as access ports and assign VLANs.

      ■   Assign **PC1** to VLAN 10.

      ■   Assign **PC3** to VLAN 30.

    b.   Issue the **show vlan brief** command to verify VLAN configuration.

```
S1# show vlan brief

VLAN Name                             Status    Ports
---- -------------------------------- --------- -------------------------------
1    default                          active    Fa0/1, Fa0/2, Fa0/3, Fa0/4
                                                Fa0/5, Fa0/7, Fa0/8, Fa0/9
                                                Fa0/10, Fa0/12, Fa0/13, Fa0/14
                                                Fa0/15, Fa0/16, Fa0/17, Fa0/18
                                                Fa0/19, Fa0/20, Fa0/21, Fa0/22
                                                Fa0/23, Fa0/24, Gig0/1, Gig0/2
10   VLAN0010                         active    Fa0/11
30   VLAN0030                         active    Fa0/6
1002 fddi-default                     active
1003 token-ring-default               active
1004 fddinet-default                  active
1005 trnet-default                    active
```

Step 3:   Test connectivity between **PC1** and **PC3**.

From **PC1**, ping **PC3**. The pings should still fail. Why were the pings unsuccessful?

_____

_____

Part 3: Configure Subinterfaces

Step 1:   Configure subinterfaces on **R1** using the 802.1Q encapsulation.

    a.   Create the subinterface G0/0.10.

        ■   Set the encapsulation type to 802.1Q and assign VLAN 10 to the subinterface.

        ■   Refer to the Address Table and assign the correct IP address to the subinterface.

    b.   Repeat for the G0/0.30 subinterface.

Step 2:   Verify Configuration.

    a.   Use the **show ip interface brief** command to verify subinterface configuration. Both subinterfaces are down. Subinterfaces are virtual interfaces that are associated with a physical interface. Therefore, in order to enable subinterfaces, you must enable the physical interface that they are associated with.

    b.   Enable the G0/0 interface. Verify that the subinterfaces are now active.

Part 4: Test Connectivity with Inter-VLAN Routing

Step 1:   Ping between **PC1** and **PC3**.

    From **PC1**, ping **PC3**. The pings should still fail.

Step 2:   Enable trunking.

    a.   On **S1**, issue the **show vlan** command. What VLAN is G0/1 assigned to? _____

    b.   Because the router was configured with multiple subinterfaces assigned to different VLANs, the switch port connecting to the router must be configured as a trunk. Enable trunking on interface G0/1.

        _____

        _____

    c.   How can you determine that the interface is a trunk port using the **show vlan** command? _____

    d.   Issue the **show interface trunk** command to verify the interface is configured as a trunk.

Step 3:   Switch to Simulation mode to monitor pings.

    a.   Switch to **Simulation** mode by clicking the **Simulation** tab or pressing **Shift+S**.

    b.   Click **Capture/Forward** to see the steps the ping takes between **PC1** and **PC3**.

    c.   You should see ARP requests and replies between **S1** and **R1**. Then ARP requests and replies between **R1** and **S3**. Then **PC1** can encapsulate an ICMP echo request with the proper data-link layer information and R1 will route the request to **PC3**.

Note: After the ARP process finishes, you may need to click **Reset Simulation** to see the ICMP process complete.

Suggested Scoring Rubric

Packet Tracer scores 60 points. The four questions are worth 10 points each.

6.3.3.7 Lab–Configuring 802.1Q Trunk-Based Inter-VLAN Routing

Topology

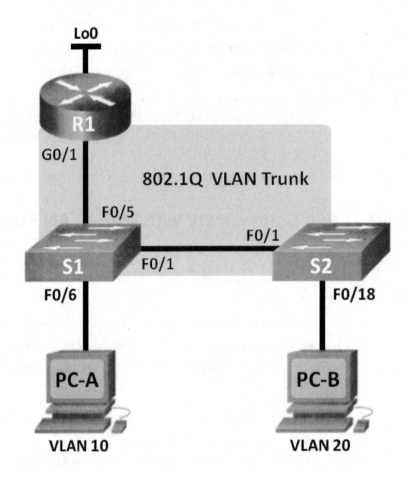

Addressing Table

Device	Interface	IP Address	Subnet Mask	Default Gateway
R1	G0/1.1	192.168.1.1	255.255.255.0	N/A
	G0/1.10	192.168.10.1	255.255.255.0	N/A
	G0/1.20	192.168.20.1	255.255.255.0	N/A
	Lo0	209.165.200.225	255.255.255.224	N/A
S1	VLAN 1	192.168.1.11	255.255.255.0	192.168.1.1
S2	VLAN 1	192.168.1.12	255.255.255.0	192.168.1.1
PC-A	NIC	192.168.10.3	255.255.255.0	192.168.10.1
PC-B	NIC	192.168.20.3	255.255.255.0	192.168.20.1

Switch Port Assignment Specifications

Ports	Assignment	Network
S1 F0/1	802.1Q Trunk	N/A
S2 F0/1	802.1Q Trunk	N/A
S1 F0/5	802.1Q Trunk	N/A
S1 F0/6	VLAN 10–Students	192.168.10.0/24
S2 F0/18	VLAN 20–Faculty	192.168.20.0/24

Objectives

Part 1: Build the Network and Configure Basic Device Settings

Part 2: Configure Switches with VLANs and Trunking

Part 3: Configure Trunk-Based Inter-VLAN Routing

Background/Scenario

A second method of providing routing and connectivity for multiple VLANs is through the use of an 802.1Q trunk between one or more switches and a single router interface. This method is also known as router-on-a-stick inter-VLAN routing. In this method, the physical router interface is divided into multiple subinterfaces that provide logical pathways to all VLANs connected.

In this lab, you will configure trunk-based inter-VLAN routing and verify connectivity to hosts on different VLANs as well as with a loopback on the router.

Note: This lab provides minimal assistance with the actual commands necessary to configure trunk-based inter-VLAN routing. However, the required configuration commands are provided in Appendix A of this lab. Test your knowledge by trying to configure the devices without referring to the appendix.

Note: The routers used with CCNA hands-on labs are Cisco 1941 Integrated Services Routers (ISRs) with Cisco IOS, Release 15.2(4)M3 (universalk9 image). The switches used are Cisco Catalyst 2960s with Cisco IOS, Release 15.0(2) (lanbasek9 image). Other routers, switches and Cisco IOS versions can be used. Depending on the model and Cisco IOS version, the commands available and output produced might vary from what is shown in the labs. Refer to the Router Interface Summary Table at the end of the lab for the correct interface identifiers.

Note: Make sure that the routers and switches have been erased and have no startup configurations. If you are unsure, contact your instructor.

Required Resources

- 1 Router (Cisco 1941 with Cisco IOS, release 15.2(4)M3 universal image or comparable)
- 2 Switches (Cisco 2960 with Cisco IOS, release 15.0(2) lanbasek9 image or comparable)
- 2 PCs (Windows 7, Vista, or XP with terminal emulation program, such as Tera Term)
- Console cables to configure the Cisco IOS devices via the console ports
- Ethernet cables as shown in the topology

Part 1: Build the Network and Configure Basic Device Settings

In Part 1, you will set up the network topology and configure basic settings on the PC hosts, switches, and router.

Step 1:   Cable the network as shown in the topology.

Step 2:   Configure PC hosts.

Step 3:   Initialize and reload the router and switches as necessary.

Step 4:   Configure basic settings for each switch.

    a.   Console into the switch and enter global configuration mode.

    b.   Copy the following basic configuration and paste it to the running-configuration on the switch.

```
no ip domain-lookup
service password-encryption
enable secret class
banner motd #
Unauthorized access is strictly prohibited. #
line con 0
password cisco
login
logging synchronous
line vty 0 15
password cisco
login
exit
```

    c.   Configure the device name as shown in the topology.

    d.   Configure the IP address listed in the Addressing Table for VLAN 1 on the switch.

    e.   Configure the default gateway on the switch.

    f.   Administratively deactivate all unused ports on the switch.

    g.   Copy the running configuration to the startup configuration.

Step 5:   Configure basic settings for the router.

    a.   Console into the router and enter global configuration mode.

    b.   Copy the following basic configuration and paste it to the running-configuration on the router.

```
no ip domain-lookup
hostname R1
service password-encryption
enable secret class
banner motd #
Unauthorized access is strictly prohibited. #
Line con 0
password cisco
login
logging synchronous
line vty 0 4
```

```
password cisco
login
```

c.   Configure the Lo0 IP address as shown in the Address Table. Do not configure sub-interfaces at this time. They will be configured in Part 3.

d.   Copy the running configuration to the startup configuration.

Part 2: Configure Switches with VLANs and Trunking

In Part 2, you will configure the switches with VLANs and trunking.

Note: The required commands for Part 2 are provided in Appendix A. Test your knowledge by trying to configure S1 and S2 without referring to the appendix.

Step 1:   Configure VLANs on S1.

a.   On S1, configure the VLANs and names listed in the Switch Port Assignment Specifications table. Write the commands you used in the space provided.

_____

_____

_____

_____

b.   On S1, configure the interface connected to R1 as a trunk. Also configure the interface connected to S2 as a trunk. Write the commands you used in the space provided.

_____

_____

c.   On S1, assign the access port for PC-A to VLAN 10. Write the commands you used in the space provided.

_____

_____

_____

Step 2:   Configure VLANs on Switch 2.

a.   On S2, configure the VLANs and names listed in the Switch Port Assignment Specifications table.

b.   On S2, verify that the VLAN names and numbers match those on S1. Write the command you used in the space provided.

_____

c.   On S2, assign the access port for PC-B to VLAN 20.

d.   On S2, configure the interface connected to S1 as a trunk.

Part 3: Configure Trunk-Based Inter-VLAN Routing

In Part 3, you will configure R1 to route to multiple VLANs by creating subinterfaces for each VLAN. This method of inter-VLAN routing is called router-on-a-stick.

Note: The required commands for Part 3 are provided in Appendix A. Test your knowledge by trying to configure trunk-based or router-on-a-stick inter-VLAN routing without referring to the appendix.

Step 1:   Configure a subinterface for VLAN 1.

    a.   Create a subinterface on R1 G0/1 for VLAN 1 using 1 as the subinterface ID. Write the command you used in the space provided.

_____

    b.   Configure the subinterface to operate on VLAN 1. Write the command you used in the space provided.

_____

    c.   Configure the subinterface with the IP address from the Address Table. Write the command you used in the space provided.

_____

Step 2:   Configure a subinterface for VLAN 10.

    a.   Create a subinterface on R1 G0/1 for VLAN 10 using 10 as the subinterface ID.

    b.   Configure the subinterface to operate on VLAN 10.

    c.   Configure the subinterface with the address from the Address Table.

Step 3:   Configure a subinterface for VLAN 20.

    a.   Create a subinterface on R1 G0/1 for VLAN 20 using 20 as the subinterface ID.

    b.   Configure the subinterface to operate on VLAN 20.

    c.   Configure the subinterface with the address from the Address Table.

Step 4:   Enable the G0/1 interface.

Enable the G0/1 interface. Write the commands you used in the space provided.

_____

Step 5:   Verify connectivity.

Enter the command to view the routing table on R1. What networks are listed?

_____

From PC-A, is it possible to ping the default gateway for VLAN 10? _____

From PC-A, is it possible to ping PC-B? _____

From PC-A, is it possible to ping Lo0? _____

From PC-A, is it possible to ping S2? _____

If the answer is **no** to any of these questions, troubleshoot the configurations and correct any errors.

Reflection

What are the advantages of trunk-based or router-on-a-stick inter-VLAN routing?

_____

_____

Router Interface Summary Table

Router Interface Summary				
Router Model	Ethernet Interface #1	Ethernet Interface #2	Serial Interface #1	Serial Interface #2
1800	Fast Ethernet 0/0 (F0/0)	Fast Ethernet 0/1 (F0/1)	Serial 0/0/0 (S0/0/0)	Serial 0/0/1 (S0/0/1)
1900	Gigabit Ethernet 0/0 (G0/0)	Gigabit Ethernet 0/1 (G0/1)	Serial 0/0/0 (S0/0/0)	Serial 0/0/1 (S0/0/1)
2801	Fast Ethernet 0/0 (F0/0)	Fast Ethernet 0/1 (F0/1)	Serial 0/1/0 (S0/1/0)	Serial 0/1/1 (S0/1/1)
2811	Fast Ethernet 0/0 (F0/0)	Fast Ethernet 0/1 (F0/1)	Serial 0/0/0 (S0/0/0)	Serial 0/0/1 (S0/0/1)
2900	Gigabit Ethernet 0/0 (G0/0)	Gigabit Ethernet 0/1 (G0/1)	Serial 0/0/0 (S0/0/0)	Serial 0/0/1 (S0/0/1)

Note: To find out how the router is configured, look at the interfaces to identify the type of router and how many interfaces the router has. There is no way to effectively list all the combinations of configurations for each router class. This table includes identifiers for the possible combinations of Ethernet and Serial interfaces in the device. The table does not include any other type of interface, even though a specific router may contain one. An example of this might be an ISDN BRI interface. The string in parentheses is the legal abbreviation that can be used in Cisco IOS commands to represent the interface.

Appendix A–Configuration Commands

Switch S1

```
S1(config)# vlan 10
S1(config-vlan)# name Students
S1(config-vlan)# vlan 20
S1(config-vlan)# name Faculty
S1(config-vlan)# exit
S1(config)# interface f0/1
S1(config-if)# switchport mode trunk
S1(config-if)# interface f0/5
S1(config-if)# switchport mode trunk
S1(config-if)# interface f0/6
S1(config-if)# switchport mode access
S1(config-if)# switchport access vlan 10
```

Switch S2

```
S2(config)# vlan 10
S2(config-vlan)# name Students
S2(config-vlan)# vlan 20
S2(config-vlan)# name Faculty
S2(config)# interface f0/1
S2(config-if)# switchport mode trunk
S2(config-if)# interface f0/18
S2(config-if)# switchport mode access
S2(config-if)# switchport access vlan 20
```

Router R1

```
R1(config)# interface g0/1.1
R1(config-subif)# encapsulation dot1Q 1
R1(config-subif)# ip address 192.168.1.1 255.255.255.0
R1(config-subif)# interface g0/1.10
R1(config-subif)# encapsulation dot1Q 10
R1(config-subif)# ip address 192.168.10.1 255.255.255.0
R1(config-subif)# interface g0/1.20
R1(config-subif)# encapsulation dot1Q 20
R1(config-subif)# ip address 192.168.20.1 255.255.255.0
R1(config-subif)# exit
R1(config)# interface g0/1
R1(config-if)# no shutdown
```

6.3.3.8 Packet Tracer–Inter-VLAN Routing Challenge

Topology

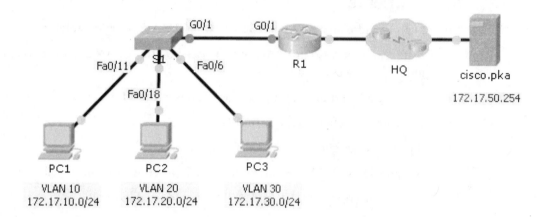

Addressing Table

Device	Interface	IP Address	Subnet Mask	Default Gateway
R1	G0/0	172.17.25.2	255.255.255.252	N/A
	G0/1.10	172.17.10.1	255.255.255.0	N/A
	G0/1.20	172.17.20.1	255.255.255.0	N/A
	G0/1.30	172.17.30.1	255.255.255.0	N/A
	G0/1.88	172.17.88.1	255.255.255.0	N/A
	G0/1.99	172.17.99.1	255.255.255.0	N/A
S1	VLAN 99	172.17.99.10	255.255.255.0	172.17.99.1
PC1	NIC	172.17.10.21	255.255.255.0	172.17.10.1
PC2	NIC	172.17.20.22	255.255.255.0	172.17.20.1
PC3	NIC	172.17.30.23	255.255.255.0	172.17.30.1

VLAN and Port Assignments Table

VLAN	Name	Interface
10	Faculty/Staff	Fa0/11-17
20	Students	Fa0/18-24
30	Guest(Default)	Fa0/6-10
88	Native	G0/1
99	Management	VLAN 99

Scenario

In this activity, you will demonstrate and reinforce your ability to implement inter-VLAN routing, including configuring IP addresses, VLANs, trunking, and subinterfaces.

Requirements

- Assign IP addressing to **R1** and **S1** based on the **Addressing Table**.

- Create, name, and assign VLANs on **S1** based on the **VLAN and Port Assignments Table**. Ports should be in access mode.

- Configure **S1** to trunk, allow only the VLANs in the **VLAN and Port Assignments Table**.

- Configure the default gateway on **S1**.

- All ports not assigned to a VLAN should be disabled.

- Configure inter-VLAN routing on **R1** based on the **Addressing Table**.

- Verify connectivity. **R1, S1**, and all PCs should be able to ping each other and the **cisco.pka** server.

6.4.1.1 Lab–The Inside Track

Objective

Explain how Layer 3 switches forward data in a small- to medium-sized business LAN.

Scenario

Your company has just purchased a three-level building. You are the network administrator and must design the company inter-VLAN routing network scheme to serve a few employees on each floor.

Floor 1 is occupied by the HR Department, Floor 2 is occupied by the IT Department, and Floor 3 is occupied by the Sales Department. All Departments must be able to communicate with each other, but at the same time have their own separate working networks.

You brought three Cisco 2960 switches and a Cisco 1941 series router from the old office location to serve network connectivity in the new building. New equipment is non-negotiable.

Refer to the PDF for this activity for further instructions.

Resources

- Software presentation program

Directions

Work with a partner to complete this activity.

Step 1: Design your topology.

    a. Use one 2960 switch per floor of your new building.

    b. Assign one department to each switch.

    c. Pick one of the switches to connect to the 1941 series router.

Step 2: Plan the VLAN scheme.

    a. Devise VLAN names and numbers for the HR, IT, and Sales Departments.

    b. Include a management VLAN, possibly named Management or Native, numbered to your choosing.

    c. Use either IPv4 or v6 as your addressing scheme for the LANs. If using IPv4, you must also use VLSM.

Step 3: Design a graphic to show your VLAN design and address scheme.

Step 4: Choose your inter-VLAN routing method.

    a. Legacy (per interface)

    b. Router-on-a-Stick

    c. Multilayer switching

Step 5:   Create a presentation justifying your inter-VLAN routing method of choice.

   a.   No more than eight slides can be created for the presentation.

   b.   Present your group's design to the class or to your instructor.

   1)   Be able to explain the method you chose. What makes it different or more desirable to your business than the other two methods?

   2)   Be able to show how data moves throughout your network. Verbally explain how the networks are able to communicate using your inter-VLAN method of choice.

6.4.1.2 Packet Tracer–Skills Integration Challenge

Topology

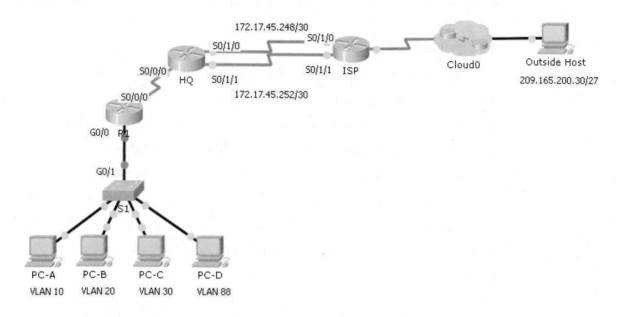

Addressing Table

Device	Interface	IP Address	Subnet Mask	Default Gateway	VLAN
R1	S0/0/0	172.31.1.2	255.255.255.0	N/A	N/A
	G0/0.10	172.31.10.1	255.255.255.0	N/A	10
	G0/0.20	172.31.20.1	255.255.255.0	N/A	20
	G0/0.30	172.31.30.1	255.255.255.0	N/A	30
	G0/0.88	172.31.88.1	255.255.255.0	N/A	88
	G0/0.99	172.31.99.1	255.255.255.0	N/A	99
S1	VLAN 88	172.31.88.33	255.255.255.0	172.31.88.1	88
PC-A	NIC	172.31.10.21	255.255.255.0	172.31.10.1	10
PC-B	NIC	172.31.20.22	255.255.255.0	172.31.20.1	20
PC-C	NIC	172.31.30.23	255.255.255.0	172.31.30.1	30
PC-D	NIC	172.31.88.24	255.255.255.0	172.31.88.1	88

VLAN Table

VLAN	Name	Interfaces
10	Sales	F0/11-15
20	Production	F0/16-20
30	Marketing	F0/5-10
88	Management	F0/21-24
99	Native	G0/1

Scenario

In this activity, you will demonstrate and reinforce your ability to configure routers for inter-VLAN communication and configure static routes to reach destinations outside of your network. Among the skills you will demonstrate are configuring inter-VLAN routing, static, and default routes.

Requirements

- Configure inter-VLAN routing on **R1** based on the **Addressing Table**.

- Configure trunking on **S1**.

- Configure four directly attached static routes on **HQ** to each VLANs 10, 20, 30, and 88.

- Configure directly attached static routes on **HQ** to reach **Outside Host**.

  - Configure the primary path through the Serial 0/1/0 interface.

  - Configure the backup route through the Serial 0/1/1 interface with a 10 AD.

- Configure a directly attached default route on **R1**.

- Verify connectivity by making sure all the PCs can ping **Outside Host**.

CHAPTER 7

Access Control Lists

One of the most important skills a network administrator needs is mastery of access control lists (ACLs). An ACL is a sequential list of permit or deny statements that apply to addresses or upper-layer protocols. ACLs provide a powerful way to control traffic into and out of a network. ACLs can be configured for all routed network protocols. In this chapter, you learn how to use standard and extended ACLs on a Cisco router as part of a security solution.

The Study Guide portion of this chapter uses a combination of matching, fill-in-the-blank, multiple-choice, and open-ended question exercises to test your knowledge and skills of basic router concepts and configuration. The Labs and Activities portion of this chapter includes all the online curriculum labs and Packet Tracer activities to ensure that you have mastered the hands-on skills needed to understand basic IP addressing and router configuration.

As you work through this chapter, use Chapter 7 in *Routing and Switching Essentials v6 Companion Guide* or use the corresponding Chapter 7 in the Routing and Switching Essentials online curriculum for assistance.

Study Guide

ACL Operation

An ACL is a series of IOS commands that control whether a router forwards or drops packets based on information found in the packet header. ACLs are among the most commonly used features of Cisco IOS software.

Traffic that enters a router interface is routed solely based on information in the routing table. When an ACL is applied to the interface, the router performs the additional task of evaluating all network packets as they pass through the interface to determine whether the packet can be forwarded. This process is called *packet filtering*. Standard IP ACLs only filter at Layer 3. Extended IP ACLs filter at Layer 3 and Layer 4.

The last statement of an ACL is always an implicit deny. Because of this implicit deny, an ACL that does not have at least one permit statement will block all traffic.

ACLs can be configured to apply to inbound traffic and outbound traffic. For inbound traffic, packets are processed before they are routed. For outbound traffic, packets are processed after they are routed to the outbound interface.

IPv4 ACLs use a wildcard mask to determine which packets will be permitted.

Calculating Wildcard Masks

A wildcard mask is a string of 32 binary digits used by the router to determine which bits of the address to examine for a match before permitting or denying the packet.

As with subnet masks, the numbers 1 and 0 in the wildcard mask identify how to treat the corresponding IP address bits. However, in a wildcard mask, these bits are used for different purposes and follow different rules. Subnet masks use binary 1s and 0s to identify the network, subnet, and host portion of an IP address. Wildcard masks use binary 1s and 0s to filter individual IP addresses or groups of IP addresses to permit or deny access to resources.

When filtering traffic for a network, the *wildcard mask* argument is simply the inverse of the subnet mask. For example, the bit pattern for 11110000 (240) becomes 00001111 (15).

For the ACL statements in Table 7-1, record the wildcard mask used to filter the specified IPv4 address or network.

Table 7-1   Determine the Correct Wildcard Mask

ACL Statement	Wildcard Mask
Permit all hosts from the 192.168.1.0/25 network	
Permit all hosts from the 10.0.0.0/16 network	
Deny all hosts from the 10.10.100.0/24 network	
Deny all hosts from the 10.20.30.128/26 network	
Permit all hosts from the 172.18.0.0/23 network	
Permit all hosts from the 192.168.5.0/27 network	
Deny host 172.18.33.1	
Deny all hosts from the 172.16.1.192/29 network	

ACL Statement	Wildcard Mask
Permit all hosts from the 172.31.64.0/18 network	
Permit host 10.10.10.1	
Deny all hosts from the 172.25.250.160/28 network	
Deny all hosts from the 172.30.128.0/20 network	
Deny all hosts from the 10.10.128.0/19 network	
Permit all hosts from the 172.18.0.0/16 network	
Permit all hosts from the 192.168.200.0/30 network	

Wildcard Mask in Operation

In Table 7-2, for each of the ACL statements and corresponding source addresses, choose whether the router will either permit or deny the packet.

Table 7-2   Determine the Permit or Deny

ACL Statement	Source Address	Permit or Deny
access-list 33 permit 198.168.100.0 0.0.0.63	198.168.100.3	
access-list 20 permit 192.168.223.64 0.0.0.15	192.168.223.72	
access-list 21 permit 192.0.2.11 0.0.0.15	192.0.2.17	
access-list 39 permit 198.168.100.64 0.0.0.63	192.168.22.100.40	
access-list 66 permit 172.16.0.0 0.0.255.255	172.17.0.5	
access-list 65 permit 172.16.1.1 0.0.0.0	172.16.1.1	
access-list 16 permit 10.10.10.0 0.0.0.255	10.10.10.33	
access-list 60 permit 10.10.0.0 0.0.255.255	10.10.33.33	
access-list 50 permit 192.168.122.128 0.0.0.63	192.168.122.195	
access-list 55 permit 192.168.15.0 0.0.0.3	192.168.15.5	
access-list 30 permit 192.168.223.32 0.0.0.31	192.168.223.60	
access-list 1 permit 192.168.155.0 0.0.0.255	192.168.155.245	
access-list 25 permit 172.18.5.0 0.0.0.255	172.18.6.20	
access-list 50 permit 192.168.155.0 0.0.0.255	192.168.156.245	
access-list 18 permit 10.10.10.0 0.0.0.63	10.10.10.50	

Guidelines for ACL Creation

Complete the ACL Operation sentences on the left using words from the Word Bank on the right. Not all words are used.

ACL Operation

a. An access control list (ACL) controls whether the router will _____ or _____ packet traffic based on packet header criteria.

b. A router with three interfaces and two network protocols (IPv4 and IPv6) can have as many as _____ active ACLs.

c. ACLs are often used in routers between internal and external networks to provide a _____.

d. For inbound ACLs, incoming packets are processed _____ they are sent to the route processor.

e. For outbound ACLs, incoming packets are processed _____ they are sent from the route processor to the outbound interface.

f. For every ACL, there is an implied deny statement; if a packet does not match any of the ACL criteria, it will be _____.

g. ACLs can filter data traffic per protocol, per direction, and per _____.

h. ACLs can filter traffic based on source/destination address, _____, and port numbers.

Word Bank

Discarded

Four

Firewall

Interface

Pathway

Deny

After

Processing

6

Protocol

12

Forwarded

Permit

Switch

Before

Guidelines for ACL Placement

Every ACL should be placed where it has the greatest impact on efficiency. The basic rules are as follows:

- Locate _____ ACLs as close to the destination as possible because these ACLs do not specify destination addresses.

- Locate _____ ACLs as close as possible to the source of the traffic to be filtered.

Use the information shown in Figure 7-1 to determine the router, interface, and direction for each scenario in Table 7-3.

Figure 7-1 . ACL Placement Topology

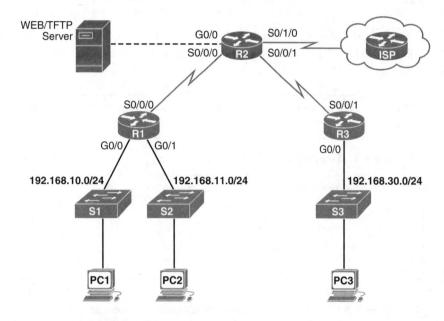

Table 7-3   ACL Placement Scenarios

Scenario	Router	Interface	Direction
Use a standard ACL to stop the 192.168.10.0/24 network from accessing the Internet through the ISP.			
Use a standard ACL to stop the 192.168.11.0/24 network from accessing the 192.168.10.0/24 network.			
Use an extended ACL to allow only TFTP and web traffic to access the WEB/TFTP server. The traffic could be from any source.			
Use an extended ACL to stop the 192.168.30.0/24 network from accessing the WEB/TFTP server.			

Standard IPv4 ACLs

To use numbered or named standard ACLs on a Cisco router, you must first create the standard ACL. Then you must apply the ACL to one of the router's processes such as an interface or Telnet lines.

Configuring Standard IPv4 ACLs

The full command syntax to configure a standard ACL is as follows:

```
Router(config)# access-list access-list-number { deny | permit | remark } source [ source-wildcard ] [ log ]
```

The following ACL statement would first add a remark and then permit traffic from the 172.16.0.0/16 network:

```
Router(config)# access-list 1 remark Permit traffic from HR LAN, 172.16.0.0/16
```

```
Router(config)# access-list 1 permit 172.16.0.0 0.0.255.255
```

In this case, the remark is not that helpful. However, in more complex configuration scenarios, the remark option can help to quickly communicate the purpose of an ACL statement.

If the policy calls for filtering traffic for a specific host, you can use the host address and 0.0.0.0 as the wildcard mask. But if you do, the IOS will drop the 0.0.0.0 and just use the host address as shown in Example 7-1.

Note: Older IOS versions convert 0.0.0.0 to the keyword **host** and prepend it before the IP address, such as **host 172.16.1.10**.

Example 7-1   Filtering One IP Address

```
R1(config)# access-list 1 deny 172.16.1.10 0.0.0.0
R1(config)# do show access-lists
Standard IP access list 1
    10 deny   172.16.1.10
R1(config)#
```

If the policy calls for filtering traffic for all sources, you can configure 0.0.0.0 255.255.255.255 as the source address and wildcard mask. The IOS will convert it to the keyword **any**, as shown in Example 7-2.

Example 7-2   Filtering All Addresses

```
R1(config)# access-list 1 deny 172.16.1.10 0.0.0.0
R1(config)# access-list 1 permit 0.0.0.0 255.255.255.255
R1(config)# do show access-lists
Standard IP access list 1
    10 deny   172.16.1.10
    20 permit any
R1(config)#
```

Note: The sequence numbers before each statement can be used to edit the statement, as discussed later.

An ACL has no impact unless it is applied to some process. To filter inbound or outbound traffic, an ACL must be applied to an interface and the direction of traffic specified. The command syntax to apply an ACL to an interface is as follows:

```
Router(config-if)# ip access-group { access-list-number | access-list-name } { in | out }
```

Naming an ACL makes it easier to understand its function. For example, an ACL configured to deny FTP could be called NO_FTP. The command syntax to enter named ACL configuration mode is as follows:

```
Router(config)# ip access-list [ standard | extended ] name
```

The *name* can be any alphanumeric string that does not begin with a number. Once in named ACL configuration mode, the router prompt changes depending on whether you chose standard or extended. The syntax for named standard ACL configuration mode is as follows:

```
Router(config-std-nacl)# [ permit | deny | remark ] { source [source-wildcard] } [log}
```

So, to reconfigure Example 7-2 with a named standard ACL and a remark, we could do something like Example 7-3.

Example 7-3   Standard Named ACL

```
R1(config)# ip access-list standard NOT_BOB
R1(config-std-nacl)# remark Stop Bob
R1(config-std-nacl)# deny host 172.16.1.10
R1(config-std-nacl)# permit any
R1(config-std-nacl)# exit
R1(config)# interface g0/0
R1(config-if)# ip access-group NOT_BOB in
R1(config-if)# do show access-lists
Standard IP access list NOT_BOB
    10 deny host 172.16.1.10
    20 permit any
R1(config-if)#
```

Use the information in Figure 7-2 to write ACL statements for the following two scenarios. Include the router prompt in your configurations.

Figure 7-2   Topology for Standard ACL Configuration Scenarios

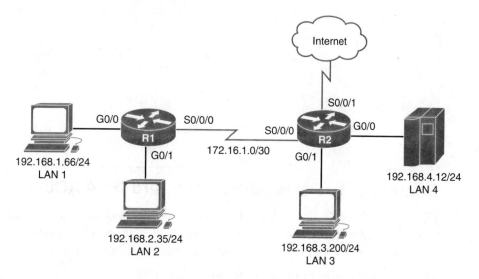

Standard ACL Scenario 1

Record the commands to configure and apply a standard ACL that will filter traffic into the 192.168.1.0 LAN. The 192.168.3.77 host should not be able to access this LAN, but all other hosts on the 192.168.3.0 and 192.168.4.0 networks should be permitted. All other traffic should be blocked.

Standard ACL Scenario 2

Record the commands to configure and apply a standard ACL that will filter traffic to host 192.168.4.12. Both the 192.168.1.66 host and all hosts in the 192.168.2.0 LAN should be permitted access to this host. All other networks should not be able to access the 192.168.4.12 host.

Modifying IPv4 ACLs

The IOS automatically adds a sequence number before the ACL statement, as you can see in the previous examples that used the **show access-lists** command. These sequence numbers can be used to delete an erroneous ACL statement and add back a correct ACL statement. The rules for using sequence numbers to edit a standard or extended numbered ACL are as follows:

1. Enter named ACL configuration mode for the ACL even if it is a numbered ACL.

2. Delete the sequence number that is in error.

3. Use the deleted sequence number to add in the correct ACL statement.

Note: For standard and extended numbered ACLs, you cannot add a new sequence number statement in the middle of the ACL.

In Example 7-4, the wrong address is currently being denied. Enter the commands to delete the erroneous statement and add back a statement to deny 192.168.1.66.

Example 7-4   Standard Numbered ACL with Error

```
R1(config)# access-list 1 deny 192.168.1.65
R1(config)# access-list 1 permit any
R1(config)# do show access-lists
Standard IP access list 1
    10 deny   192.168.1.65
    20 permit any
R1(config)#
```

Securing vty Ports with a Standard IPv4 ACL

Filtering Telnet or Secure Shell (SSH) traffic is usually considered an extended IP ACL function because it filters a higher-level protocol. However, because the **access-class** command is used to filter incoming or outgoing Telnet/SSH sessions by source address, you can use a standard ACL.

The command syntax of the **access-class** command is:

```
Router(config-line)# access-class access-list-number { in [ vrf-also ] | out }
```

The parameter **in** restricts incoming connections between the addresses in the access list and the Cisco device, and the parameter **out** restricts outgoing connections between a particular Cisco device and the addresses in the access list.

Record the commands to configure an ACL to permit host 192.168.2.35 and then apply the ACL to all Telnet lines.

R1(config)# _____

_____

_____

Troubleshoot ACLs

When troubleshooting ACLs, it is important to first understand precisely how the router processes and filters packets. In addition, you should check for several common errors. The most common errors are entering ACLs in the wrong order and not applying adequate criteria to the ACL rules.

When processing packets, a router looks twice to see whether an ACL needs to be evaluated—inbound and outbound. In Figure 7-3, label each stage in the ACL processing flowchart with one of the following processing steps. All processing steps are used. Some processing steps are used more than once.

Figure 7-3   Processing Flowchart for an ACL

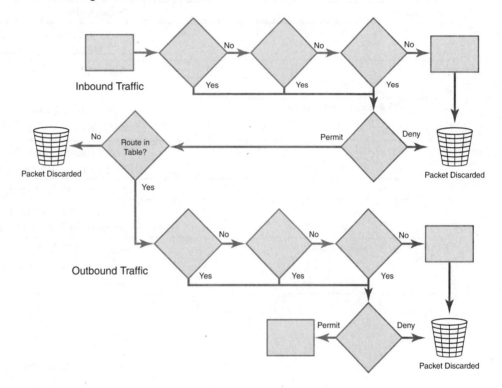

Processing Steps:

Implicitly Deny Any

Inbound Interface

Match First ACL Statement

Match Second ACL Statement

Match Third ACL Statement

Outbound Interface

Permit or Deny

Labs and Activities

Command Reference

In Table 7-4, record the command, including the correct router or switch prompt, that fits the description. Fill in any blanks with the appropriate missing information.

Table 7-4   Commands for Chapter 7, "Access Control Lists"

Command	Description
	Configure ACL 10 to permit the 172.16.2.0/24 network.
	Add "Admin allowed" as a comment to ACL 10.
`R1(config)# interface g0/0`	Apply ACL 10 for traffic entering the router interface.
	Enter the command to verify the configured ACLs on a router (not **show run**).
	Name a standard ACL VTY-ACL.
	Add an ACE to the standard named ACL permitting host 10.1.1.1.
`R1(config)# line vty 0 15`	Apply VTY-ACL to allow VTY lines to receive connections from the permitted host.

7.0.1.2 Permit Me to Assist You

Objective

Explain the purpose and operation of ACLs.

Scenario

- Each individual in the class will record five questions they would ask a candidate who is applying for a security clearance for a network assistant position within a small- to medium-sized business. The list of questions should be listed in order of importance to selecting a good candidate for the job. The preferred answers will also be recorded.

- After three minutes of brainstorming the list of questions, the instructor will ask two students to serve as interviewers. These two students will use only their list of questions and answers for the next part of this activity. The instructor will explain to only the two interviewers that they have the discretion, at any time, to stop the process and state "you are all permitted to the next level of interviews" or "I am sorry, but you do not have the qualifications to continue to the next level of interviews." The interviewer does not need to complete all of the questions on the list.

- The rest of the class will be split in half and assigned to one of the interviewers.

- Once everyone is settled into their group with an interviewer, the group application interviews will begin.

- The two selected interviewers will ask the first question on the list that they created; an example would be "are you over the age of 18?" If the applicant does not meet the age requirement, as specified by the interviewer's original questions and answers, the applicant will be eliminated from the pool of applicants and must move to another area within the room where they will observe the rest of the application process.

  The next question will then be asked by the interviewer. If applicants answer correctly, they may stay with the applicant group. The entire class will then get together and discuss their observations regarding the process to permit or deny them the opportunity to continue on to the next level of interviews.

Reflection

1. What factors did you consider when devising your list of criteria for network assistant security clearance?

   _____

2. How difficult was it to devise five security questions to deliver during the interviews? Why were you asked to list your questions in order of importance to selecting a good candidate?

   _____

3. Why would the process of elimination be stopped, even if there were still a few applicants available?

   _____

4. How could this scenario and the results be applied to network traffic?

   _____

Packet Tracer
☐ Activity

7.1.1.4 Packet Tracer–Access Control List Demonstration

Topology

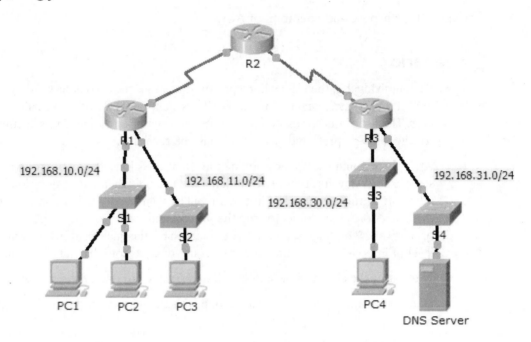

Objectives

Part 1: Verify Local Connectivity and Test Access Control List

Part 2: Remove Access Control List and Repeat Test

Background

In this activity, you will observe how an access control list (ACL) can be used to prevent a ping from reaching hosts on remote networks. After removing the ACL from the configuration, the pings will be successful.

Part 1: Verify Local Connectivity and Test Access Control List

Step 1:   Ping devices on the local network to verify connectivity.

    a.   From the command prompt of **PC1**, ping **PC2**.

    b.   From the command prompt of **PC1**, ping **PC3**.

       Why were the pings successful? _____

       _____

Step 2: Ping devices on remote networks to test ACL functionality.

    a. From the command prompt of **PC1**, ping **PC4**.

    b. From the command prompt of **PC1**, ping the **DNS Server**.

    Why did the pings fail? (Hint: Use simulation mode or view the router configurations to investigate.) _____

_____

Part 2: Remove ACL and Repeat Test

Step 1: Use show commands to investigate the ACL configuration.

    a. Use the **show run** and **show access-lists** commands to view the currently configured ACLs. To quickly view the current ACLs, use **show access-lists**. Enter the **show access-lists** command, followed by a space and a question mark (?) to view the available options:

```
R1#show access-lists ?
  <1-199>  ACL number
  WORD     ACL name
  <cr>
```

    If you know the ACL number or name, you can filter the **show** output further. However, **R1** only has one ACL; therefore, the **show access-lists** command will suffice.

```
R1#show access-lists
Standard IP access list 11
    10 deny 192.168.10.0 0.0.0.255
    20 permit any
```

    The first line of the ACL prevents any packets originating in the **192.168.10.0/24** network, which includes Internet Control Message Protocol (ICMP) echoes (ping requests). The second line of the ACL allows all other **ip** traffic from **any** source to traverse the router.

    b. For an ACL to impact router operation, it must be applied to an interface in a specific direction. In this scenario, the ACL is used to filter traffic exiting an interface. Therefore, all traffic leaving the specified interface of R1 will be inspected against ACL 11.

    Although you can view IP information with the **show ip interface** command, it may be more efficient in some situations to simply use the **show run** command.

    Using one or both of these commands, to which interface and direction is the ACL applied?

_____

Step 2: Remove access list 11 from the configuration.

    You can remove ACLs from the configuration by issuing the **no access list** [*number of the ACL*] command. The **no access-list** command deletes all ACLs configured on the router. The **no access-list** [*number of the ACL*] command removes only a specific ACL.

    a. Under the Serial0/0/0 interface, remove access-list 11 previously applied to the interface as an **outgoing** filter:

```
R1(config)# int se0/0/0
R1(config-if)#no ip access-group 11 out
```

b. In global configuration mode, remove the ACL by entering the following command:

```
R1(config)# no access-list 11
```

c. Verify that **PC1** can now ping the **DNS Server** and **PC4**.

Suggested Scoring Rubric

Question Location	Possible Points	Earned Points
Part 1, Step 1 b.	50	
Part 1, Step 2 b.	40	
Part 2, Step 2 b.	10	
Total Score	100	

7.2.1.6 Packet Tracer–Configuring Numbered Standard IPv4 ACLs

Topology

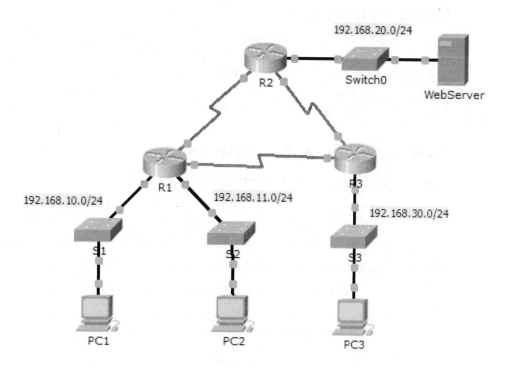

Addressing Table

Device	Interface	IP Address	Subnet Mask	Default Gateway
R1	G0/0	192.168.10.1	255.255.255.0	N/A
	G0/1	192.168.11.1	255.255.255.0	N/A
	S0/0/0	10.1.1.1	255.255.255.252	N/A
	S0/0/1	10.3.3.1	255.255.255.252	N/A
R2	G0/0	192.168.20.1	255.255.255.0	N/A
	S0/0/0	10.1.1.2	255.255.255.252	N/A
	S0/0/1	10.2.2.1	255.255.255.252	N/A
R3	G0/0	192.168.30.1	255.255.255.0	N/A
	S0/0/0	10.3.3.2	255.255.255.252	N/A
	S0/0/1	10.2.2.2	255.255.255.252	N/A
PC1	NIC	192.168.10.10	255.255.255.0	192.168.10.1
PC2	NIC	192.168.11.10	255.255.255.0	192.168.11.1
PC3	NIC	192.168.30.10	255.255.255.0	192.168.30.1
WebServer	NIC	192.168.20.254	255.255.255.0	192.168.20.1

Objectives

Part 1: Plan an ACL Implementation

Part 2: Configure, Apply, and Verify a Standard ACL

Background/Scenario

Standard access control lists (ACLs) are router configuration scripts that control whether a router permits or denies packets based on the source address. This activity focuses on defining filtering criteria, configuring standard ACLs, applying ACLs to router interfaces, and verifying and testing the ACL implementation. The routers are already configured, including IP addresses and Enhanced Interior Gateway Routing Protocol (EIGRP) routing.

Part 1: Plan an ACL Implementation

Step 1:   Investigate the current network configuration.

Before applying any ACLs to a network, it is important to confirm that you have full connectivity. Verify that the network has full connectivity by choosing a PC and pinging other devices on the network. You should be able to successfully ping every device.

Step 2:   Evaluate two network policies and plan ACL implementations.

   a.   The following network policies are implemented on R2:

   ■   The 192.168.11.0/24 network is not allowed access to the WebServer on the 192.168.20.0/24 network.

   ■   All other access is permitted.

   To restrict access from the 192.168.11.0/24 network to the WebServer at 192.168.20.254 without interfering with other traffic, an ACL must be created on R2. The access list must be placed on the outbound interface to the WebServer. A second rule must be created on R2 to permit all other traffic.

   b.   The following network policies are implemented on R3:

   ■   The 192.168.10.0/24 network is not allowed to communicate with the 192.168.30.0/24 network.

   ■   All other access is permitted.

   To restrict access from the 192.168.10.0/24 network to the 192.168.30/24 network without interfering with other traffic, an access list will need to be created on R3. The ACL must be placed on the outbound interface to PC3. A second rule must be created on R3 to permit all other traffic.

Part 2: Configure, Apply, and Verify a Standard ACL

Step 1:   Configure and apply a numbered standard ACL on R2.

   a.   Create an ACL using the number 1 on R2 with a statement that denies access to the 192.168.20.0/24 network from the 192.168.11.0/24 network.

```
R2(config)# access-list 1 deny 192.168.11.0 0.0.0.255
```

b. By default, an access list denies all traffic that does not match any rules. To permit all other traffic, configure the following statement:

```
R2(config)# access-list 1 permit any
```

c. For the ACL to actually filter traffic, it must be applied to some router operation. Apply the ACL by placing it for outbound traffic on the Gigabit Ethernet 0/0 interface.

```
R2(config)# interface GigabitEthernet0/0
R2(config-if)# ip access-group 1 out
```

Step 2: Configure and apply a numbered standard ACL on R3.

a. Create an ACL using the number 1 on **R3** with a statement that denies access to the 192.168.30.0/24 network from the **PC1** (192.168.10.0/24) network.

```
R3(config)# access-list 1 deny 192.168.10.0 0.0.0.255
```

b. By default, an ACL denies all traffic that does not match any rules. To permit all other traffic, create a second rule for ACL 1.

```
R3(config)# access-list 1 permit any
```

c. Apply the ACL by placing it for outbound traffic on the Gigabit Ethernet 0/0 interface.

```
R3(config)# interface GigabitEthernet0/0
R3(config-if)# ip access-group 1 out
```

Step 3: Verify ACL configuration and functionality.

a. On **R2** and **R3**, enter the **show access-list** command to verify the ACL configurations. Enter the **show run** or **show ip interface gigabitethernet 0/0** command to verify the ACL placements.

b. With the two ACLs in place, network traffic is restricted according to the policies detailed in Part 1. Use the following tests to verify the ACL implementations:

- A ping from 192.168.10.10 to 192.168.11.10 succeeds.

- A ping from 192.168.10.10 to 192.168.20.254 succeeds.

- A ping from 192.168.11.10 to 192.168.20.254 fails.

- A ping from 192.168.10.10 to 192.168.30.10 fails.

- A ping from 192.168.11.10 to 192.168.30.10 succeeds.

- A ping from 192.168.30.10 to 192.168.20.254 succeeds.

7.2.1.7 Packet Tracer–Configuring Named Standard IPv4 ACLs

Topology

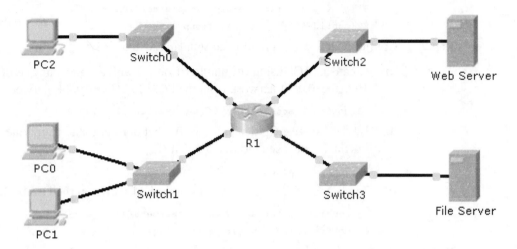

Addressing Table

Device	Interface	IP Address	Subnet Mask	Default Gateway
R1	F0/0	192.168.10.1	255.255.255.0	N/A
	F0/1	192.168.20.1	255.255.255.0	N/A
	E0/0/0	192.168.100.1	255.255.255.0	N/A
	E0/1/0	192.168.200.1	255.255.255.0	N/A
File Server	NIC	192.168.200.100	255.255.255.0	192.168.200.1
Web Server	NIC	192.168.100.100	255.255.255.0	192.168.100.1
PC0	NIC	192.168.20.3	255.255.255.0	192.168.20.1
PC1	NIC	192.168.20.4	255.255.255.0	192.168.20.1
PC2	NIC	192.168.10.3	255.255.255.0	192.168.10.1

Objectives

Part 1: Configure and Apply a Named Standard ACL

Part 2: Verify the ACL Implementation

Background/Scenario

The senior network administrator has tasked you to create a standard named ACL to prevent access to a file server. All clients from one network and one specific workstation from a different network should be denied access.

Part 1: Configure and Apply a Named Standard ACL

Step 1:   Verify connectivity before the ACL is configured and applied.

All three workstations should be able to ping both the **Web Server** and **File Server**.

Step 2:   Configure a named standard ACL.

Configure the following named ACL on **R1**.

```
R1(config)# ip access-list standard File_Server_Restrictions
R1(config-std-nacl)# permit host 192.168.20.4
R1(config-std-nacl)# deny any
```

Note: For scoring purposes, the ACL name is case sensitive.

Step 3:   Apply the named ACL.

   a.   Apply the ACL outbound on the interface Fast Ethernet 0/1.

```
R1(config-if)# ip access-group File_Server_Restrictions out
```

   b.   Save the configuration.

Part 2: Verify the ACL Implementation

Step 1:   Verify the ACL configuration and application to the interface.

Use the **show access-lists** command to verify the ACL configuration. Use the **show run** or **show ip interface fastethernet 0/1** command to verify that the ACL is applied correctly to the interface.

Step 2:   Verify that the ACL is working properly.

All three workstations should be able to ping the **Web Server**, but only **PC1** should be able to ping the **File Server**.

7.2.2.6 Lab–Configuring and Verifying Standard IPv4 ACLs

Topology

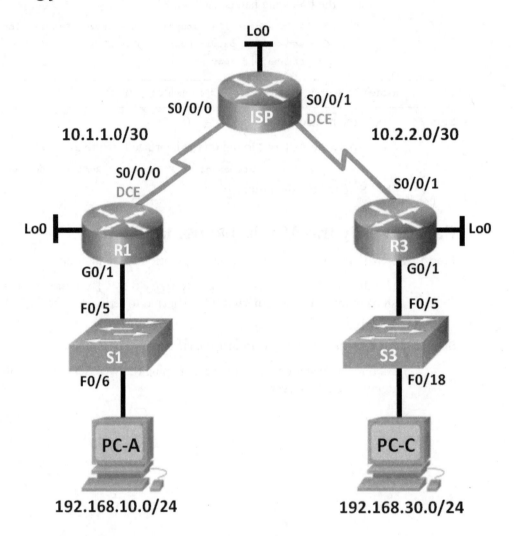

Addressing Table

Device	Interface	IP Address	Subnet Mask	Default Gateway
R1	G0/1	192.168.10.1	255.255.255.0	N/A
	Lo0	192.168.20.1	255.255.255.0	N/A
	S0/0/0 (DCE)	10.1.1.1	255.255.255.252	N/A
ISP	S0/0/0	10.1.1.2	255.255.255.252	N/A
	S0/0/1 (DCE)	10.2.2.2	255.255.255.252	N/A
	Lo0	209.165.200.225	255.255.255.224	N/A
R3	G0/1	192.168.30.1	255.255.255.0	N/A

Device	Interface	IP Address	Subnet Mask	Default Gateway
	Lo0	192.168.40.1	255.255.255.0	N/A
	S0/0/1	10.2.2.1	255.255.255.252	N/A
S1	VLAN 1	192.168.10.11	255.255.255.0	192.168.10.1
S3	VLAN 1	192.168.30.11	255.255.255.0	192.168.30.1
PC-A	NIC	192.168.10.3	255.255.255.0	192.168.10.1
PC-C	NIC	192.168.30.3	255.255.255.0	192.168.30.1

Objectives

Part 1: Set Up the Topology and Initialize Devices

- Set up equipment to match the network topology.

- Initialize and reload the routers and switches.

Part 2: Configure Devices and Verify Connectivity

- Assign a static IP address to PCs.

- Configure basic settings on routers.

- Configure basic settings on switches.

- Configure OSPF routing on R1, ISP, and R3.

- Verify connectivity between devices.

Part 3: Configure and Verify Standard Numbered and Named ACLs

- Configure, apply, and verify a numbered standard ACL.

- Configure, apply, and verify a named ACL.

Part 4: Modify a Standard ACL

- Modify and verify a named standard ACL.

- Test the ACL.

Background/Scenario

Network security is an important issue when designing and managing IP networks. The ability to configure proper rules to filter packets, based on established security policies, is a valuable skill.

In this lab, you will set up filtering rules for two offices represented by R1 and R3. Management has established some access policies between the LANs located at R1 and R3, which you must implement. The ISP router sitting between R1 and R3 will not have any ACLs placed on it. You would not be allowed any administrative access to an ISP router because you can only control and manage your own equipment.

Note: The routers used with CCNA hands-on labs are Cisco 1941 Integrated Services Routers (ISRs) with Cisco IOS Release 15.2(4)M3 (universalk9 image). The switches used are Cisco Catalyst 2960s with Cisco IOS Release 15.0(2) (lanbasek9 image). Other routers, switches, and Cisco IOS versions can be used. Depending on the model and Cisco IOS version, the commands available and output produced might vary from what is shown in the labs. Refer to the Router Interface Summary Table at the end of the lab for the correct interface identifiers.

Note: Make sure that the routers and switches have been erased and have no startup configurations. If you are unsure, contact your instructor.

Required Resources

- 3 Routers (Cisco 1941 with Cisco IOS Release 15.2(4)M3 universal image or comparable)

- 2 Switches (Cisco 2960 with Cisco IOS Release 15.0(2) lanbasek9 image or comparable)

- 2 PCs (Windows 7, Vista, or XP with terminal emulation program, such as Tera Term)

- Console cables to configure the Cisco IOS devices via the console ports

- Ethernet and serial cables as shown in the topology

Part 1: Set Up the Topology and Initialize Devices

In Part 1, you set up the network topology and clear any configurations, if necessary.

Step 1: Cable the network as shown in the topology.

Step 2: Initialize and reload the routers and switches.

Part 2: Configure Devices and Verify Connectivity

In Part 2, you configure basic settings on the routers, switches, and PCs. Refer to the Topology and Addressing Table for device names and address information.

Step 1: Configure IP addresses on PC-A and PC-C.

Step 2: Configure basic settings for the routers.

    a. Console into the router and enter global configuration mode.

    b. Copy the following basic configuration and paste it to the running configuration on the router.

```
no ip domain-lookup
hostname R1
service password-encryption
enable secret class
banner motd #
Unauthorized access is strictly prohibited. #
Line con 0
password cisco
login
logging synchronous
line vty 0 4
password cisco
login
```

    c. Configure the device name as shown in the topology.

    d. Create loopback interfaces on each router as shown in the Addressing Table.

    e. Configure interface IP addresses as shown in the Topology and Addressing Table.

    f. Assign a clock rate of **128000** to the DCE serial interfaces.

g. Enable Telnet access.

h. Copy the running configuration to the startup configuration.

Step 3: (Optional) Configure basic settings on the switches.

a. Console into the switch and enter global configuration mode.

b. Copy the following basic configuration and paste it to the running configuration on the switch.

```
no ip domain-lookup
service password-encryption
enable secret class
banner motd #
Unauthorized access is strictly prohibited. #
Line con 0
password cisco
login
logging synchronous
line vty 0 15
password cisco
login
exit
```

c. Configure the device name as shown in the topology.

d. Configure the management interface IP address as shown in the Topology and Addressing Table.

e. Configure a default gateway.

f. Enable Telnet access.

g. Copy the running configuration to the startup configuration.

Step 4: Configure Rip routing on R1, ISP, and R3.

a. Configure RIP version 2 and advertise all networks on R1, ISP, and R3. The OSPF configuration for R1 and ISP is included for reference.

```
R1(config)# router rip
R1(config-router)# version 2
R1(config-router)# network 192.168.10.0
R1(config-router)# network 192.168.20.0
R1(config-router)# network 10.1.1.0

ISP(config)# router rip
ISP(config-router)# version 2
ISP(config-router)# network 209.165.200.224
ISP(config-router)# network 10.1.1.0
ISP(config-router)# network 10.2.2.0
```

b. After configuring Rip on R1, ISP, and R3, verify that all routers have complete routing tables, listing all networks. Troubleshoot if this is not the case.

Step 5:   Verify connectivity between devices.

Note: It is very important to test whether connectivity is working before you configure and apply access lists! You want to ensure that your network is properly functioning before you start to filter traffic.

  a. From PC-A, ping PC-C and the loopback interface on R3. Were your pings successful?

  _____

  b. From R1, ping PC-C and the loopback interface on R3. Were your pings successful?

  _____

  c. From PC-C, ping PC-A and the loopback interface on R1. Were your pings successful?

  _____

  d. From R3, ping PC-A and the loopback interface on R1. Were your pings successful?

  _____

Part 3: Configure and Verify Standard Numbered and Named ACLs

Step 1:   Configure a numbered standard ACL.

Standard ACLs filter traffic based on the source IP address only. A typical best practice for standard ACLs is to configure and apply it as close to the destination as possible. For the first access list, create a standard numbered ACL that allows traffic from all hosts on the 192.168.10.0/24 network and all hosts on the 192.168.20.0/24 network to access all hosts on the 192.168.30.0/24 network. The security policy also states that a **deny any** access control entry (ACE), also referred to as an ACL statement, should be present at the end of all ACLs.

What wildcard mask would you use to allow all hosts on the 192.168.10.0/24 network to access the 192.168.30.0/24 network?

_____

Following Cisco's recommended best practices, on which router would you place this ACL?

_____

On which interface would you place this ACL? In what direction would you apply it?

_____

  a. Configure the ACL on R3. Use 1 for the access list number.

```
R3(config)# access-list 1 remark Allow R1 LANs Access
R3(config)# access-list 1 permit 192.168.10.0 0.0.0.255
R3(config)# access-list 1 permit 192.168.20.0 0.0.0.255
R3(config)# access-list 1 deny any
```

  b. Apply the ACL to the appropriate interface in the proper direction.

```
R3(config)# interface g0/1
R3(config-if)# ip access-group 1 out
```

  c. Verify a numbered ACL.

The use of various **show** commands can aid you in verifying both the syntax and placement of your ACLs in your router.

To see access list 1 in its entirety with all ACEs, which command would you use?

_____

What command would you use to see where the access list was applied and in what direction?

---

1) On R3, issue the **show access-lists 1** command.

```
R3# show access-list 1

Standard IP access list 1

    10 permit 192.168.10.0, wildcard bits 0.0.0.255

    20 permit 192.168.20.0, wildcard bits 0.0.0.255

    30 deny    any
```

2) On R3, issue the **show ip interface g0/1** command.

```
R3# show ip interface g0/1

GigabitEthernet0/1 is up, line protocol is up

  Internet address is 192.168.30.1/24

  Broadcast address is 255.255.255.255

  Address determined by non-volatile memory

  MTU is 1500 bytes

  Helper address is not set

  Directed broadcast forwarding is disabled

  Multicast reserved groups joined: 224.0.0.10

  Outgoing access list is 1

  Inbound access list is not set

  Output omitted
```

3) Test the ACL to see if it allows traffic from the 192.168.10.0/24 network access to the 192.168.30.0/24 network. From the PC-A command prompt, ping the PC-C IP address. Were the pings successful? _____

4) Test the ACL to see if it allows traffic from the 192.168.20.0/24 network access to the 192.168.30.0/24 network. You must do an extended ping and use the loopback 0 address on R1 as your source. Ping PC-C's IP address. Were the pings successful? _____

```
R1# ping

Protocol [ip]:

Target IP address: 192.168.30.3

Repeat count [5]:

Datagram size [100]:

Timeout in seconds [2]:

Extended commands [n]: y

Source address or interface: 192.168.20.1

Type of service [0]:

Set DF bit in IP header? [no]:

Validate reply data? [no]:

Data pattern [0xABCD]:
```

```
Loose, Strict, Record, Timestamp, Verbose[none]:

Sweep range of sizes [n]:

Type escape sequence to abort.

Sending 5, 100-byte ICMP Echos to 192.168.30.3, timeout is 2 seconds:

Packet sent with a source address of 192.168.20.1

!!!!!

Success rate is 100 percent (5/5), round-trip min/avg/max = 28/29/32 ms
```

d. From the R1 prompt, ping PC-C's IP address again.

```
R1# ping 192.168.30.3
```

Was the ping successful? Why or why not?

_____

_____

_____

Step 2: Configure a named standard ACL.

Create a named standard ACL that conforms to the following policy: allow traffic from all hosts on the 192.168.40.0/24 network access to all hosts on the 192.168.10.0/24 network. Also, only allow host PC-C access to the 192.168.10.0/24 network. The name of this access list should be called BRANCH-OFFICE-POLICY.

Following Cisco's recommended best practices, on which router would you place this ACL?

_____

On which interface would you place this ACL? In what direction would you apply it?

_____

a. Create the standard named ACL BRANCH-OFFICE-POLICY on R1.

```
R1(config)# ip access-list standard BRANCH-OFFICE-POLICY
R1(config-std-nacl)# permit host 192.168.30.3
R1(config-std-nacl)# permit 192.168.40.0 0.0.0.255
R1(config-std-nacl)# end
R1#
*Feb 15 15:56:55.707: %SYS-5-CONFIG_I: Configured from console by console
```

Looking at the first permit ACE in the access list, what is another way to write this?

_____

b. Apply the ACL to the appropriate interface in the proper direction.

```
R1# config t
R1(config)# interface g0/1
R1(config-if)# ip access-group BRANCH-OFFICE-POLICY out
```

c. Verify a named ACL.

1) On R1, issue the **show access-lists** command.

```
R1# show access-lists
Standard IP access list BRANCH-OFFICE-POLICY
    10 permit 192.168.30.3
    20 permit 192.168.40.0, wildcard bits 0.0.0.255
```

Is there any difference between this ACL on R1 with the ACL on R3? If so, what is it?

_____

_____

_____

_____

_____

2) On R1, issue the **show ip interface g0/1** command.

```
R1# show ip interface g0/1
GigabitEthernet0/1 is up, line protocol is up
  Internet address is 192.168.10.1/24
  Broadcast address is 255.255.255.255
  Address determined by non-volatile memory
  MTU is 1500 bytes
  Helper address is not set
  Directed broadcast forwarding is disabled
  Multicast reserved groups joined: 224.0.0.10
  Outgoing access list is BRANCH-OFFICE-POLICY
  Inbound access list is not set
<Output omitted>
```

3) Test the ACL. From the command prompt on PC-C, ping PC-A's IP address. Were the pings successful? _____

4) Test the ACL to ensure that only the PC-C host is allowed access to the 192.168.10.0/24 network. You must do an extended ping and use the G0/1 address on R3 as your source. Ping PC-A's IP address. Were the pings successful? _____

```
R3# ping
Protocol [ip]:
Target IP address: 192.168.10.3
Repeat count [5]:
Datagram size [100]:
Timeout in seconds [2]:
Extended commands [n]: y
Source address or interface: 192.168.30.1
Type of service [0]:
Set DF bit in IP header? [no]:
Validate reply data? [no]:
Data pattern [0xABCD]:
Loose, Strict, Record, Timestamp, Verbose[none]:
Sweep range of sizes [n]:
```

```
Type escape sequence to abort.

Sending 5, 100-byte ICMP Echos to 192.168.10.3, timeout is 2 seconds:

Packet sent with a source address of 192.168.30.1

U.U.U
```

5) Test the ACL to see if it allows traffic from the 192.168.40.0/24 network access to the 192.168.10.0/24 network. You must perform an extended ping and use the loopback 0 address on R3 as your source. Ping PC-A's IP address. Were the pings successful? _____

```
R3# ping

Protocol [ip]:

Target IP address: 192.168.10.3

Repeat count [5]:

Datagram size [100]:

Timeout in seconds [2]:

Extended commands [n]: y

Source address or interface: 192.168.40.1

Type of service [0]:

Set DF bit in IP header? [no]:

Validate reply data? [no]:

Data pattern [0xABCD]:

Loose, Strict, Record, Timestamp, Verbose[none]:

Sweep range of sizes [n]:

Type escape sequence to abort.

Sending 5, 100-byte ICMP Echos to 192.168.10.3, timeout is 2 seconds:

Packet sent with a source address of 192.168.40.1

!!!!!

Success rate is 100 percent (5/5), round-trip min/avg/max = 32/40/60 ms
```

Part 4: Modify a Standard ACL

It is common in business for security policies to change. For this reason, ACLs may need to be modified. In Part 4, you will change one of the previous ACLs you configured to match a new management policy being put in place.

Management has decided that users from the 209.165.200.224/27 network should be allowed full access to the 192.168.10.0/24 network. Management also wants ACLs on all of their routers to follow consistent rules. A **deny any** ACE should be placed at the end of all ACLs. You must modify the BRANCH-OFFICE-POLICY ACL.

You will add two additional lines to this ACL. There are two ways you could do this:

OPTION 1: Issue a **no ip access-list standard BRANCH-OFFICE-POLICY** command in global configuration mode. This would effectively take the whole ACL out of the router. Depending upon the router IOS, one of the following scenarios would occur: all filtering of packets would be cancelled and all packets would be allowed through the router; or, because you did not take off the **ip access-group** command on the G0/1 interface, filtering is still in place. Regardless, when the ACL is gone, you could retype the whole ACL, or cut and paste it in from a text editor.

OPTION 2: You can modify ACLs in place by adding or deleting specific lines within the ACL itself. This can come in handy, especially with ACLs that have many lines of code. The retyping of the whole ACL or cutting and pasting can easily lead to errors. Modifying specific lines within the ACL is easily accomplished.

Note: For this lab, use Option 2.

Step 1:   Modify a named standard ACL.

 a.   From R1 privileged EXEC mode, issue a **show access-lists** command.

```
R1# show access-lists
Standard IP access list BRANCH-OFFICE-POLICY
    10 permit 192.168.30.3 (8 matches)
    20 permit 192.168.40.0, wildcard bits 0.0.0.255 (5 matches)
```

 b.   Add two additional lines at the end of the ACL. From global config mode, modify the ACL, BRANCH-OFFICE-POLICY.

```
R1#(config)# ip access-list standard BRANCH-OFFICE-POLICY
R1(config-std-nacl)# 30 permit 209.165.200.224 0.0.0.31
R1(config-std-nacl)# 40 deny any
R1(config-std-nacl)# end
```

 c.   Verify the ACL.

  1)   On R1, issue the **show access-lists** command.

```
R1# show access-lists
Standard IP access list BRANCH-OFFICE-POLICY
    10 permit 192.168.30.3 (8 matches)
    20 permit 192.168.40.0, wildcard bits 0.0.0.255 (5 matches)
    30 permit 209.165.200.224, wildcard bits 0.0.0.31
    40 deny   any
```

  Do you have to apply the BRANCH-OFFICE-POLICY to the G0/1 interface on R1?

  _____

  _____

  2)   From the ISP command prompt, issue an extended ping. Test the ACL to see if it allows traffic from the 209.165.200.224/27 network access to the 192.168.10.0/24 network. You must do an extended ping and use the loopback 0 address on ISP as your source. Ping PC-A's IP address. Were the pings successful? _____

Reflection

 1.   As you can see, standard ACLs are very powerful and work quite well. Why would you ever have the need for using extended ACLs?

 _____

 _____

 _____

 _____

2. Typically, more typing is required when using a named ACL as opposed to a numbered ACL. Why would you choose named ACLs over numbered?

_____

_____

_____

_____

Router Interface Summary Table

	Router Interface Summary			
Router Model	**Ethernet Interface #1**	**Ethernet Interface #2**	**Serial Interface #1**	**Serial Interface #2**
1800	Fast Ethernet 0/0 (F0/0)	Fast Ethernet 0/1 (F0/1)	Serial 0/0/0 (S0/0/0)	Serial 0/0/1 (S0/0/1)
1900	Gigabit Ethernet 0/0 (G0/0)	Gigabit Ethernet 0/1 (G0/1)	Serial 0/0/0 (S0/0/0)	Serial 0/0/1 (S0/0/1)
2801	Fast Ethernet 0/0 (F0/0)	Fast Ethernet 0/1 (F0/1)	Serial 0/1/0 (S0/1/0)	Serial 0/1/1 (S0/1/1)
2811	Fast Ethernet 0/0 (F0/0)	Fast Ethernet 0/1 (F0/1)	Serial 0/0/0 (S0/0/0)	Serial 0/0/1 (S0/0/1)
2900	Gigabit Ethernet 0/0 (G0/0)	Gigabit Ethernet 0/1 (G0/1)	Serial 0/0/0 (S0/0/0)	Serial 0/0/1 (S0/0/1)

Note: To find out how the router is configured, look at the interfaces to identify the type of router and how many interfaces the router has. There is no way to effectively list all the combinations of configurations for each router class. This table includes identifiers for the possible combinations of Ethernet and Serial interfaces in the device. The table does not include any other type of interface, even though a specific router may contain one. An example of this might be an ISDN BRI interface. The string in parentheses is the legal abbreviation that can be used in Cisco IOS commands to represent the interface.

7.2.3.3 Packet Tracer–Configuring an IPv4 ACL on VTY Lines

Topology

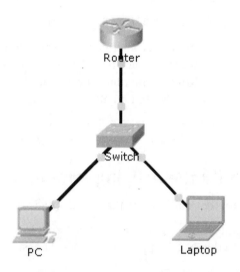

Addressing Table

Device	Interface	IP Address	Subnet Mask	Default Gateway
Router	F0/0	10.0.0.254	255.0.0.0	N/A
PC	NIC	10.0.0.1	255.0.0.0	10.0.0.254
Laptop	NIC	10.0.0.2	255.0.0.0	10.0.0.254

Objectives

Part 1: Configure and Apply an ACL to VTY Lines

Part 2: Verify the ACL Implementation

Background

As network administrator, you must have remote access to your router. This access should not be available to other users of the network. Therefore, you will configure and apply an access control list (ACL) that allows PC access to the Telnet lines, but denies all other source IP addresses.

Part 1: Configure and Apply an ACL to VTY Lines

Step 1:   Verify Telnet access before the ACL is configured.

Both computers should be able to Telnet to the **Router**. The password is **cisco**.

Step 2:   Configure a numbered standard ACL.

Configure the following numbered ACL on **Router**.

```
Router(config)# access-list 99 permit host 10.0.0.1
```

Because we do not want to permit access from any other computers, the implicit deny property of the access list satisfies our requirements.

Step 3:   Place a named standard ACL on the router.

Access to the **Router** interfaces must be allowed, while Telnet access must be restricted. Therefore, we must place the ACL on Telnet lines 0 through 4. From the configuration prompt of **Router**, enter line configuration mode for lines 0–4 and use the **access-class** command to apply the ACL to all the VTY lines:

```
Router(config)# line vty 0 15
Router(config-line)# access-class 99 in
```

Part 2: Verify the ACL Implementation

Step 1:   Verify the ACL configuration and application to the VTY lines.

Use the **show access-lists** to verify the ACL configuration. Use the **show run** command to verify the ACL is applied to the VTY lines.

Step 2:   Verify that the ACL is working properly.

Both computers should be able to ping the **Router**, but only **PC** should be able to Telnet to it.

7.2.3.4 Lab–Configuring and Verifying VTY Restrictions

Topology

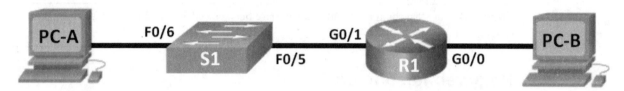

Addressing Table

Device	Interface	IP Address	Subnet Mask	Default Gateway
R1	G0/0	192.168.0.1	255.255.255.0	N/A
	G0/1	192.168.1.1	255.255.255.0	N/A
S1	VLAN 1	192.168.1.2	255.255.255.0	192.168.1.1
PC-A	NIC	192.168.1.3	255.255.255.0	192.168.1.1
PC-B	NIC	192.168.0.3	255.255.255.0	192.168.0.1

Objectives

Part 1: Configure Basic Device Settings

Part 2: Configure and Apply the Access Control List on R1

Part 3: Verify the Access Control List Using Telnet

Part 4: Challenge—Configure and Apply the Access Control List on S1

Background/Scenario

It is a good practice to restrict access to the router management interfaces, such as the console and vty lines. An access control list (ACL) can be used to allow access for specific IP addresses, ensuring that only the administrator PCs have permission to telnet or SSH into the router.

Note: In the Cisco device outputs, ACL is abbreviated as access-list.

In this lab, you will create and apply a named standard ACL to restrict remote access to the router vty lines.

After the ACL has been created and applied, you will test and verify the ACL by accessing the router from different IP addresses using Telnet.

This lab will provide the commands necessary for creating and applying the ACL.

Note: The routers used with CCNA hands-on labs are Cisco 1941 Integrated Services Routers (ISRs) with Cisco IOS Release 15.2(4)M3 (universalk9 image). The switches used are Cisco Catalyst 2960s with Cisco IOS Release 15.0(2) (lanbasek9 image). Other routers, switches, and Cisco IOS versions can be used. Depending on the model and Cisco IOS version, the commands available and output produced might vary from what is shown in the labs. Refer to the Router Interface Summary Table at the end of the lab for the correct interface identifiers.

Note: Make sure that the routers and switches have been erased and have no startup configurations. If you are unsure, contact your instructor.

Required Resources

- 1 Router (Cisco 1941 with Cisco IOS Release 15.2(4)M3 universal image or comparable)
- 1 Switch (Cisco 2960 with Cisco IOS Release 15.0(2) lanbasek9 image or comparable)
- 2 PCs (Windows 7, Vista, or XP with terminal emulation program, such as Tera Term)
- Console cables to configure the Cisco IOS devices via the console ports
- Ethernet cables as shown in the topology

Note: The Gigabit Ethernet interfaces on Cisco 1941 routers are autosensing and an Ethernet straight-through cable may be used between the router and PC-B. If using another model Cisco router, it may be necessary to use an Ethernet crossover cable.

Part 1: Configure Basic Device Settings

In Part 1, you will set up the network topology and configure the interface IP addresses, device access, and passwords on the router.

Step 1: Cable the network as shown in the topology diagram.

Step 2: Configure the PC-A and PC-B network settings according to the Addressing Table.

Step 3: Initialize and reload the router and switch.

    a. Console into the router and enter global configuration mode.

    b. Copy the following basic configuration and paste it to the running configuration on the router.

```
no ip domain-lookup
hostname R1
service password-encryption
enable secret class
banner motd #
Unauthorized access is strictly prohibited. #
Line con 0
password cisco
login
logging synchronous
line vty 0 4
password cisco
login
```

    c. Configure IP addresses on the interfaces listed in the Addressing Table.

d. Save the running configuration to the startup configuration file.

e. Console into the switch and enter global configuration mode.

f. Copy the following basic configuration and paste it to the running configuration on the switch.

```
no ip domain-lookup
hostname S1
service password-encryption
enable secret class
banner motd #
Unauthorized access is strictly prohibited. #
Line con 0
password cisco
login
logging synchronous
line vty 0 15
password cisco
login
exit
```

g. Configure IP address on VLAN1 interface listed in the Addressing Table.

h. Configure the default gateway for the switch.

i. Save the running configuration to the startup configuration file.

Part 2: Configure and Apply the Access Control List on R1

In Part 2, you will configure a named standard ACL and apply it to the router virtual terminal lines to restrict remote access to the router.

Step 1: Configure and apply a standard named ACL.

a. Console into the router R1 and enable privileged EXEC mode.

b. From global configuration mode, view the command options under **ip access-list** by using a space and a question mark.

```
R1(config)# ip access-list ?
  extended     Extended Access List
  helper       Access List acts on helper-address
  log-update   Control access list log updates
  logging      Control access list logging
  resequence   Resequence Access List
  standard     Standard Access List
```

c. View the command options under **ip access-list standard** by using a space and a question mark.

```
R1(config)# ip access-list standard ?
  <1-99>       Standard IP access-list number
  <1300-1999>  Standard IP access-list number (expanded range)
  WORD         Access-list name
```

d. Add **ADMIN-MGT** to the end of the **ip access-list standard** command and press Enter. You are now in the standard named access-list configuration mode (config-std-nacl).

```
R1(config)# ip access-list standard ADMIN-MGT
R1(config-std-nacl)#
```

e. Enter your ACL permit or deny access control entry (ACE), also known as an ACL statement, one line at a time. Remember that there is an implicit **deny any** at the end of the ACL, which effectively denies all traffic. Enter a question mark to view your command options.

```
R1(config-std-nacl)# ?
Standard Access List configuration commands:
  <1-2147483647>  Sequence Number
  default         Set a command to its defaults
  deny            Specify packets to reject
  exit            Exit from access-list configuration mode
  no              Negate a command or set its defaults
  permit          Specify packets to forward
  remark          Access list entry comment
```

f. Create a permit ACE for Administrator PC-A at 192.168.1.3 and an additional permit ACE to allow other reserved administrative IP addresses from 192.168.1.4 to 192.168.1.7. Notice how the first permit ACE signifies a single host by using the **host** keyword. The ACE **permit 192.168.1.3 0.0.0.0** could have been used instead. The second permit ACE allows hosts 192.168.1.4 through 192.168.1.7, by using the 0.0.0.3 wildcard, which is the inverse of a 255.255.255.252 subnet mask.

```
R1(config-std-nacl)# permit host 192.168.1.3
R1(config-std-nacl)# permit 192.168.1.4 0.0.0.3
R1(config-std-nacl)# exit
```

You do not need to enter a deny ACE because there is an implicit **deny any** ACE at the end of the ACL.

g. Now that the named ACL is created, apply it to the vty lines.

```
R1(config)# line vty 0 15
R1(config-line)# access-class ADMIN-MGT in
R1(config-line)# exit
```

Part 3: Verify the Access Control List Using Telnet

In Part 3, you will use Telnet to access the router, verifying that the named ACL is functioning correctly.

Note: SSH is more secure than Telnet; however, SSH requires that the network device be configured to accept SSH connections. Telnet is used with this lab for convenience.

a. Open a command prompt on PC-A and verify that you can communicate with the router by issuing a **ping** command.

```
C:\Users\user1> ping 192.168.1.1

Pinging 192.168.1.1 with 32 bytes of data:
Reply from 192.168.1.1: bytes=32 time=5ms TTL=64
Reply from 192.168.1.1: bytes=32 time=1ms TTL=64
Reply from 192.168.1.1: bytes=32 time=1ms TTL=64
Reply from 192.168.1.1: bytes=32 time=1ms TTL=64
```

```
Ping statistics for 192.168.1.1:
    Packets: Sent = 4, Received = 4, Lost = 0 (0% loss),
Approximate round trip times in milli-seconds:
    Minimum = 1ms, Maximum = 5ms, Average = 2ms
C:\Users\user1>
```

b. Using the command prompt on PC-A, launch the Telnet client program to telnet into the router. Enter the login and then the enable passwords. You should be successfully logged in, see the banner message, and receive an R1 router command prompt.

```
C:\Users\user1> telnet 192.168.1.1

Unauthorized access is prohibited!

User Access Verification

Password:
R1>enable
Password:
R1#
```

Was the Telnet connection successful? _____

c. Type **exit** at the command prompt and press Enter to exit the Telnet session.

d. Change your IP address to test if the named ACL blocks non-permitted IP addresses. Change the IPv4 address to 192.168.1.100 on PC-A.

e. Attempt to telnet into R1 at 192.168.1.1 again. Was the Telnet session successful?

_____

What message was received? _____

f. Change the IP address on PC-A to test if the named ACL permits a host with an IP address from the 192.168.1.4 to 192.168.1.7 range to telnet into the router. After changing the IP address on PC-A, open a Windows command prompt and attempt to telnet into router R1.

Was the Telnet session successful?

_____

_____

g. From privileged EXEC mode on R1, type the **show ip access-lists** command and press Enter. From the command output, notice how the Cisco IOS automatically assigns line numbers to the ACL ACEs in increments of 10 and shows the number of times each permit ACE has been successfully matched (in parentheses).

```
R1# show ip access-lists
Standard IP access list ADMIN-MGT
    10 permit 192.168.1.3 (2 matches)
    20 permit 192.168.1.4, wildcard bits 0.0.0.3 (2 matches)
```

Because two successful Telnet connections to the router were established, and each Telnet session was initiated from an IP address that matches one of the permit ACEs, there are matches for each permit ACE.

Why do you think that there are two matches for each permit ACE when only one connection from each IP address was initiated?

_____

_____

_____

_____

How would you determine at what point the Telnet protocol causes the two matches during the Telnet connection?

_____

_____

_____

h. On R1, enter into global configuration mode.

i. Enter into access-list configuration mode for the ADMIN-MGT named access list and add a **deny any** ACE to the end of the access list.

```
R1(config)# ip access-list standard ADMIN-MGT
R1(config-std-nacl)# deny any
R1(config-std-nacl)# exit
```

Note: Because there is an implicit **deny any** ACE at the end of all ACLs, adding an explicit **deny any** ACE is unnecessary. However, the explicit **deny any** at the end of the ACL can still be useful to the network administrator to log or simply know how many times the **deny any** access-list ACE was matched.

j. Try to telnet from PC-B to R1. This creates a match to the **deny any** ACE in the ADMIN-MGT named access list.

k. From privileged EXEC mode, type **show ip access-lists** command and press Enter. You should now see multiple matches to the **deny any** ACE.

```
R1# show ip access-lists
Standard IP access list ADMIN-MGT
    10 permit 192.168.1.3 (2 matches)
    20 permit 192.168.1.4, wildcard bits 0.0.0.3 (2 matches)
    30 deny any (3 matches)
```

The failed Telnet connection produces more matches to the explicit deny ACE than a successful one. Why do you think this happens?

_____

_____

Part 4: Challenge–Configure and Apply the Access Control List on S1

Step 1:   Configure and apply a standard named ACL for the vty lines on S1.

a. Without referring back to the R1 configuration commands, try to configure the ACL on S1, allowing only the PC-A IP address.

b. Apply the ACL to the S1 vty lines. Remember that there are more vty lines on a switch than a router.

Step 2:   Test the vty ACL on S1.

Telnet from each of the PCs to verify that the vty ACL is working properly. You should be able to telnet to S1 from PC-A, but not from PC-B.

Reflection

1. As evidenced by the remote vty access, ACLs are powerful content filters that can be applied to more than just inbound and outbound network interfaces. What other ways might ACLs be applied?

   _____

   _____

2. Does an ACL applied to a vty remote management interface improve the security of Telnet connection? Does this make Telnet a more viable remote access management tool?

   _____

   _____

   _____

3. Why does it make sense to apply an ACL to vty lines instead of specific interfaces?

   _____

   _____

   _____

Router Interface Summary Table

Router Interface Summary				
Router Model	Ethernet Interface #1	Ethernet Interface #2	Serial Interface #1	Serial Interface #2
1800	Fast Ethernet 0/0 (F0/0)	Fast Ethernet 0/1 (F0/1)	Serial 0/0/0 (S0/0/0)	Serial 0/0/1 (S0/0/1)
1900	Gigabit Ethernet 0/0 (G0/0)	Gigabit Ethernet 0/1 (G0/1)	Serial 0/0/0 (S0/0/0)	Serial 0/0/1 (S0/0/1)
2801	Fast Ethernet 0/0 (F0/0)	Fast Ethernet 0/1 (F0/1)	Serial 0/1/0 (S0/1/0)	Serial 0/1/1 (S0/1/1)
2811	Fast Ethernet 0/0 (F0/0)	Fast Ethernet 0/1 (F0/1)	Serial 0/0/0 (S0/0/0)	Serial 0/0/1 (S0/0/1)
2900	Gigabit Ethernet 0/0 (G0/0)	Gigabit Ethernet 0/1 (G0/1)	Serial 0/0/0 (S0/0/0)	Serial 0/0/1 (S0/0/1)

Note: To find out how the router is configured, look at the interfaces to identify the type of router and how many interfaces the router has. There is no way to effectively list all the combinations of configurations for each router class. This table includes identifiers for the possible combinations of Ethernet and Serial interfaces in the device. The table does not include any other type of interface, even though a specific router may contain one. An example of this might be an ISDN BRI interface. The string in parentheses is the legal abbreviation that can be used in Cisco IOS commands to represent the interface.

7.3.2.4 Packet Tracer–Troubleshooting Standard IPv4 ACLs

Topology

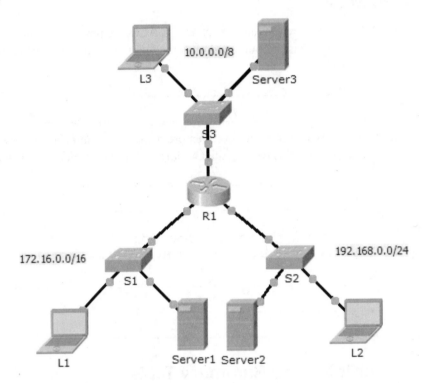

Addressing Table

Device	Interface	IP Address	Subnet Mask	Default Gateway
R1	G0/0	10.0.0.1	255.0.0.0	N/A
	G0/1	172.16.0.1	255.255.0.0	N/A
	G0/2	192.168.0.1	255.255.255.0	N/A
Server1	NIC	172.16.255.254	255.255.0.0	172.16.0.1
Server2	NIC	192.168.0.254	255.255.255.0	192.168.0.1
Server3	NIC	10.255.255.254	255.0.0.0	10.0.0.1
L1	NIC	172.16.0.2	255.255.0.0	172.16.0.1
L2	NIC	192.168.0.2	255.255.255.0	192.168.0.1
L3	NIC	10.0.0.2	255.0.0.0	10.0.0.1

Objectives

Part 1: Troubleshoot ACL Issue 1

Part 2: Troubleshoot ACL Issue 2

Part 3: Troubleshoot ACL Issue 3

Scenario

This network is meant to have the following three policies implemented:

- Hosts from the 192.168.0.0/24 network are unable to access network 10.0.0.0/8.

- L3 can't access any devices in network 192.168.0.0/24.

- L3 can't access **Server1** or **Server2**. L3 should only access **Server3**.

- Hosts from the 172.16.0.0/16 network have full access to **Server1**, **Server2** and **Server3**.

Note: All FTP usernames and passwords are "cisco".

No other restrictions should be in place. Unfortunately, the rules that have been implemented are not working correctly. Your task is to find and fix the errors related to the access lists on **R1**.

Part 1: Troubleshoot ACL Issue 1

Hosts from the 192.168.0.0/24 network should not be able to access any devices on the 10.0.0.0/8 network. This is not currently the case.

Step 1:   Determine the ACL problem.

As you perform the following tasks, compare the results to what you would expect from the ACL.

a.   Using **L2**, attempt to access FTP and HTTP services of **Server1**, **Server2**, and **Server3**.

b.   Using **L2**, ping **Server1**, **Server2**, and **Server3**.

c.   View the running configuration on **R1**. Examine access list **FROM_192** and its placement on the interfaces. Is the access list placed on the correct interface and in the correct direction? Is there any statement in the list that permits or denies traffic to other networks? Are the statements in the correct order?

d.   Perform other tests, as necessary.

Step 2:   Implement a solution.

Make the necessary adjustments to **FROM_192**, or to its placement, to fix the problem.

Step 3:   Verify that the problem is resolved and document the solution.

If the problem is resolved, document the solution; otherwise return to Step 1.

Part 2: Troubleshoot ACL Issue 2

L3 should not be able to reach **Server1** or **Server2**. This is not currently the case.

Step 1:   Determine the ACL problem.

As you perform the following tasks, compare the results to what you would expect from the ACL.

a.   Using **L3**, attempt to access FTP and HTTP services of **Server1**, **Server2**, and **Server3**.

b.   Using **L3**, ping **Server1**, **Server2**, and **Server3**.

    c. View the running configuration on **R1**. Examine access list **FROM_10** and its placement on the interfaces. Is the access list placed on the correct interface and in the correct direction? Is there any statement in the list that permits or denies traffic to other networks? Are the statements in the correct order?

    d. Run other tests as necessary.

Step 2:   Implement a solution.

Make the necessary adjustments to access list **FROM_10,** or to its placement, to fix the problem.

Step 3:   Verify the problem is resolved and document the solution.

If the problem is resolved, document the solution; otherwise return to Step 1.

_____

_____

Part 3: Troubleshoot ACL Issue 3

Hosts from the 172.16.0.0/16 network should have full access to **Server1**, **Server2** and **Server3** but this is not currently the case, as **L1** can't communicate to **Server2** or **Server3**.

Step 1:   Determine the ACL problem.

As you perform the following tasks, compare the results to the expectations of the ACL.

    a. Using **L1**, attempt to access FTP and HTTP services of **Server1**, **Server2**, and **Server3**.

    b. Using **L1**, ping **Server1**, **Server2**, and **Server3**.

    c. View the running configuration on **R1**. Examine access list **FROM_172** and its placement on the interfaces. Is the access list placed on the correct port in the correct direction? Is there any statement in the list that permits or denies traffic to other networks? Are the statements in the correct order?

    d. Run other tests as necessary.

Step 2:   Implement a solution.

Make an adjustment to access list **FROM_172** or to its placements to fix the problem.

Step 3:   Verify the problem is resolved and document the solution.

If the problem is resolved, document the solution; otherwise return to Step 1.

_____

_____

Part 4: Reflection (Optional)

Access-lists pose a logical problem that often has more than one solution. Can you think of a different set of rules or placements that would yield the same required access filtering?

_____

Suggested Scoring Rubric

Question Location	Possible Points	Earned Points
Documentation Score	10	
Packet Tracer Score	90	
Total Score	100	

7.3.2.5 Lab–Troubleshooting Standard IPv4 ACL Configuration and Placement

Topology

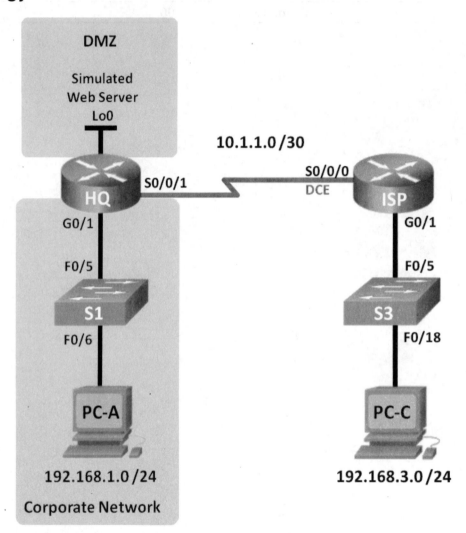

Addressing Table

Device	Interface	IP Address	Subnet Mask	Default Gateway
HQ	G0/1	192.168.1.1	255.255.255.0	N/A
	S0/0/1	10.1.1.2	255.255.255.252	N/A
	Lo0	192.168.4.1	255.255.255.0	N/A
ISP	G0/1	192.168.3.1	255.255.255.0	N/A
	S0/0/0 (DCE)	10.1.1.1	255.255.255.252	N/A
S1	VLAN 1	192.168.1.11	255.255.255.0	192.168.1.1
S3	VLAN 1	192.168.3.11	255.255.255.0	192.168.3.1
PC-A	NIC	192.168.1.3	255.255.255.0	192.168.1.1
PC-C	NIC	192.168.3.3	255.255.255.0	192.168.3.1

Objectives

Part 1: Build the Network and Configure Basic Device Settings

Part 2: Troubleshoot Internal Access

Part 3: Troubleshoot Remote Access

Background/Scenario

An access control list (ACL) is a series of IOS commands that can provide basic traffic filtering on a Cisco router. ACLs are used to select the types of traffic to be processed. A single ACL statement is called an access control entry (ACE). The ACEs in the ACL are evaluated from top to bottom with an implicit deny all ACE at the end of the list. ACLs can also control the types of traffic into or out of a network by the source and destination hosts or network. To process the desired traffic correctly, the placement of the ACL is critical.

In this lab, a small company has added a web server to the network to allow customers to access confidential information. The company network is divided into two zones: corporate network zone and demilitarized zone (DMZ). The corporate network zone houses private servers and internal clients. The DMZ houses the externally accessible web server (simulated by Lo0 on HQ). Because the company can only administer its own HQ router, all ACLs must be applied to the HQ router.

- ACL 101 is implemented to limit the traffic out of the corporate network zone. This zone houses the private servers and internal clients (192.168.1.0/24). No other network should be able to access it.

- ACL 102 is used to limit the traffic into the corporate network. Only responses to requests that originated from within the corporate network are allowed back into that network. This includes TCP-based requests from internal hosts such as Web and FTP. ICMP is allowed into the network for troubleshooting purposes, so that incoming ICMP messages generated in response to pings can be received by internal hosts.

- ACL 121 controls outside traffic to the DMZ and corporate network. Only HTTP traffic is allowed to the DMZ web server (simulated by Lo0 on R1). Other network related traffic, such as RIP, is allowed from outside networks. Furthermore, valid internal private addresses, such as 192.168.1.0, loopback addresses, such as 127.0.0.0, and multicast addresses are denied entrance to the corporate network to prevent malicious network attacks from outside users.

Note: The routers used with CCNA hands-on labs are Cisco 1941 Integrated Services Routers (ISRs) with Cisco IOS Release 15.2(4)M3 (universalk9 image). The switches used are Cisco Catalyst 2960s with Cisco IOS Release 15.0(2) (lanbasek9 image). Other routers, switches and Cisco IOS versions can be used. Depending on the model and Cisco IOS version, the commands available and output produced might vary from what is shown in the labs. Refer to the Router Interface Summary Table at the end of the lab for the correct interface identifiers.

Note: Make sure that the routers and switches have been erased and have no startup configurations. If you are unsure, contact your instructor.

Required Resources

- 2 Routers (Cisco 1941 with Cisco IOS Release 15.2(4)M3 universal image or comparable)

- 2 Switches (Cisco 2960 with Cisco IOS Release 15.0(2) lanbasek9 image or comparable)

- 2 PCs (Windows 7, Vista, or XP with terminal emulation program, such as Tera Term)
- Console cables to configure the Cisco IOS devices via the console ports
- Ethernet and serial cables as shown in the topology

Part 1: Build the Network and Configure Basic Device Settings

In Part 1, you set up the network topology and configure the routers and switches with some basic settings, such as passwords and IP addresses. Preset configurations are also provided for the initial router configurations. You will also configure the IP settings for the PCs in the topology.

Step 1: Cable the network as shown in the topology.

Step 2: Configure PC hosts.

Step 3: Initialize and reload the routers and switches as necessary.

Step 4: (Optional) Configure basic settings for each switch.

    a. Console into the switch and enter global configuration mode.

    b. Copy the following basic configuration and paste it to the running configuration on each switch.

```
no ip domain-lookup
service password-encryption
enable secret class
banner motd #
Unauthorized access is strictly prohibited. #
Line con 0
password cisco
login
logging synchronous
line vty 0 15
password cisco
login
exit
```

    c. Configure host names as shown in the Topology.

    d. Configure IP address and default gateway in the Addressing Table.

    e. Copy the running configuration to the startup configuration.

Step 5: Configure basic settings for each router.

    a. Console into the router and enter global configuration mode.

    b. Copy the following basic configuration and paste it to the running configuration on the router.

```
no ip domain-lookup
service password-encryption
enable secret class
banner motd #
Unauthorized access is strictly prohibited. #
Line con 0
password cisco
login
```

```
                    logging synchronous
                    line vty 0 4
                    password cisco
                    login
```

    c.   Configure the host name as shown in the topology.

    d.   Copy the running configuration to the startup configuration.

Step 6:   Configure HTTP access and user credentials on HQ router.

Local user credentials are configured to access the simulated web server (192.168.4.1).

```
HQ(config)# ip http server
HQ(config)# username admin privilege 15 secret adminpass
HQ(config)# ip http authentication local
```

Step 7:   Load additional router configurations.

The configurations for the routers ISP and HQ are provided for you. There are errors within these configurations, and it is your job to determine the incorrect configurations and correct them.

Router ISP

```
hostname ISP
interface GigabitEthernet0/1
 ip address 192.168.3.1 255.255.255.0
 no shutdown
interface Serial0/0/0
 ip address 10.1.1.1 255.255.255.252
 clock rate 128000
 no shutdown
router rip
 version 2
 network 10.1.1.0
 network 192.168.3.0
 no auto-summary
end
```

Router HQ

```
hostname HQ
interface Loopback0
 ip address 192.168.4.1 255.255.255.0
interface GigabitEthernet0/1
 ip address 192.168.1.1 255.255.255.0
 ip access-group 101 out

 ip access-group 102 in

 no shutdown
interface Serial0/0/1
 ip address 10.1.1.2 255.255.255.252
```

```
        ip access-group 121 in
        no shutdown
router rip
 version 2
 network 10.1.1.0
 network 192.168.1.0
 network 192.168.4.0
 no auto-summary
access-list 101 permit ip 192.168.11.0 0.0.0.255 any

access-list 101 deny ip any any
access-list 102 permit tcp any any established
access-list 102 permit icmp any any echo-reply
access-list 102 permit icmp any any unreachable
access-list 102 deny ip any any
access-list 121 permit tcp any host 192.168.4.1 eq 89

access-list 121 deny icmp any host 192.168.4.11

access-list 121 deny ip 192.168.1.0 0.0.0.255 any
access-list 121 deny ip 127.0.0.0 0.255.255.255 any
access-list 121 deny ip 224.0.0.0 31.255.255.255 any
access-list 121 permit ip any any
access-list 121 deny ip any any
end
```

Part 2: Troubleshoot Internal Access

In Part 2, the ACLs on router HQ are examined to determine if they are configured correctly.

Step 1: Troubleshoot ACL 101

ACL 101 is implemented to limit the traffic out of the corporate network zone. This zone houses only internal clients and private servers. Only 192.168.1.0/24 network can exit this corporate network zone.

a. Can PC-A ping its default gateway? _____

b. After verifying that the PC-A was configured correctly, examine the HQ router to find possible configuration errors by viewing the summary of ACL 101. Enter the command **show access-lists 101.**

```
HQ# show access-lists 101
Extended IP access list 101
    10 permit ip 192.168.11.0 0.0.0.255 any
    20 deny ip any any
```

c. Are there any problems with ACL 101?

d. Examine the default gateway interface for the 192.168.1.0 /24 network. Verify that the ACL 101 is applied in the correct direction on the G0/1 interface. Enter the **show ip interface g0/1** command.

```
HQ# show ip interface g0/1
GigabitEthernet0/1 is up, line protocol is up
  Internet address is 192.168.1.1/24
  Broadcast address is 255.255.255.255
  Address determined by setup command
  MTU is 1500 bytes
  Helper address is not set
  Directed broadcast forwarding is disabled
  Multicast reserved groups joined: 224.0.0.10
  Outgoing access list is 101
  Inbound  access list is 102
```

Is the direction for interface G0/1 configured correctly for ACL 101?

_____

e. Correct the errors found regarding ACL 101 and verify the traffic from network 192.168.1.0 /24 can exit the corporate network. Record the commands used to correct the errors.

_____

_____

_____

_____

_____

f. Verify PC-A can ping its default gateway interface.

Step 2: Troubleshoot ACL 102

ACL 102 is implemented to limit traffic into the corporate network. Traffic originating from the outside network is not allowed onto the corporate network. Remote traffic is allowed into the corporate network if the established traffic originated from the internal network. ICMP reply messages are allowed for troubleshooting purposes.

a. Can PC-A ping PC-C? _____

b. Examine the HQ router to find possible configuration errors by viewing the summary of ACL 102. Enter the command **show access-lists 102**.

```
HQ# show access-lists 102
Extended IP access list 102
    10 permit tcp any any established
    20 permit icmp any any echo-reply
    30 permit icmp any any unreachable
    40 deny ip any any (57 matches)
```

c. Are there any problems with ACL 102?

_____

d. Verify that the ACL 102 is applied in the correct direction on G0/1 interface. Enter the **show ip interface g0/1** command.

```
HQ# show ip interface g0/1
GigabitEthernet0/1 is up, line protocol is up
   Internet address is 192.168.1.1/24
   Broadcast address is 255.255.255.255
   Address determined by setup command
   MTU is 1500 bytes
   Helper address is not set
   Directed broadcast forwarding is disabled
   Multicast reserved groups joined: 224.0.0.10
   Outgoing access list is 101
   Inbound  access list is 101
```

e. Are there any problems with the application of ACL 102 to interface G0/1?

_____

f. Correct any errors found regarding ACL 102. Record the commands used to correct the errors.

_____

_____

g. Can PC-A ping PC-C now? _____

Part 3: Troubleshoot Remote Access

In Part 3, ACL 121 is configured to prevent spoofing attacks from the outside networks and allow only remote HTTP access to the web server (192.168.4.1) in DMZ.

a. Verify ACL 121 has been configured correctly. Enter the **show ip access-list 121** command.

```
HQ# show ip access-lists 121
Extended IP access list 121
    10 permit tcp any host 192.168.4.1 eq 89
    20 deny icmp any host 192.168.4.11
    30 deny ip 192.168.1.0 0.0.0.255 any
    40 deny ip 127.0.0.0 0.255.255.255 any
    50 deny ip 224.0.0.0 31.255.255.255 any
    60 permit ip any any (354 matches)
    70 deny ip any any
```

Are there any problems with this ACL?

_____

_____

b. Verify that the ACL 121 is applied in the correct direction on the R1 S0/0/1 interface. Enter the **show ip interface s0/0/1** command.

```
HQ# show ip interface s0/0/1
Serial0/0/1 is up, line protocol is up
   Internet address is 10.1.1.2/30
   Broadcast address is 255.255.255.255
<output omitted>
```

```
Multicast reserved groups joined: 224.0.0.10
Outgoing access list is not set
Inbound  access list is 121
```

Are there any problems with the application of this ACL?

_____

_____

c. If any errors were found, make and record the necessary configuration changes to ACL 121.

_____

_____

_____

_____

_____

d. Verify that PC-C can only access the simulated web server on HQ by using the web browser. Provide the username **admin** and password **adminpass** to access the web server (192.168.4.1).

Reflection

1. How should the ACL statement be ordered? From general to specific or vice versa?

_____

2. If you delete an ACL by using the **no access-list** command and the ACL is still applied to the interface, what happens? _____

Router Interface Summary Table

Router Interface Summary				
Router Model	Ethernet Interface #1	Ethernet Interface #2	Serial Interface #1	Serial Interface #2
1800	Fast Ethernet 0/0 (F0/0)	Fast Ethernet 0/1 (F0/1)	Serial 0/0/0 (S0/0/0)	Serial 0/0/1 (S0/0/1)
1900	Gigabit Ethernet 0/0 (G0/0)	Gigabit Ethernet 0/1 (G0/1)	Serial 0/0/0 (S0/0/0)	Serial 0/0/1 (S0/0/1)
2801	Fast Ethernet 0/0 (F0/0)	Fast Ethernet 0/1 (F0/1)	Serial 0/1/0 (S0/1/0)	Serial 0/1/1 (S0/1/1)
2811	Fast Ethernet 0/0 (F0/0)	Fast Ethernet 0/1 (F0/1)	Serial 0/0/0 (S0/0/0)	Serial 0/0/1 (S0/0/1)
2900	Gigabit Ethernet 0/0 (G0/0)	Gigabit Ethernet 0/1 (G0/1)	Serial 0/0/0 (S0/0/0)	Serial 0/0/1 (S0/0/1)

Note: To find out how the router is configured, look at the interfaces to identify the type of router and how many interfaces the router has. There is no way to effectively list all the combinations of configurations for each router class. This table includes identifiers for the possible combinations of Ethernet and Serial interfaces in the device. The table does not include any other type of interface, even though a specific router may contain one. An example of this might be an ISDN BRI interface. The string in parentheses is the legal abbreviation that can be used in Cisco IOS commands to represent the interface.

7.4.1.1 Lab–FTP Denied

Objective

Implement packet filtering using extended IPv4 ACLs according to networking requirements (to include named and numbered ACLs).

Scenario

It was recently reported that viruses are on the rise within your small- to medium-sized business network. Your network administrator has been tracking network performance and has determined that one particular host is constantly downloading files from a remote FTP server. This host just may be the virus source perpetuating throughout the network!

Use Packet Tracer to complete this activity. Write a <u>named</u> ACL to deny the host access to the FTP server. Apply the ACL to the most effective interface on the router.

To complete the physical topology, you must use:

- One PC host station

- Two switches

- One Cisco 1941 series Integrated Services Router

- One server

Using the Packet Tracer text tool, record the ACL you prepared. Validate that the ACL works to deny access to the FTP server by trying to access the FTP server's address. Observe what happens while in simulation mode.

Save your file and be prepared to share it with another student, or with the entire class.

Reflection

1. What was the most difficult part of completing this modeling activity?

_____

2. How often do you think network administrators need to change their ACLs on their networks?

_____

3. Why would you consider using a named extended ACL instead of a regular extended ACL?

_____

7.4.1.2 Packet Tracer–Skills Integration Challenge

Topology

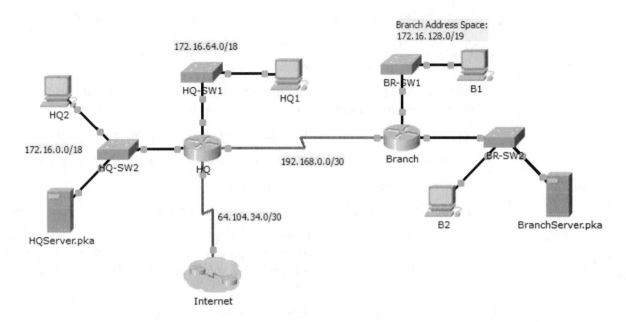

Addressing Table

Device	Interface	IP Address	Subnet Mask	Default Gateway
HQ	G0/0	172.16.127.254	255.255.192.0	N/A
	G0/1	172.16.63.254	255.255.192.0	N/A
	S0/0/0	192.168.0.1	255.255.255.252	N/A
	S0/0/1	64.104.34.2	255.255.255.252	64.104.34.1
Branch	G0/0			N/A
	G0/1			N/A
	S0/0/0	192.168.0.2	255.255.255.252	N/A
HQ1	NIC	172.16.64.1	255.255.192.0	172.16.127.254
HQ2	NIC	172.16.0.2	255.255.192.0	172.16.63.254
HQServer.pka	NIC	172.16.0.1	255.255.192.0	172.16.63.254
B1	NIC			
B2	NIC	172.16.128.2	255.255.240.0	172.16.143.254
BranchServer.pka	NIC	172.16.128.1	255.255.240.0	172.16.143.254

Scenario

In this challenge activity, you will finish the addressing scheme, configure routing, and implement named access control lists.

Requirements

a. Divide 172.16.128.0/19 into two equal subnets for use on **Branch**.

Assign the last usable address of the second subnet to the Gigabit Ethernet 0/0 interface.

Assign the last usable address of the first subnet to the Gigabit Ethernet 0/1 interface.

Document the addressing in the Addressing Table.

Configure **Branch** with appropriate addressing

b. Configure **B1** with appropriate addressing using the first available address of the network to which it is attached. Document the addressing in the Addressing Table.

c. Configure **HQ** and **Branch** with RIPv2 routing according to the following criteria:

- Advertise all three attached networks. Do not advertise the link to the Internet.

- Configure appropriate interfaces as passive.

d. Set a default route on **HQ** that directs traffic to S0/0/1 interface. Redistribute the route to **Branch**.

e. Design a named access list **HQServer** to prevent any computers attached to the Gigabit Ethernet 0/0 interface of the **Branch** router from accessing **HQServer.pka**. All other traffic is permitted. Configure the access list on the appropriate router, apply it to the appropriate interface and in the appropriate direction.

f. Design a named access list **BranchServer** to prevent any computers attached to the Gigabit Ethernet 0/0 interface of the **HQ** router from accessing the **Branch** server. All other traffic is permitted. Configure the access list on the appropriate router, apply it to the appropriate interface and in the appropriate direction.

Every device that connects to a network needs a unique IP address. Because computers and users in an organization often change locations, managing static IP address assignments can be difficult and time consuming. Although some devices should always be statically assigned IP addressing information, Dynamic Host Configuration Protocol (DHCP) installed on a server helps manage the addressing of the majority of devices in the enterprise. DHCP is available for both IPv4 (DHCPv4) and IPv6 (DHCPv6).

The Study Guide portion of this chapter uses a combination of matching, fill-in-the-blank, multiple-choice, and open-ended question exercises to test your knowledge and skills of basic DHCP concepts and configuration. The Labs and Activities portion of this chapter includes all the online curriculum labs and Packet Tracer activities to ensure that you have mastered the hands-on skills needed to understand basic IP addressing and router configuration.

As you work through this chapter, use Chapter 8 in *Routing and Switching Essentials v6 Companion Guide* or use the corresponding Chapter 8 in the Routing and Switching Essentials online curriculum for assistance.

Study Guide

Dynamic Host Configuration Protocol v4

DHCPv4 assigns IPv4 addresses and other network configuration information dynamically. Because desktop clients usually make up the bulk of network nodes, DHCPv4 is an extremely useful and time-saving tool for network administrators.

DHCPv4 Operation

DHCPv4 uses four messages between the DHCP server and a client set to use DHCP for IPv4 addressing configuration. In Figure 8-1, label each DHCP message type sent between the server and client when originating a lease.

Figure 8-1   DHCPv4 Lease-Origination Operation

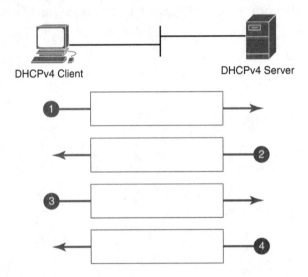

Configuring a Cisco Device as a DHCPv4 Server

Use the following steps to configure a Cisco router or switch to act as a DHCPv4 server:

Step 1.   Exclude statically assigned IPv4 addresses.

Typically, some IPv4 addresses in a pool are assigned to network devices that require static address assignments. To exclude these addresses, use the **ip dhcp excluded-address** *first-address* [*last-address*] global configuration command.

Step 2.   Configure a DHCPv4 pool name.

Use the **ip dhcp pool** *pool-name* global configuration command to create a pool with the specified name. The router will then be in DHCPv4 configuration mode as indicated by the prompt changing to Router(dhcp-config)#.

Step 3.   Configure the DHCPv4 pool settings.

Some settings are required and others are optional. In Table 8-1, record the command syntax for the two required DHCPv4 settings and four optional DHCPv4 settings.

Table 8-1   DHCPv4 Pool Settings

Required Tasks	Command Syntax
Define the address pool.	
Define the default router or gateway.	

Optional Tasks	Command Syntax
Define a DNS server.	
Define a domain name.	
Define the duration of the DHCP lease.	
Define the NetBIOS WINS server.	

Refer to Figure 8-2. Record the commands to configure R1 as the DHCP server for the 172.16.1.0/24 LAN. Exclude the first ten IP addresses. Use an appropriate name. Include a setting for the DNS server and the domain R1.com.

Figure 8-2   DHCPv4 Configuration Topology

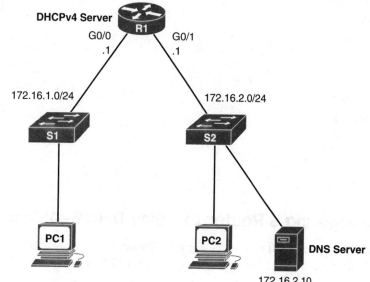

```
R1(config)# _____

_____

_____

_____

_____

_____
```

To verify DHCP settings, use the **show run** command to see the configuration. There are also two other DHCP show commands you can use. Record the commands that display the following information:

```
R1# _____

Bindings from all pools not associated with VRF:
IP address          Client-ID/            Lease expiration      Type
                    Hardware address/
                    User name
172.16.1.11         0100.5056.be8e.bb     Jul 05 2011 12:35 AM  Automatic
```

```
R1# _____

Memory usage              49491

Address pools             1

Database agents           0

Automatic bindings        3

Manual bindings           0

Expired bindings          0

Malformed messages        0

Secure arp entries        0


Message                   Received

BOOTREQUEST               0

DHCPDISCOVER              3

DHCPREQUEST               3

DHCPDECLINE               0

DHCPRELEASE               0

DHCPINFORM                6


Message                   Sent

BOOTREPLY                 0

DHCPOFFER                 3

DHCPACK                   9

DHCPNAK                   0

R1#
```

Configuring a Router to Relay DHCPv4 Requests

Refer to Figure 8-3. It is just like Figure 8-2 except that now there is a DHCP server on the 172.16.2.0/24 LAN that provides addressing services to both 172.16.1.0/24 and 172.16.2.0/24.

Figure 8-3   DHCPv4 Topology with a Dedicated DHCPv4 Server

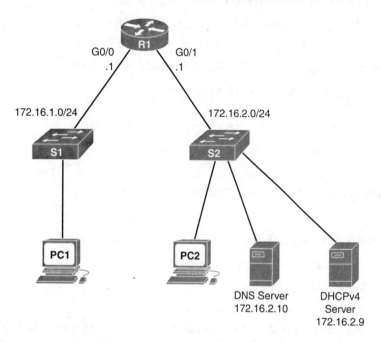

Assume the DHCP pool for 172.16.1.0/24 has been removed from R1. Record the commands to configure R1 to send DHCP requests to the new DHCP server.

```
R1(config)# _____
_____
```

What eight UDP services does this command forward?

_____

_____

Configuring a Router as a DHCPv4 Client

Commonly, routers receive IP addressing from a DHCP server. This is particularly true in small office/home office (SOHO) networks. Refer to Figure 8-4. Record the commands to configure SOHO to request IPv4 addressing for its G0/1 interface.

Figure 8-4   Configuring a Router as a DHCPv4 Client

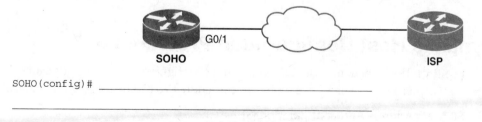

```
SOHO(config)# _____
_____
_____
```

Troubleshooting DHCPv4

DHCPv4 problems are most commonly the result of configuration issues. Because of the number of potentially problematic areas, use a systematic approach to troubleshooting.

Troubleshooting Task 1: Resolve IPv4 Address Conflicts

Why might an address conflict occur?

_____

_____

_____

What command will display DHCP address conflicts?

SOHO# _____

Troubleshooting Task 2: Verify Physical Connectivity

What commands are helpful to ensure interfaces are active?

SOHO# _____

SOHO# _____

Troubleshooting Task 3: Test Connectivity Using a Static IP Address

When troubleshooting any DHCPv4 issue, verify network connectivity by configuring static IPv4 address information on a client workstation. If the workstation is unable to reach network resources with a statically configured IPv4 address, the root cause of the problem is not DHCPv4. At this point, network connectivity troubleshooting is required.

Troubleshooting Task 4: Verify Switch Port Configuration

What are some potential reasons why a switch in between the DHCPv4 server and client might be the cause of the problem?

_____

Troubleshooting Task 5: Test DHCPv4 Operation on the Same Subnet or VLAN

It is important to distinguish whether DHCPv4 is functioning correctly when the client is on the same subnet or VLAN as the DHCPv4 server. If DHCPv4 is working correctly when the client is on the same subnet or VLAN, the problem may be the DHCP relay agent. If the problem persists even with testing DHCPv4 on the same subnet or VLAN as the DHCPv4 server, the problem may actually be with the DHCPv4 server.

Dynamic Host Configuration Protocol v6

Similar to IPv4, IPv6 global unicast addresses can be configured manually or dynamically. However, there are two methods in which IPv6 global unicast addresses can be assigned dynamically:

- Stateless Address Autoconfiguration (SLAAC)
- Dynamic Host Configuration Protocol for IPv6 (stateful DHCPv6)

SLAAC and DHCPv6

SLAAC uses ICMPv6 Router Solicitation and Router Advertisement messages to provide addressing and other configuration information that would normally be provided by a DHCP server. Briefly describe these two messages.

_____

_____

_____

_____

_____

Explain the two ways a client can create its own unique interface ID from the information in an RA.

_____

_____

After the client creates an interface ID, what process does it use to ensure that it is unique?

_____

_____

_____

A router will always respond to an RS from a client. However, the RA message reply can have one of three options for the client. Briefly describe these three options.

_____

_____

_____

_____

_____

_____

What are the default values for the M and O flags in the RA message, and what do they mean?

_____

What is the command to configure an interface for stateless DHCPv6?

_____

What does this command do to the RA message?

_____

What is the command to configure an interface for stateful DHCPv6?

_____

What does this command do to the RA message?

_____

In Figure 8-5, label each DHCPv6 message type sent between the server and client when originating a lease.

Figure 8-5 DHCPv6 Lease-Origination Operation

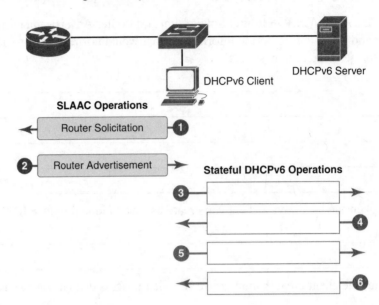

Configuring a Router as a Stateless DHCPv6 Server

To configure a router as a DHCPv6 server, you must complete four steps:

Step 1. Enable IPv6 routing.

The **ipv6 unicast-routing** command is required before the router will send ICMPv6 RA messages.

Step 2. Configure a DHCPv6 pool.

Use the **ipv6 dhcp pool** *pool-name* global configuration command to create a pool and enter DHCPv6 configuration mode, which is identified by the Router(config-dhcpv6)# prompt.

Step 3. Configure the DHCPv6 settings.

The stateless DHCPv6 server can be configured to provide other information that might not have been included in the RA message such as DNS server address (**dns-server** *dns-server*) and the domain name (**domain-name** *domain-name*).

Step 4. Configure the DHCPv6 interface.

Bind the pool to the interface with the **ipv6 dhcp server** *pool-name* command, and change the O flag with the **ipv6 nd other-config-flag** command.

Refer to Figure 8-6. Record the commands to configure R1 as the DHCPv6 server for the 2001:DB8:1:1::/64 LAN. Use an appropriate name. Include a setting for the DNS server and the domain R1.com.

Figure 8-6   DHCPv6 Configuration Topology

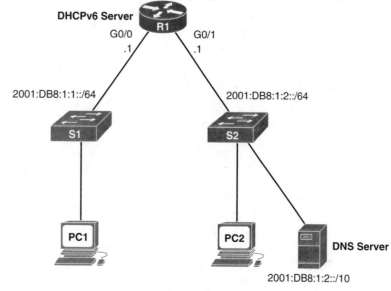

```
R1(config)# _____

_____

_____

_____

_____

_____

_____
```

What are the commands to configure a router interface as a DHCPv6 client?

_____

_____

Configuring a Router as a Stateful DHCPv6 Server

Configuring a router as a stateful DHCPv6 server is similar to configuring a stateless server. The most significant difference is that a stateful server also includes IPv6 addressing information similar to a DHCPv4 server and you set the M flag instead of the O flag.

What is the command to define the DHCPv6 pool with IPv6 addressing information?

_____

_____

For the previous configuration, add the commands to configure the IPv6 addressing information for infinite lifetime, set the O flag back to 0, and set the M flag to 1.

```
R1(config)# _____

_____

_____

_____

_____

_____
```

If the DHCPv6 server is located on a different network than the client, you can configure the IPv6 router as a DHCPv6 relay agent. What is the command to configure a router as a DHCPv6 relay agent?

_____

Labs and Activities

Command Reference

In Table 8-2, record the command, including the correct router or switch prompt, that fits the description. Fill in any blanks with the appropriate missing information.

Table 8-2   Commands for Chapter 8, "DHCP"

Command	Description
	Exclude the IP address range 10.1.1.1 to 10.1.1.10 from the DHCP pool.
	Create a DHCPv4 pool named MYPOOL.
	Define the network 10.1.1.0/24 as the address pool.
	Set 10.1.1.1 as the gateway for a host that belongs to the 10.1.1.0/24 network.
	Set the domain to mydomain.com.
	Set the DNS server to 10.1.1.10.
	Set the lease to never expire.
	Display the current IPv4 addresses that are assigned from the pool.
	Display DHCPv4 server statistics.
	Configure the interface to relay DHCP requests to 10.1.1.5.
	Configure the interface to request IPv4 addressing information from a DHCPv4 server.
	Display any current DHCPv4 address conflicts.
	Create a DHCPv6 pool named STATELESS.
	Configure the interface to use STATELESS as the DHCPv6 pool.
	Configure the interface for stateless DHCPv6.
	Create a DHCPv6 pool named STATEFUL.
	Define the network 2001:DB8:10:10::/64 as the address pool with an infinite lifetime.
	Configure the interface for stateful DHCPv6.
	Display the current IPv6 addresses that are assigned from the pool.
	Configure the interface to relay DHCPv6 requests to 2001:DB8:10:10::5.

8.1.2.4 Lab–Configuring Basic DHCPv4 on a Router

Topology

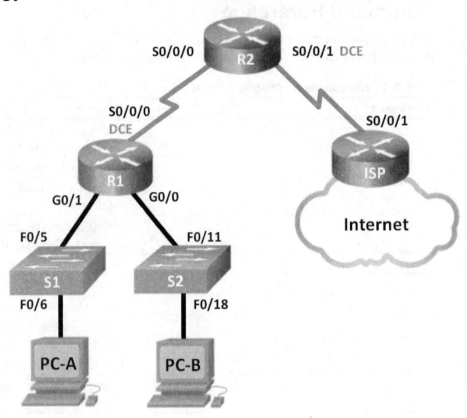

Addressing Table

Device	Interface	IP Address	Subnet Mask	Default Gateway
R1	G0/0	192.168.0.1	255.255.255.0	N/A
	G0/1	192.168.1.1	255.255.255.0	N/A
	S0/0/0 (DCE)	192.168.2.253	255.255.255.252	N/A
R2	S0/0/0	192.168.2.254	255.255.255.252	N/A
	S0/0/1 (DCE)	209.165.200.226	255.255.255.224	N/A
ISP	S0/0/1	209.165.200.225	255.255.255.224	N/A
PC-A	NIC	DHCP	DHCP	DHCP
PC-B	NIC	DHCP	DHCP	DHCP

Objectives

Part 1: Build the Network and Configure Basic Device Settings

Part 2: Configure a DHCPv4 Server and a DHCP Relay Agent

Background/Scenario

The Dynamic Host Configuration Protocol (DHCP) is a network protocol that lets network administrators manage and automate the assignment of IP addresses. Without DHCP, the administrator must manually assign and configure IP addresses, preferred DNS servers, and default gateways. As the network grows in size, this becomes an administrative problem when devices are moved from one internal network to another.

In this scenario, the company has grown in size, and the network administrators can no longer assign IP addresses to devices manually. Your job is to configure the R2 router to assign IPv4 addresses on two different subnets connected to router R1.

Note: This lab provides minimal assistance with the actual commands necessary to configure DHCP. However, the required commands are provided in Appendix A. Test your knowledge by trying to configure the devices without referring to the appendix.

Note: The routers used with CCNA hands-on labs are Cisco 1941 Integrated Services Routers (ISRs) with Cisco IOS Release 15.2(4)M3 (universalk9 image). The switches used are Cisco Catalyst 2960s with Cisco IOS Release 15.0(2) (lanbasek9 image). Other routers, switches and Cisco IOS versions can be used. Depending on the model and Cisco IOS version, the commands available and output produced might vary from what is shown in the labs. Refer to the Router Interface Summary Table at the end of this lab for the correct interface identifiers.

Note: Make sure that the routers and switches have been erased and have no startup configurations. If you are unsure, contact your instructor.

Required Resources

- 3 Routers (Cisco 1941 with Cisco IOS Release 15.2(4)M3 universal image or comparable)
- 2 Switches (Cisco 2960 with Cisco IOS Release 15.0(2) lanbasek9 image or comparable)
- 2 PCs (Windows 7, Vista, or XP with terminal emulation program, such as Tera Term)
- Console cables to configure the Cisco IOS devices via the console ports
- Ethernet and serial cables as shown in the topology

Part 1: Build the Network and Configure Basic Device Settings

In Part 1, you will set up the network topology and configure the routers and switches with basic settings, such as passwords and IP addresses. You will also configure the IP settings for the PCs in the topology.

Step 1: Cable the network as shown in the topology.

Step 2: Initialize and reload the routers and switches.

Step 3: Configure basic settings for each router.

    a. Console into the router and enter global configuration mode.

    b. Copy the following basic configuration and paste it to the running-configuration on the router.

```
no ip domain-lookup
service password-encryption
```

```
enable secret class
banner motd #
Unauthorized access is strictly prohibited. #
line con 0
password cisco
login
logging synchronous
line vty 0 4
password cisco
login
```

c. Configure the host name as shown in the topology.

d. Configure the IPv4 addresses on the router as shown in the topology.

e. Set the DCE serial interfaces with a clock rate of 128000.

Step 4: Configure dynamic, default, and static routing on the routers.

a. Configure RIPv2 for R1.

```
R1(config)# router rip
R1(config-router)# version 2
R1(config-router)# network 192.168.0.0
R1(config-router)# network 192.168.1.0
R1(config-router)# network 192.168.2.252
R1(config-router)# no auto-summary
```

b. Configure RIPv2 and a default route to the ISP on R2.

```
R2(config)# router rip
R1(config-router)# version 2
R2(config-router)# network 192.168.2.252
R2(config-router)# default-information originate
R2(config-router)# exit
R2(config)# ip route 0.0.0.0 0.0.0.0 209.165.200.225
```

c. Configure a summary static route on ISP to reach the networks on the R1 and R2 routers.

```
ISP(config)# ip route 192.168.0.0 255.255.252.0 209.165.200.226
```

d. Copy the running configuration to the startup configuration.

Step 5: Verify network connectivity between the routers.

If any pings between routers fail, correct the errors before proceeding to the next step. Use **show ip route** and **show ip interface brief** to locate possible issues.

Step 6: Verify the host PCs are configured for DHCP.

Part 2: Configure a DHCPv4 Server and a DHCP Relay Agent

To automatically assign address information on the network, you will configure R2 as a DHCPv4 server and R1 as a DHCP relay agent.

Step 1: Configure DHCPv4 server settings on router R2.

On R2, you will configure a DHCP address pool for each of the R1 LANs. Use the pool name **R1G0** for the G0/0 LAN and **R1G1** for the G0/1 LAN. You will also configure the addresses to be excluded from the address pools. Best practice dictates that excluded addresses be configured first, to guarantee that they are not accidentally leased to other devices.

Exclude the first 9 addresses in each R1 LAN starting with .1. All other addresses should be available in the DHCP address pool. Make sure that each DHCP address pool includes a default gateway, the domain **ccna-lab.com**, a DNS server (209.165.200.225), and a lease time of 2 days.

On the lines below, write the commands necessary for configuring DHCP services on router R2, including the DHCP-excluded addresses and the DHCP address pools.

Note: The required commands for Part 2 are provided in Appendix A. Test your knowledge by trying to configure DHCP on R1 and R2 without referring to the appendix.

_____

_____

_____

_____

_____

_____

_____

_____

_____

_____

_____

_____

_____

_____

_____

On PC-A or PC-B, open a command prompt and enter the **ipconfig /all** command. Did either of the host PCs receive an IP address from the DHCP server? Why?

_____

Step 2:   Configure R1 as a DHCP relay agent.

Configure IP helper addresses on R1 to forward all DHCP requests to the R2 DHCP server.

On the lines below, write the commands necessary to configure R1 as a DHCP relay agent for the R1 LANs.

_____

_____

_____

_____

Step 3:   Record IP settings for PC-A and PC-B.

On PC-A and PC-B, issue the **ipconfig /all** command to verify that the PCs have received IP address information from the DHCP server on R2. Record the IP and MAC address for each PC.

_____

Based on the DHCP pool that was configured on R2, what are the first available IP addresses that PC-A and PC-B can lease?

_____

Step 4:   Verify DHCP services and address leases on R2.

    a.   On R2, enter the **show ip dhcp binding** command to view DHCP address leases.

        Along with the IP addresses that were leased, what other piece of useful client identification information is in the output?

        _____

    b.   On R2, enter the **show ip dhcp server statistics** command to view the DHCP pool statistics and message activity.

        How many types of DHCP messages are listed in the output?

        _____

    c.   On R2, enter the **show ip dhcp pool** command to view the DHCP pool settings.

        In the output of the **show ip dhcp pool** command, what does the current index refer to?

        _____

    d.   On R2, enter the **show run | section dhcp** command to view the DHCP configuration in the running configuration.

    e.   On R1, enter the **show run interface** command for interfaces G0/0 and G0/1 to view the DHCP relay configuration in the running configuration.

Reflection

What do you think is the benefit of using DHCP relay agents instead of multiple routers acting as DHCP servers?

_____

_____

_____

_____

Router Interface Summary Table

Router Model	Ethernet Interface #1	Ethernet Interface #2	Serial Interface #1	Serial Interface #2
1800	Fast Ethernet 0/0 (F0/0)	Fast Ethernet 0/1 (F0/1)	Serial 0/0/0 (S0/0/0)	Serial 0/0/1 (S0/0/1)
1900	Gigabit Ethernet 0/0 (G0/0)	Gigabit Ethernet 0/1 (G0/1)	Serial 0/0/0 (S0/0/0)	Serial 0/0/1 (S0/0/1)
2801	Fast Ethernet 0/0 (F0/0)	Fast Ethernet 0/1 (F0/1)	Serial 0/1/0 (S0/1/0)	Serial 0/1/1 (S0/1/1)
2811	Fast Ethernet 0/0 (F0/0)	Fast Ethernet 0/1 (F0/1)	Serial 0/0/0 (S0/0/0)	Serial 0/0/1 (S0/0/1)
2900	Gigabit Ethernet 0/0 (G0/0)	Gigabit Ethernet 0/1 (G0/1)	Serial 0/0/0 (S0/0/0)	Serial 0/0/1 (S0/0/1)

Note: To find out how the router is configured, look at the interfaces to identify the type of router and how many interfaces the router has. There is no way to effectively list all the combinations of configurations for each router class. This table includes identifiers for the possible combinations of Ethernet and Serial interfaces in the device. The table does not include any other type of interface, even though a specific router may contain one. An example of this might be an ISDN BRI interface. The string in parentheses is the legal abbreviation that can be used in Cisco IOS commands to represent the interface.

Appendix A – DHCP Configuration Commands

Router R1

```
R1(config)# interface g0/0
R1(config-if)# ip helper-address 192.168.2.254
R1(config-if)# exit
R1(config-if)# interface g0/1
R1(config-if)# ip helper-address 192.168.2.254
```

Router R2

```
R2(config)# ip dhcp excluded-address 192.168.0.1 192.168.0.9
R2(config)# ip dhcp excluded-address 192.168.1.1 192.168.1.9
R2(config)# ip dhcp pool R1G1
R2(dhcp-config)# network 192.168.1.0 255.255.255.0
R2(dhcp-config)# default-router 192.168.1.1
R2(dhcp-config)# dns-server 209.165.200.225
R2(dhcp-config)# domain-name ccna-lab.com
R2(dhcp-config)# lease 2
R2(dhcp-config)# exit
R2(config)# ip dhcp pool R1G0
R2(dhcp-config)# network 192.168.0.0 255.255.255.0
R2(dhcp-config)# default-router 192.168.0.1
R2(dhcp-config)# dns-server 209.165.200.225
R2(dhcp-config)# domain-name ccna-lab.com
R2(dhcp-config)# lease 2
```

8.1.2.5 Lab–Configuring Basic DHCPv4 on a Switch

Topology

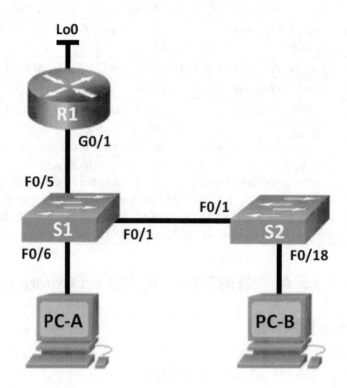

Addressing Table

Device	Interface	IP Address	Subnet Mask
R1	G0/1	192.168.1.10	255.255.255.0
	Lo0	209.165.200.225	255.255.255.224
S1	VLAN 1	192.168.1.1	255.255.255.0
	VLAN 2	192.168.2.1	255.255.255.0

Objectives

Part 1: Build the Network and Configure Basic Device Settings

Part 2: Change the SDM Preference

■ Set the SDM preference to lanbase-routing on S1.

Part 3: Configure DHCPv4

■ Configure DHCPv4 for VLAN 1.

■ Verify DHCPv4 and connectivity.

Part 4: Configure DHCP for Multiple VLANs

- Assign ports to VLAN 2.
- Configure DHCPv4 for VLAN 2.
- Verify DHCPv4 and connectivity.

Part 5: Enable IP Routing

- Enable IP routing on the switch.
- Create static routes.

Background/Scenario

A Cisco 2960 switch can function as a DHCPv4 server. The Cisco DHCPv4 server assigns and manages IPv4 addresses from identified address pools that are associated with specific VLANs and switch virtual interfaces (SVIs). The Cisco 2960 switch can also function as a Layer 3 device and route between VLANs and a limited number of static routes. In this lab, you will configure DHCPv4 for both single and multiple VLANs on a Cisco 2960 switch, enable routing on the switch to allow for communication between VLANs, and add static routes to allow for communication between all hosts.

Note: This lab provides minimal assistance with the actual commands necessary to configure DHCP. However, the required commands are provided in Appendix A. Test your knowledge by trying to configure the devices without referring to the appendix.

Note: The routers used with CCNA hands-on labs are Cisco 1941 Integrated Services Routers (ISRs) with Cisco IOS Release 15.2(4)M3 (universalk9 image). The switches used are Cisco Catalyst 2960s with Cisco IOS Release 15.0(2) (lanbasek9 image). Other routers, switches and Cisco IOS versions can be used. Depending on the model and Cisco IOS version, the commands available and output produced might vary from what is shown in the labs. Refer to the Router Interface Summary Table at the end of this lab for the correct interface identifiers.

Note: Make sure that the router and switches have been erased and have no startup configurations. If you are unsure, contact your instructor.

Required Resources

- 1 Router (Cisco 1941 with Cisco IOS Release 15.2(4)M3 universal image or comparable)
- 2 Switches (Cisco 2960 with Cisco IOS Release 15.0(2) lanbasek9 image or comparable)
- 2 PCs (Windows 7, Vista, or XP with terminal emulation program, such as Tera Term)
- Console cables to configure the Cisco IOS devices via the console ports
- Ethernet cables as shown in the topology

Part 1: Build the Network and Configure Basic Device Settings

Step 1:   Cable the network as shown in the topology.

Step 2:   Initialize and reload the router and switches.

Step 3: Configure basic setting on devices.

    a. Console into the router and enter global configuration mode.

    b. Copy the following basic configuration and paste it to the running-configuration on the router.

```
no ip domain-lookup
service password-encryption
enable secret class
banner motd #
Unauthorized access is strictly prohibited. #
line con 0
password cisco
login
logging synchronous
line vty 0 4
password cisco
login
```

    c. Console into the switches and enter global configuration mode.

    d. Copy the following basic configuration and paste it to the running-configuration on the switches.

```
no ip domain-lookup
service password-encryption
enable secret class
banner motd #
Unauthorized access is strictly prohibited. #
line con 0
password cisco
login
logging synchronous
line vty 0 15
password cisco
login
exit
```

    e. Assign device names as shown in the topology.

    f. Configure the IP addresses on R1 G0/1 and Lo0 interfaces, according to the Addressing Table.

    g. Configure the IP addresses on S1 VLAN 1 and VLAN 2 interfaces, according to the Addressing Table.

    h. Save the running configuration to the startup configuration file.

Part 2: Change the SDM Preference

The Cisco Switch Database Manager (SDM) provides multiple templates for the Cisco 2960 switch. The templates can be enabled to support specific roles depending on how the switch is used in the network. In this lab, the sdm lanbase-routing template is enabled to allow the switch to route between VLANs and to support static routing.

Step 1:   Display the SDM preference on S1.

On S1, issue the **show sdm prefer** command in privileged EXEC mode. If the template has not been changed from the factory default, it should still be the **default** template. The **default** template does not support static routing. If IPv6 addressing has been enabled, the template will be **dual-ipv4-and-ipv6 default**.

```
S1# show sdm prefer
The current template is "default" template.
The selected template optimizes the resources in
the switch to support this level of features for
0 routed interfaces and 255 VLANs.

  number of unicast mac addresses:              8K
  number of IPv4 IGMP groups:                   0.25K
  number of IPv4/MAC qos aces:                  0.125k
  number of IPv4/MAC security aces:             0.375k
```

What is the current template? _____

Step 2:   Change the SDM Preference on S1.

a.   Set the SDM preference to **lanbase-routing**. (If lanbase-routing is the current template, please proceed to Part 3.) From global configuration mode, issue the **sdm prefer lanbase-routing** command.

```
S1(config)# sdm prefer lanbase-routing
Changes to the running SDM preferences have been stored, but cannot take effect
until the next reload.
Use 'show sdm prefer' to see what SDM preference is currently active.
```

Which template will be available after reload? _____

b.   The switch must be reloaded for the template to be enabled.

```
S1# reload

System configuration has been modified. Save? [yes/no]: no
Proceed with reload? [confirm]
```

Note: The new template will be used after reboot even if the running configuration has not been saved. To save the running configuration, answer yes to save the modified system configuration.

Step 3:   Verify the lanbase-routing template is loaded.

Issue the **show sdm prefer** command to verify that the lanbase-routing template has been loaded on S1.

```
S1# show sdm prefer
The current template is "lanbase-routing" template.
The selected template optimizes the resources in
the switch to support this level of features for
0 routed interfaces and 255 VLANs.

  number of unicast mac addresses:              4K
  number of IPv4 IGMP groups + multicast routes: 0.25K
```

```
number of IPv4 unicast routes:                0.75K
  number of directly-connected IPv4 hosts:    0.75K
  number of indirect IPv4 routes:             16
number of IPv6 multicast groups:              0.375k
number of directly-connected IPv6 addresses:  0.75K
  number of indirect IPv6 unicast routes:     16
number of IPv4 policy based routing aces:     0
number of IPv4/MAC qos aces:                  0.125k
number of IPv4/MAC security aces:             0.375k
number of IPv6 policy based routing aces:     0
number of IPv6 qos aces:                      0.375k
number of IPv6 security aces:                 127
```

Part 3: Configure DHCPv4

In Part 3, you will configure DHCPv4 for VLAN 1, check IP settings on host computers to validate DHCP functionality, and verify connectivity for all devices in VLAN 1.

Step 1: Configure DHCP for VLAN 1.

    a. Exclude the first 10 valid host addresses from network 192.168.1.0/24. Write the command you used in the space provided.

    _____

    b. Create a DHCP pool named **DHCP1**. Write the command you used in the space provided.

    _____

    c. Assign the network 192.168.1.0/24 for available addresses. Write the command you used in the space provided.

    _____

    d. Assign the default gateway as 192.168.1.1. Write the command you used in the space provided.

    _____

    e. Assign the DNS server as 192.168.1.9. Write the command you used in the space provided.

    _____

    f. Assign a lease time of 3 days. Write the command you used in the space provided.

    _____

    g. Save the running configuration to the startup configuration file.

Step 2: Verify DHCP and connectivity.

    a. On PC-A and PC-B, open the command prompt and issue the **ipconfig** command. If IP information is not present, or if it is incomplete, issue the **ipconfig /release** command, followed by the **ipconfig /renew** command.

For PC-A, list the following:

IP Address: _____

Subnet Mask: _____

Default Gateway: _____

For PC-B, list the following:

IP Address: _____

Subnet Mask: _____

Default Gateway: _____

b. Test connectivity by pinging from PC-A to the default gateway, PC-B, and R1.

From PC-A, is it possible to ping the VLAN 1 default gateway? _____

From PC-A, is it possible to ping PC-B? _____

From PC-A, is it possible to ping R1 G0/1? _____

If the answer is no to any of these questions, troubleshoot the configurations and correct the error.

Part 4: Configure DHCPv4 for Multiple VLANs

In Part 4, you will assign PC-A to a port accessing VLAN 2, configure DHCPv4 for VLAN 2, renew the IP configuration of PC-A to validate DHCPv4, and verify connectivity within the VLAN.

Step 1: Assign a port to VLAN 2.

Place port F0/6 into VLAN 2. Write the command you used in the space provided.

_____

_____

Step 2: Configure DHCPv4 for VLAN 2

a. Exclude the first 10 valid host addresses from network 192.168.2.0. Write the command you used in the space provided.

_____

b. Create a DHCP pool named **DHCP2**. Write the command you used in the space provided.

_____

c. Assign the network 192.168.2.0/24 for available addresses. Write the command you used in the space provided.

_____

d. Assign the default gateway as 192.168.2.1. Write the command you used in the space provided.

_____

e. Assign the DNS server as 192.168.2.9. Write the command you used in the space provided.

_____

f. Assign a lease time of 3 days. Write the command you used in the space provided.

_____

g. Save the running configuration to the startup configuration file.

Step 3: Verify DHCPv4 and connectivity.

a. On PC-A, open the command prompt and issue the **ipconfig /release** command, followed by the **ipconfig /renew** command.

For PC-A, list the following:

IP Address: _____

Subnet Mask: _____

Default Gateway: _____

b. Test connectivity by pinging from PC-A to the VLAN 2 default gateway and PC-B.

From PC-A, is it possible to ping the default gateway? _____

From PC-A, is it possible to ping PC-B? _____

Were these pings successful? Why?

_____

_____

c. Issue the **show ip route** command on S1.

What was the result of this command?

_____

_____

Part 5: Enable IP Routing

In Part 5, you will enable IP routing on the switch, which will allow for inter-VLAN communication. For all networks to communicate, static routes on S1 and R1 must be implemented.

Step 1: Enable IP routing on S1.

a. From global configuration mode, use the **ip routing** command to enable routing on S1.

```
S1(config)# ip routing
```

b. Verify inter-VLAN connectivity.

From PC-A, is it possible to ping PC-B? _____

What function is the switch performing?

_____

    c. View the routing table information for S1.

    What route information is contained in the output of this command?

_____

_____

    d. View the routing table information for R1.

    What route information is contained in the output of this command?

_____

_____

    e. From PC-A, is it possible to ping R1? _____

    From PC-A, is it possible to ping Lo0? _____

    Consider the routing table of the two devices, what must be added to communicate between all networks?

_____

Step 2: Assign static routes.

Enabling IP routing allows the switch to route between VLANs assigned on the switch. For all VLANs to communicate with the router, static routes must be added to the routing table of both the switch and the router.

    a. On S1, create a default static route to R1. Write the command you used in the space provided.

_____

    b. On R1, create a static route to VLAN 2. Write the command you used in the space provided.

_____

    c. View the routing table information for S1.

    How is the default static route represented?

_____

    d. View the routing table information for R1.

    How is the static route represented?

_____

    e. From PC-A, is it possible to ping R1? _____

    From PC-A, is it possible to ping Lo0? _____

Reflection

  1. In configuring DHCPv4, why would you exclude the static addresses prior to setting up the DHCPv4 pool?

_____

_____

2. If multiple DHCPv4 pools are present, how does the switch assign the IP information to hosts?

3. Besides switching, what functions can the Cisco 2960 switch perform?

Router Interface Summary Table

Router Interface Summary				
Router Model	Ethernet Interface #1	Ethernet Interface #2	Serial Interface #1	Serial Interface #2
1800	Fast Ethernet 0/0 (F0/0)	Fast Ethernet 0/1 (F0/1)	Serial 0/0/0 (S0/0/0)	Serial 0/0/1 (S0/0/1)
1900	Gigabit Ethernet 0/0 (G0/0)	Gigabit Ethernet 0/1 (G0/1)	Serial 0/0/0 (S0/0/0)	Serial 0/0/1 (S0/0/1)
2801	Fast Ethernet 0/0 (F0/0)	Fast Ethernet 0/1 (F0/1)	Serial 0/1/0 (S0/1/0)	Serial 0/1/1 (S0/1/1)
2811	Fast Ethernet 0/0 (F0/0)	Fast Ethernet 0/1 (F0/1)	Serial 0/0/0 (S0/0/0)	Serial 0/0/1 (S0/0/1)
2900	Gigabit Ethernet 0/0 (G0/0)	Gigabit Ethernet 0/1 (G0/1)	Serial 0/0/0 (S0/0/0)	Serial 0/0/1 (S0/0/1)

Note: To find out how the router is configured, look at the interfaces to identify the type of router and how many interfaces the router has. There is no way to effectively list all the combinations of configurations for each router class. This table includes identifiers for the possible combinations of Ethernet and Serial interfaces in the device. The table does not include any other type of interface, even though a specific router may contain one. An example of this might be an ISDN BRI interface. The string in parentheses is the legal abbreviation that can be used in Cisco IOS commands to represent the interface.

Appendix A: Configuration Commands

Configure DHCPv4

```
S1(config)# ip dhcp excluded-address 192.168.1.1 192.168.1.10
S1(config)# ip dhcp pool DHCP1
S1(dhcp-config)# network 192.168.1.0 255.255.255.0
S1(dhcp-config)# default-router 192.168.1.1
S1(dhcp-config)# dns-server 192.168.1.9
S1(dhcp-config)# lease 3
```

Configure DHCPv4 for Multiple VLANs

```
S1(config)# interface f0/6
S1(config-if)# switchport access vlan 2
S1(config)# ip dhcp excluded-address 192.168.2.1 192.168.2.10
S1(config)# ip dhcp pool DHCP2
S1(dhcp-config)# network 192.168.2.0 255.255.255.0
S1(dhcp-config)# default-router 192.168.2.1
S1(dhcp-config)# dns-server 192.168.2.9
S1(dhcp-config)# lease 3
```

Enable IP Routing

```
S1(config)# ip routing
S1(config)# ip route 0.0.0.0 0.0.0.0 192.168.1.10
R1(config)# ip route 192.168.2.0 255.255.255.0 g0/1
```

8.1.3.3 Packet Tracer–Configuring DHCP Using Cisco IOS

Topology

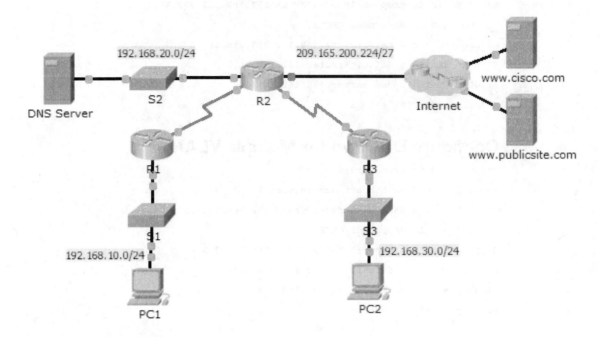

Addressing Table

Device	Interface	IPv4 Address	Subnet Mask	Default Gateway
R1	G0/0	192.168.10.1	255.255.255.0	N/A
	S0/0/0	10.1.1.1	255.255.255.252	N/A
R2	G0/0	192.168.20.1	255.255.255.0	N/A
	G0/1	DHCP Assigned	DHCP Assigned	N/A
	S0/0/0	10.1.1.2	255.255.255.252	N/A
	S0/0/1	10.2.2.2	255.255.255.252	N/A
R3	G0/0	192.168.30.1	255.255.255.0	N/A
	S0/0/1	10.2.2.1	255.255.255.0	N/A
PC1	NIC	DHCP Assigned	DHCP Assigned	DHCP Assigned
PC2	NIC	DHCP Assigned	DHCP Assigned	DHCP Assigned
DNS Server	NIC	192.168.20.254	255.255.255.0	192.168.20.1

Objectives

Part 1: Configure a Router as a DHCP Server

Part 2: Configure DHCP Relay

Part 3: Configure a Router as a DHCP Client

Part 4: Verify DHCP and Connectivity

Scenario

A dedicated DHCP server is scalable and relatively easy to manage, but it can be costly to have one at every location in a network. However, a Cisco router can be configured to provide DHCP services without the need for a dedicated server. As the network technician for your company, you are tasked with configuring a Cisco router as a DHCP server to provide dynamic allocation of addresses to clients on the network. You are also required to configure the edge router as a DHCP client so that it receives an IP address from the ISP network.

Part 1: Configure a Router as a DHCP Server

Step 1:   Configure the excluded IPv4 addresses.

Configure **R2** to exclude the first 10 addresses from the R1 and R3 LANs. All other addresses should be available in the DHCP address pool.

Step 2:   Create a DHCP pool on R2 for the R1 LAN.

    a.   Create a DHCP pool named R1-LAN (case-sensitive).

    b.   Configure the DHCP pool to include the network address, the default gateway, and the IP address of the DNS server.

Step 3:   Create a DHCP pool on R2 for the R3 LAN.

    a.   Create a DHCP pool named R3-LAN (case-sensitive).

    b.   Configure the DHCP pool to include the network address, the default gateway, and the IP address of the DNS server.

Part 2: Configure DHCP Relay

Step 1: Configure R1 and R3 as a DHCP relay agent.

Step 2: Set PC1 and PC2 to receive IP addressing information from DHCP.

Part 3: Configure R2 as a DHCP Client

a. Configure the Gigabit Ethernet 0/1 interface on R2 to receive IP addressing from DHCP and activate the interface.

Note: Use Packet Tracer's Fast Forward Time feature to speed up the process or wait until R2 forms an EIGRP adjacency with the ISP router.

---

b. Use the **show ip interface brief** command to verify that R2 received an IP address from DHCP.

Part 4: Verify DHCP and Connectivity

Step 1: Verify DHCP bindings.

```
R2# show ip dhcp binding
IP address        Client-ID/          Lease expiration      Type
                  Hardware address
192.168.10.11     0002.4AA5.1470      --                    Automatic
192.168.30.11     0004.9A97.2535      --                    Automatic
```

Step 2: Verify configurations.

Verify that **PC1** and **PC2** can now ping each other and all other devices.

8.1.4.4 Lab–Troubleshooting DHCPv4

Topology

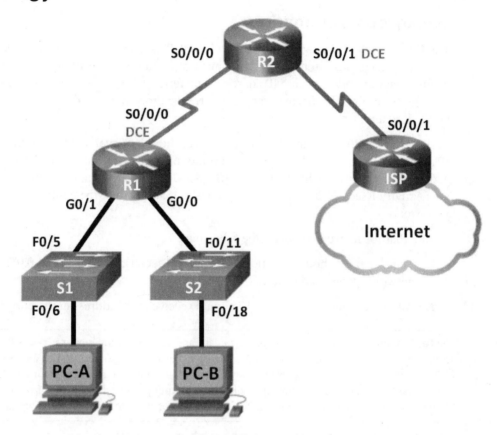

Addressing Table

Device	Interface	IP Address	Subnet Mask	Default Gateway
R1	G0/0	192.168.0.1	255.255.255.128	N/A
	G0/1	192.168.1.1	255.255.255.0	N/A
	S0/0/0 (DCE)	192.168.0.253	255.255.255.252	N/A
R2	S0/0/0	192.168.0.254	255.255.255.252	N/A
	S0/0/1 (DCE)	209.165.200.226	255.255.255.252	N/A
ISP	S0/0/1	209.165.200.225	255.255.255.252	N/A
S1	VLAN 1	192.168.1.2	255.255.255.0	192.168.1.1
S2	VLAN 1	192.168.0.2	255.255.255.128	192.168.0.1
PC-A	NIC	DHCP	DHCP	DHCP
PC-B	NIC	DHCP	DHCP	DHCP

Objectives

Part 1: Build the Network and Configure Basic Device Settings

Part 2: Troubleshoot DHCPv4 Issues

Background/Scenario

The Dynamic Host Configuration Protocol (DHCP) is a network protocol that lets the network administrators manage and automate the assignment of IP addresses. Without DHCP, the administrator must manually assign and configure IP addresses, preferred DNS servers, and the default gateway. As the network grows in size, this becomes an administrative problem when devices are moved from one internal network to another.

In this scenario, the company has grown in size, and the network administrators can no longer assign IP addresses to devices manually. The R2 router has been configured as a DHCP server to assign IP addresses to the host devices on router R1 LANs. Several errors in the configuration have resulted in connectivity issues. You are asked to troubleshoot and correct the configuration errors and document your work.

Ensure that the network supports the following:

1. The router R2 should function as the DHCP server for the 192.168.0.0/25 and 192.168.1.0/24 networks connected to R1.

2. All PCs connected to S1 and S2 should receive an IP address in the correct network via DHCP.

Note: The routers used with CCNA hands-on labs are Cisco 1941 Integrated Services Routers (ISRs) with Cisco IOS Release 15.2(4)M3 (universalk9 image). The switches used are Cisco Catalyst 2960s with Cisco IOS Release 15.0(2) (lanbasek9 image). Other routers, switches and Cisco IOS versions can be used. Depending on the model and Cisco IOS version, the commands available and output produced might vary from what is shown in the labs. Refer to the Router Interface Summary Table at the end of this lab for the correct interface identifiers.

Note: Make sure that the routers and switches have been erased and have no startup configurations. If you are unsure, contact your instructor.

Required Resources

- 3 Routers (Cisco 1941 with Cisco IOS Release 15.2(4)M3 universal image or comparable)
- 2 Switches (Cisco 2960 with Cisco IOS Release 15.0(2) lanbasek9 image or comparable)
- 2 PCs (Windows 7, Vista, or XP with terminal emulation program, such as Tera Term)
- Console cables to configure the Cisco IOS devices via the console ports
- Ethernet and serial cables as shown in the topology

Part 1: Build the Network and Configure Basic Device Settings

In Part 1, you will set up the network topology and configure the routers and switches with basic settings, such as passwords and IP addresses. You will also configure the IP settings for the PCs in the topology.

Step 1:   Cable the network as shown in the topology.

Step 2:   Initialize and reload the routers and switches.

Step 3:   Configure basic settings for each router.

    a.   Disable DNS lookup.

    b.   Configure device names as shown in the topology.

    c.   Assign **class** as the privileged EXEC password.

    d.   Assign **cisco** as the console and vty passwords.

    e.   Configure **logging synchronous** to prevent console messages from interrupting command entry.

    f.   Configure the IP addresses for all the router interfaces.

    g.   Set clock rate to **128000** for all DCE router interfaces.

    h.   Configure RIP for R1.

```
R1(config)# router rip
R1(config-router)# version 2
R1(config-router)# network 192.168.0.0
R1(config-router)# network 192.168.1.0
R1(config-router)# no auto-summary
R1(config-router)# exit
```

    i.   Configure RIP and a static default route on R2.

```
R2(config)# router rip
R2(config-router)# version 2
R2(config-router)# network 192.168.0.0
R2(config-router)# default-information originate
R2(config-router)# no auto-summary
R2(config-router)# exit
R2(config)# ip route 0.0.0.0 0.0.0.0 209.165.200.225
```

    j.   Configure a summary static route on ISP to the networks on R1 and R2 routers.

```
ISP(config)# ip route 192.168.0.0 255.255.254.0 209.165.200.226
```

Step 4:   Verify network connectivity between the routers.

If any pings between the routers fail, correct the errors before proceeding to the next step. Use **show ip route** and **show ip interface brief** to locate possible issues.

Step 5:   Configure basic settings for each switch.

    a.   Disable DNS lookup.

    b.   Configure device name as shown in the topology.

    c.   Configure the IP address for the VLAN 1 interface and the default gateway for each switch.

    d.   Assign **class** as the privileged EXEC mode password.

    e.   Assign **cisco** as the console and vty passwords.

    f.   Configure **logging synchronous** for the console line.

Step 6:   Verify the hosts are configured for DHCP.

Step 7:   Load the initial DHCP configuration for R1 and R2.

Router R1

```
interface GigabitEthernet0/1
 ip helper-address 192.168.0.253
```

Router R2

```
ip dhcp excluded-address 192.168.11.1 192.168.11.9
ip dhcp excluded-address 192.168.0.1 192.168.0.9
ip dhcp pool R1G1
 network 192.168.1.0 255.255.255.0
 default-router 192.168.1.1
ip dhcp pool R1G0
 network 192.168.0.0 255.255.255.128
 default-router 192.168.11.1
```

Part 2: Troubleshoot DHCPv4 Issues

After configuring routers R1 and R2 with DHCPv4 settings, several errors in the DHCP configurations were introduced and resulted in connectivity issues. R2 is configured as a DHCP server. For both pools of DHCP addresses, the first nine addresses are reserved for the routers and switches. R1 relays the DHCP information to all the R1 LANs. Currently, PC-A and PC-B have no access to the network. Use the **show** and **debug** commands to determine and correct the network connectivity issues.

Step 1:   Record IP settings for PC-A and PC-B.

a.   For PC-A and PC-B, at the command prompt, enter **ipconfig /all** to display the IP and MAC addresses.

b.   Record the IP and MAC addresses in the table below. The MAC address can be used to determine which PC is involved in the debug message.

IP Address/Subnet Mask	MAC Address
PC-A	
PC-B	

Step 2:   Troubleshoot DHCP issues for the 192.168.1.0/24 network on router R1.
Router R1 is a DHCP relay agent for all the R1 LANs. In this step, only the DHCP process for the 192.168.1.0/24 network will be examined. The first nine addresses are reserved for other network devices, such as routers, switches, and servers.

a.   Use a DHCP **debug** command to observe the DHCP process on R2 router.

```
R2# debug ip dhcp server events
```

b.   On R1, display the running configuration for the G0/1 interface.

```
R1# show run interface g0/1
interface GigabitEthernet0/1
 ip address 192.168.1.1 255.255.255.0
```

```
ip helper-address 192.168.0.253
duplex auto
speed auto
```

If there are any DHCP relay issues, record any commands that are necessary to correct the configurations errors.

_____

_____

_____

c. In a command prompt on PC-A, type **ipconfig /renew** to receive an address from the DHCP server. Record the configured IP address, subnet mask, and default gateway for PC-A.

_____

d. Observe the debug messages on R2 router for the DHCP renewal process for PC-A. The DHCP server attempted to assign 192.168.1.1/24 to PC-A. This address is already in use for G0/1 interface on R1. The same issue occurs with IP address 192.168.1.2/24 because this address has been assigned to S1 in the initial configuration. Therefore, an IP address of 192.168.1.3/24 has been assigned to PC-A. The DHCP assignment conflict indicates there may be an issue with the excluded-address statement on the DHCP server configuration on R2.

```
*Mar  5 06:32:16.939: DHCPD: Sending notification of DISCOVER:
*Mar  5 06:32:16.939:   DHCPD: htype 1 chaddr 0050.56be.768c
*Mar  5 06:32:16.939:   DHCPD: circuit id 00000000
*Mar  5 06:32:16.939: DHCPD: Seeing if there is an internally specified pool
class:
*Mar  5 06:32:16.939:   DHCPD: htype 1 chaddr 0050.56be.768c
*Mar  5 06:32:16.939:   DHCPD: circuit id 00000000
*Mar  5 06:32:16.943: DHCPD: Allocated binding 2944C764
*Mar  5 06:32:16.943: DHCPD: Adding binding to radix tree (192.168.1.1)
*Mar  5 06:32:16.943: DHCPD: Adding binding to hash tree
*Mar  5 06:32:16.943: DHCPD: assigned IP address 192.168.1.1 to client
0100.5056.be76.8c.
*Mar  5 06:32:16.951: %DHCPD-4-PING_CONFLICT: DHCP address conflict:  server
pinged 192.168.1.1.
*Mar  5 06:32:16.951: DHCPD: returned 192.168.1.1 to address pool R1G1.
*Mar  5 06:32:16.951: DHCPD: Sending notification of DISCOVER:
*Mar  5 06:32:16.951:   DHCPD: htype 1 chaddr 0050.56be.768c
*Mar  5 06:32:16.951:   DHCPD: circuit id 00000000
*Mar  5 06:32:1
R2#6.951: DHCPD: Seeing if there is an internally specified pool class:
*Mar  5 06:32:16.951:   DHCPD: htype 1 chaddr 0050.56be.768c
*Mar  5 06:32:16.951:   DHCPD: circuit id 00000000
*Mar  5 06:32:16.951: DHCPD: Allocated binding 31DC93C8
*Mar  5 06:32:16.951: DHCPD: Adding binding to radix tree (192.168.1.2)
*Mar  5 06:32:16.951: DHCPD: Adding binding to hash tree
*Mar  5 06:32:16.951: DHCPD: assigned IP address 192.168.1.2 to client
0100.5056.be76.8c.
*Mar  5 06:32:18.383: %DHCPD-4-PING_CONFLICT: DHCP address conflict:  server
pinged 192.168.1.2.
*Mar  5 06:32:18.383: DHCPD: returned 192.168.1.2 to address pool R1G1.
```

```
*Mar  5 06:32:18.383: DHCPD: Sending notification of DISCOVER:
*Mar  5 06:32:18.383:   DHCPD: htype 1 chaddr 0050.56be.6c89
*Mar  5 06:32:18.383:   DHCPD: circuit id 00000000
*Mar  5 06:32:18.383: DHCPD: Seeing if there is an internally specified pool
class:
*Mar  5 06:32:18.383:   DHCPD: htype 1 chaddr 0050.56be.6c89
*Mar  5 06:32:18.383:   DHCPD: circuit id 00000000
*Mar  5 06:32:18.383: DHCPD: Allocated binding 2A40E074
*Mar  5 06:32:18.383: DHCPD: Adding binding to radix tree (192.168.1.3)
*Mar  5 06:32:18.383: DHCPD: Adding binding to hash tree
*Mar  5 06:32:18.383: DHCPD: assigned IP address 192.168.1.3 to client
0100.5056.be76.8c.
<output omitted>
```

e. Display the DHCP server configuration on R2. The first nine addresses for 192.168.1.0/24 network are not excluded from the DHCP pool.

```
R2# show run | section dhcp
ip dhcp excluded-address 192.168.11.1 192.168.11.9
ip dhcp excluded-address 192.168.0.1 192.168.0.9
ip dhcp pool R1G1
 network 192.168.1.0 255.255.255.0
 default-router 192.168.1.1
ip dhcp pool R1G0
 network 192.168.0.0 255.255.255.128
 default-router 192.168.1.1
```

Record the commands to resolve the issue on R2.

_____

_____

f. At the command prompt on PC-A, type **ipconfig /release** to return the 192.168.1.3 address back to the DHCP pool. The process can be observed in the debug message on R2.

```
*Mar  5 06:49:59.563: DHCPD: Sending notification of TERMINATION:
*Mar  5 06:49:59.563:   DHCPD: address 192.168.1.3 mask 255.255.255.0
*Mar  5 06:49:59.563:   DHCPD: reason flags: RELEASE
*Mar  5 06:49:59.563:   DHCPD: htype 1 chaddr 0050.56be.768c
*Mar  5 06:49:59.563:   DHCPD: lease time remaining (secs) = 85340
*Mar  5 06:49:59.563: DHCPD: returned 192.168.1.3 to address pool R1G1.
```

g. At the command prompt on PC-A, type **ipconfig /renew** to be assigned a new IP address from the DHCP server. Record the assigned IP address and default gateway information.

_____

The process can be observed in the debug message on R2.

```
*Mar  5 06:50:11.863: DHCPD: Sending notification of DISCOVER:
*Mar  5 06:50:11.863:   DHCPD: htype 1 chaddr 0050.56be.768c
*Mar  5 06:50:11.863:   DHCPD: circuit id 00000000
*Mar  5 06:50:11.863: DHCPD: Seeing if there is an internally specified pool
class:
*Mar  5 06:50:11.863:   DHCPD: htype 1 chaddr 0050.56be.768c
*Mar  5 06:50:11.863:   DHCPD: circuit id 00000000
```

```
*Mar  5 06:50:11.863: DHCPD: requested address 192.168.1.3 has already been
assigned.
*Mar  5 06:50:11.863: DHCPD: Allocated binding 3003018C
*Mar  5 06:50:11.863: DHCPD: Adding binding to radix tree (192.168.1.10)
*Mar  5 06:50:11.863: DHCPD: Adding binding to hash tree
*Mar  5 06:50:11.863: DHCPD: assigned IP address 192.168.1.10 to client
0100.5056.be76.8c.
<output omitted>
```

h. Verify network connectivity.

Can PC-A ping the assigned default gateway? _____

Can PC-A ping the R2 router? _____

Can PC-A ping the ISP router? _____

Step 3: Troubleshoot DHCP issues for 192.168.0.0/25 network on R1.

Router R1 is a DHCP relay agent for all the R1 LANs. In this step, only the DHCP process for the 192.168.0.0/25 network is examined. The first nine addresses are reserved for other network devices.

a. Use a DHCP **debug** command to observe the DHCP process on R2.

```
R2# debug ip dhcp server events
```

b. Display the running configuration for the G0/0 interface on R1 to identify possible DHCP issues.

```
R1# show run interface g0/0
interface GigabitEthernet0/0
 ip address 192.168.0.1 255.255.255.128
 duplex auto
 speed auto
```

Record the issues and any commands that are necessary to correct the configuration errors.

_____

_____

_____

c. From the command prompt on PC-B, type **ipconfig /renew** to receive an address from the DHCP server. Record the configured IP address, subnet mask, and default gateway for PC-B.

_____

d. Observe the debug messages on R2 router for the renewal process for PC-A. The DHCP server assigned 192.168.0.10/25 to PC-B.

```
*Mar  5 07:15:09.663: DHCPD: Sending notification of DISCOVER:
*Mar  5 07:15:09.663:   DHCPD: htype 1 chaddr 0050.56be.f6db
*Mar  5 07:15:09.663:   DHCPD: circuit id 00000000
*Mar  5 07:15:09.663: DHCPD: Seeing if there is an internally specified pool
class:
*Mar  5 07:15:09.663:   DHCPD: htype 1 chaddr 0050.56be.f6db
*Mar  5 07:15:09.663:   DHCPD: circuit id 00000000
*Mar  5 07:15:09.707: DHCPD: Sending notification of ASSIGNMENT:
```

```
*Mar  5 07:15:09.707:   DHCPD: address 192.168.0.10 mask 255.255.255.128
*Mar  5 07:15:09.707:   DHCPD: htype 1 chaddr 0050.56be.f6db
*Mar  5 07:15:09.707:   DHCPD: lease time remaining (secs) = 86400
```

e. Verify network connectivity.

Can PC-B ping the DHCP assigned default gateway? _____

Can PC-B ping its default gateway (192.168.0.1)? _____

Can PC-B ping the R2 router? _____

Can PC-B ping the ISP router? _____

f. If any issues failed in step e, record the problems and any commands to resolve the issues.

_____

_____

g. Release and renew the IP configurations on PC-B. Repeat Step e to verify network connectivity.

h. Discontinue the debug process by using the **undebug all** command.

```
R2# undebug all
All possible debugging has been turned off
```

Reflection

What are the benefits of using DHCP?

_____

_____

Router Interface Summary Table

	Router Interface Summary			
Router Model	Ethernet Interface #1	Ethernet Interface #2	Serial Interface #1	Serial Interface #2
1800	Fast Ethernet 0/0 (F0/0)	Fast Ethernet 0/1 (F0/1)	Serial 0/0/0 (S0/0/0)	Serial 0/0/1 (S0/0/1)
1900	Gigabit Ethernet 0/0 (G0/0)	Gigabit Ethernet 0/1 (G0/1)	Serial 0/0/0 (S0/0/0)	Serial 0/0/1 (S0/0/1)
2801	Fast Ethernet 0/0 (F0/0)	Fast Ethernet 0/1 (F0/1)	Serial 0/1/0 (S0/1/0)	Serial 0/1/1 (S0/1/1)
2811	Fast Ethernet 0/0 (F0/0)	Fast Ethernet 0/1 (F0/1)	Serial 0/0/0 (S0/0/0)	Serial 0/0/1 (S0/0/1)
2900	Gigabit Ethernet 0/0 (G0/0)	Gigabit Ethernet 0/1 (G0/1)	Serial 0/0/0 (S0/0/0)	Serial 0/0/1 (S0/0/1)

Note: To find out how the router is configured, look at the interfaces to identify the type of router and how many interfaces the router has. There is no way to effectively list all the combinations of configurations for each router class. This table includes identifiers for the possible combinations of Ethernet and Serial interfaces in the device. The table does not include any other type of interface, even though a specific router may contain one. An example of this might be an ISDN BRI interface. The string in parentheses is the legal abbreviation that can be used in Cisco IOS commands to represent the interface.

8.2.3.5 Lab–Configuring Stateless and Stateful DHCPv6

Topology

Addressing Table

Device	Interface	IPv6 Address	Prefix Length	Default Gateway
R1	G0/1	2001:DB8:ACAD:A::1	64	N/A
S1	VLAN 1	Assigned by SLAAC	64	Assigned by SLAAC
PC-A	NIC	Assigned by SLAAC and DHCPv6	64	Assigned by R1

Objectives

Part 1: Build the Network and Configure Basic Device Settings

Part 2: Configure the Network for SLAAC

Part 3: Configure the Network for Stateless DHCPv6

Part 4: Configure the Network for Stateful DHCPv6

Background/Scenario

The dynamic assignment of IPv6 global unicast addresses can be configured in three ways:

- Stateless Address Autoconfiguration (SLAAC) only
- Stateless Dynamic Host Configuration Protocol for IPv6 (DHCPv6)
- Stateful DHCPv6

With SLAAC (pronounced slack), a DHCPv6 server is not needed for hosts to acquire IPv6 addresses. It can be used to receive additional information that the host needs, such as the domain name and the domain name server (DNS) address. When SLAAC is used to assign the IPv6 host addresses and DHCPv6 is used to assign other network parameters, it is called Stateless DHCPv6.

With Stateful DHCPv6, the DHCP server assigns all information, including the host IPv6 address.

Determination of how hosts obtain their dynamic IPv6 addressing information is dependent on flag settings contained within the router advertisement (RA) messages.

In this lab, you will initially configure the network to use SLAAC. After connectivity has been verified, you will configure DHCPv6 settings and change the network to use Stateless DHCPv6. After verification that Stateless DHCPv6 is functioning correctly, you will change the configuration on R1 to use Stateful DHCPv6. Wireshark will be used on PC-A to verify all three dynamic network configurations.

Note: The routers used with CCNA hands-on labs are Cisco 1941 Integrated Services Routers (ISRs) with Cisco IOS Release 15.2(4)M3 (universalk9 image). The switches used are Cisco Catalyst 2960s with Cisco IOS Release 15.0(2) (lanbasek9 image). Other routers, switches and Cisco IOS versions can be used. Depending on the model and Cisco IOS version, the commands available and output produced might vary from what is shown in the labs. Refer to the Router Interface Summary Table at the end of this lab for the correct interface identifiers.

Note: Make sure that the router and switch have been erased and have no startup configurations. If you are unsure, contact your instructor.

Note: The default bias template (used by the Switch Database Manager (SDM)) does not provide IPv6 address capabilities. Verify that SDM is using either the dual-ipv4-and-ipv6 template or the lanbase-routing template. The new template will be used after reboot even if the config is not saved.

```
S1# show sdm prefer
```

Follow these steps to assign the **dual-ipv4-and-ipv6** template as the default SDM template:

```
S1# config t
S1(config)# sdm prefer dual-ipv4-and-ipv6 default
S1(config)# end
S1# reload
```

Required Resources

- 1 Router (Cisco 1941 with Cisco IOS Release 15.2(4)M3 universal image or comparable)

- 1 Switch (Cisco 2960 with Cisco IOS Release 15.0(2) lanbasek9 image or comparable)

- 1 PC (Windows 7 or Vista with Wireshark and terminal emulation program, such as Tera Term)

- Console cables to configure the Cisco IOS devices via the console ports

- Ethernet cables as shown in the topology

Note: DHCPv6 client services are disabled on Windows XP. It is recommended to use a Windows 7 host for this lab.

Part 1: Build the Network and Configure Basic Device Settings

In Part 1, you will set up the network topology and configure basic settings, such as device names, passwords and interface IP addresses.

Step 1:   Cable the network as shown in the topology.

Step 2:   Initialize and reload the router and switch as necessary.

Step 3:   Configure R1.

   a.   Console into R1 and enter global configuration mode.

   b.   Copy the following basic configuration and paste it to the running-configuration on R1.

```
no ip domain-lookup
service password-encryption
```

```
hostname R1
enable secret class
banner motd #
Unauthorized access is strictly prohibited. #
line con 0
password cisco
login
logging synchronous
line vty 0 4
password cisco
login
```

    c. Save the running configuration to the startup configuration.

Step 4: Configure S1.

    a. Console into S1 and enter global configuration mode.

    b. Copy the following basic configuration and paste it to the running-configuration on S1.

```
no ip domain-lookup
service password-encryption
hostname S1
enable secret class
banner motd #
Unauthorized access is strictly prohibited. #
line con 0
password cisco
login
logging synchronous
line vty 0 15
password cisco
login
exit
```

    c. Administratively disable all inactive interfaces.

    d. Save running configuration to the startup configuration.

Part 2: Configure the Network for SLAAC

Step 1: Prepare PC-A.

    a. Verify that the IPv6 protocol has been enabled on the Local Area Connection Properties window. If the Internet Protocol Version 6 (TCP/IPv6) check box is not checked, click to enable it.

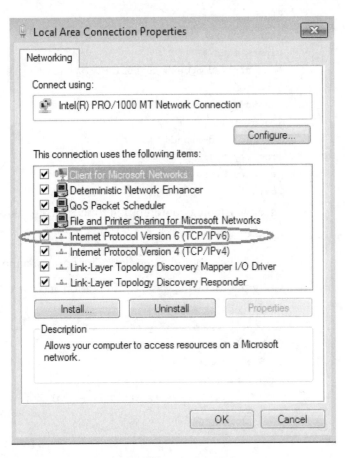

b. Start a Wireshark capture of traffic on the NIC.

c. Filter the data capture to see only RA messages. This can be done by filtering on IPv6 packets with a destination address of FF02::1, which is the all-unicast client group address. The filter entry used with Wireshark is **ipv6.dst==ff02::1**, as shown here.

Step 2: Configure R1.

 a. Enable IPv6 unicast routing.

 b. Assign the IPv6 unicast address to interface G0/1 according to the Addressing Table.

 c. Assign FE80::1 as the IPv6 link-local address for interface G0/1.

 d. Activate interface G0/1.

Step 3: Verify that R1 is part of the all-router multicast group.

Use the **show ipv6 interface g0/1** command to verify that G0/1 is part of the All-router multicast group (FF02::2). RA messages are not sent out G0/1 without that group assignment.

```
R1# show ipv6 interface g0/1
GigabitEthernet0/1 is up, line protocol is up
  IPv6 is enabled, link-local address is FE80::1
  No Virtual link-local address(es):
  Global unicast address(es):
    2001:DB8:ACAD:A::1, subnet is 2001:DB8:ACAD:A::/64
```

```
        Joined group address(es):
          FF02::1
          FF02::2
          FF02::1:FF00:1
        MTU is 1500 bytes
        ICMP error messages limited to one every 100 milliseconds
        ICMP redirects are enabled
        ICMP unreachables are sent
        ND DAD is enabled, number of DAD attempts: 1
        ND reachable time is 30000 milliseconds (using 30000)
        ND advertised reachable time is 0 (unspecified)
        ND advertised retransmit interval is 0 (unspecified)
        ND router advertisements are sent every 200 seconds
        ND router advertisements live for 1800 seconds
        ND advertised default router preference is Medium
        Hosts use stateless autoconfig for addresses.
```

Step 4:   Configure S1.

Use the **ipv6 address autoconfig** command on VLAN 1 to obtain an IPv6 address through SLAAC.

```
S1(config)# interface vlan 1
S1(config-if)# ipv6 address autoconfig
S1(config-if)# end
```

Step 5:   Verify that SLAAC provided a unicast address to S1.

Use the **show ipv6 interface** command to verify that SLAAC provided a unicast address to VLAN1 on S1.

```
S1# show ipv6 interface
Vlan1 is up, line protocol is up
  IPv6 is enabled, link-local address is FE80::ED9:96FF:FEE8:8A40
  No Virtual link-local address(es):
  Stateless address autoconfig enabled
  Global unicast address(es):
    2001:DB8:ACAD:A:ED9:96FF:FEE8:8A40, subnet is 2001:DB8:ACAD:A::/64 [EUI/CAL/PRE]
      valid lifetime 2591988 preferred lifetime 604788
  Joined group address(es):
    FF02::1
    FF02::1:FFE8:8A40
  MTU is 1500 bytes
  ICMP error messages limited to one every 100 milliseconds
  ICMP redirects are enabled
  ICMP unreachables are sent
  Output features: Check hwidb
  ND DAD is enabled, number of DAD attempts: 1
  ND reachable time is 30000 milliseconds (using 30000)
  ND NS retransmit interval is 1000 milliseconds
  Default router is FE80::1 on Vlan1
```

Step 6:   Verify that SLAAC provided IPv6 address information on PC-A.

   a.   From a command prompt on PC-A, issue the **ipconfig /all** command. Verify that PC-A is showing an IPv6 address with the 2001:db8:acad:a::/64 prefix. The Default Gateway should have the FE80::1 address.

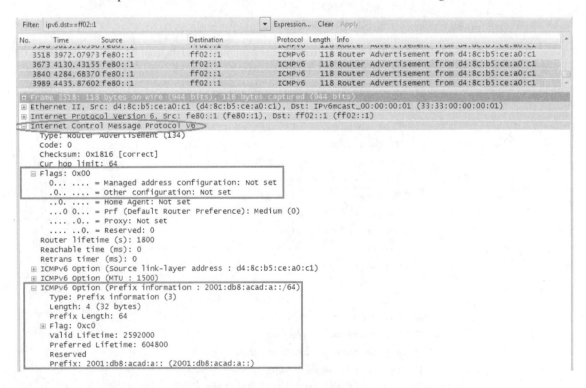

   b.   From Wireshark, look at one of the RA messages that were captured. Expand the Internet Control Message Protocol v6 layer to view the Flags and Prefix information. The first two flags control DHCPv6 usage and are not set if DHCPv6 is not configured. The prefix information is also contained within this RA message.

Part 3: Configure the Network for Stateless DHCPv6

Step 1:   Configure an IPv6 DHCP server on R1.

   a.   Create an IPv6 DHCP pool.

```
R1(config)# ipv6 dhcp pool IPV6POOL-A
```

b. Assign a domain name to the pool.

```
R1(config-dhcpv6)# domain-name ccna-statelessDHCPv6.com
```

c. Assign a DNS server address.

```
R1(config-dhcpv6)# dns-server 2001:db8:acad:a::abcd
R1(config-dhcpv6)# exit
```

d. Assign the DHCPv6 pool to the interface.

```
R1(config)# interface g0/1
R1(config-if)# ipv6 dhcp server IPV6POOL-A
```

e. Set the DHCPv6 network discovery (ND) **other-config-flag.**

```
R1(config-if)# ipv6 nd other-config-flag
R1(config-if)# end
```

Step 2: Verify DHCPv6 settings on interface G0/1 on R1.

Use the **show ipv6 interface g0/1** command to verify that the interface is now part of the IPv6 multicast all-DHCPv6-servers group (FF02::1:2). The last line of the output from this **show** command verifies that the other-config-flag has been set.

```
R1# show ipv6 interface g0/1
GigabitEthernet0/1 is up, line protocol is up
  IPv6 is enabled, link-local address is FE80::1
  No Virtual link-local address(es):
  Global unicast address(es):
    2001:DB8:ACAD:A::1, subnet is 2001:DB8:ACAD:A::/64
  Joined group address(es):
    FF02::1
    FF02::2
    FF02::1:2
    FF02::1:FF00:1
    FF05::1:3
  MTU is 1500 bytes
  ICMP error messages limited to one every 100 milliseconds
  ICMP redirects are enabled
  ICMP unreachables are sent
  ND DAD is enabled, number of DAD attempts: 1
  ND reachable time is 30000 milliseconds (using 30000)
  ND advertised reachable time is 0 (unspecified)
  ND advertised retransmit interval is 0 (unspecified)
  ND router advertisements are sent every 200 seconds
  ND router advertisements live for 1800 seconds
  ND advertised default router preference is Medium
  Hosts use stateless autoconfig for addresses.
  Hosts use DHCP to obtain other configuration.
```

Step 3: View network changes to PC-A.

Use the **ipconfig /all** command to review the network changes. Notice that additional information, including the domain name and DNS server information, has been retrieved from the DHCPv6 server. However, the IPv6 global unicast and link-local addresses were obtained previously from SLAAC.

```
Ethernet adapter Local Area Connection:

   Connection-specific DNS Suffix  . : ccna-statelessDHCPv6.com
   Description . . . . . . . . . . . : Intel(R) PRO/1000 MT Network Connection
   Physical Address. . . . . . . . . : 00-50-56-BE-76-8C
   DHCP Enabled. . . . . . . . . . . : Yes
   Autoconfiguration Enabled . . . . : Yes
   IPv6 Address. . . . . . . . . . . : 2001:db8:acad:a:24ba:a0a0:9f0:ff88(Prefer
red)
   Temporary IPv6 Address. . . . . . : 2001:db8:acad:a:103a:4344:4b5e:ab1d(Prefe
rred)
   Link-local IPv6 Address . . . . . : fe80::24ba:a0a0:9f0:ff88%11(Preferred)
   Autoconfiguration IPv4 Address. . : 169.254.255.136(Preferred)
   Subnet Mask . . . . . . . . . . . : 255.255.0.0
   Default Gateway . . . . . . . . . : fe80::1%11
   DHCPv6 IAID . . . . . . . . . . . : 234884137
   DHCPv6 Client DUID. . . . . . . . : 00-01-00-01-17-F6-72-3D-00-0C-29-8D-54-44

   DNS Servers . . . . . . . . . . . : 2001:db8:acad:a::abcd
   NetBIOS over Tcpip. . . . . . . . : Enabled
   Connection-specific DNS Suffix Search List :
                                       ccna-statelessDHCPv6.com

Tunnel adapter isatap.{E2FC1866-B195-460A-BF40-F04F42A38FFE}:

   Media State . . . . . . . . . . . : Media disconnected
   Connection-specific DNS Suffix  . : ccna-statelessDHCPv6.com
   Description . . . . . . . . . . . : Microsoft ISATAP Adapter
   Physical Address. . . . . . . . . : 00-00-00-00-00-00-00-E0
   DHCP Enabled. . . . . . . . . . . : No
   Autoconfiguration Enabled . . . . : Yes
```

Step 4: View the RA messages in Wireshark.

Scroll down to the last RA message that is displayed in Wireshark and expand it to view the ICMPv6 flag settings. Notice that the other configuration flag is set to **1**.

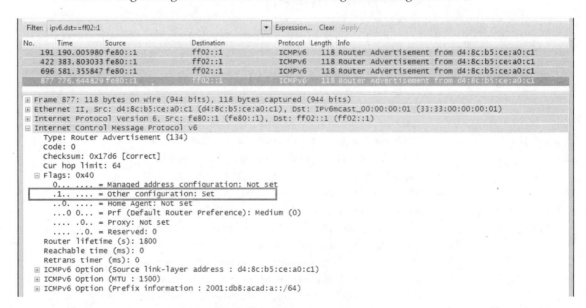

Step 5: Verify that PC-A did not obtain its IPv6 address from a DHCPv6 server.

Use the **show ipv6 dhcp binding** and **show ipv6 dhcp pool** commands to verify that PC-A did not obtain an IPv6 address from the DHCPv6 pool.

```
R1# show ipv6 dhcp binding
R1# show ipv6 dhcp pool
DHCPv6 pool: IPV6POOL-A
   DNS server: 2001:DB8:ACAD:A::ABCD
```

```
Domain name: ccna-statelessDHCPv6.com
Active clients: 0
```

Step 6:   Reset PC-A IPv6 network settings.

    a.   Shut down interface F0/6 on S1.

Note: Shutting down the interface F0/6 prevents PC-A from receiving a new IPv6 address before you reconfigure R1 for Stateful DHCPv6 in Part 4.

```
S1(config)# interface f0/6
S1(config-if)# shutdown
```

    b.   Stop Wireshark capture of traffic on the PC-A NIC.

    c.   Reset the IPv6 settings on PC-A to remove the Stateless DHCPv6 settings.

        1.   Open the Local Area Connection Properties window, deselect the **Internet Protocol Version 6 (TCP/IPv6)** check box, and click **OK** to accept the change.

        2.   Open the Local Area Connection Properties window again. Click to enable the **Internet Protocol Version 6 (TCP/IPv6)** check box, and then click **OK** to accept the change.

Part 4: Configure the Network for Stateful DHCPv6

Step 1:   Prepare PC-A.

    a.   Start a Wireshark capture of traffic on the NIC.

    b.   Filter the data capture to see only RA messages. This can be done by filtering on IPv6 packets with a destination address of FF02::1, which is the all-unicast client group address.

Step 2:   Change the DHCPv6 pool on R1.

    a.   Add the network prefix to the pool.

```
R1(config)# ipv6 dhcp pool IPV6POOL-A
R1(config-dhcpv6)# address prefix 2001:db8:acad:a::/64
```

    b.   Change the domain name to **ccna-statefulDHCPv6.com**.

Note: You must remove the old domain name. It is not replaced by the domain-name command.

```
R1(config-dhcpv6)# no domain-name ccna-statelessDHCPv6.com
R1(config-dhcpv6)# domain-name ccna-StatefulDHCPv6.com
R1(config-dhcpv6)# end
```

    c.   Verify DHCPv6 pool settings.

```
R1# show ipv6 dhcp pool
DHCPv6 pool: IPV6POOL-A
  Address allocation prefix: 2001:DB8:ACAD:A::/64 valid 172800 preferred 86400
(0 in use, 0 conflicts)
  DNS server: 2001:DB8:ACAD:A::ABCD
  Domain name: ccna-StatefulDHCPv6.com
  Active clients: 0
```

d. Enter debug mode to verify the Stateful DHCPv6 address assignment.

```
R1# debug ipv6 dhcp detail
    IPv6 DHCP debugging is on (detailed)
```

Step 3: Set the flag on G0/1 for Stateful DHCPv6.

Note: Shutting down the G0/1 interface before making changes ensures that an RA message is sent when the interface is activated.

```
R1(config)# interface g0/1
R1(config-if)# shutdown
R1(config-if)# ipv6 nd managed-config-flag
R1(config-if)# no shutdown
R1(config-if)# end
```

Step 4: Enable interface F0/6 on S1.

Now that R1 has been configured for Stateful DHCPv6, you can reconnect PC-A to the network by activating interface F0/6 on S1.

```
S1(config)# interface f0/6
S1(config-if)# no shutdown
S1(config-if)# end
```

Step 5: Verify Stateful DHCPv6 settings on R1.

a. Issue the **show ipv6 interface g0/1** command to verify that the interface is in Stateful DHCPv6 mode.

```
R1# show ipv6 interface g0/1
GigabitEthernet0/1 is up, line protocol is up
  IPv6 is enabled, link-local address is FE80::1
  No Virtual link-local address(es):
  Global unicast address(es):
    2001:DB8:ACAD:A::1, subnet is 2001:DB8:ACAD:A::/64
  Joined group address(es):
    FF02::1
    FF02::2
    FF02::1:2
    FF02::1:FF00:1
    FF05::1:3
  MTU is 1500 bytes
  ICMP error messages limited to one every 100 milliseconds
  ICMP redirects are enabled
  ICMP unreachables are sent
  ND DAD is enabled, number of DAD attempts: 1
  ND reachable time is 30000 milliseconds (using 30000)
  ND advertised reachable time is 0 (unspecified)
  ND advertised retransmit interval is 0 (unspecified)
  ND router advertisements are sent every 200 seconds
  ND router advertisements live for 1800 seconds
  ND advertised default router preference is Medium
  Hosts use DHCP to obtain routable addresses.
  Hosts use DHCP to obtain other configuration.
```

b. In a command prompt on PC-A, type **ipconfig /release6** to release the currently assigned IPv6 address. Then type **ipconfig /renew6** to request an IPv6 address from the DHCPv6 server.

c. Issue the **show ipv6 dhcp pool** command to verify the number of active clients.

```
R1# show ipv6 dhcp pool
DHCPv6 pool: IPV6POOL-A
  Address allocation prefix: 2001:DB8:ACAD:A::/64 valid 172800 preferred 86400
(1 in use, 0 conflicts)
  DNS server: 2001:DB8:ACAD:A::ABCD
  Domain name: ccna-StatefulDHCPv6.com
  Active clients: 1
```

d. Issue the **show ipv6 dhcp binding** command to verify that PC-A received its IPv6 unicast address from the DHCP pool. Compare the client address to the link-local IPv6 address on PC-A using the **ipconfig /all** command. Compare the address provided by the **show** command to the IPv6 address listed with the **ipconfig /all** command on PC-A.

```
R1# show ipv6 dhcp binding
Client: FE80::D428:7DE2:997C:B05A
  DUID: 0001000117F6723D000C298D5444
  Username : unassigned
  IA NA: IA ID 0x0E000C29, T1 43200, T2 69120
    Address: 2001:DB8:ACAD:A:B55C:8519:8915:57CE
            preferred lifetime 86400, valid lifetime 172800
            expires at Mar 07 2013 04:09 PM (171595 seconds)
```

```
Ethernet adapter Local Area Connection:

   Connection-specific DNS Suffix  . : ccna-StatefulDHCPv6.com
   Description . . . . . . . . . . . : Intel(R) PRO/1000 MT Network Connection
   Physical Address. . . . . . . . . : 00-50-56-BE-6C-89
   DHCP Enabled. . . . . . . . . . . : Yes
   Autoconfiguration Enabled . . . . : Yes
   IPv6 Address. . . . . . . . . . . : 2001:db8:acad:a:b55c:8519:8915:57ce(Prefe
rred)
   Lease Obtained. . . . . . . . . . : Tuesday, March 05, 2013 11:53:11 AM
   Lease Expires . . . . . . . . . . : Thursday, March 07, 2013 11:53:11 AM
   IPv6 Address. . . . . . . . . . . : 2001:db8:acad:a:d428:7de2:997c:b05a(Prefe
rred)
   Temporary IPv6 Address. . . . . . : 2001:db8:acad:a:dd37:1e42:948c:225b(Prefe
rred)
   Link-local IPv6 Address . . . . . : fe80::d428:7de2:997c:b05a%11(Preferred)
   Autoconfiguration IPv4 Address. . : 169.254.176.90(Preferred)
   Subnet Mask . . . . . . . . . . . : 255.255.0.0
   Default Gateway . . . . . . . . . : fe80::1%11
   DHCPv6 IAID . . . . . . . . . . . : 234884137
   DHCPv6 Client DUID. . . . . . . . : 00-01-00-01-17-F6-72-3D-00-0C-29-8D-54-44

   DNS Servers . . . . . . . . . . . : 2001:db8:acad:a::abcd
   NetBIOS over Tcpip. . . . . . . . : Enabled
   Connection-specific DNS Suffix Search List :
                                       ccna-StatefulDHCPv6.com
```

e. Issue the **undebug all** command on R1 to stop debugging DHCPv6.

Note: Typing u all is the shortest form of this command and is useful to know if you are trying to stop debug messages from continually scrolling down your terminal session screen. If multiple debugs are in process, the undebug all command stops all of them.

```
R1# u all
All possible debugging has been turned off
```

f. Review the debug messages that appeared on your R1 terminal screen.

1) Examine the solicit message from PC-A requesting network information.

```
*Mar  5 16:42:39.775: IPv6 DHCP: Received SOLICIT from
FE80::D428:7DE2:997C:B05A on GigabitEthernet0/1
*Mar  5 16:42:39.775: IPv6 DHCP: detailed packet contents
*Mar  5 16:42:39.775:   src FE80::D428:7DE2:997C:B05A (GigabitEthernet0/1)
*Mar  5 16:42:39.775:   dst FF02::1:2
*Mar  5 16:42:39.775:   type SOLICIT(1), xid 1039238
*Mar  5 16:42:39.775:   option ELAPSED-TIME(8), len 2
*Mar  5 16:42:39.775:     elapsed-time 6300
*Mar  5 16:42:39.775:   option CLIENTID(1), len 14
```

2) Examine the reply message sent back to PC-A with the DHCP network information.

```
*Mar  5 16:42:39.779: IPv6 DHCP: Sending REPLY to FE80::D428:7DE2:997C:B05A on
GigabitEthernet0/1
*Mar  5 16:42:39.779: IPv6 DHCP: detailed packet contents
*Mar  5 16:42:39.779:   src FE80::1
*Mar  5 16:42:39.779:   dst FE80::D428:7DE2:997C:B05A (GigabitEthernet0/1)
*Mar  5 16:42:39.779:   type REPLY(7), xid 1039238
*Mar  5 16:42:39.779:   option SERVERID(2), len 10
*Mar  5 16:42:39.779:     00030001FC994775C3E0
*Mar  5 16:42:39.779:   option CLIENTID(1), len 14
*Mar  5 16:42:39.779:     00010001
R1#17F6723D000C298D5444
*Mar  5 16:42:39.779:   option IA-NA(3), len 40
*Mar  5 16:42:39.779:     IAID 0x0E000C29, T1 43200, T2 69120
*Mar  5 16:42:39.779:     option IAADDR(5), len 24
*Mar  5 16:42:39.779:       IPv6 address 2001:DB8:ACAD:A:B55C:8519:8915:57CE
*Mar  5 16:42:39.779:       preferred 86400, valid 172800
*Mar  5 16:42:39.779:   option DNS-SERVERS(23), len 16
*Mar  5 16:42:39.779:     2001:DB8:ACAD:A::ABCD
*Mar  5 16:42:39.779:   option DOMAIN-LIST(24), len 26
*Mar  5 16:42:39.779:     ccna-StatefulDHCPv6.com
```

Step 6: Verify Stateful DHCPv6 on PC-A

a. Stop the Wireshark capture on PC-A.

b. Expand the most recent RA message listed in Wireshark. Verify that the **Managed address configuration** flag has been set.

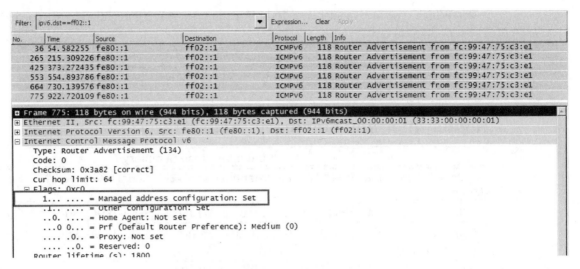

c. Change the filter in Wireshark to view **DHCPv6** packets only by typing **dhcpv6**, and then **Apply** the filter. Highlight the last DHCPv6 reply listed and expand the DHCPv6 information. Examine the DHCPv6 network information that is contained in this packet.

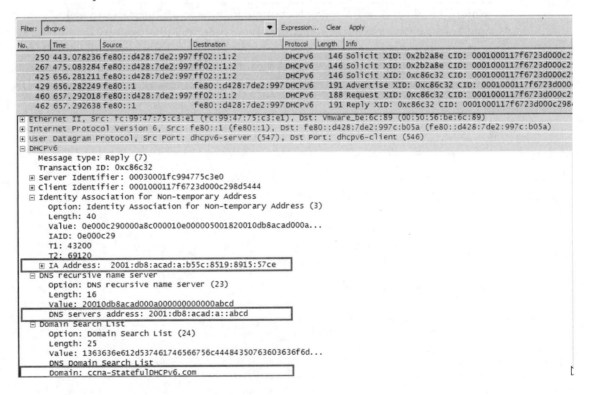

Reflection

1. What IPv6 addressing method uses more memory resources on the router configured as a DHCPv6 server, Stateless DHCPv6 or Stateful DHCPv6? Why?

2. Which type of dynamic IPv6 address assignment is recommended by Cisco, Stateless DHCPv6 or Stateful DHCPv6?

_____

_____

Router Interface Summary Table

Router Interface Summary				
Router Model	Ethernet Interface #1	Ethernet Interface #2	Serial Interface #1	Serial Interface #2
1800	Fast Ethernet 0/0 (F0/0)	Fast Ethernet 0/1 (F0/1)	Serial 0/0/0 (S0/0/0)	Serial 0/0/1 (S0/0/1)
1900	Gigabit Ethernet 0/0 (G0/0)	Gigabit Ethernet 0/1 (G0/1)	Serial 0/0/0 (S0/0/0)	Serial 0/0/1 (S0/0/1)
2801	Fast Ethernet 0/0 (F0/0)	Fast Ethernet 0/1 (F0/1)	Serial 0/1/0 (S0/1/0)	Serial 0/1/1 (S0/1/1)
2811	Fast Ethernet 0/0 (F0/0)	Fast Ethernet 0/1 (F0/1)	Serial 0/0/0 (S0/0/0)	Serial 0/0/1 (S0/0/1)
2900	Gigabit Ethernet 0/0 (G0/0)	Gigabit Ethernet 0/1 (G0/1)	Serial 0/0/0 (S0/0/0)	Serial 0/0/1 (S0/0/1)

Note: To find out how the router is configured, look at the interfaces to identify the type of router and how many interfaces the router has. There is no way to effectively list all the combinations of configurations for each router class. This table includes identifiers for the possible combinations of Ethernet and Serial interfaces in the device. The table does not include any other type of interface, even though a specific router may contain one. An example of this might be an ISDN BRI interface. The string in parentheses is the legal abbreviation that can be used in Cisco IOS commands to represent the interface.

8.2.4.4 Lab–Troubleshooting DHCPv6

Topology

Addressing Table

Device	Interface	IPv6 Address	Prefix Length	Default Gateway
R1	G0/1	2001:DB8:ACAD:A::1	64	N/A
S1	VLAN 1	Assigned by SLAAC	64	Assigned by SLAAC
PC-A	NIC	Assigned by SLAAC and DHCPv6	64	Assigned by SLAAC

Objectives

Part 1: Build the Network and Configure Basic Device Settings

Part 2: Troubleshoot IPv6 Connectivity

Part 3: Troubleshoot Stateless DHCPv6

Background/Scenario

The ability to troubleshoot network issues is a very useful skill for network administrators. It is important to understand IPv6 address groups and how they are used when troubleshooting a network. Knowing what commands to use to extract IPv6 network information is necessary to effectively troubleshoot.

In this lab, you will load configurations on R1 and S1. These configurations will contain issues that prevent Stateless DHCPv6 from functioning on the network. You will troubleshoot R1 and S1 to resolve these issues.

Note: The routers used with CCNA hands-on labs are Cisco 1941 Integrated Services Routers (ISRs) with Cisco IOS Release 15.2(4)M3 (universalk9 image). The switches used are Cisco Catalyst 2960s with Cisco IOS Release 15.0(2) (lanbasek9 image). Other routers, switches and Cisco IOS versions can be used. Depending on the model and Cisco IOS version, the commands available and output produced might vary from what is shown in the labs. Refer to the Router Interface Summary Table at the end of this lab for the correct interface identifiers.

Note: Make sure that the router and switch have been erased and have no startup configurations. If you are unsure, contact your instructor.

Note: The default bias template used by the Switch Database Manager (SDM) does not provide IPv6 address capabilities. Verify that SDM is using either the dual-ipv4-and-ipv6 template or the lanbase-routing template. The new template will be used after reboot even if the configuration is not saved.

```
S1# show sdm prefer
```

Follow this configuration to assign the **dual-ipv4-and-ipv6** template as the default SDM template:

```
S1# config t
S1(config)# sdm prefer dual-ipv4-and-ipv6 default
S1(config)# end
S1# reload
```

Required Resources

- 1 Router (Cisco 1941 with Cisco IOS Release 15.2(4)M3 universal image or comparable)

- 1 Switch (Cisco 2960 with Cisco IOS Release 15.0(2) lanbasek9 image or comparable)

- 1 PC (Windows 7, Vista, or XP with terminal emulation program, such as Tera Term)

- Console cables to configure the Cisco IOS devices via the console ports

- Ethernet cables as shown in the topology

Part 1: Build the Network and Configure Basic Device Settings

In Part 1, you will set up the network topology and clear any configurations if necessary. You will configure basic settings on the router and switch. Then you will load the provided IPv6 configurations before you start troubleshooting.

Step 1:   Cable the network as shown in the topology.

Step 2:   Initialize and reload the router and the switch.

Step 3:   Configure basic settings on the router and switch.

    a.   Disable DNS lookup.

    b.   Configure device names as shown in the topology.

    c.   Encrypt plain text passwords.

    d.   Create a MOTD banner warning users that unauthorized access is prohibited.

    e.   Assign **class** as the encrypted privileged EXEC mode password.

    f.   Assign **cisco** as the console and vty passwords and enable login.

    g.   Configure **logging synchronous** to prevent console messages from interrupting command entry.

Step 4:   Load the IPv6 configuration to R1.

```
ip domain name ccna-lab.com
ipv6 dhcp pool IPV6POOL-A
 dns-server 2001:DB8:ACAD:CAFE::A
 domain-name ccna-lab.com
interface g0/0
 no ip address
 shutdown
 duplex auto
 speed auto
interface g0/1
```

```
    no ip address
    duplex auto
    speed auto
    ipv6 address FE80::1 link-local
    ipv6 address 2001:DB8:ACAD:A::11/64
end
```

Step 5: Load the IPv6 configuration to S1.

```
interface range f0/1-24
  shutdown
interface range g0/1-2
  shutdown
interface Vlan1
  shutdown
end
```

Step 6: Save the running configurations on R1 and S1.

Step 7: Verify that IPv6 is enabled on PC-A.

Verify that IPv6 has been enabled in the Local Area Connection Properties window on PC-A.

Part 2: Troubleshoot IPv6 Connectivity

In Part 2, you will test and verify Layer 3 IPv6 connectivity on the network. Continue troubleshooting the network until Layer 3 connectivity has been established on all devices. Do not continue to Part 3 until you have successfully completed Part 2.

Step 1: Troubleshoot IPv6 interfaces on R1.

   a. According to the topology, which interface must be active on R1 for network connectivity to be established? Record any commands used to identify which interfaces are active.

   _____

   b. If necessary, take the steps required to bring up the interface. Record the commands used to correct the configuration errors and verify that the interface is active.

   _____

   _____

   ```
   R1(config)# interface g0/1
   R1(config-if)# no shutdown
   ```

   c. Identify the IPv6 addresses configured on R1. Record the addresses found and the commands used to view the IPv6 addresses.

   _____

   _____

d. Determine if a configuration error has been made. If any errors are identified, record all the commands used to correct the configuration.

_____

_____

_____

```
R1(config)# interface g0/1
R1(config-if)# no ipv6 address 2001:db8:acad:a::11/64
R1(config-if)# ipv6 address 2001:db8:acad:a::1/64
```

e. On R1, what multicast group is needed for SLAAC to function?

_____

f. What command is used to verify that R1 is a member of that group?

_____

g. If R1 is not a member of the multicast group that is needed for SLAAC to function correctly, make the necessary changes to the configuration so that it joins the group. Record any commands necessary to correct the configurations errors.

_____

```
R1(config)# ipv6 unicast-routing
```

h. Re-issue the command to verify that interface G0/1 has joined the all-routers multicast group (FF02::2).

Note: If you are unable to join the all-routers multicast group, you may need to save your current configuration and reload the router.

Step 2:   Troubleshoot S1.

a. Are the interfaces needed for network connectivity active on S1? _____

Record any commands that are used to activate necessary interfaces on S1.

_____

_____

_____

```
S1(config)# interface range f0/5-6
S1(config-if)# no shutdown
S1(config-if)# interface vlan 1
S1(config-if)# no shutdown
```

b. What command could you use to determine if an IPv6 unicast address has been assigned to S1?

_____

c. Does S1 have an IPv6 unicast address configured? If so, what is it?

_____

d. If S1 is not receiving a SLAAC address, make the necessary configuration changes to allow it to receive one. Record the commands used.

_____

_____

```
S1(config)# interface vlan 1
S1(config-if)# ipv6 address autoconfig
```

e. Re-issue the command that verifies that the interface now receives a SLAAC address.

f. Can S1 ping the IPv6 unicast address assigned to the G0/1 interface assigned to R1?

_____

Step 3:   Troubleshoot PC-A.

a. Issue the command used on PC-A to verify the IPv6 address assigned. Record the command.

_____

b. What is the IPv6 unicast address SLAAC is providing to PC-A?

_____

c. Can PC-A ping the default gateway address that was assigned by SLAAC?

_____

d. Can PC-A ping the management interface on S1?

_____

_____

_____

_____

Note: Continue troubleshooting until you can ping R1 and S1 from PC-A.

Part 3: Troubleshoot Stateless DHCPv6

In Part 3, you will test and verify that Stateless DHCPv6 is working correctly on the network. You will need to use the correct IPv6 CLI commands on the router to determine if Stateless DHCPv6 is working. You may want to use debug to help determine if the DHCP server is being solicited.

Step 1:   Determine if Stateless DHCPv6 is functioning correctly.

a. What is the name of the IPv6 DHCP pool? How did you determine this?

_____

_____

b. What network information is listed in the DHCPv6 pool?

_____

_____

    c. Was the DHCPv6 information assigned to PC-A? How did you determine this?

_____

_____

Step 2: Troubleshoot R1.

    a. What commands can be used to determine if R1 is configured for Stateless DHCPv6?

_____

_____

    b. Is the G0/1 interface on R1 in Stateless DHCPv6 mode?

_____

_____

    c. What command can be used to have R1 join the all-DHCPv6 server group?

_____

_____

    d. Verify that the all-DHCPv6 server group is configured for interface G0/1.

    e. Will PC-A receive the DHCP information now? Explain?

_____

_____

    f. What is missing from the configuration of G0/1 that causes hosts to use the DCHP server to retrieve other network information?

_____

    g. Reset the IPv6 settings on PC-A.

       1. Open the Local Area Connection Properties window, deselect the Internet Protocol Version 6 (TCP/IPv6) check box, and then click **OK** to accept the change.

       2. Open the Local Area Connection Properties window again, click the Internet Protocol Version 6 (TCP/IPv6) check box, and then click **OK** to accept the change.

    h. Issue the command to verify changes have been made on PC-A.

Note: Continue troubleshooting until PC-A receives the additional DHCP information from R1.

Reflection

    1. What command is needed in the DHCPv6 pool for Stateful DHCPv6 that is not needed for Stateless DHCPv6? Why?

_____

_____

_____

2. What command is needed on the interface to change the network to use Stateful DHCPv6 instead of Stateless DHCPv6?

_____

_____

Router Interface Summary Table

Router Interface Summary				
Router Model	Ethernet Interface #1	Ethernet Interface #2	Serial Interface #1	Serial Interface #2
1800	Fast Ethernet 0/0 (F0/0)	Fast Ethernet 0/1 (F0/1)	Serial 0/0/0 (S0/0/0)	Serial 0/0/1 (S0/0/1)
1900	Gigabit Ethernet 0/0 (G0/0)	Gigabit Ethernet 0/1 (G0/1)	Serial 0/0/0 (S0/0/0)	Serial 0/0/1 (S0/0/1)
2801	Fast Ethernet 0/0 (F0/0)	Fast Ethernet 0/1 (F0/1)	Serial 0/1/0 (S0/1/0)	Serial 0/1/1 (S0/1/1)
2811	Fast Ethernet 0/0 (F0/0)	Fast Ethernet 0/1 (F0/1)	Serial 0/0/0 (S0/0/0)	Serial 0/0/1 (S0/0/1)
2900	Gigabit Ethernet 0/0 (G0/0)	Gigabit Ethernet 0/1 (G0/1)	Serial 0/0/0 (S0/0/0)	Serial 0/0/1 (S0/0/1)

Note: To find out how the router is configured, look at the interfaces to identify the type of router and how many interfaces the router has. There is no way to effectively list all the combinations of configurations for each router class. This table includes identifiers for the possible combinations of Ethernet and Serial interfaces in the device. The table does not include any other type of interface, even though a specific router may contain one. An example of this might be an ISDN BRI interface. The string in parentheses is the legal abbreviation that can be used in Cisco IOS commands to represent the interface.

8.3.1.1 Lab–IoE and DHCP

Objective

Configure DHCP for IPv4 or IPv6 on a Cisco 1941 router.

Scenario

This chapter presents the concept of using the DHCP process in a small- to medium-sized business network; however, DHCP also has other uses!

With the advent of the Internet of Everything (IoE), any device in your home capable of wired or wireless connectivity to a network will be able to be accessed from just about anywhere.

Using Packet Tracer for this modeling activity, perform the following tasks:

- Configure a Cisco 1941 router (or DHCP-server-capable ISR device) for IPv4 or IPv6 DHCP addressing.

- Think of five devices in your home you would like to receive IP addresses from the router's DHCP service. Set the end devices to claim DHCP addresses from the DHCP server.

- Show output validating that each end device secures an IP address from the server. Save your output information via a screen capture program or use the **PrtScrn** key command.

- Present your findings to a fellow classmate or to the class.

Required Resources

Packet Tracer software

Reflection

1. Why would a user want to use a Cisco 1941 router to configure DHCP on his home network? Wouldn't a smaller ISR be good enough to use as a DHCP server?

_____

2. How do you think small- to medium-sized businesses are able to use DHCP IP address allocation in the IoE and IPv6 network world? Brainstorm and record five possible answers.

_____

8.3.1.2 Packet Tracer–Skills Integration Challenge

Topology

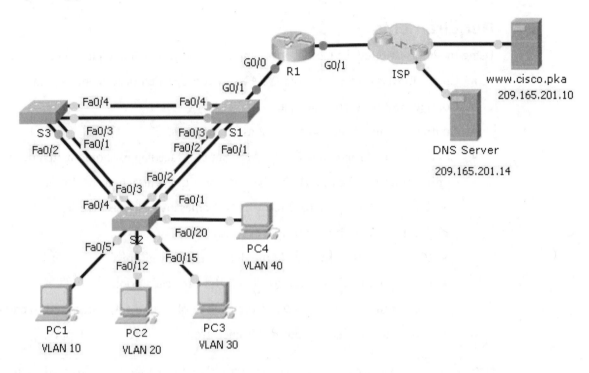

Addressing Table

Device	Interface	IP Address	Subnet Mask	Default Gateway
R1	G0/0.10	172.31.10.1	255.255.255.224	N/A
	G0/0.20	172.31.20.1	255.255.255.240	N/A
	G0/0.30	172.31.30.1	255.255.255.128	N/A
	G0/0.40	172.31.40.1	255.255.255.192	N/A
	G0/1	DHCP Assigned	DHCP Assigned	N/A
PC1	NIC	DHCP Assigned	DHCP Assigned	DHCP Assigned
PC2	NIC	DHCP Assigned	DHCP Assigned	DHCP Assigned
PC3	NIC	DHCP Assigned	DHCP Assigned	DHCP Assigned
PC4	NIC	DHCP Assigned	DHCP Assigned	DHCP Assigned

VLAN Port Assignments and DHCP Information

Ports	VLAN Number - Name	DHCP Pool Name	Network
Fa0/5 – 0/9	VLAN 10 - Sales	VLAN_10	172.31.10.0/27
Fa0/10 – Fa0/14	VLAN 20 - Production	VLAN_20	172.31.20.0/28
Fa0/15 – Fa0/19	VLAN 30 - Marketing	VLAN_30	172.31.30.0/25
Fa0/20 - Fa0/24	VLAN 40 - HR	VLAN_40	172.31.40.0/26

Scenario

In this culminating activity, you will configure VLANs, trunks, DHCP Server, DHCP relay agents, and configure a router as a DHCP client.

Requirements

Using the information in the tables above, implement the following requirements:

- Create VLANs on **S2** and assign VLANs to appropriate ports. Names are case-sensitive.
- Configure **S2** ports for trunking.
- Configure all non-trunk ports on **S2** as access ports.
- Configure **R1** to route between VLANs. Subinterface names should match the VLAN number.
- Configure **R1** to act as a DHCP server for the VLANs attached to S2.
    - Create a DHCP pool for each VLAN. Names are case-sensitive.
    - Assign the appropriate addresses to each pool.
    - Configure DHCP to provide the default gateway address
    - Configure the DNS server 209.165.201.14 for each pool.
    - Prevent the first 10 addresses from each pool from being distributed to end devices.
- Verify that each PC has an address assigned from the correct DHCP pool.

Note: DHCP address assignments may take some time. Click Fast Forward Time to speed up the process.

- Configure **R1** as a DHCP client so that it receives an IP address from the ISP network.
- Verify all devices can now ping each other and **www.cisco.pka**.

CHAPTER 9

NAT for IPv4

All public IPv4 addresses that traverse the Internet must be registered with a Regional Internet Registry (RIR). Only the registered holder of a public Internet address can assign that address to a network device. With the proliferation of personal computing and the advent of the World Wide Web, it soon became obvious that 4.3 billion IPv4 addresses would not be enough. The long-term solution was to eventually be IPv6. But for the short term, several solutions were implemented by the IETF, including Network Address Translation (NAT) and RFC 1918 private IPv4 addresses.

The Study Guide portion of this chapter uses a combination of matching, fill-in-the-blank, multiple-choice, and open-ended question exercises to test your knowledge and skills of NAT for IPv4 concepts and configuration. The Labs and Activities portion of this chapter includes all the online curriculum labs and Packet Tracer activities to ensure that you have mastered the hands-on skills needed to understand basic IP addressing and router configuration.

As you work through this chapter, use Chapter 9 in *Routing and Switching Essentials v6 Companion Guide* or use the corresponding Chapter 9 in the Routing and Switching Essentials online curriculum for assistance.

Study Guide

NAT Operation

There are not enough public IPv4 addresses to assign a unique address to each device connected to the Internet. Networks are commonly implemented using private IPv4 addresses.

NAT Characteristics

Fill in the table with the private addresses defined by RFC 1918.

Class	Address Range	CIDR Prefix
A		
B		
C		

Briefly explain the following terms:

- Inside local address: _____
- Inside global address: _____
- Outside global address: _____

  _____
- Outside local address: _____

  _____

In Figure 9-1, label each type of NAT address.

Figure 9-1   Identify NAT Address Types

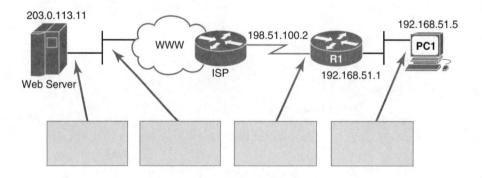

Types and Benefits of NAT

Briefly describe the three types of NAT:

- Static address translation (static NAT): _____

_____

- Dynamic address translation (dynamic NAT): _____

_____

- Port Address Translation (PAT): _____

_____

When is it appropriate to use static NAT?

_____

_____

_____

What is the difference between dynamic NAT and PAT?

_____

_____

_____

List and explain at least three advantages and three disadvantages to using NAT.

Advantages:

_____

_____

_____

_____

Disadvantages:

_____

_____

_____

_____

_____

Configuring NAT

Configuring NAT is straightforward if you follow a few simple steps. Static NAT and dynamic NAT configurations vary slightly. Adding PAT to a dynamic NAT is as simple as adding a keyword to the configuration.

Configuring Static NAT

Use the following steps to configure static NAT:

Step 1.   Create a map between the inside local IP address and the inside global IP address with the **ip nat inside source static** *local-ip global-ip* global configuration command.

Step 2.   Configure the inside interface of the LAN to which the device is attached to participate in NAT with the **ip nat inside** interface configuration command.

Step 3.   Configure the outside interface where NAT translation will occur with the **ip nat outside** interface configuration command.

Refer to the topology in Figure 9-2 to configure static NAT.

Figure 9-2   Static NAT Configuration Topology

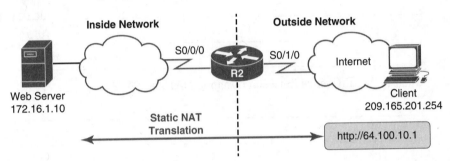

The web server uses an inside local address 172.16.1.10 that needs to be translated to the inside global address 64.100.10.1. Record the command including router prompt to configure the static translation on R2.

_____

Record the commands including router prompt to configure the inside interface.

_____

_____

Record the commands including router prompt to configure the outside interface.

_____

_____

Packet Tracer Exercise 9-1: Configuring Static NAT

Now you are ready to use Packet Tracer to apply your knowledge about static NAT configuration. Download and open the file LSG02-0901.pka found at the companion website for this book. Refer to the Introduction of this book for specifics on accessing files.

Note: The following instructions are also contained in the Packet Tracer exercise.

In this Packet Tracer activity, you will configure and verify static NAT. Use the commands you documented in the "Configuring Static NAT" section to help you complete the activity.

Requirements

- Configure R2 to statically NAT the inside address 172.16.1.10 to the outside address 64.100.10.1.

- Configure the appropriate interfaces for NAT.

- Verify that the outside client can ping the web server at 64.100.10.1.

Your completion percentage should be 100%. If not, click **Check Results** to see which required components are not yet completed.

Configuring Dynamic NAT

Use the following steps to configure dynamic NAT:

Step 1. Define the pool of addresses that will be used for dynamic translation using the **ip nat pool** *name start-ip end-ip* {**netmask** *netmask* | **prefix-length** *prefix-length*} global configuration command.

Step 2. Configure an ACL to specify which inside local addresses will be translated using a standard ACL.

Step 3. Bind the NAT pool to the ACL with the **ip nat inside source list** *ACL-number* **pool** *name* global configuration command.

Step 4. Configure the inside interface of the LAN to which the device is attached to participate in NAT with the **ip nat inside** interface configuration command.

Step 5. Configure the outside interface where NAT translation will occur with the **ip nat outside** interface configuration command.

Refer to the topology in Figure 9-3 to configure dynamic NAT.

Figure 9-3   Dynamic NAT Configuration Topology

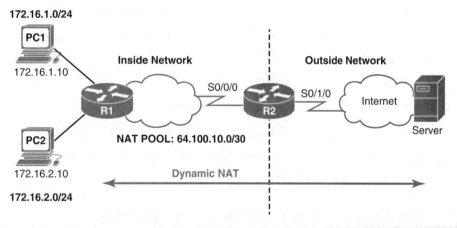

The pool of available addresses is 64.100.10.0/30. Record the command including router prompt to configure the NAT pool with an appropriate name.

The two LANs, 172.16.1.0/24 and 172.16.2.0/24, need to be translated. No other addresses are allowed. Record the command including router prompt to configure a standard ACL number 1.

_____

_____

Record the command including router prompt to bind the NAT pool to the ACL.

_____

Record the commands including router prompt to configure the inside interface.

_____

Record the commands including router prompt to configure the outside interface.

_____

_____

Packet Tracer Exercise 9-2: Configuring Dynamic NAT

Now you are ready to use Packet Tracer to apply your knowledge about static NAT configuration. Download and open the file LSG02-0902.pka found at the companion website for this book. Refer to the Introduction of this book for specifics on accessing files.

Note: The following instructions are also contained in the Packet Tracer exercise.

In this Packet Tracer activity, you will configure and verify dynamic NAT. Use the commands you documented in the "Configuring Dynamic NAT" section to help you complete the activity.

Requirements

- Configure R2 with a pool named NAT. Use the address 64.100.10.0/30.
- Configure ACL 1 to permit the two LANs. Configure the statement for 172.16.1.0/24 first. Only use two statements.
- Bind the NAT pool to the ACL.
- Configure the appropriate interfaces for NAT.
- Verify that PC1 and PC2 can ping the server at 209.165.201.254.

Your completion percentage should be 100%. If not, click **Check Results** to see which required components are not yet completed.

Configuring Port Address Translation

Configuring Port Address Translation (PAT) is just like configuring dynamic NAT except you add the keyword **overload** to your binding configuration:

```
Router(config)# ip nat inside source list ACL-number pool name overload
```

However, a more common solution in a small business enterprise network is to simply overload the IP address on the gateway router. In fact, this is what a home router does "out of the box."

To configure NAT to overload the public IP address on an interface, use the following command:

```
Router(config)# ip nat inside source list ACL-number interface type number overload
```

In this case, of course, there is no pool configuration.

Refer to the topology in Figure 9-4 to configure PAT.

Figure 9-4   Dynamic NAT Configuration Topology

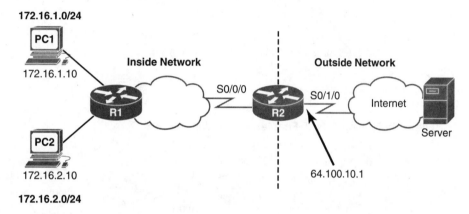

R2 is using the public IP address 64.100.10.1 on the Serial 0/1/0 interface. Record the command including router prompt to bind the ACL you configured for dynamic NAT to the Serial 0/1/0 interface.

_____

That's it! The rest of the commands are the same as dynamic NAT. However, the process of translating inbound and outbound packets is a bit more involved. PAT maintains a table of inside and outside addresses mapped to port numbers to track connections between the source and destination.

The series of Figures 9-5 through 9-8 illustrate the PAT process overloading an interface address. Use the options in Table 9-1 to fill in the source address (SA), destination address (DA), and corresponding port numbers as the packet travels from source to destination and back.

Table 9-1   Addresses and Port Numbers

64.100.10.2	192.168.51.5	1268	209.165.201.11
1150	53	192.168.51.1	80

Figure 9-5   Hop 1: PC1 to NAT-Enabled R1

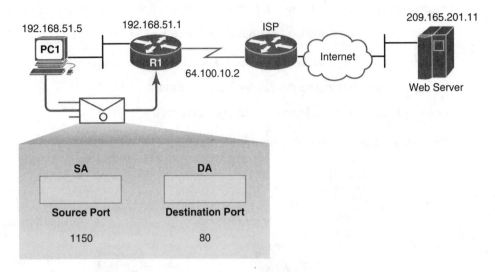

Figure 9-6   Hop 2: NAT-Enabled R1 to Web Server

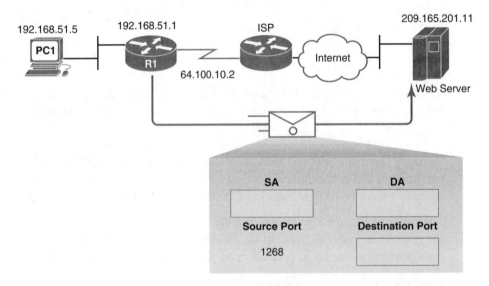

Figure 9-7   Hop 3: Web Server to NAT-Enabled R1

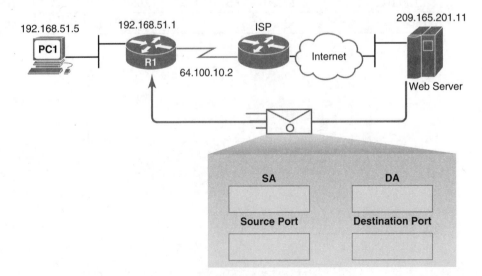

Figure 9-8   Hop 4: NAT-Enabled R1 to PC1

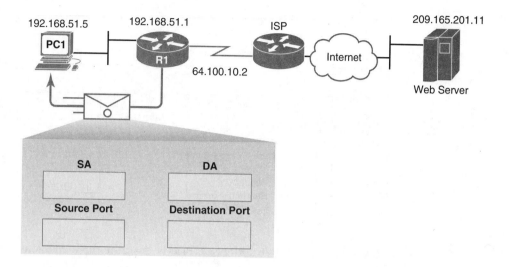

A Word About Port Forwarding

Because NAT hides internal addresses, peer-to-peer connections work only from the inside out, where NAT can map outgoing requests against incoming replies. The problem is that NAT does not allow requests initiated from the outside. To resolve this problem, you can configure port forwarding to identify specific ports that can be forwarded to inside hosts.

The port forwarding configuration is commonly done in a GUI. However, you can also configure port forwarding in the Cisco IOS adding the following command to your NAT configuration:

```
Router(config)# ip nat inside source static {tcp | udp } {local-ip local-port global-ip glob-
al-port} [extendable]}
```

Note: Several parameters are not shown in the syntax because they are beyond the scope of this course.

NAT and IPv6

IPv6 includes both its own IPv6 private address space and NAT, which are implemented differently than they are for IPv4. IPv6 uses a unique local address (ULA) for communication within a local site.

In Figure 9-9, label the missing parts of the IPv6 ULA address structure.

Figure 9-9   IPv6 Unique Local Address Structure

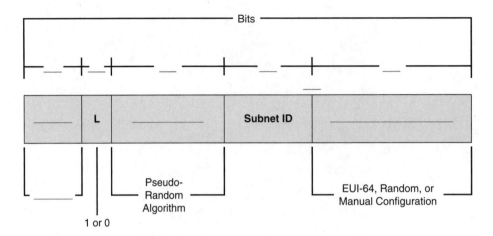

ULAs are also known as local IPv6 addresses. Briefly describe three characteristics of ULAs.

_____

_____

_____

_____

_____

What is the main purpose of NAT64?

_____

Briefly describe the three transition strategies to move from IPv4 to IPv6.

_____

_____

_____

_____

Troubleshooting NAT

When there are IPv4 connectivity problems in a NAT environment, determining the cause of the problem is often difficult. The first step in solving the problem is to rule out NAT as the cause. Follow these steps to verify that NAT is operating as expected:

Step 1.   Review the purpose of the NAT configuration. Is there a static NAT implementation? Are the addresses in the dynamic pool actually valid? Are the inside and outside interfaces correctly identified?

Step 2.   Verify that correct translations exist in the translation table using the **show ip nat translations** command.

Step 3.   Use the **clear ip nat translations *** and **debug ip nat** commands to verify that NAT is operating as expected. Check to see whether dynamic entries are re-created after they are cleared.

Step 4.   Review in detail what is happening to the packet, and verify that routers have the correct routing information to move the packet.

Labs and Activities

Command Reference

In Table 9-2, record the command, including the correct router or switch prompt, that fits the description. Fill in any blanks with the appropriate missing information.

Table 9-2   Commands for Chapter 9, "NAT for IPv4"

Command	Description
	Statically translate 10.10.10.10 to 192.0.2.1.
	Configure a NAT pool MYNAT for 192.0.2.8/29
	Bind ACL 5 to MYNAT pool.
	Assign NAT to the internal interface.
	Assign NAT to the external interface.
	Bind NAT to ACL 5 and to use the s0/0/0 interface with PAT.

9.0.1.2 Lab–Conceptual NAT

Objective

Describe NAT characteristics.

Scenario

You work for a large university or school system. Because you are the network administrator, many professors, administrative workers, and other network administrators need your assistance with their networks on a daily basis. They call you at all working hours of the day and, because of the number of telephone calls, you cannot complete your regular network administration tasks.

You need to find a way to limit when you take calls and from whom. You also need to mask your telephone number so that when you call someone, another number is displayed to the recipient.

This scenario describes a very common problem for most small- to medium-sized businesses. Visit "How Network Address Translation Works" located at http://computer.howstuffworks.com/nat.htm/ printable to view more information about how the digital world handles these types of workday interruptions.

Use the PDF provided accompanying this activity to reflect further on how a process, known as NAT, could be the answer to this scenario's challenge.

Resources

Internet connection

Directions

Step 1:   Read Information on the Internet site.

    a.   Go to "How Network Address Translation Works" located at http://computer.howstuff-works.com/nat.htm/printable

    b.   Read the information provided to introduce the basic concepts of NAT.

    c.   Record five facts you find to be interesting about the NAT process.

Step 2:   View the NAT graphics.

    a.   On the same Internet page, look at the types of NAT that are available for configuration on most networks.

    b.   Define the four NAT types:

        Static NAT

        Dynamic NAT

        NAT Overload

        NAT Overlap

Step 3:   Meet together in a full-class setting.

   a.   Report your five NAT facts to the class.

   b.   As other students state their interesting facts to the class, check off the stated fact if you already recorded it.

   c.   If a student reports a fact to the class that you did not record, add it to your list.

9.1.2.6 Packet Tracer–Investigating NAT Operation

Topology

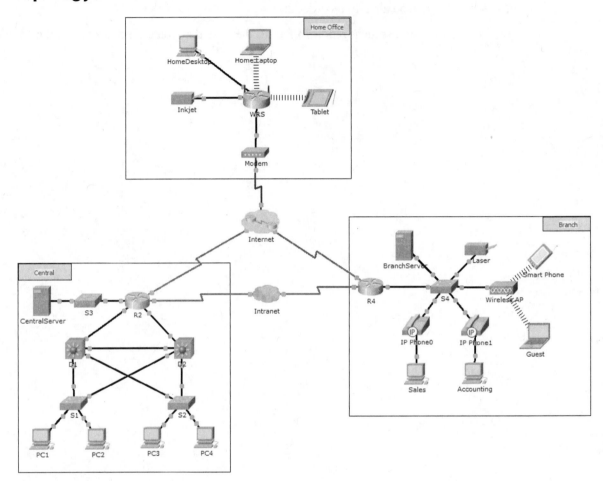

Objectives

Part 1: Investigate NAT Operation Across the Intranet

Part 2: Investigate NAT Operation Across the Internet

Part 3: Conduct Further Investigations

Scenario

As a frame travels across a network, the MAC addresses may change. IP addresses can also change when a packet is forwarded by a device configured with NAT. In this activity, we will investigate what happens to IP addresses during the NAT process.

Part 1: Investigate NAT Operation Across the Intranet

Step 1:   Wait for the network to converge.

It might take a few minutes for everything in the network to converge. You can speed the process up by clicking on Fast Forward Time.

Step 2:   Generate an HTTP request from any PC in the Central domain.

    a.   Open the Web browser of any PC in the **Central** domain and type the following without pressing enter or clicking **Go: http://branchserver.pka.**

    b.   Switch to **Simulation** mode and edit the filters to show only HTTP requests.

    c.   Click **Go** in the browser; a PDU envelope will appear.

    d.   Click **Capture/Forward** until the PDU is over **D1** or **D2**. Record the source and destination IP addresses. To what devices do those addresses belong?

    _____

    e.   Click **Capture/Forward** until the PDU is over **R2**. Record the source and destination IP addresses in the outbound packet. To what devices do those addresses belong?

    _____

    _____

    f.   Login to R2 using '**class**' to enter privileged EXEC and show the running configuration. The address came from the following address pool:

```
ip nat pool R2Pool 64.100.100.3 64.100.100.31 netmask 255.255.255.224
```

    g.   Click **Capture/Forward** until the PDU is over **R4**. Record the source and destination IP addresses in the outbound packet. To what devices do those addresses belong?

    _____

    _____

    h.   Click **Capture/Forward** until the PDU is over **Branchserver.pka**. Record the source and destination TCP port addresses in the outbound segment.

    i.   On both **R2** and **R4**, run the following command and match the IP addresses and ports recorded above to the correct line of output:

```
R2# show ip nat translations
R4# show ip nat translations
```

    j.   What do the inside local IP addresses have in common?

    _____

    k.   Did any private addresses cross the Intranet? _____

    l.   Return to **Realtime** mode.

Part 2: Investigate NAT Operation Across the Internet

Step 1:   Generate an HTTP request from any computer in the home office.

    a.   Open the Web browser of any computer in the home office and type the following without pressing enter or clicking **Go: http://centralserver.pka.**

b. Switch to **Simulation** mode. The filters should already be set to show only HTTP requests.

c. Click **Go** in the browser; a PDU envelope will appear.

d. Click **Capture/Forward** until the PDU is over **WRS**. Record the inbound source and destination IP addresses and the outbound source and destination addresses. To what devices do those addresses belong? _____

_____

e. Click **Capture/Forward** until the PDU is over **R2**. Record the source and destination IP addresses in the outbound packet. To what devices do those addresses belong?

_____

f. On **R2**, run the following command and match the IP addresses and ports recorded above to the correct line of output:

```
R2# show ip nat translations
```

g. Return to **Realtime** mode. Did all of the web pages appear in the browsers? _____

Part 3: Conduct Further Investigations

a. Experiment with more packets, both HTTP and HTTPS. There are many questions to consider such as:

- Do the NAT translation tables grow?

- Does WRS have a pool of addresses?

- Is this how the computers in the classroom connect to the Internet?

- Why does NAT use four columns of addresses and ports?

Suggested Scoring Rubric

Activity Section	Question Location	Possible Points	Earned Points
Part 1: Request a Web Page Across the Intranet	Step 2d	12	
	Step 2e	12	
	Step 2g	13	
	Step 2j	12	
	Step 2k	12	
	Part 1 Total	61	
Part 2: Request a Web Page Across the Internet	Step 1d	13	
	Step 1e	13	
	Step 1g	13	
	Part 2 Total	39	
	Total Score	100	

9.2.1.4 Packet Tracer–Configuring Static NAT

Topology

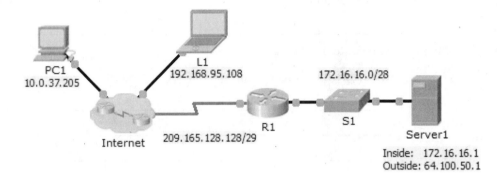

Objectives

Part 1: Test Access without NAT

Part 2: Configure Static NAT

Part 3: Test Access with NAT

Scenario

In IPv4 configured networks, clients and servers use private addressing. Before packets with private addressing can cross the Internet, they need to be translated to public addressing. Servers that are accessed from outside the organization are usually assigned both a public and a private static IP address. In this activity, you will configure static NAT so that outside devices can access an inside server at its public address.

Part 1: Test Access without NAT

Step 1:   Attempt to connect to Server1 using Simulation Mode.

    a.   From **PC1** or **L1**, attempt to connect to the **Server1** Web page at 172.16.16.1. Use the Web browser to browse **Server1** at 172.16.16.1. The attempts should fail.

    b.   From **PC1**, ping the **R1** S0/0/0 interface. The ping should succeed.

Step 2:   View the R1 routing table and running-config.

    a.   View the running configuration of **R1**. Note that there are no commands referring to NAT.

    b.   Verify that the routing table does not contain entries referring to the IP addresses used by **PC1** and **L1**.

    c.   Verify that NAT is not being used by **R1**.

```
R1# show ip nat translations
```

Part 2: Configure Static NAT

Step 1:   Configure static NAT statements.

Refer to the Topology. Create a static NAT translation to map the **Server1** inside address to its outside address.

_____

Step 2:   Configure interfaces.

Configure the correct inside and outside interfaces.

_____

_____

_____

_____

Part 3: Test Access with NAT

Step 1:   Verify connectivity to the Server1 Web page.

a.   Open the command prompt on **PC1** or **L1**, attempt to ping the public address for **Server1**. Pings should succeed.

b.   Verify that both **PC1** and **L1** can now access the **Server1** Web page.

Step 2:   View NAT translations.

Use the following commands to verify the static NAT configuration:

```
show running-config
show ip nat translations
show ip nat statistics
```

9.2.2.5 Packet Tracer–Configuring Dynamic NAT

Topology

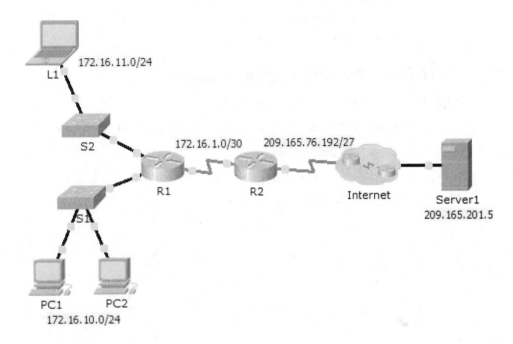

Objectives

Part 1: Configure Dynamic NAT

Part 2: Verify NAT Implementation

Part 1: Configure Dynamic NAT

Step 1:   Configure traffic that will be permitted.

On **R2**, configure one statement for ACL 1 to permit any address belonging to 172.16.0.0/16.

_____

Step 2:   Configure a pool of addresses for NAT.

Configure **R2** with a NAT pool that uses all four addresses in the 209.165.76.196/30 address space.

_____

_____

Notice in the topology there are 3 network ranges that would be translated based on the ACL created. What will happen if more than 2 devices attempt to access the Internet?

_____

_____

Step 3:   Associate ACL1 with the NAT pool.

```
R2(config)# ip nat inside source list 1 pool any-name-here
```

Step 4:   Configure the NAT interfaces.

Configure **R2** interfaces with the appropriate inside and outside NAT commands.

```
R2(config)# interface s0/0/0
R2(config-if)# ip nat outside
R2(config-if)# interface s0/0/1
R2(config-if)# ip nat inside
```

Part 2: Verify NAT Implementation

Step 1:   Access services across the Internet.

From the Web browser of **L1**, **PC1**, or **PC2**, access the Web page for **Server1**.

Step 2:   View NAT translations.

View the NAT translations on **R2**.

```
R2# show ip nat translations
```

9.2.2.6 Lab–Configuring Dynamic and Static NAT

Topology

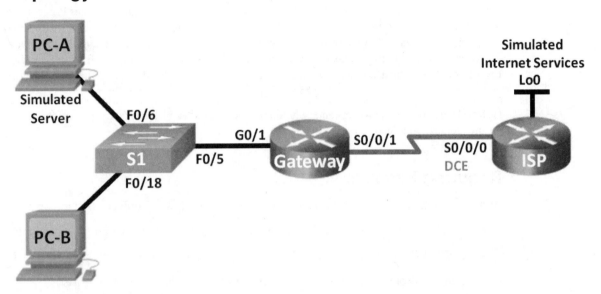

Addressing Table

Device	Interface	IP Address	Subnet Mask	Default Gateway
Gateway	G0/1	192.168.1.1	255.255.255.0	N/A
	S0/0/1	209.165.201.18	255.255.255.252	N/A
ISP	S0/0/0 (DCE)	209.165.201.17	255.255.255.252	N/A
	Lo0	192.31.7.1	255.255.255.255	N/A
PC-A (Simulated Server)	NIC	192.168.1.20	255.255.255.0	192.168.1.1
PC-B	NIC	192.168.1.21	255.255.255.0	192.168.1.1

Objectives

Part 1: Build the Network and Verify Connectivity

Part 2: Configure and Verify Static NAT

Part 3: Configure and Verify Dynamic NAT

Background/Scenario

Network Address Translation (NAT) is the process where a network device, such as a Cisco router, assigns a public address to host devices inside a private network. The main reason to use NAT is to reduce the number of public IP addresses that an organization uses because the number of available IPv4 public addresses is limited.

In this lab, an ISP has allocated the public IP address space of 209.165.200.224/27 to a company. This provides the company with 30 public IP addresses. The addresses 209.165.200.225 to 209.165.200.241

are for static allocation and 209.165.200.242 to 209.165.200.254 are for dynamic allocation. A static route is used from the ISP to the gateway router, and a default route is used from the gateway to the ISP router. The ISP connection to the Internet is simulated by a loopback address on the ISP router.

Note: The routers used with CCNA hands-on labs are Cisco 1941 Integrated Services Routers (ISRs) with Cisco IOS Release 15.2(4)M3 (universalk9 image). The switches used are Cisco Catalyst 2960s with Cisco IOS Release 15.0(2) (lanbasek9 image). Other routers, switches and Cisco IOS versions can be used. Depending on the model and Cisco IOS version, the commands available and output produced might vary from what is shown in the labs. Refer to the Router Interface Summary Table at the end of this lab for the correct interface identifiers.

Note: Make sure that the routers and switch have been erased and have no startup configurations. If you are unsure, contact your instructor.

Required Resources

- 2 Routers (Cisco 1941 with Cisco IOS Release 15.2(4)M3 universal image or comparable)
- 1 Switch (Cisco 2960 with Cisco IOS Release 15.0(2) lanbasek9 image or comparable)
- 2 PCs (Windows 7, Vista, or XP with terminal emulation program, such as Tera Term)
- Console cables to configure the Cisco IOS devices via the console ports
- Ethernet and serial cables as shown in the topology

Part 1: Build the Network and Verify Connectivity

In Part 1, you will set up the network topology and configure basic settings, such as the interface IP addresses, static routing, device access, and passwords.

Step 1: Cable the network as shown in the topology.

Attach the devices as shown in the topology diagram, and cable as necessary.

Step 2: Configure PC hosts.

Step 3: Initialize and reload the routers and switches as necessary.

Step 4: Configure basic settings for each router.

    a. Console into the router and enter global configuration mode.

    b. Copy the following basic configuration and paste it to the running-configuration on the router.

```
no ip domain-lookup
service password-encryption
enable secret class
banner motd #
Unauthorized access is strictly prohibited. #
line con 0
password cisco
login
logging synchronous
line vty 0 4
password cisco
login
```

       c.   Configure the host name as shown in the topology.

       d.   Copy the running configuration to the startup configuration.

Step 5:   Create a simulated web server on ISP.

       a.   Create a local user named **webuser** with an encrypted password of **webpass**.

```
ISP(config)# username webuser privilege 15 secret webpass
```

       b.   Enable the HTTP server service on ISP.

```
ISP(config)# ip http server
```

       c.   Configure the HTTP service to use the local user database.

```
ISP(config)# ip http authentication local
```

Step 6:   Configure static routing.

       a.   Create a static route from the ISP router to the Gateway router using the assigned public network address range 209.165.200.224/27.

```
ISP(config)# ip route 209.165.200.224 255.255.255.224 209.165.201.18
```

       b.   Create a default route from the Gateway router to the ISP router.

```
Gateway(config)# ip route 0.0.0.0 0.0.0.0 209.165.201.17
```

Step 7:   Save the running configuration to the startup configuration.

Step 8:   Verify network connectivity.

       a.   From the PC hosts, ping the G0/1 interface on the Gateway router. Troubleshoot if the pings are unsuccessful.

       b.   Display the routing tables on both routers to verify that the static routes are in the routing table and configured correctly on both routers.

Part 2: Configure and Verify Static NAT

Static NAT uses a one-to-one mapping of local and global addresses, and these mappings remain constant. Static NAT is particularly useful for web servers or devices that must have static addresses that are accessible from the Internet.

Step 1:   Configure a static mapping.

A static map is configured to tell the router to translate between the private inside server address 192.168.1.20 and the public address 209.165.200.225. This allows a user from the Internet to access PC-A. PC-A is simulating a server or device with a constant address that can be accessed from the Internet.

```
Gateway(config)# ip nat inside source static 192.168.1.20 209.165.200.225
```

Step 2:   Specify the interfaces.

Issue the **ip nat inside** and **ip nat outside** commands to the interfaces.

```
Gateway(config)# interface g0/1
Gateway(config-if)# ip nat inside
Gateway(config-if)# interface s0/0/1
Gateway(config-if)# ip nat outside
```

Step 3: Test the configuration.

   a. Display the static NAT table by issuing the **show ip nat translations** command.

```
Gateway# show ip nat translations
Pro Inside global      Inside local     Outside local    Outside global
--- 209.165.200.225    192.168.1.20     ---              ---
```

   What is the translation of the Inside local host address?

   192.168.1.20 = _____

   The Inside global address is assigned by?

   _____

   The Inside local address is assigned by?

   _____

   b. From PC-A, ping the Lo0 interface (192.31.7.1) on ISP. If the ping was unsuccessful, troubleshoot and correct the issues. On the Gateway router, display the NAT table.

```
Gateway# show ip nat translations
Pro Inside global      Inside local     Outside local    Outside global
icmp 209.165.200.225:1 192.168.1.20:1   192.31.7.1:1     192.31.7.1:1
--- 209.165.200.225    192.168.1.20     ---              ---
```

   A NAT entry was added to the table with ICMP listed as the protocol when PC-A sent an ICMP request (ping) to 192.31.7.1 on ISP.

   What port number was used in this ICMP exchange? _____

Note: It may be necessary to disable the PC-A firewall for the ping to be successful.

   c. From PC-A, telnet to the ISP Lo0 interface and display the NAT table.

```
Pro Inside global        Inside local       Outside local    Outside global
icmp 209.165.200.225:1   192.168.1.20:1     192.31.7.1:1     192.31.7.1:1
tcp 209.165.200.225:1034 192.168.1.20:1034  192.31.7.1:23    192.31.7.1:23
--- 209.165.200.225      192.168.1.20       ---              ---
```

Note: The NAT for the ICMP request may have timed out and been removed from the NAT table.

   What was the protocol used in this translation? _____

   What are the port numbers used?

   Inside global/local: _____

   Outside global/local: _____

   d. Because static NAT was configured for PC-A, verify that pinging from ISP to PC-A at the static NAT public address (209.165.200.225) is successful.

   e. On the Gateway router, display the NAT table to verify the translation.

```
Gateway# show ip nat translations
Pro Inside global       Inside local      Outside local       Outside global
icmp 209.165.200.225:12 192.168.1.20:12   209.165.201.17:12   209.165.201.17:12
--- 209.165.200.225     192.168.1.20      ---                 ---
```

Notice that the Outside local and Outside global addresses are the same. This address is the ISP remote network source address. For the ping from the ISP to succeed, the Inside global static NAT address 209.165.200.225 was translated to the Inside local address of PC-A (192.168.1.20).

f. Verify NAT statistics by using the **show ip nat statistics** command on the Gateway router.

```
Gateway# show ip nat statistics
Total active translations: 2 (1 static, 1 dynamic; 1 extended)
Peak translations: 2, occurred 00:02:12 ago
Outside interfaces:
  Serial0/0/1
Inside interfaces:
  GigabitEthernet0/1
Hits: 39  Misses: 0
CEF Translated packets: 39, CEF Punted packets: 0
Expired translations: 3
Dynamic mappings:

Total doors: 0
Appl doors: 0
Normal doors: 0
Queued Packets: 0
```

Note: This is only a sample output. Your output may not match exactly.

Part 3: Configure and Verify Dynamic NAT

Dynamic NAT uses a pool of public addresses and assigns them on a first-come, first-served basis. When an inside device requests access to an outside network, dynamic NAT assigns an available public IPv4 address from the pool. Dynamic NAT results in a many-to-many address mapping between local and global addresses.

Step 1: Clear NATs.

Before proceeding to add dynamic NATs, clear the NATs and statistics from Part 2.

```
Gateway# clear ip nat translation *
Gateway# clear ip nat statistics
```

Step 2: Define an access control list (ACL) that matches the LAN private IP address range.

ACL 1 is used to allow 192.168.1.0/24 network to be translated.

```
Gateway(config)# access-list 1 permit 192.168.1.0 0.0.0.255
```

Step 3: Verify that the NAT interface configurations are still valid.

Issue the **show ip nat statistics** command on the Gateway router to verify the NAT configurations.

Step 4: Define the pool of usable public IP addresses.

```
Gateway(config)# ip nat pool public_access 209.165.200.242 209.165.200.254 netmask
255.255.255.224
```

Step 5:   Define the NAT from the inside source list to the outside pool.

Note: Remember that NAT pool names are case sensitive and the pool name entered here must match that used in the previous step.

```
Gateway(config)# ip nat inside source list 1 pool public_access
```

Step 6:   Test the configuration.

a.   From PC-B, ping the Lo0 interface (192.31.7.1) on ISP. If the ping was unsuccessful, troubleshoot and correct the issues. On the Gateway router, display the NAT table.

```
Gateway# show ip nat translations
Pro Inside global       Inside local      Outside local     Outside global
--- 209.165.200.225     192.168.1.20      ---               ---
icmp 209.165.200.242:1 192.168.1.21:1     192.31.7.1:1      192.31.7.1:1
--- 209.165.200.242     192.168.1.21      ---               ---
```

What is the translation of the Inside local host address for PC-B?

192.168.1.21 = _____

A dynamic NAT entry was added to the table with ICMP as the protocol when PC-B sent an ICMP message to 192.31.7.1 on ISP.

What port number was used in this ICMP exchange? _____

b.   From PC-B, open a browser and enter the IP address of the ISP-simulated web server (Lo0 interface). When prompted, log in as **webuser** with a password of **webpass**.

c.   Display the NAT table.

```
Pro Inside global         Inside local       Outside local     Outside global
--- 209.165.200.225       192.168.1.20       ---               ---
tcp 209.165.200.242:1038 192.168.1.21:1038 192.31.7.1:80      192.31.7.1:80
tcp 209.165.200.242:1039 192.168.1.21:1039 192.31.7.1:80      192.31.7.1:80
tcp 209.165.200.242:1040 192.168.1.21:1040 192.31.7.1:80      192.31.7.1:80
tcp 209.165.200.242:1041 192.168.1.21:1041 192.31.7.1:80      192.31.7.1:80
tcp 209.165.200.242:1042 192.168.1.21:1042 192.31.7.1:80      192.31.7.1:80
tcp 209.165.200.242:1043 192.168.1.21:1043 192.31.7.1:80      192.31.7.1:80
tcp 209.165.200.242:1044 192.168.1.21:1044 192.31.7.1:80      192.31.7.1:80
tcp 209.165.200.242:1045 192.168.1.21:1045 192.31.7.1:80      192.31.7.1:80
tcp 209.165.200.242:1046 192.168.1.21:1046 192.31.7.1:80      192.31.7.1:80
tcp 209.165.200.242:1047 192.168.1.21:1047 192.31.7.1:80      192.31.7.1:80
tcp 209.165.200.242:1048 192.168.1.21:1048 192.31.7.1:80      192.31.7.1:80
tcp 209.165.200.242:1049 192.168.1.21:1049 192.31.7.1:80      192.31.7.1:80
tcp 209.165.200.242:1050 192.168.1.21:1050 192.31.7.1:80      192.31.7.1:80
tcp 209.165.200.242:1051 192.168.1.21:1051 192.31.7.1:80      192.31.7.1:80
tcp 209.165.200.242:1052 192.168.1.21:1052 192.31.7.1:80      192.31.7.1:80
--- 209.165.200.242       192.168.1.22       ---               ---
```

What protocol was used in this translation? _____

What port numbers were used?

Inside: _____

Outside: _____

What well-known port number and service was used? _____

d. Verify NAT statistics by using the **show ip nat statistics** command on the Gateway router.

```
Gateway# show ip nat statistics
Total active translations: 3 (1 static, 2 dynamic; 1 extended)
Peak translations: 17, occurred 00:06:40 ago
Outside interfaces:
  Serial0/0/1
Inside interfaces:
  GigabitEthernet0/1
Hits: 345  Misses: 0
CEF Translated packets: 345, CEF Punted packets: 0
Expired translations: 20
Dynamic mappings:
-- Inside Source
[Id: 1] access-list 1 pool public_access refcount 2
 pool public_access: netmask 255.255.255.224
        start 209.165.200.242 end 209.165.200.254
        type generic, total addresses 13, allocated 1 (7%), misses 0

Total doors: 0
Appl doors: 0
Normal doors: 0
Queued Packets: 0
```

Note: This is only a sample output. Your output may not match exactly.

Step 7:   Remove the static NAT entry.

In Step 7, the static NAT entry is removed and you can observe the NAT entry.

a. Remove the static NAT from Part 2. Enter **yes** when prompted to delete child entries.

```
Gateway(config)# no ip nat inside source static 192.168.1.20 209.165.200.225

Static entry in use, do you want to delete child entries? [no]: yes
```

b. Clear the NATs and statistics.

c. Ping the ISP (192.31.7.1) from both hosts.

d. Display the NAT table and statistics.

```
Gateway# show ip nat statistics
Total active translations: 4 (0 static, 4 dynamic; 2 extended)
Peak translations: 15, occurred 00:00:43 ago
Outside interfaces:
  Serial0/0/1
Inside interfaces:
  GigabitEthernet0/1
Hits: 16  Misses: 0
```

```
CEF Translated packets: 285, CEF Punted packets: 0
Expired translations: 11
Dynamic mappings:
-- Inside Source
[Id: 1] access-list 1 pool public_access refcount 4
 pool public_access: netmask 255.255.255.224
        start 209.165.200.242 end 209.165.200.254
        type generic, total addresses 13, allocated 2 (15%), misses 0

Total doors: 0
Appl doors: 0
Normal doors: 0
Queued Packets: 0

Gateway# show ip nat translation
Pro Inside global       Inside local      Outside local      Outside global
icmp 209.165.200.243:512 192.168.1.20:512 192.31.7.1:512     192.31.7.1:512
--- 209.165.200.243     192.168.1.20      ---                ---
icmp 209.165.200.242:512 192.168.1.21:512 192.31.7.1:512     192.31.7.1:512
--- 209.165.200.242     192.168.1.21      ---                ---
```

Note: This is only a sample output. Your output may not match exactly.

Reflection

1. Why would NAT be used in a network?

_____

_____

_____

2. What are the limitations of NAT?

_____

_____

_____

Router Interface Summary Table

Router Interface Summary			
Router Model	Ethernet Interface #1	Ethernet Interface #2	Serial Interface #1	Serial Interface #2
1800	Fast Ethernet 0/0 (F0/0)	Fast Ethernet 0/1 (F0/1)	Serial 0/0/0 (S0/0/0)	Serial 0/0/1 (S0/0/1)
1900	Gigabit Ethernet 0/0 (G0/0)	Gigabit Ethernet 0/1 (G0/1)	Serial 0/0/0 (S0/0/0)	Serial 0/0/1 (S0/0/1)
2801	Fast Ethernet 0/0 (F0/0)	Fast Ethernet 0/1 (F0/1)	Serial 0/1/0 (S0/1/0)	Serial 0/1/1 (S0/1/1)

Router Interface Summary			
Router Model	**Ethernet Interface #1**	**Ethernet Interface #2**	**Serial Interface #1**	**Serial Interface #2**
2811	Fast Ethernet 0/0 (F0/0)	Fast Ethernet 0/1 (F0/1)	Serial 0/0/0 (S0/0/0)	Serial 0/0/1 (S0/0/1)
2900	Gigabit Ethernet 0/0 (G0/0)	Gigabit Ethernet 0/1 (G0/1)	Serial 0/0/0 (S0/0/0)	Serial 0/0/1 (S0/0/1)

Note: To find out how the router is configured, look at the interfaces to identify the type of router and how many interfaces the router has. There is no way to effectively list all the combinations of configurations for each router class. This table includes identifiers for the possible combinations of Ethernet and Serial interfaces in the device. The table does not include any other type of interface, even though a specific router may contain one. An example of this might be an ISDN BRI interface. The string in parentheses is the legal abbreviation that can be used in Cisco IOS commands to represent the interface.

Packet Tracer
☐ Activity

9.2.3.6 Packet Tracer–Implementing Static and Dynamic NAT

Topology

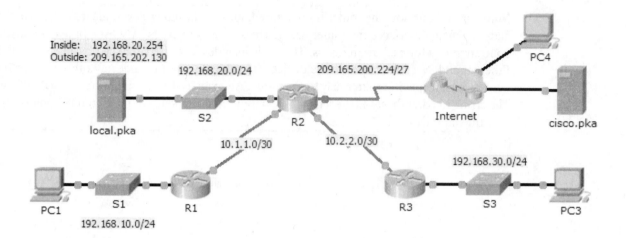

Inside: 192.168.20.254
Outside: 209.165.202.130

192.168.20.0/24

209.165.200.224/27

local.pka   S2   R2   Internet   cisco.pka   PC4

10.1.1.0/30   10.2.2.0/30

192.168.30.0/24

PC1   S1   R1   R3   S3   PC3

192.168.10.0/24

Objectives

Part 1: Configure Dynamic NAT with PAT

Part 2: Configure Static NAT

Part 3: Verify NAT Implementation

Part 1: Configure Dynamic NAT with PAT

Step 1:   Configure traffic that will be permitted for NAT translations.

On **R2**, configure a standard ACL named **R2NAT** that uses three statements to permit, in order, the following private address spaces: 192.168.10.0/24, 192.168.20.0/24, and 192.168.30.0/24.

_____

_____

_____

_____

Step 2:   Configure a pool of addresses for NAT.

Configure R2 with a NAT pool named R2POOL that uses the first address in the 209.165.202.128/30 address space. The second address is used for static NAT later in Part 2.

_____

_____

Step 3:   Associate the named ACL with the NAT pool and enable PAT.

```
R2(config)# ip nat inside source list R2NAT pool R2POOL overload
```

Step 4:   Configure the NAT interfaces.

Configure **R2** interfaces with the appropriate inside and outside NAT commands.

```
R2(config)# inte fa0/0
R2(config-if)# ip nat inside
R2(config-if)# inte s0/0/0
R2(config-if)# ip nat inside
R2(config-if)# inte s0/0/1
R2(config-if)# ip nat inside
R2(config-if)# inte s0/1/0
R2(config-if)# ip nat outside
```

Part 2: Configure Static NAT

Refer to the Topology. Create a static NAT translation to map the **local.pka** inside address to its outside address.

Part 3: Verify NAT Implementation

Step 1:   Access services across the Internet.

   a.   From the Web browser of **PC1**, or **PC3**, access the Web page for **cisco.pka**.

   b.   From the Web browser for **PC4**, access the Web page for **local.pka**.

Step 2:   View NAT translations.

View the NAT translations on **R2**.

```
R2# show ip nat translations
```

9.2.3.7 Lab–Configuring Port Address Translation (PAT)

Topology

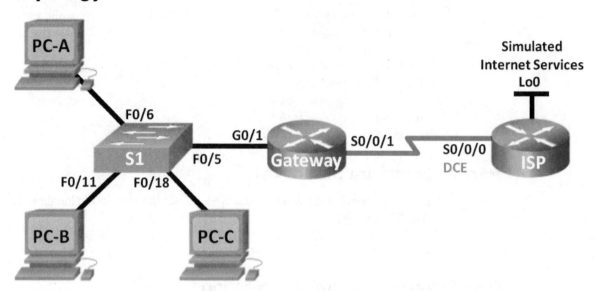

Addressing Table

Device	Interface	IP Address	Subnet Mask	Default Gateway
Gateway	G0/1	192.168.1.1	255.255.255.0	N/A
	S0/0/1	209.165.201.18	255.255.255.252	N/A
ISP	S0/0/0 (DCE)	209.165.201.17	255.255.255.252	N/A
	Lo0	192.31.7.1	255.255.255.255	N/A
PC-A	NIC	192.168.1.20	255.255.255.0	192.168.1.1
PC-B	NIC	192.168.1.21	255.255.255.0	192.168.1.1
PC-C	NIC	192.168.1.22	255.255.255.0	192.168.1.1

Objectives

Part 1: Build the Network and Verify Connectivity

Part 2: Configure and Verify NAT Pool Overload

Part 3: Configure and Verify PAT

Background/Scenario

In the first part of the lab, your company is allocated the public IP address range of 209.165.200.224/29 by the ISP. This provides the company with six public IP addresses. Dynamic NAT pool overload uses a pool of IP addresses in a many-to-many relationship. The router uses the first IP address in the pool and assigns connections using the IP address plus a unique port number. After the maximum number of translations for a single IP address have been reached on the router (platform and hardware specific), it uses the next IP address in the pool. NAT pool overload is a form of port address translation (PAT) that overloads a group of public IPv4 addresses.

In Part 2, the ISP has allocated a single IP address, 209.165.201.18, to your company for use on the Internet connection from the company Gateway router to the ISP. You will use the PAT to convert multiple internal addresses into the one usable public address. You will test, view, and verify that the translations are taking place, and you will interpret the NAT/PAT statistics to monitor the process.

Note: The routers used with CCNA hands-on labs are Cisco 1941 Integrated Services Routers (ISRs) with Cisco IOS Release 15.2(4)M3 (universalk9 image). The switches used are Cisco Catalyst 2960s with Cisco IOS Release 15.0(2) (lanbasek9 image). Other routers, switches and Cisco IOS versions can be used. Depending on the model and Cisco IOS version, the commands available and output produced might vary from what is shown in the labs. Refer to the Router Interface Summary Table at the end of this lab for the correct interface identifiers.

Note: Make sure that the routers and switch have been erased and have no startup configurations. If you are unsure, contact your instructor.

Required Resources

- 2 Routers (Cisco 1941 with Cisco IOS Release 15.2(4)M3 universal image or comparable)

- 1 Switch (Cisco 2960 with Cisco IOS Release 15.0(2) lanbasek9 image or comparable)

- 3 PCs (Windows 7, Vista, or XP with terminal emulation program, such as Tera Term)

- Console cables to configure the Cisco IOS devices via the console ports

- Ethernet and serial cables as shown in the topology

Part 1: Build the Network and Verify Connectivity

In Part 1, you will set up the network topology and configure basic settings, such as the interface IP addresses, static routing, device access, and passwords.

Step 1:   Cable the network as shown in the topology.

Step 2:   Configure PC hosts.

Step 3:   Initialize and reload the routers and switches.

Step 4:   Configure basic settings for each router.

    a.   Console into the router and enter global configuration mode.

    b.   Copy the following basic configuration and paste it to the running-configuration on the router.

```
no ip domain-lookup
service password-encryption
enable secret class
banner motd #
Unauthorized access is strictly prohibited. #
Line con 0
password cisco
login
logging synchronous
```

```
line vty 0 4
password cisco
login
```

c. Configure the host name as shown in the topology.

d. Copy the running configuration to the startup configuration.

Step 5: Configure static routing.

a. Create a static route from the ISP router to the Gateway router.

```
ISP(config)# ip route 209.165.200.224 255.255.255.248 209.165.201.18
```

b. Create a default route from the Gateway router to the ISP router.

```
Gateway(config)# ip route 0.0.0.0 0.0.0.0 209.165.201.17
```

Step 6: Verify network connectivity.

a. From the PC hosts, ping the G0/1 interface on the Gateway router. Troubleshoot if the pings are unsuccessful.

b. Verify that the static routes are configured correctly on both routers.

Part 2: Configure and Verify NAT Pool Overload

In Part 2, you will configure the Gateway router to translate the IP addresses from the 192.168.1.0/24 network to one of the six usable addresses in the 209.165.200.224/29 range.

Step 1: Define an access control list that matches the LAN private IP addresses.

ACL 1 is used to allow the 192.168.1.0/24 network to be translated.

```
Gateway(config)# access-list 1 permit 192.168.1.0 0.0.0.255
```

Step 2: Define the pool of usable public IP addresses.

```
Gateway(config)# ip nat pool public_access 209.165.200.225  209.165.200.230 netmask
255.255.255.248
```

Step 3: Define the NAT from the inside source list to the outside pool.

```
Gateway(config)# ip nat inside source list 1 pool public_access overload
```

Step 4: Specify the interfaces.

Issue the **ip nat inside** and **ip nat outside** commands to the interfaces.

```
Gateway(config)# interface g0/1
Gateway(config-if)# ip nat inside
Gateway(config-if)# interface s0/0/1
Gateway(config-if)# ip nat outside
```

Step 5: Verify the NAT pool overload configuration.

a. From each PC host, ping the 192.31.7.1 address on the ISP router.

b. Display NAT statistics on the Gateway router.

```
Gateway# show ip nat statistics
Total active translations: 3 (0 static, 3 dynamic; 3 extended)
Peak translations: 3, occurred 00:00:25 ago
Outside interfaces:
  Serial0/0/1
Inside interfaces:
  GigabitEthernet0/1
```

```
Hits: 24  Misses: 0
CEF Translated packets: 24, CEF Punted packets: 0
Expired translations: 0
Dynamic mappings:
-- Inside Source
[Id: 1] access-list 1 pool public_access refcount 3
 pool public_access: netmask 255.255.255.248
        start 209.165.200.225 end 209.165.200.230
        type generic, total addresses 6, allocated 1 (16%), misses 0

Total doors: 0
Appl doors: 0
Normal doors: 0
Queued Packets: 0
```

c. Display NATs on the Gateway router.

```
Gateway# show ip nat translations
Pro Inside global      Inside local     Outside local     Outside global
icmp 209.165.200.225:0 192.168.1.20:1   192.31.7.1:1      192.31.7.1:0
icmp 209.165.200.225:1 192.168.1.21:1   192.31.7.1:1      192.31.7.1:1
icmp 209.165.200.225:2 192.168.1.22:1   192.31.7.1:1      192.31.7.1:2
```

Note: Depending on how much time has elapsed since you performed the pings from each PC, you may not see all three translations. ICMP translations have a short timeout value.

How many Inside local IP addresses are listed in the sample output above? _____

How many Inside global IP addresses are listed? _____

How many port numbers are paired with the Inside global addresses? _____

What would be the result of pinging the Inside local address of PC-A from the ISP router? Why?

_____

_____

Part 3: Configure and Verify PAT

In Part 3, you will configure PAT by using an interface instead of a pool of addresses to define the outside address. Not all of the commands in Part 2 will be reused in Part 3.

Step 1: Clear NATs and statistics on the Gateway router.

Step 2: Verify the configuration for NAT.

a. Verify that statistics have been cleared.

b. Verify that the outside and inside interfaces are configured for NATs.

c. Verify that the ACL is still configured for NATs.

What command did you use to confirm the results from Steps a to c?

_____

Step 3: Remove the pool of useable public IP addresses.

> Gateway(config)# **no ip nat pool public_access 209.165.200.225 209.165.200.230 netmask 255.255.255.248**

Step 4: Remove the NAT translation from inside source list to outside pool.

> Gateway(config)# **no ip nat inside source list 1 pool public_access overload**

Step 5: Associate the source list with the outside interface.

> Gateway(config)# **ip nat inside source list 1 interface serial 0/0/1 overload**

Step 6: Test the PAT configuration.

   a. From each PC, ping the 192.31.7.1 address on the ISP router.

   b. Display NAT statistics on the Gateway router.

```
Gateway# show ip nat statistics
Total active translations: 3 (0 static, 3 dynamic; 3 extended)
Peak translations: 3, occurred 00:00:19 ago
Outside interfaces:
  Serial0/0/1
Inside interfaces:
  GigabitEthernet0/1
Hits: 24  Misses: 0
CEF Translated packets: 24, CEF Punted packets: 0
Expired translations: 0
Dynamic mappings:
-- Inside Source
[Id: 2] access-list 1 interface Serial0/0/1 refcount 3

Total doors: 0
Appl doors: 0
Normal doors: 0
Queued Packets: 0
```

   c. Display NAT translations on Gateway.

```
Gateway# show ip nat translations
Pro Inside global      Inside local      Outside local      Outside global
icmp 209.165.201.18:3  192.168.1.20:1    192.31.7.1:1       192.31.7.1:3
icmp 209.165.201.18:1  192.168.1.21:1    192.31.7.1:1       192.31.7.1:1
icmp 209.165.201.18:4  192.168.1.22:1    192.31.7.1:1       192.31.7.1:4
```

Reflection

What advantages does PAT provide?

Router Interface Summary Table

Router Interface Summary				
Router Model	Ethernet Interface #1	Ethernet Interface #2	Serial Interface #1	Serial Interface #2
1800	Fast Ethernet 0/0 (F0/0)	Fast Ethernet 0/1 (F0/1)	Serial 0/0/0 (S0/0/0)	Serial 0/0/1 (S0/0/1)
1900	Gigabit Ethernet 0/0 (G0/0)	Gigabit Ethernet 0/1 (G0/1)	Serial 0/0/0 (S0/0/0)	Serial 0/0/1 (S0/0/1)
2801	Fast Ethernet 0/0 (F0/0)	Fast Ethernet 0/1 (F0/1)	Serial 0/1/0 (S0/1/0)	Serial 0/1/1 (S0/1/1)
2811	Fast Ethernet 0/0 (F0/0)	Fast Ethernet 0/1 (F0/1)	Serial 0/0/0 (S0/0/0)	Serial 0/0/1 (S0/0/1)
2900	Gigabit Ethernet 0/0 (G0/0)	Gigabit Ethernet 0/1 (G0/1)	Serial 0/0/0 (S0/0/0)	Serial 0/0/1 (S0/0/1)

Note: To find out how the router is configured, look at the interfaces to identify the type of router and how many interfaces the router has. There is no way to effectively list all the combinations of configurations for each router class. This table includes identifiers for the possible combinations of Ethernet and Serial interfaces in the device. The table does not include any other type of interface, even though a specific router may contain one. An example of this might be an ISDN BRI interface. The string in parentheses is the legal abbreviation that can be used in Cisco IOS commands to represent the interface.

9.2.4.4 Packet Tracer–Configuring Port Forwarding on a Wireless Router

Topology

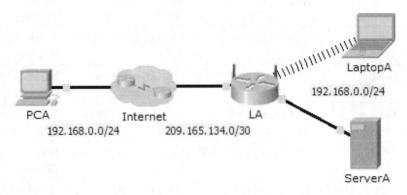

Addressing Table

Device	Interface	IP Address	Subnet Mask
LA	Internet	209.165.134.1	255.255.255.252
	LAN	192.168.0.1	255.255.255.0

Objectives

Part 1: Configure Port Forwarding

Part 2: Verify Remote Connectivity to ServerA

Scenario

Your friend wants to play a game with you on your server. Both of you are at your respective homes, connected to the Internet. You need to configure your SOHO (Small Office, Home Office) router to port forward HTTP requests to your server so that your friend can access the game lobby Web page.

Part 1: Configure Port Forwarding

a. From the Web browser on **LaptopA**, access **LA** by entering the LAN IP address, 192.168.0.1. The username is **admin** and the password is **cisco123**.

b. Click **Applications & Gaming**. In the first dropdown on the left, choose **HTTP** and then enter 192.168.0.2 in the "To IP Address" column. This configures **LA** to forward port 80 to 192.168.0.2. Check the **Enabled** box next to the address column.

c. Scroll to the bottom and click **Save Settings**.

Part 2: Verify Remote Connectivity to ServerA

From the Web browser on **PCA**, enter the Internet IP address for **LA**. The game server Web page should appear.

9.3.1.4 Packet Tracer–Verifying and Troubleshooting NAT Configurations

Topology

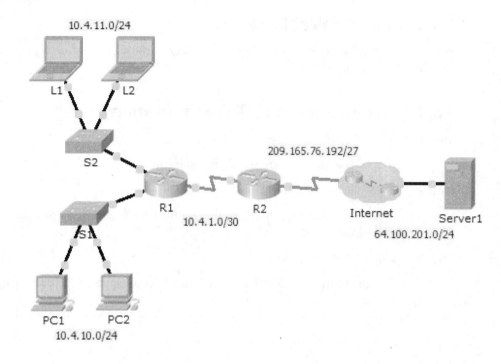

Addressing Table

Device	Interface	IP Address	Subnet Mask	Default Gateway
R1	G0/0	10.4.10.254	255.255.255.0	N/A
	G0/1	10.4.11.254	255.255.255.0	N/A
	S0/0/1	10.4.1.2	255.255.255.252	N/A
R2	S0/0/0	209.165.76.194	255.255.255.224	N/A
	S0/0/1	10.4.1.1	255.255.255.252	N/A
Server1	NIC	64.100.201.5	255.255.255.0	64.100.201.1
PC1	NIC	10.4.10.1	255.255.255.0	10.4.10.254
PC2	NIC	10.4.10.2	255.255.255.0	10.4.10.254
L1	NIC	10.4.11.1	255.255.255.0	10.4.11.254
L2	NIC	10.4.11.2	255.255.255.0	10.4.11.254

Objectives

Part 1: Isolate Problems

Part 2: Troubleshoot NAT Configuration

Part 3: Verify Connectivity

Scenario

A contractor restored an old configuration to a new router running NAT. But, the network has changed and a new subnet was added after the old configuration was backed up. It is your job to get the network working again.

Part 1: Isolate Problems

Ping **Server1** from **PC1**, **PC2**, **L1**, **L2**, and **R2**. Record the success of each ping. Ping any other machines as needed.

Part 2: Troubleshoot NAT Configuration

Step 1: View the NAT translations on R2.

If NAT is working, there should be table entries.

Step 2: Show the running configuration of R2.

The NAT inside port should align with the private address, while the NAT outside port should align with the public address.

Step 3: Correct the interfaces.

Assign the **ip nat inside** and **ip nat outside** commands to the correct ports.

_____

_____

_____

_____

Step 4: Ping Server1 from PC1, PC2, L1, L2, and R2.

Record the success of each ping. Ping any other machines as needed.

Step 5: View the NAT translations on R2.

If NAT is working, there should be table entries.

Step 6: Show Access-list 101 on R2.

The wildcard mask should encompass both the 10.4.10.0 network and the 10.4.11.0 network.

Step 7: Correct the Access-list.

Delete access-list 101 and replace it with a similar list that is also one statement in length. The only difference should be the wildcard.

_____

_____

Part 3: Verify Connectivity

Step 1:   Verify connectivity to Server1.

Record the success of each ping. All hosts should be able to ping **Server1**, **R1**, and **R2**. Troubleshoot if the pings are not successful.

Step 2:   View the NAT translations on R2.

NAT should display many table entries.

9.3.1.5 Lab–Troubleshooting NAT Configurations

Topology

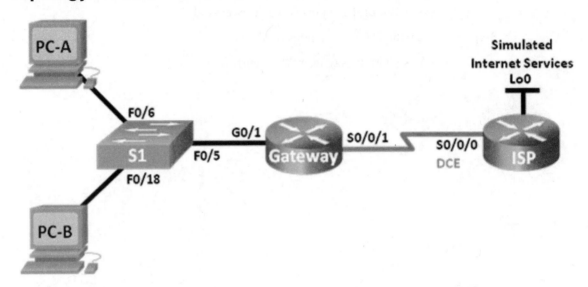

Addressing Table

Device	Interface	IP Address	Subnet Mask	Default Gateway
Gateway	G0/1	192.168.1.1	255.255.255.0	N/A
	S0/0/1	209.165.200.225	255.255.255.252	N/A
ISP	S0/0/0 (DCE)	209.165.200.226	255.255.255.252	N/A
	Lo0	198.133.219.1	255.255.255.255	N/A
PC-A	NIC	192.168.1.3	255.255.255.0	192.168.1.1
PC-B	NIC	192.168.1.4	255.255.255.0	192.168.1.1

Objectives

Part 1: Build the Network and Configure Basic Device Settings

Part 2: Troubleshoot Static NAT

Part 3: Troubleshoot Dynamic NAT

Background/Scenario

In this lab, the Gateway router was configured by an inexperienced network administrator at your company. Several errors in the configuration have resulted in NAT issues. Your boss has asked you to troubleshoot and correct the NAT errors and document your work. Ensure that the network supports the following:

- PC-A acts as a web server with a static NAT and will be reachable from the outside using the 209.165.200.254 address.

- PC-B acts as a host computer and dynamically receives an IP address from the created pool of addresses called NAT_POOL, which uses the 209.165.200.240/29 range.

Note: The routers used with CCNA hands-on labs are Cisco 1941 Integrated Services Routers (ISRs) with Cisco IOS Release 15.2(4)M3 (universalk9 image). The switches used are Cisco Catalyst 2960s with Cisco IOS Release 15.0(2) (lanbasek9 image). Other routers, switches and Cisco IOS versions can be used. Depending on the model and Cisco IOS version, the commands available and output produced might vary from what is shown in the labs. Refer to the Router Interface Summary Table at the end of this lab for the correct interface identifiers.

Note: Make sure that the routers and switch have been erased and have no startup configurations. If you are unsure, contact your instructor.

Required Resources

- 2 Routers (Cisco 1941 with Cisco IOS Release 15.2(4)M3 universal image or comparable)

- 1 Switch (Cisco 2960 with Cisco IOS Release 15.0(2) lanbasek9 image or comparable)

- 2 PCs (Windows 7, Vista, or XP with terminal emulation program, such as Tera Term)

- Console cables to configure the Cisco IOS devices via the console ports

- Ethernet and serial cables as shown in the topology

Part 1: Build the Network and Configure Basic Device Settings

In Part 1, you will set up the network topology and configure the routers with basic settings. Additional NAT-related configurations are provided. The NAT configurations for the Gateway router contain errors that you will identify and correct as you proceed through the lab.

Step 1: Cable the network as shown in the topology.

Step 2: Configure PC hosts.

Step 3: Initialize and reload the switch and routers.

Step 4: Configure basic settings for each router.

    a. Console into the router and enter global configuration mode.

    b. Copy the following basic configuration and paste it to the running-configuration on the router.

```
no ip domain-lookup
service password-encryption
enable secret class
banner motd #
Unauthorized access is strictly prohibited. #
line con 0
password cisco
login
logging synchronous
line vty 0 4
password cisco
login
```

    c. Configure the host name as shown in the topology.

    d. Copy the running configuration to the startup configuration.

Step 5: Configure static routing.

    a. Create a static route from the ISP router to the Gateway router that was assigned public network address range 209.165.200.224/27.

```
ISP(config)# ip route 209.165.200.224 255.255.255.224 s0/0/0
```

    b. Create a default route from the Gateway router to the ISP router.

```
Gateway(config)# ip route 0.0.0.0 0.0.0.0 s0/0/1
```

Step 6: Load router configurations.

The configurations for the routers are provided for you. There are errors with the configuration for the Gateway router. Identify and correct the configuration errors.

Gateway Router Configuration

```
interface g0/1
 ip nat outside
 no shutdown
interface s0/0/0
 ip nat outside
interface s0/0/1
 no shutdown
ip nat inside source static 192.168.2.3 209.165.200.254
ip nat pool NAT_POOL 209.165.200.241 209.165.200.246 netmask 255.255.255.248
ip nat inside source list NAT_ACL pool NATPOOL
ip access-list standard NAT_ACL
 permit 192.168.10.0 0.0.0.255
banner motd $AUTHORIZED ACCESS ONLY$
end
```

Step 7: Save the running configuration to the startup configuration.

Part 2: Troubleshoot Static NAT

In Part 2, you will examine the static NAT for PC-A to determine if it is configured correctly. You will troubleshoot the scenario until the correct static NAT is verified.

    a. To troubleshoot issues with NAT, use the **debug ip nat** command. Turn on NAT debugging to see translations in real-time across the Gateway router.

```
Gateway# debug ip nat
```

    b. From PC-A, ping Lo0 on the ISP router. Do any NAT debug translations appear on the Gateway router?

_____

    c. On the Gateway router, enter the command that allows you to see all current NAT translations on the Gateway router. Write the command in the space below.

_____

Why are you seeing a NAT translation in the table, but none occurred when PC-A pinged the ISP loopback interface? What is needed to correct the issue?

_____

d. Record any commands that are necessary to correct the static NAT configuration error.

_____

_____

e. From PC-A, ping Lo0 on the ISP router. Do any NAT debug translations appear on the Gateway router?

_____

f. On the Gateway router, enter the command that allows you to observe the total number of current NATs. Write the command in the space below.

_____

Is the static NAT occurring successfully? Why?

_____

g. On the Gateway router, enter the command that allows you to view the current configuration of the router. Write the command in the space below.

_____

h. Are there any problems with the current configuration that prevent the static NAT from occurring?

_____

i. Record any commands that are necessary to correct the static NAT configuration errors.

_____

_____

_____

_____

_____

_____

_____

j. From PC-A, ping Lo0 on the ISP router. Do any NAT debug translations appear on the Gateway router?

_____

k. Use the **show ip nat translations verbose** command to verify static NAT functionality.

Note: The timeout value for ICMP is very short. If you do not see all the translations in the output, redo the ping.

Is the static NAT translation occurring successfully? _____

If static NAT is not occurring, repeat the steps above to troubleshoot the configuration.

Part 3: Troubleshoot Dynamic NAT

    a. From PC-B, ping Lo0 on the ISP router. Do any NAT debug translations appear on the Gateway router?

    _____

    b. On the Gateway router, enter the command that allows you to view the current configuration of the router. Are there any problems with the current configuration that prevent dynamic NAT from occurring?

    _____

    c. Record any commands that are necessary to correct the dynamic NAT configuration errors.

    _____

    _____

    _____

    _____

    _____

    d. From PC-B, ping Lo0 on the ISP router. Do any NAT debug translations appear on the Gateway router?

    _____

    e. Use the **show ip nat statistics** to view NAT usage.

    Is the NAT occurring successfully? _____

    What percentage of dynamic addresses has been allocated? _____

    f. Turn off all debugging using the **undebug all** command.

Reflection

    1. What is the benefit of a static NAT?

    _____

    _____

    2. What issues would arise if 10 host computers in this network were attempting simultaneous Internet communication?

    _____

    _____

Router Interface Summary Table

Router Interface Summary			
Router Model	**Ethernet Interface #1**	**Ethernet Interface #2**	**Serial Interface #1** **Serial Interface #2**
1800	Fast Ethernet 0/0 (F0/0)	Fast Ethernet 0/1 (F0/1)	Serial 0/0/0 (S0/0/0) Serial 0/0/1 (S0/0/1)
1900	Gigabit Ethernet 0/0 (G0/0)	Gigabit Ethernet 0/1 (G0/1)	Serial 0/0/0 (S0/0/0) Serial 0/0/1 (S0/0/1)

| Router Interface Summary | | | |
Router Model	Ethernet Interface #1	Ethernet Interface #2	Serial Interface #1	Serial Interface #2
2801	Fast Ethernet 0/0 (F0/0)	Fast Ethernet 0/1 (F0/1)	Serial 0/1/0 (S0/1/0)	Serial 0/1/1 (S0/1/1)
2811	Fast Ethernet 0/0 (F0/0)	Fast Ethernet 0/1 (F0/1)	Serial 0/0/0 (S0/0/0)	Serial 0/0/1 (S0/0/1)
2900	Gigabit Ethernet 0/0 (G0/0)	Gigabit Ethernet 0/1 (G0/1)	Serial 0/0/0 (S0/0/0)	Serial 0/0/1 (S0/0/1)

Note: To find out how the router is configured, look at the interfaces to identify the type of router and how many interfaces the router has. There is no way to effectively list all the combinations of configurations for each router class. This table includes identifiers for the possible combinations of Ethernet and Serial interfaces in the device. The table does not include any other type of interface, even though a specific router may contain one. An example of this might be an ISDN BRI interface. The string in parentheses is the legal abbreviation that can be used in Cisco IOS commands to represent the interface.

Lab 9.4.1.1–NAT Check

Objective

Configure, verify, and analyze static NAT, dynamic NAT, and NAT with overloading.

Scenario

Network address translation is not currently included in your company's network design. It has been decided to configure some devices to use NAT services for connecting to the mail server.

Before deploying NAT live on the network, you prototype it using a network simulation program.

Resources

- Packet Tracer software
- Word processing or presentation software

Directions

Step 1:   Create a very small network topology using Packet Tracer, including, at minimum:

    a.   Two 1941 routers, interconnected

    b.   Two LAN switches, one per router

    c.   One mail server, connected to the LAN on one router

    d.   One PC or laptop, connected to the LAN on the other router

Step 2:   Address the topology.

    a.   Use private addressing for all networks, hosts, and device.

    b.   DHCP addressing of the PC or laptop is optional.

    c.   Static addressing of the mail server is mandatory.

Step 3:   Configure a routing protocol for the network.

Step 4:   Validate full network connectivity without NAT services.

    a.   Ping from one end of the topology and back to ensure the network is functioning fully.

    b.   Troubleshoot and correct any problems preventing full network functionality.

Step 5:   Configure NAT services on either router from the host PC or laptop to the mail server.

Step 6:   Produce output validating NAT operations on the simulated network.

    a.   Use the **show ip nat statistics, show access-lists,** and **show ip nat translations** commands to gather information about NAT's operation on the router.

    b.   Copy and paste or save screenshots of the topology and output information to a word processing or presentation document.

Step 7:   Explain the NAT design and output to another group or to the class.

9.4.1.2 Packet Tracer–Skills Integration Challenge

Topology

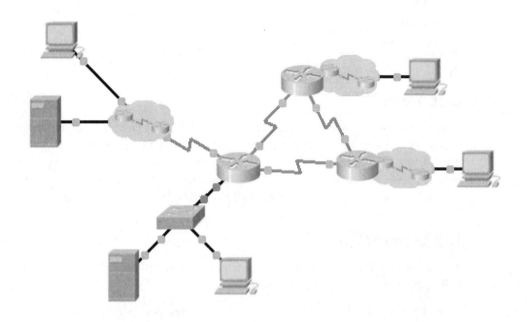

Addressing Table

Device	Interface	IP Address	Subnet Mask	Default Gateway
	G0/0.15			N/A
	G0/0.30			N/A
	G0/0.45			N/A
	G0/0.60			N/A
	S0/0/0		255.255.255.252	N/A
	S0/0/1		255.255.255.252	N/A
	S0/1/0		255.255.255.252	N/A
	G0/0			N/A
	S0/0/0		255.255.255.252	N/A
	S0/0/1		255.255.255.252	N/A
	G0/0			N/A
	S0/0/0		255.255.255.252	N/A
	S0/0/1		255.255.255.252	N/A
	VLAN 60			
	NIC	DHCP Assigned	DHCP Assigned	DHCP Assigned

VLANs and Port Assignments Table

VLAN Number–Name	Port Assignment	Network
15–Servers	F0/11–F0/20	
30–PCs	F0/1–F0/10	
45–Native	G0/1	
60–Management	VLAN 60	

Scenario

This culminating activity includes many of the skills that you have acquired during this course. First, you will complete the documentation for the network. Make sure you have a printed version of the instructions. During implementation, you will configure VLANs, trunking, port security, and SSH remote access on a switch. You will then implement inter-VLAN routing and NAT on a router. Finally, you will use your documentation to verify your implementation by testing end-to-end connectivity.

Documentation

You are required to fully document the network. You will need a print out of this instruction set, which will include an unlabeled topology diagram:

- Label all the device names, network addresses, and other important information that Packet Tracer generated.

- Complete the **Addressing Table** and **VLANs and Port Assignments Table**.

- Fill in any blanks in the **Implementation** and **Verification** steps. The information is supplied when you launch the Packet Tracer activity.

Implementation

Note: All devices in the topology except [[R1Name]], [[S1Name]], and [[PC1Name]] are fully configured. You do not have access to the other routers. You can access all the servers and PCs for testing purposes.

Implement the following requirements using your documentation:

[[S1Name]]

- Configure remote management access including IP addressing and SSH:

    - Domain is cisco.com

    - User [[UserText]] with password [[UserPass]]

    - Crypto key length of 1024

    - SSH version 2, limited to 2 authentication attempts and a 60 second timeout

    - Clear text passwords should be encrypted.

- Configure, name, and assign VLANs. Ports should be manually configured as access ports.

- Configure trunking.

- Implement port security:

  - On Fa0/1, allow 2 MAC addresses that are automatically added to the configuration file when detected. The port should not be disabled, but a syslog message should be captured if a violation occurs.

  - Disable all other unused ports.

  [[R1Name]]

- Configure inter-VLAN routing.

- Configure DHCP services for VLAN 30. Use **LAN** as the case-sensitive name for the pool.

- Implement routing:

  - Use RIPv2 as the routing protocol.

  - Configure one network statement for the entire **[[DisplayNet]]** address space.

  - Disable interfaces that should not send RIPv2 messages.

  - Configure a default route to the Internet.

- Implement NAT:

  - Configure a standard, one statement ACL number 1. All IP addresses belonging to the **[[DisplayNet]]** address space are allowed.

  - Refer to your documentation and configure static NAT for the File Server.

  - Configure dynamic NAT with PAT using a pool name of your choice, a /30 mask, and these two public addresses:

  [[NATPoolText]]

  [[PC1Name]]

  Verify **[[PC1Name]]** has received full addressing information from **[[R1Name]]**.

Verification

All devices should now be able to ping all other devices. If not, troubleshoot your configurations to isolate and solve problems. A few tests include:

- Verify remote access to **[[S1Name]]** by using SSH from a PC.

- Verify VLANs are assigned to appropriate ports and port security is in force.

- Verify OSPF neighbors and a complete routing table.

- Verify NAT translations and statistics.

  - **Outside Host** should be able to access **File Server** at the public address.

  - Inside PCs should be able to access **Web Server**.

- Document any problems you encountered and the solutions in the **Troubleshooting Documentation** table below.

Troubleshooting Documentation

Problem	Solution

Suggested Scoring Rubric

Packet Tracer scores 70 points. Documentation is worth 30 points.

CHAPTER 10

Device Discovery, Management, and Maintenance

Most of your CCNA studies have focused on implementing networking technologies. But what if there is currently no design or implementation to do in your job as network administrator? What if the network is already up and running? What if the network documentation is incomplete or out of date? What if you don't know where your configuration files or IOS image backups are stored? Then you will mostly likely start to engage is some activities to rectify the situation. This chapter focuses on some protocols and basic procedures that network administrators use to perform device discovery, management, and maintenance tasks.

The Study Guide portion of this chapter uses a combination of matching, fill-in-the-blank, multiple-choice, and open-ended question exercises to test your knowledge and skills in device discovery, management, and maintenance. The Labs and Activities portion of this chapter includes all the online curriculum labs and Packet Tracer activities to ensure that you have mastered the hands-on skills needed to understand basic IP addressing and router configuration.

As you work through this chapter, use Chapter 10 in *Routing and Switching Essentials v6 Companion Guide* or use the corresponding Chapter 10 in the Routing and Switching Essentials online curriculum for assistance.

Study Guide

Device Discovery

Cisco Discovery Protocol (CDP) and Link Layer Discover Protocol (LLDP) are both capable of discovering information about directly connected devices. CDP is a Cisco proprietary Layer 2 protocol that is used to gather information about Cisco devices that share the same data link. CDP is media and protocol independent and runs on all Cisco devices, such as routers, switches, and access servers. Cisco devices also support LLDP, which is a vendor-neutral neighbor discovery protocol similar to CDP. LLDP works with network devices, such as routers, switches, and wireless LAN access points. Both protocols advertise device identity and capabilities to other devices across Layer 2 links.

Draw and Label the Network Topology

Use the command output in Example 10-1 to answer the following questions.

What command was used to generate the output? _____

How many devices are in the network? _____

What are the type and platform of devices? _____

What CDP command would allow you to record the IP addresses of connected devices?

_____

Based on the command output in Example 10-1, use the space provided in Figure 10-1 to draw and label the topology. Include all the devices, the links between the devices, device names, and interface labels.

Example 10-1   CDP Command Output

```
London# _____

Capability Codes: R - Router, T - Trans Bridge, B - Source Route Bridge
                  S - Switch, H - Host, I - IGMP, r - Repeater, P - Phone

Device ID    Local Intrfce   Holdtme    Capability   Platform   Port ID
LdSw         Gig 0/0          154          S          2960       Gig 0/1
HK1          Ser 0/0/0        124          R          C1900      Ser 0/0/0
HK2          Ser 0/0/1        179          R          C1900      Ser 0/0/1

HK1# _____

Capability Codes: R - Router, T - Trans Bridge, B - Source Route Bridge
                  S - Switch, H - Host, I - IGMP, r - Repeater, P - Phone

Device ID    Local Intrfce   Holdtme    Capability   Platform   Port ID
London       Ser 0/0/0        145          R          C1900      Ser 0/0/0
Sw1          Gig 0/0          148          S          2960       Gig 0/1

HK2# _____

Capability Codes: R - Router, T - Trans Bridge, B - Source Route Bridge
                  S - Switch, H - Host, I - IGMP, r - Repeater, P - Phone

Device ID    Local Intrfce   Holdtme    Capability   Platform   Port ID
Sw1          Gig 0/1          128          S          2960       Gig 0/2
London       Ser 0/0/1        125          R          C1900      Ser 0/0/1
```

Figure 10-1   Network Topology

Compare CDP and LLDP

In Table 10-1, indicate the protocol for each characteristic listed.

Table 10-1   CDP and LLDP Characteristics

Field	CDP	LLDP
Requires two commands on the interface to transmit and receive packets		
Used to gather information about Cisco devices that share the same data link		
Works with network devices, such as routers, switches, and wireless LAN access points, across multiple manufacturers' devices		
A vendor-neutral neighbor discovery protocol to run on local area networks		
Media and protocol independent, runs on all Cisco devices		
This protocol advertises its identity and capabilities to other devices and receives the information from physically connected Layer 2 devices from multiple manufacturers		
Advertisements share information about the type of device that is discovered, the names of the devices, and the number and type of interfaces		

Device Management

Device management protocols for this course include Network Time Protocol (NTP) and syslog.

NTP Implementation

What are the two methods for setting the date and time on a router or a switch?

_____

_____

What is the command to manually set the time and date to December 1, 2017 3:00 PM?

_____

_____

_____

What command will display the current time and date shown in Example 10-2?

Example 10-2   Displaying the Current Time and Date

```
Router# _____
*15:0:19.942 UTC Fri Dec 1 2017
```

NTP networks use a hierarchical system of time sources. Each level in this hierarchical system is called a stratum. Stratum _____ devices are high-precision timekeeping devices. Stratum _____ devices are directly connected to one or more of these high-precision timekeeping devices. Stratum _____ devices, such as NTP clients, synchronize their time using NTP packets from stratum _____ NTP servers.

In Example 10-3, what command was used to determine that the clock was manually set?

Example 10-3   Determining How the Clock Was Configured

```
Router# _____
*15:10:32.713 UTC Fri Dec 1 2017
Time source is user configuration
```

The NTP server is at 10.10.10.10. Record the command, including router prompt, that would configure RTA to synchronize with the NTP server.

_____

Syslog Operation

Developed in the 1980s and documented as RFC 3164, syslog uses UDP port 514 to send notifications across IP networks to a syslog server. Briefly describe the three main syslog functions.

_____

_____

_____

List the four destinations these messages can be sent to.

_____

_____

_____

_____

Because you have configured many routers by now, one of the more common messages you have seen is the interface "up" and "up" message, as shown in Example 10-4.

Example 10-4   Syslog Message: Interface Is "Up" and "Up"

```
000039: *Nov 13 15:20:39.999: %LINK-3-UPDOWN: Interface GigabitEthernet0/0, changed state
to up

000040: *Nov 13 15:20:40.999: %LINEPROTO-5-UPDOWN: Line protocol on Interface
GigabitEthernet0/0, changed state to up
```

In Table 10-2, use the second line of output from Example 10-4 to provide an example of each field in the syslog message format.

Table 10-2   Syslog Message Format

Field	Example
Sequence Number	
Timestamp	
Facility	
Severity	
Mnemonic	
Description	

By default, the Sequence Number field is not shown. Record the command, including the router prompt, to add this field to syslog messages.

```
Router(config)# _____
```

Syslog Configuration

Using the topology and addressing shown in Figure 10-2, record the commands, including the router prompt, to configure the logging service on RTA with the following requirements:

- All logging messages should be sent to the console and to the buffer as well as the syslog server.

- Only log messages with severity 5 or lower.

- The source interface for logged messages should always be the G0/0 interface.

Figure 10-2   Syslog Configuration Topology

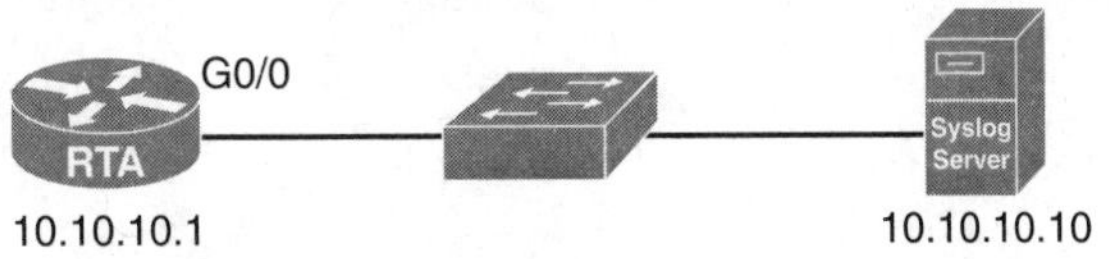

```
RTA# _____
    _____
    _____
    _____
    _____
    _____
```

What command will display the messages logged to RAM?

_____

Device Maintenance

Device maintenance includes ensuring that Cisco IOS images and configuration files are backed up in a safe location in the event that the device memory is corrupted or erased, either maliciously or inadvertently. Maintenance also includes keeping the IOS image up to date. The device maintenance section of the chapter includes topics for file maintenance, image management, and software licensing.

Router and Switch File Maintenance

In addition to implementing and securing a small network, it is also the job of the network administrator to manage configuration files. Managing the configuration files is important for purposes of backup and retrieval in the event of a device failure. This section includes a Packet Tracer activity and several important labs you should complete.

Indicate the commands used to generate the output in Example 10-5.

Example 10-5   Cisco IOS File System Commands

```
Router# _____
File Systems:


        Size(b)       Free(b)       Type   Flags   Prefixes
            -             -         opaque    rw    archive:
            -             -         opaque    rw    system:
            -             -         opaque    rw    ʹtmpsys:
            -             -         opaque    rw    null:
            -             -         network   rw    tftp:
*     256610304     112222208       disk     rw    flash0: flash:#
            -             -          disk     rw    flash1:
        262136        249536        nvram    rw    nvram:
            -             -         opaque    wo    syslog:
            -             -         opaque    rw    xmodem:
            -             -         opaque    rw    ymodem:
            -             -         network   rw    rcp:
            -             -         network   rw    http:
            -             -         network   rw    ftp:
            -             -         network   rw    scp:
            -             -         opaque    ro    tar:
            -             -         network   rw    https:
            -             -         opaque    ro    cns:
        127090688      59346944     usbflash  rw    usbflash0:
```

```
Router# _____
Directory of flash0:/


    1  -rw-    68831808   Apr 3 2013 21:53:06 +00:00  c1900-universalk9-mz.SPA.152-4.M3.bin
    2  -rw-        2903   Aug 9 2012 16:12:34 +00:00  cpconfig-19xx.cfg
    3  -rw-     3000320   Aug 9 2012 16:12:46 +00:00  cpexpress.tar
    4  -rw-        1038   Aug 9 2012 16:12:56 +00:00  home.shtml
    5  -rw-      122880   Aug 9 2012 16:13:04 +00:00  home.tar
    6  -rw-     1697952   Aug 9 2012 16:13:18 +00:00  securedesktop-ios-3.1.1.45-k9.pkg
    7  -rw-      415956   Aug 9 2012 16:13:30 +00:00  sslclient-win-1.1.4.176.pkg
    8  -rw-        1389   Feb 6 2013 17:40:08 +00:00  my-running-config


256487424 bytes total (182394880 bytes free)


Router# _____
Router# _____
Directory of nvram:/


  253  -rw-        1279               <no date>  startup-config
  254  ----           5               <no date>  private-config
  255  -rw-        1279               <no date>  underlying-config
    1  -rw-        2945               <no date>  cwmp_inventory
    4  ----           0               <no date>  rf_cold_starts
    5  ----          92               <no date>  persistent-data
    6  -rw-          17               <no date>  ecfm_ieee_mib
    7  -rw-         559               <no date>  IOS-Self-Sig#1.cer
    8  -rw-         559               <no date>  IOS-Self-Sig#2.cer
    9  -rw-         559               <no date>  IOS-Self-Sig#3.cer
   10  -rw-         559               <no date>  IOS-Self-Sig#4.cer
   11  -rw-         559               <no date>  IOS-Self-Sig#5.cer
   12  -rw-         559               <no date>  IOS-Self-Sig#6.cer
   13  -rw-         559               <no date>  IOS-Self-Sig#7.cer
   14  -rw-         559               <no date>  IOS-Self-Sig#8.cer
   15  -rw-           0               <no date>  ifIndex-table
Router# _____
Router# pwd
flash0:/
```

ISO System Files

With the ISR G2 devices, IOS image selection has been made easier because all features are included in the universal image. Features are activated through licensing. List and describe the two types of universal images supported in the ISR G2:

_____

_____

_____

_____

The IP Base technology package is installed by default. What are the other three packages that can be activated using licensing?

_____

_____

_____

Each licensing key is unique to the Cisco device. What three pieces of information must you provide to obtain a licensing key to unlock other technology packages?

_____

_____

_____

IOS Image Management

To back up an IOS image to a TFTP server, complete the following steps:

Step 1.   Ping the TFTP server to test connectivity.

Step 2.   Verify the TFTP server has enough memory to accept the image file. Use the **show flash** command to determine the size of the image.

Step 3.   Copy the image to the TFTP server using the **copy** *source-url destination-url* command.

In Figure 10-3, you are copying the image c1900-universalk9-mz.SPA.152-4.M1.bin from RTA to the TFTP server at 10.10.10.10. Record the commands, including the router prompt, to complete this task.

Figure 10-3   Backing Up an IOS to a TFTP Server

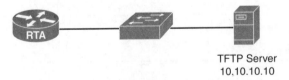

TFTP Server
10.10.10.10

Software Licensing

The feature sets that you enable with licensing keys are called _____. What are the four _____ available?

_____

_____

_____

_____

On which Cisco ISR G2 platforms can these licenses be used?

_____

What command enables you to view the licenses currently supported on the router?

_____

What are the three major steps to activate a new software package or feature on the router?

_____

_____

_____

What two things are needed to obtain a license?

_____

How is the UDI constructed?

_____

What command displays the UDI?

_____

What command installs the license?

_____

License Verification and Management

After installing a license, you must reboot the router before the technology package is active and ready to use.

What two commands are used in Example 10-6 to verify the licenses installed?

Example 10-6   Verifying License Installation

```
Router# _____ | begin License Info:
License Info:

License UDI:


-----------------------------------------------------------
Device#   PID              SN

-----------------------------------------------------------
```

```
*0        CISCO1941/K9          FTX163283RZ




Technology Package License Information for Module:'c1900'


----------------------------------------------------------------
Technology     Technology-package         Technology-package
               Current      Type          Next reboot
----------------------------------------------------------------
ipbase         ipbasek9      Permanent     ipbasek9
security       securityk9    EvalRightToUse securityk9
data           None          None          None


Configuration register is 0x2102


Router# show license detail
Index 1 Feature: ipbasek9
       Period left: Life time
       License Type: Permanent
       License State: Active, In Use
       License Count: Non-Counted
       License Priority: Medium
Index 2 Feature: securityk9
       Period left: 8  weeks 1  day
       Period Used: 2  days 0  hour
       License Type: EvalRightToUse
       License State: Active, In Use
       License Count: Non-Counted
       License Priority: Low
Index 3 Feature: datak9
       Period left: Not Activated
       Period Used: 0  minute  0  second
       License Type: EvalRightToUse
       License State: Not in Use, EULA not accepted
       License Count: Non-Counted
       License Priority: None
<output omitted>
```

In Example 10-6, the datak9 technology package is not in use. Record the commands, including the router prompt, to accept the EULA and activate the datak9 package.

_____

_____

What message do you receive when activate a package?

_____

To back up your license files, save them to flash. Record the command, including the router prompt, to save the license files to flash.

_____

Complete the following steps to uninstall a license:

Step 1.   Disable the technology package. Record the command, including the router prompt, to disable the datak9 technology package.

_____

Step 2.   After reloading the router, clear the license from storage. Record the commands, including the router prompt, to clear the datak9 technology package.

_____

_____

_____

Labs and Activities

Command Reference

In Table 10-3, record the command, including the correct router or switch prompt, that fits the description. Fill in any blanks with the appropriate missing information.

Table 10-3   Commands for Chapter 10, "Device Discovery, Management, and Maintenance"

Command	Description
	Configure a router to enable CDP globally
	Enable CDP on an interface
	Verify the CDP status on the router.
	View abbreviated output of CDP neighbors
	View CDP neighbors' information including the IP address and IOS image.
	Configure a router to enable LLDP globally.
	Enable an interface to send LLDP packets.
	Enable an interface to process LLDP packets.
	View abbreviated output of LLDP neighbors.
	View LLDP neighbors information including the IP address and IOS image.
	Manually set the clock to 8:00PM, March 15, 2018.
	Verify the NTP synchronization (two possible commands).
	Force logged events to display the date and time.
	View the default logging services on a router.
	Set the router to log messages to the syslog server at 172.16.20.15.
	Configure the router to log all messages from level 3 to level 0.
	Only log messages from the S0/0/0 interface.
	You are recovering a password. The router is in ROMMON mode. Set the configuration register to 0x2142.
	You have completed a password recovery. Set the configuration register to 0x2102.
	Accept the end user license agreement.
	Set the securityk9 package to load on the next reboot of a Cisco 1941 router.

10.1.1.4 Packet Tracer–Map a Network Using CDP

Topology

Admin-PC   S1   Edge1   Remote Branch Office

Addressing Table

Device	Interface	IP Address	Subnet Mask	Local Interface and Connected Neighbor
Edge1	G0/0	192.168.1.1	255.255.255.0	G0/1 - S1
	S0/0/0			S0/0/0 - ISP
	S0/0/1	209.165.200.10		S0/0/1 - ISP

Objectives

Map a network using CDP and SSH remote access.

Background/Scenario

A senior network administrator requires you to map the Remote Branch Office network and discover the name of a recently installed switch that still needs an IP address to be configured. Your task is to create a map of the branch office network. You must record all of the network device names, IP addresses and subnet masks, and physical interfaces interconnecting the network devices, as well as the name of the switch that does not have an IP address.

To map the network, you will use SSH for remote access and the Cisco Discovery Protocol (CDP) to discover information about neighboring network devices, like routers and switches. Because CDP is a Layer 2 protocol, it can be used to discover information about devices that do not have IP addresses.

You will record the gathered information to complete the Addressing Table and provide a topology diagram of the Remote Branch Office network.

You will need the IP address for the remote branch office, which is 209.165.200.10. The local and remote administrative usernames and passwords are:

Local Network

Username: **admin01**

Password: **S3cre7P@55**

Branch Office Network

Username: **branchadmin**

Password: **S3cre7P@55**

Part 1: Use SSH to Remotely Access Network Devices

In Part 1, you will use the Admin-PC to remotely access the Edge1 gateway router. Next, from the Edge1 router you will SSH into the Remote Branch Office.

    a. On the Admin-PC, open a command prompt.

    b. SSH into the gateway router at 192.168.1.1 using the username **admin01** and the password **S3cre7P@55**.

```
PC> ssh -l admin01 192.168.1.1
Open
Password:

Edge1#
```

Note: Notice that you are placed directly into privileged EXEC mode. This is because the admin01 user account is set to privilege level 15.

---

    c. Use the **show ip interface brief** and **show interfaces** commands to document the Edge1 router's physical interfaces, IP addresses, and subnet masks in the Addressing Table.

```
Edge1# show ip interface brief
Edge1# show interfaces
```

    d. Using the Edge1 router's CLI, you will SSH into the Remote Branch Office at 209.165.200.10 with the username **branchadmin** and the same password:

```
Edge1# ssh -l branchadmin 209.165.200.10
Open
Password:

Branch-Edge#
```

After connecting to the Remote Branch Office at 209.165.200.10 what piece of previously missing information can now be added to the Addressing Table above?

Part 2: Use CDP to Discover Neighboring Devices

You are now remotely connected to the Branch-Edge router. Using CDP, begin looking for connected network devices.

a. Issue the **show ip interface brief** and **show interfaces** commands to document the Branch-Edge router's network interfaces, IP addresses, and subnet masks. Add the missing information to the Addressing Table to map the network:

```
Branch-Edge# show ip interface brief

Branch-Edge# show interfaces
```

b. Security best practice recommends only running CDP when needed, so CDP may need to be turned on. Use a **show cdp** command to test its status.

```
Branch-Edge# show cdp
% CDP is not enabled
```

c. You need to turn on CDP, but it is a good idea to only broadcast CDP information to internal network devices and not to external networks. To do this, disable CDP on the s0/0/1 interface and then turn on the CDP protocol.

```
Branch-Edge# configure terminal
Branch-Edge(config)# interface s0/0/1
Branch-Edge(config-if)# no cdp enable
Branch-Edge(config-if)# exit
Branch-Edge(config)# cdp run
```

d. Issue a **show cdp neighbors** command to find any neighboring network devices.

Note: CDP will only show connected Cisco devices that are also running CDP.

```
Branch-Edge# show cdp neighbors
```

Is there a neighboring network device? What type of device is it? What is its name? On what interface is it connected? Is the device's IP address listed? Record the information in the Addressing Table.

---

e. To find the IP address of the neighboring device use the **show cdp neighbors detail** command and record the ip address:

```
Branch-Edge# show cdp neighbors detail
```

Aside from the neighboring device's IP address, what other piece of potentially sensitive information is listed?

---

f. Now that you know the IP address of the neighbor device, you need to connect to it with SSH in order to discover other devices that may be its neighbors.

Note: To connect with SSH use the same Remote Branch Office username and password.

```
Branch-Edge# ssh -l branchadmin <the ip address of the neighbor device>
```

After successfully connecting with SSH, what does the command prompt show?

---

g. You are remotely connected to the next neighbor. Use the **show cdp neighbors** command and the **show cdp neighbors detail** command to discover other connected neighbor devices.

What types of network devices neighbor this device? Record any newly discovered devices in the Addressing Table. Include their hostname, interfaces, and IP addresses.

h. Continue discovering new network devices using SSH and the show CDP commands. Eventually, you will reach the end of the network and there will be no more devices to discover.

What is the name of the switch that does not have an IP address on the network?

i. Draw a topology of the Remote Branch Office network using the information you have gathered using CDP.

Suggested Scoring Rubric

Activity Section	Possible Points	Earned Points
Part 1 Question	2	
Question d	2	
Part 2 Questions	8	
Question d	2	
Question e	1	
Question f	1	
Question g	2	
Question h	2	
Packet Tracer	10	
Addressing Scheme Documentation	60	
Topology Documentation	20	
Total Points	100	

10.1.2.5 Lab–Configure CDP and LLDP

Topology

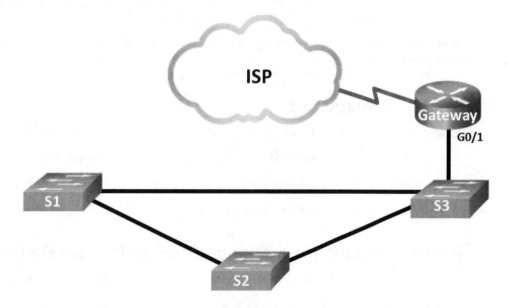

Addressing Table

Device	Interface	IP Address	Subnet Mask
Gateway	G0/1	192.168.1.254	255.255.255.0
	S0/0/1	209.165.200.226	255.255.255.252
ISP	S0/0/1 (DCE)	209.165.200.225	255.255.255.252

Objectives

Part 1: Build the Network and Configure Basic Device Settings

Part 2: Network Discovery with CDP

Part 3: Network Discovery with LLDP

Background/Scenario

Cisco Discovery Protocol (CDP) is a Cisco proprietary protocol for network discovery on the data link layer. It can share information such as device names and IOS versions, with other physically connected Cisco devices. Link Layer Discovery Protocol (LLDP) is vendor-neutral protocol using on the data link layer for network discovery. It is mainly used with network devices in the local area network (LAN). The network devices advertise information, such as their identities and capabilities to their neighbors.

In this lab, you must document the ports that are connected to other switches using CDP and LLDP. You will document your findings in a network topology diagram. You will also enable or disable these discovery protocols as necessary.

Note: The routers used with CCNA hands-on labs are Cisco 1941 Integrated Services Routers (ISRs) with Cisco IOS Release 15.2(4)M3 (universalk9 image). The switches used are Cisco Catalyst 2960s with Cisco IOS Release 15.0(2) (lanbasek9 image). Other routers, switches, and Cisco IOS versions can be used. Depending on the model and Cisco IOS version, the commands available and the output produced might vary from what is shown in the labs. Refer to the Router Interface Summary Table at the end of this lab for the correct interface identifiers.

Note: Make sure that the routers and switches have been erased and have no startup configurations. If you are unsure, contact your instructor.

Required Resources

- 1 Router (Cisco 1941 with Cisco IOS Release 15.2(4)M3 universal image or comparable)

- 3 Switches (Cisco 2960 with Cisco IOS Release 15.0(2) lanbasek9 image or comparable)

- Console cables to configure the Cisco IOS devices via the console ports

- Ethernet cables as shown in the topology

Part 1: Build the Network and Configure Basic Device Settings

In Part 1, you will set up the network topology and configure basic settings on the router and switches.

Step 1: Cable the network as shown in the topology.

The Ethernet ports used on the switches are not specified in the topology. You may choose to use any Ethernet ports to cable the switches as shown in the topology diagram.

Step 2: Initialize and reload the network devices as necessary.

Step 3: Configure basic device settings for the switches.

    a. Console into the device and enable privileged EXEC mode.

    b. Enter configuration mode.

    c. Disable DNS lookup to prevent the switch from attempting to translate incorrectly entered commands as though they were host names.

    d. Configure the hostname according to the topology.

    e. Verify that the switchports with connected Ethernet cables are enabled.

    f. Save the running configuration to the startup configuration file.

Step 4: Configure basic device settings for the routers.

    a. Console into the device and enable privileged EXEC mode.

    b. Enter configuration mode.

    c. Copy and paste the following configurations into the routers.

    ISP:

```
hostname ISP
no ip domain lookup
interface Serial0/0/1
  ip address 209.165.200.225 255.255.255.252
  no shutdown
```

Gateway:

```
hostname Gateway
no ip domain lookup
interface GigabitEthernet0/1
 ip address 192.168.1.254 255.255.255.0
 ip nat inside
 no shutdown
interface Serial0/0/1
 ip address 209.165.200.226 255.255.255.252
 ip nat outside
 no shutdown
ip nat inside source list 1 interface Serial0/0/1 overload
access-list 1 permit 192.168.1.0 0.0.0.255
```

d. Save the running configuration to the startup configuration file.

Part 2: Network Discovery with CDP

On Cisco devices, CDP is enabled by default. You will use CDP to discover the ports that are currently connected.

a. On router Gateway, enter the **show cdp** command in the privileged EXEC mode to verify that CDP is currently enabled on router Gateway.

```
Gateway# show cdp
Global CDP information:
        Sending CDP packets every 60 seconds
        Sending a holdtime value of 180 seconds
        Sending CDPv2 advertisements is  enabled
```

How often are CDP packets sent?

_____

If CDP is disabled on Gateway, enable CDP by issuing the **cdp run** command in the global configuration mode.

```
Gateway(config)# cdp run
Gateway(config)# end
```

b. Issue the **show cdp interface** to list the interfaces that are participating in CDP advertisements.

```
Gateway# show cdp interface
Embedded-Service-Engine0/0 is administratively down, line protocol is down
  Encapsulation ARPA
  Sending CDP packets every 60 seconds
  Holdtime is 180 seconds
GigabitEthernet0/0 is administratively down, line protocol is down
  Encapsulation ARPA
  Sending CDP packets every 60 seconds
  Holdtime is 180 seconds
GigabitEthernet0/1 is up, line protocol is up
  Encapsulation ARPA
  Sending CDP packets every 60 seconds
  Holdtime is 180 seconds
```

```
Serial0/0/0 is administratively down, line protocol is down
  Encapsulation HDLC
  Sending CDP packets every 60 seconds
  Holdtime is 180 seconds
Serial0/0/1 is up, line protocol is up
  Encapsulation HDLC
  Sending CDP packets every 60 seconds
  Holdtime is 180 seconds

cdp enabled interfaces : 5
interfaces up         : 2
interfaces down       : 3
```

How many interfaces are participating in the CDP advertisement? Which interfaces are up?

_____

c. Issue the **show cdp neighbors** command to determine the CDP neighbors.

```
Gateway# show cdp neighbors
Capability Codes: R - Router, T - Trans Bridge, B - Source Route Bridge
                  S - Switch, H - Host, I - IGMP, r - Repeater, P - Phone,
                  D - Remote, C - CVTA, M - Two-port Mac Relay

Device ID       Local Intrfce   Holdtme    Capability  Platform  Port ID
ISP             Ser 0/0/1       158          R B S I   CISCO1941 Ser 0/0/1
S3              Gig 0/1         170              S I   WS-C2960- Fas 0/5
```

d. For more details on CDP neighbors, issue the **show cdp neighbors detail** command.

```
Gateway# show cdp neighbors detail
-------------------------
Device ID: ISP
Entry address(es):
  IP address: 209.165.200.225
Platform: Cisco CISCO1941/K9,  Capabilities: Router Source-Route-Bridge Switch
IGMP
Interface: Serial0/0/1,  Port ID (outgoing port): Serial0/0/1
Holdtime : 143 sec

Version :
Cisco IOS Software, C1900 Software (C1900-UNIVERSALK9-M), Version 15.4(3)M2,
RELEASE SOFTWARE (fc2)
Technical Support: http://www.cisco.com/techsupport
Copyright (c) 1986-2015 by Cisco Systems, Inc.
Compiled Fri 06-Feb-15 17:01 by prod_rel_team

advertisement version: 2
Management address(es):
  IP address: 209.165.200.225


-------------------------
Device ID: S3
```

```
Entry address(es):
Platform: cisco WS-C2960-24TT-L,  Capabilities: Switch IGMP
Interface: GigabitEthernet0/1,  Port ID (outgoing port): FastEthernet0/5
Holdtime : 158 sec

Version :
Cisco IOS Software, C2960 Software (C2960-LANBASEK9-M), Version 15.0(2)SE7,
RELEASE SOFTWARE (fc1)
Technical Support: http://www.cisco.com/techsupport
Copyright (c) 1986-2014 by Cisco Systems, Inc.
Compiled Thu 23-Oct-14 14:49 by prod_rel_team

advertisement version: 2
Protocol Hello:  OUI=0x00000C, Protocol ID=0x0112; payload len=27, value=000000
00FFFFFFFF010221FF0000000000000CD996E87400FF0000
VTP Management Domain: ''
Native VLAN: 1
Duplex: full
```

e. What can you learn about ISP and S3 from the outputs of the **show cdp neighbors detail** command?

_____

_____

f. Configure the SVI on S3. Use an available IP address in 192.168.1.0/24 network. Configure 192.168.1.254 as the default gateway.

```
S3(config)# interface vlan 1
S3(config-if)# ip address 192.168.1.3 255.255.255.0
S3(config-if)# no shutdown
S3(config-if)# exit
S3(config)# ip default-gateway 192.168.1.254
```

g. Issue the **show cdp neighbors detail** command on Gateway. What additional information is available?

_____

h. For security reasons, it is a good idea to turn off CDP on an interface facing an external network. Issue the **no cdp enable** in the interface configuration mode on the S0/0/1 interface on Gateway.

```
Gateway(config)# interface s0/0/1
Gateway(config-if)# no cdp enable
Gateway(config-if)# end
```

To verify that CDP has been turned off on the interface S0/0/1, issue the **show cdp neighbors** or **show cdp interface** command. You may need to wait for the hold time to expire. The hold time is the amount of time the network devices will hold the CDP packets until the devices discard them.

```
Gateway# show cdp neighbors
Capability Codes: R - Router, T - Trans Bridge, B - Source Route Bridge
                  S - Switch, H - Host, I - IGMP, r - Repeater, P - Phone,
                  D - Remote, C - CVTA, M - Two-port Mac Relay
```

Device ID	Local Intrfce	Holdtme	Capability	Platform	Port ID
S3	Gig 0/1	161	S I	WS-C2960-	Fas 0/5

The interface S0/0/1 on Gateway no longer has a CDP adjacency with the ISP router. But it still has CDP adjacencies with other interfaces.

```
Gateway# show cdp interface
Embedded-Service-Engine0/0 is administratively down, line protocol is down
  Encapsulation ARPA
  Sending CDP packets every 60 seconds
  Holdtime is 180 seconds
GigabitEthernet0/0 is administratively down, line protocol is down
  Encapsulation ARPA
  Sending CDP packets every 60 seconds
  Holdtime is 180 seconds
GigabitEthernet0/1 is up, line protocol is up
  Encapsulation ARPA
  Sending CDP packets every 60 seconds
  Holdtime is 180 seconds
Serial0/0/0 is administratively down, line protocol is down
  Encapsulation HDLC
  Sending CDP packets every 60 seconds
  Holdtime is 180 seconds

 cdp enabled interfaces : 4
 interfaces up          : 1
 interfaces down        : 3
```

i. To disable CDP globally, issue the **no cdp run** command in the global configuration mode.

```
Gateway# conf t
Gateway(config)# no cdp run
Gateway(config)# end
```

Which command(s) would you use to verify that CDP has been disabled?

_____

j. Enable CDP globally on Gateway. How many interfaces are CDP enabled? Which interfaces are CDP disabled?

_____

k. Console into all the switches and use the CDP commands to determine the Ethernet ports that connected to other devices. An example of the CDP commands for S3 is displayed below.

```
S3# show cdp neighbors
Capability Codes: R - Router, T - Trans Bridge, B - Source Route Bridge
                  S - Switch, H - Host, I - IGMP, r - Repeater, P - Phone,
                  D - Remote, C - CVTA, M - Two-port Mac Relay
```

Device ID	Local Intrfce	Holdtme	Capability	Platform	Port ID
Gateway	Fas 0/5	143	R B S I	CISCO1941	Gig 0/1
S2	Fas 0/2	173	S I	WS-C2960-	Fas 0/4
S1	Fas 0/4	171	S I	WS-C2960-	Fas 0/4

Part 3: Network Discovery with LLDP

On Cisco devices, LLDP may be enabled by default. You will use LLDP to discover the ports that are currently connected.

a. On Gateway, enter the **show lldp** command in the privileged EXEC mode.

```
Gateway# show lldp
% LLDP is not enabled
```

If LLDP is disabled, enter the **lldp run** command in the global configuration mode.

```
Gateway(config)# lldp run
```

b. Use the **show lldp** command to verify that LLDP is enabled on Gateway.

```
Gateway# show lldp

Global LLDP Information:
    Status: ACTIVE
    LLDP advertisements are sent every 30 seconds
    LLDP hold time advertised is 120 seconds
    LLDP interface reinitialization delay is 2 seconds
```

Issue the **show lldp neighbors** command. Which devices are neighbors to Gateway?

_____

c. If there are no LLDP neighbors for Gateway, enable LLDP on the switches and ISP. Issue **lldp run** in the global configuration mode on the devices.

```
S1(config)# lldp run
S2(config)# lldp run
S3(config)# lldp run
ISP(config)# lldp run
```

d. Issue the **show lldp neighbors** command on the switches and router to list the LLDP enabled ports. The output for Gateway is shown below.

```
Gateway# show lldp neighbors
Capability codes:
    (R) Router, (B) Bridge, (T) Telephone, (C) DOCSIS Cable Device
    (W) WLAN Access Point, (P) Repeater, (S) Station, (O) Other

Device ID          Local Intf     Hold-time  Capability      Port ID
S3                 Gi0/1          120        B               Fa0/5

Total entries displayed: 1
```

e. Issue the **show lldp neighbors detail** command on Gateway.

```
Gateway# show lldp neighbors detail
------------------------------------------------
Local Intf: Gi0/1
Chassis id: 0cd9.96e8.7400
Port id: Fa0/5
Port Description: FastEthernet0/5
System Name: S3

System Description:
Cisco IOS Software, C2960 Software (C2960-LANBASEK9-M), Version 15.0(2)SE7,
```

```
RELEASE SOFTWARE (fc1)
Technical Support: http://www.cisco.com/techsupport
Copyright (c) 1986-2014 by Cisco Systems, Inc.
Compiled Thu 23-Oct-14 14:49 by prod_rel_team

Time remaining: 103 seconds
System Capabilities: B
Enabled Capabilities: B
Management Addresses:
    IP: 192.168.1.3
Auto Negotiation - supported, enabled
Physical media capabilities:
    100base-TX(FD)
    100base-TX(HD)
    10base-T(FD)
    10base-T(HD)
Media Attachment Unit type: 16
Vlan ID: 1


Total entries displayed: 1
```

What port is used on S3 to connect to the Gateway router?

_____

f. Use the **show** command outputs from CDP and LLDP to document the connected ports in the network topology.

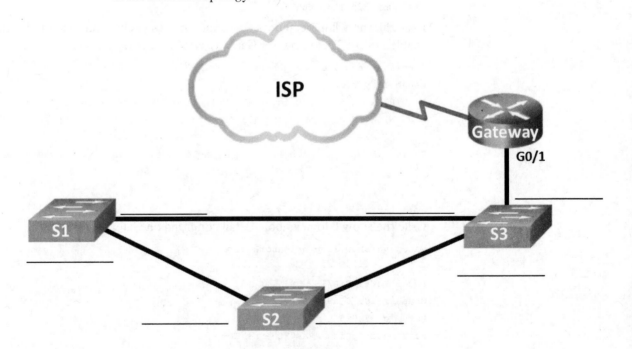

Reflection

Within a network, on which interfaces should you not use discovery protocols? Explain.

_____

_____

_____

_____

Router Interface Summary Table

Router Interface Summary				
Router Model	**Ethernet Interface #1**	**Ethernet Interface #2**	**Serial Interface #1**	**Serial Interface #2**
1800	Fast Ethernet 0/0 (F0/0)	Fast Ethernet 0/1 (F0/1)	Serial 0/0/0 (S0/0/0)	Serial 0/0/1 (S0/0/1)
1900	Gigabit Ethernet 0/0 (G0/0)	Gigabit Ethernet 0/1 (G0/1)	Serial 0/0/0 (S0/0/0)	Serial 0/0/1 (S0/0/1)
2801	Fast Ethernet 0/0 (F0/0)	Fast Ethernet 0/1 (F0/1)	Serial 0/1/0 (S0/1/0)	Serial 0/1/1 (S0/1/1)
2811	Fast Ethernet 0/0 (F0/0)	Fast Ethernet 0/1 (F0/1)	Serial 0/0/0 (S0/0/0)	Serial 0/0/1 (S0/0/1)
2900	Gigabit Ethernet 0/0 (G0/0)	Gigabit Ethernet 0/1 (G0/1)	Serial 0/0/0 (S0/0/0)	Serial 0/0/1 (S0/0/1)

Note: To find out how the router is configured, look at the interfaces to identify the type of router and how many interfaces the router has. There is no way to effectively list all the combinations of configurations for each router class. This table includes identifiers for the possible combinations of Ethernet and Serial interfaces in the device. The table does not include any other type of interface, even though a specific router may contain one. An example of this might be an ISDN BRI interface. The string in parentheses is the legal abbreviation that can be used in Cisco IOS commands to represent the interface.

10.2.1.4 Packet Tracer–Configure and Verify NTP

Topology

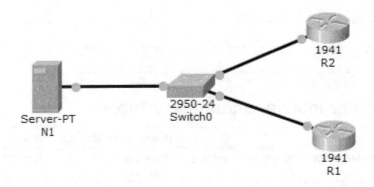

Addressing Table

Device	Interface	IP Address	Subnet Mask
N1	NIC	209.165.200.225	255.255.255.0
R1	G0/0	209.165.200.226	255.255.255.0
R2	G0/0	209.165.200.227	255.255.255.0

Objectives

In this activity, you will configure NTP on R1 and R2 to allow time synchronization.

Background/Scenario

Network Time Protocol (NTP) synchronizes the time of day among a set of distributed time servers and clients. While there are a number of applications that require synchronized time, this lab will focus on correlating events that are listed in the system log and other time-specific events from multiple network devices. NTP uses the User Datagram Protocol (UDP) as its transport protocol. All NTP communications use Coordinated Universal Time (UTC).

An NTP server usually receives its time from an authoritative time source, such as an atomic clock attached to a time server It then distributes this time across the network. NTP is extremely efficient; no more than one packet per minute is necessary to synchronize two machines to within a millisecond of each other.

Step 1:   Configuring the NTP Server

   a.   Server N1 is already configured as the NTP Server for this topology. Verify its configuration under **Services > NTP**.

   b.   From R1, ping N1 (209.165.200.225) to verify connectivity. The ping should be successful.

   c.   Repeat the ping to N1 from R2 to verify connectivity to N1.

Step 2:   Configuring the NTP Clients

Cisco devices can be configured to refer to an NTP server to synchronize their clocks. This is important to keep time consistent among all devices. Configure R1 and R2 as NTP clients so their clocks are synchronized. Both R1 and R2 will use N1 server as their NTP server. To configure R1 and R2 as NTP clients, issue the commands below:

a.   Use the **ntp server** command to specify an NTP server, as shown below:

```
R1# conf t
R1(config)# ntp server 209.165.200.225
```

```
R2# conf t
R2(config)# ntp server 209.165.200.225
```

b.   Check the clock on R1 and R2 again to verify that they are synchronized:

```
R1# show clock
*12:02:18:619 UTC Tue Dec 8 2015
```

```
R2# show clock
*12:02:20:422 UTC Tue Dec 8 2015
```

Note: When working on physical routers, allow a few minutes before R1 and R2 clocks are synchronized.

Are the clocks synchronized?

_____

Packet Tracer
☐ Activity

10.2.3.5 Packet Tracer–Configuring Syslog and NTP

Topology

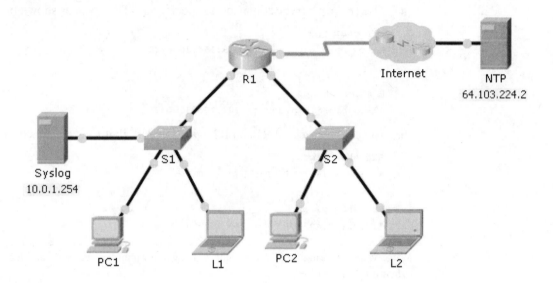

Objectives

Part 1: Configure Syslog Service

Part 2: Generate Logged Events

Part 3: Manually Set Switch Clocks

Part 4: Configure NTP Service

Part 5: Verify Timestamped Logs

Scenario

In this activity, you will enable and use the Syslog service and the NTP service so that the network administrator is able to monitor the network more effectively.

Part 1: Configure Syslog Service

Step 1:   Enable the Syslog service.

   a.   Click **Syslog**, then the **Services** tab.

   b.   Turn the **Syslog** service on and move the window so you can monitor activity.

Step 2:   Configure the intermediary devices to use the Syslog service.

   a.   Configure **R1** to send log events to the **Syslog** server.

   ```
   R1(config)# logging 10.0.1.254
   ```

   b.   Configure S1 to send log events to the **Syslog** server.

c. Configure **S2** to send log events to the **Syslog** server.

Part 2: Generate Logged Events

Step 1: Change the status of interfaces to create event logs.

a. Configure a Loopback 0 interface on **R1** then disable it.

b. Turn off **PC1** and **PC2**. Turn them on again.

Step 2: Examine the Syslog events.

a. Look at the Syslog events.

Note: All of the events have been recorded; however, the time stamps are incorrect.

b. Clear the log before proceeding to the next part.

Part 3: Manually Set Switch Clocks

Step 1: Manually set the clocks on the switches.

Manually set the clock on **S1** and **S2** to the current date and approximate time. An example is provided.

```
S1# clock set 11:47:00 July 10 2013
```

Step 2: Enable the logging timestamp service on the switches.

Configure **S1** and **S2** to send its timestamp with logs it sends to the **Syslog** server.

```
S1(config)# service timestamps log datetime msec
```

Part 4: Configure NTP Service

Step 1: Enable the NTP service.

In this activity, we are assuming that the NTP service is being hosted on a public Internet server. If the NTP server was private, authentication could also be used.

a. Open the **Services** tab of the **NTP** server.

b. Turn the NTP service on and note the date and time that is displayed.

Step 2: Automatically set the clock on the router.

Set the clock on **R1** to the date and time according to the NTP server.

```
R1(config)# ntp server 64.103.224.2
```

Step 3: Enable the logging timestamp service of the router.

Configure **R1** to send its timestamp with the logs that it sends to the **Syslog** server.

Part 5: Verify Timestamped Logs

Step 1: Change the status of interfaces to create event logs.

    a. Re-enable and then disable the Loopback 0 interface on R1.

_____

_____

_____

    b. Turn off laptops **L1** and **L2**. Turn them on again.

Step 2: Examine the Syslog events.

Look at the Syslog events.

_____

Note: All of the events have been recorded and the time stamps are correct as configured.

_____

Note: R1 uses the clock settings from the NTP server, and S1 and S2 use the clock settings configured by you in Part 3.

10.2.3.6 Lab–Configuring Syslog and NTP

Topology

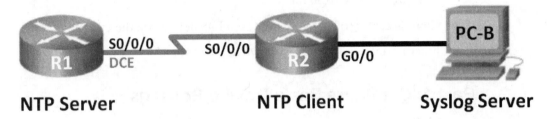

Addressing Table

Device	Interface	IP Address	Subnet Mask	Default Gateway
R1	S0/0/0 (DCE)	10.1.1.1	255.255.255.252	N/A
R2	S0/0/0	10.1.1.2	255.255.255.252	N/A
	G0/0	172.16.2.1	255.255.255.0	N/A
PC-B	NIC	172.16.2.3	255.255.255.0	172.16.2.1

Objectives

Part 1: Configure Basic Device Settings

Part 2: Configure NTP

Part 3: Configure Syslog

Background/Scenario

Syslog messages that are generated by the network devices can be collected and archived on a syslog server. The information can be used for monitoring, debugging, and troubleshooting purposes. The administrator can control where the messages are stored and displayed. Syslog messages can be time-stamped for analysis of the sequence of network events; therefore, it is important to synchronize the clock across the network devices with a Network Time Protocol (NTP) server.

In this lab, you will configure R1 as the NTP server and R2 as a Syslog and NTP client. The syslog server application, such as Tftp32d or other similar program, will be running on PC-B. Furthermore, you will control the severity level of log messages that are collected and archived on the syslog server.

Note: The routers used with CCNA hands-on labs are Cisco 1941 Integrated Services Routers (ISRs) with Cisco IOS Release 15.2(4)M3 (universalk9 image). Other routers and Cisco IOS versions can be used. Depending on the model and Cisco IOS version, the commands available and output produced might vary from what is shown in the labs. Refer to the Router Interface Summary Table at the end of this lab for the correct interface identifiers.

Note: Make sure that the routers have been erased and have no startup configurations. If you are unsure, contact your instructor.

Required Resources

- 2 Routers (Cisco 1941 with Cisco IOS Release 15.2(4)M3 universal image or comparable)
- 1 PC (Windows 7, Vista, or XP with terminal emulation program, such as Tera Term, and Syslog software, such as Tftpd32)
- Console cables to configure the Cisco IOS devices via the console ports
- Ethernet and serial cables as shown in the topology

Part 1: Configure Basic Device Settings

In Part 1, you will set up the network topology and configure basic settings, such as the interface IP addresses, routing, device access, and passwords.

Step 1:   Cable the network as shown in the topology.

Step 2:   Initialize and reload the routers as necessary.

Step 3:   Configure basic settings for each router.

    a.   Console into the router and enter global configuration mode.

    b.   Copy the following basic configuration and paste it to the running-configuration on the router.

```
no ip domain-lookup
service password-encryption
enable secret class
banner motd #
Unauthorized access is strictly prohibited. #
line con 0
password cisco
login
logging synchronous
line vty 0 4
password cisco
login
```

    c.   Configure the host name as shown in the topology.

    d.   Apply the IP addresses to Serial and Gigabit Ethernet interfaces according to the Addressing Table and activate the physical interfaces.

    e.   Set the clock rate to **128000** for the DCE serial interface.

Step 4:   Configure routing.

Enable RIPv2 on the routers. Add all the networks into the RIPv2 process.

Step 5:   Configure PC-B.

Configure the IP address and default gateway for PC-B according to the Addressing Table.

Step 6:   Verify end-to-end connectivity.

Verify that each device is able to ping every other device in the network successfully. If not, troubleshoot until there is end-to-end connectivity.

Step 7:   Save the running configuration to the startup configuration.

Part 2: Configure NTP

In Part 2, you will configure R1 as the NTP server and R2 as the NTP client of R1. Synchronized time is important for syslog and debug functions. If the time is not synchronized, it is difficult to determine what network event caused the message.

Step 1:   Display the current time.

Issue the **show clock** command to display the current time on R1.

```
R1# show clock
*12:30:06.147 UTC Tue May 14 2013
```

Record the information regarding the current time displayed in the following table.

Date	
Time	
Time Zone	

Step 2:   Set the time.

Use the **clock set** command to set the time on R1. The following is an example of setting the date and time.

```
R1# clock set 9:39:00 05 july 2013
R1#
*Jul  5 09:39:00.000: %SYS-6-CLOCKUPDATE: System clock has been updated from
12:30:54 UTC Tue May 14 2013 to 09:39:00 UTC Fri Jul 5 2013, configured from console
by console.
```

Note: The time can also be set using the clock timezone command in the global configuration mode. For more information regarding this command, research the clock timezone command at www.cisco.com to determine the zone for your region.

Step 3:   Configure the NTP master.

Configure R1 as the NTP master by using the **ntp master** *stratum-number* command in global configuration mode. The stratum number indicates the number of NTP hops away from an authoritative time source. In this lab, the number 5 is the stratum level of this NTP server.

```
R1(config)# ntp master 5
```

Step 4:   Configure the NTP client.

  a.   Issue **show clock** command on R2. Record the current time displayed on R2 in the following table.

Date	
Time	
Time Zone	

Configure R2 as the NTP client. Use the **ntp server** command to point to the IP address or hostname of the NTP server. The **ntp update-calendar** command periodically updates the calendar with NTP time.

```
R2(config)# ntp server 10.1.1.1
R2(config)# ntp update-calendar
```

Step 5:   Verify NTP configuration.

   a.   Use the **show ntp associations** command to verify that R2 has an NTP association with R1.

```
R2# show ntp associations

   address         ref clock       st   when  poll reach delay offset   disp
*~10.1.1.1       127.127.1.1      5    11    64   177 11.312 -0.018  4.298
 * sys.peer, # selected, + candidate, - outlyer, x falseticker, ~ configured
```

   b.   Issue **show clock** on R1 and R2 to compare the timestamp.

Note: It could take a few minutes before the timestamp on R2 is synchronized with R1.

```
R1# show clock
09:43:32.799 UTC Fri Jul 5 2013
R2# show clock
09:43:37.122 UTC Fri Jul 5 2013
```

Part 3: Configure Syslog

Syslog messages from network devices can be collected and archived on a syslog server. In this lab, Tftpd32 will be used as the syslog server software. The network administrator can control the types of messages that can be sent to the syslog server.

Step 1:   (Optional) Install syslog server.

   If a syslog server is not already installed on the PC, download and install the latest version of a syslog server, such as Tftpd32, on the PC. The latest version of Tftpd32 can be found at the following link:

   http://tftpd32.jounin.net/

Step 2:   Start the syslog server on PC-B.

   After starting the Tftpd32 application, click the **Syslog server** tab.

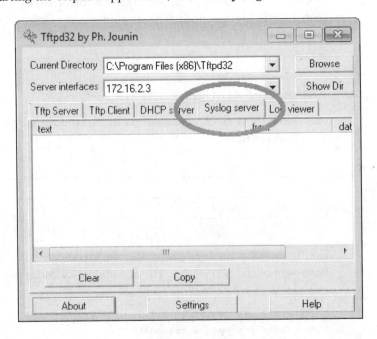

Step 3:   Verify that the timestamp service is enabled on R2.

Use the **show run** command to verify that the timestamp service is enabled for logging on R2.

```
R2# show run | include timestamp
service timestamps debug datetime msec
service timestamps log datetime msec
```

If the timestamp service is not enabled, use the following command to enable it.

```
R2(config)# service timestamps log datetime msec
```

Step 4:   Configure R2 to log messages to the syslog server.

Configure R2 to send Syslog messages to the syslog server, PC-B. The IP address of the PC-B syslog server is 172.16.2.3.

```
R2(config)# logging host 172.16.2.3
```

Step 5:   Display the default logging settings.

Use the **show logging** command to display the default logging settings.

```
R2# show logging
Syslog logging: enabled (0 messages dropped, 2 messages rate-limited, 0 flushes, 0
overruns, xml disabled, filtering disabled)

No Active Message Discriminator.



No Inactive Message Discriminator.


    Console logging: level debugging, 47 messages logged, xml disabled,
                     filtering disabled
    Monitor logging: level debugging, 0 messages logged, xml disabled,
                     filtering disabled
    Buffer logging:  level debugging, 47 messages logged, xml disabled,
                     filtering disabled
    Exception Logging: size (4096 bytes)
    Count and timestamp logging messages: disabled
    Persistent logging: disabled

No active filter modules.

    Trap logging: level informational, 49 message lines logged
        Logging to 172.16.2.3  (udp port 514, audit disabled,
             link up),
         6 message lines logged,
         0 message lines rate-limited,
         0 message lines dropped-by-MD,
         xml disabled, sequence number disabled
         filtering disabled
    Logging Source-Interface:      VRF Name:
```

What is the IP address of the syslog server? _____

What protocol and port is syslog using? _____

At what level is trap logging enabled? _____

Step 6:   Configure and observe the effect of logging severity levels on R2.

a.   Use the **logging trap ?** command to determine the various trap levels availability. When configuring a level, the messages sent to the syslog server are the trap level configured and any lower levels.

```
R2(config)# logging trap ?
  <0-7>          Logging severity level
  alerts         Immediate action needed       (severity=1)
  critical       Critical conditions           (severity=2)
  debugging      Debugging messages            (severity=7)
  emergencies    System is unusable            (severity=0)
  errors         Error conditions              (severity=3)
  informational  Informational messages        (severity=6)
  notifications  Normal but significant conditions (severity=5)
  warnings       Warning conditions            (severity=4)
  <cr>
```

If the **logging trap warnings** command was issued, which severity levels of messages are logged?

_____

b.   Change the logging severity level to 4.

```
R2(config)# logging trap warnings
```

or

```
R2(config)# logging trap 4
```

c.   Create interface Loopback0 on R2 and observe the log messages on both the terminal window and the syslog server window on PC-B.

```
R2(config)# interface lo 0
R2(config-if)#
Jul  5 09:57:47.162: %LINK-3-UPDOWN: Interface Loopback0, changed state to up
Jul  5 09:57:48.162: %LINEPROTO-5-UPDOWN: Line protocol on Interface Loopback0,
changed state to up
```

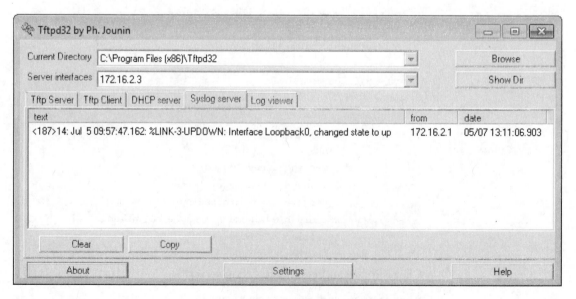

d. Remove the Loopback 0 interface on R2 and observe the log messages.

```
R2(config-if)# no interface lo 0
R2(config)#
Jul  5 10:02:58.910: %LINK-5-CHANGED: Interface Loopback0, changed state to
administratively down
Jul  5 10:02:59.910: %LINEPROTO-5-UPDOWN: Line protocol on Interface Loopback0,
changed state to down
```

At severity level 4, are there any log messages on the syslog server? If any log messages appeared, explain what appeared and why.

_____

_____

_____

_____

e. Change the logging severity level to 6.

```
R2(config)# logging trap informational
```

or

```
R2(config)# logging trap 6
```

f. Clear the syslog entries on PC-B. Click **Clear** in the Tftpd32 dialog box.

g. Create the Loopback 1 interface on R2.

```
R2(config)# interface lo 1
Jul  5 10:05:46.650: %LINK-3-UPDOWN: Interface Loopback1, changed state to up
Jul  5 10:05:47.650: %LINEPROTO-5-UPDOWN: Line protocol on Interface Loopback1,
changed state to up
```

h. Remove the Loopback 1 interface from R2.

```
R2(config-if)# no interface lo 1
R2(config-if)#
Jul  5 10:08:29.742: %LINK-5-CHANGED: Interface Loopback1, changed state to
administratively down
Jul  5 10:08:30.742: %LINEPROTO-5-UPDOWN: Line protocol on Interface Loopback1,
changed state to down
```

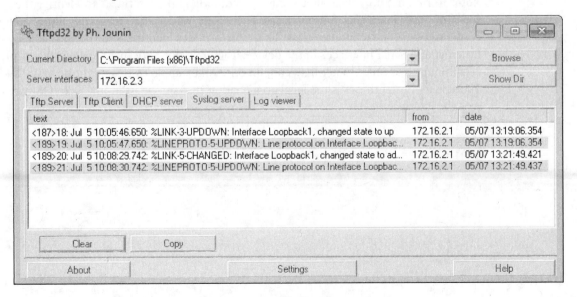

    i. Observe the syslog server output. Compare this result with the results at trapping level 4. What is your observation?

_____

_____

_____

Reflection

What is the problem with setting the level of severity too high (lowest level number) or too low (highest level number) for syslog?

_____

_____

_____

Router Interface Summary Table

Router Interface Summary				
Router Model	Ethernet Interface #1	Ethernet Interface #2	Serial Interface #1	Serial Interface #2
1800	Fast Ethernet 0/0 (F0/0)	Fast Ethernet 0/1 (F0/1)	Serial 0/0/0 (S0/0/0)	Serial 0/0/1 (S0/0/1)
1900	Gigabit Ethernet 0/0 (G0/0)	Gigabit Ethernet 0/1 (G0/1)	Serial 0/0/0 (S0/0/0)	Serial 0/0/1 (S0/0/1)
2801	Fast Ethernet 0/0 (F0/0)	Fast Ethernet 0/1 (F0/1)	Serial 0/1/0 (S0/1/0)	Serial 0/1/1 (S0/1/1)
2811	Fast Ethernet 0/0 (F0/0)	Fast Ethernet 0/1 (F0/1)	Serial 0/0/0 (S0/0/0)	Serial 0/0/1 (S0/0/1)
2900	Gigabit Ethernet 0/0 (G0/0)	Gigabit Ethernet 0/1 (G0/1)	Serial 0/0/0 (S0/0/0)	Serial 0/0/1 (S0/0/1)

Note: To find out how the router is configured, look at the interfaces to identify the type of router and how many interfaces the router has. There is no way to effectively list all the combinations of configurations for each router class. This table includes identifiers for the possible combinations of Ethernet and Serial interfaces in the device. The table does not include any other type of interface, even though a specific router may contain one. An example of this might be an ISDN BRI interface. The string in parentheses is the legal abbreviation that can be used in Cisco IOS commands to represent the interface.

10.3.1.8 Packet Tracer–Backing Up Configuration Files

Topology

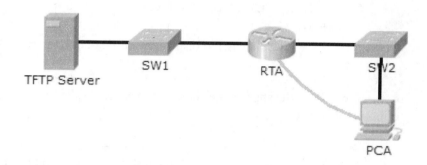

Objectives

Part 1: Establish Connectivity to TFTP Server

Part 2: Transfer Configuration from TFTP Server

Part 3: Backup Configuration and IOS to TFTP Server

Background/Scenario

This activity is designed to show how to restore a configuration from a backup and then perform a new backup. Due to an equipment failure, a new router has been put in place. Fortunately backup configuration files have been saved to a Trivial File Transfer Protocol (TFTP) Server. You are required to restore the files from the TFTP Server to get the router back online with as little down time as possible.

Part 1: Establish Connectivity to the TFTP Server

Note: Because this is a new router, initial configuration will be performed using a console connection to the router.

- **a.** Click **PCA**, then the **Desktop** tab, followed by **Terminal** to access the **RTA** command line.

- **b.** Configure and activate the **Gigabit Ethernet 0/0** interface. The IP address should match the default gateway for the **TFTP Server**.

- **c.** Test connectivity to **TFTP Server**. Troubleshoot, if necessary.

Part 2: Transfer Configuration from the TFTP Server

- **a.** From privileged EXEC mode, issue the following command:

```
Router# copy tftp running-config
Address or name of remote host []? 172.16.1.2
Source filename []? RTA-confg
Destination filename [running-config]? <cr>
```

The router should return the following:

```
Accessing tftp://172.16.1.2/RTA-confg...
Loading RTA-confg from 172.16.1.2: !
[OK - 785 bytes]
785 bytes copied in 0 secs
RTA#
%SYS-5-CONFIG_I: Configured from console by console
RTA#
```

b. Issue the command to display the current configuration. What changes were made?

_____

c. Issue the appropriate **show** command to display the interface status. Are all interfaces active?

_____

d. Correct any issues related to interface problems and test connectivity.

Part 3: Backup Configuration and IOS to TFTP Server

a. Change the hostname of **RTA** to **RTA-1**.

b. Save the configuration to NVRAM.

c. Copy the configuration to the **TFTP Server** using the **copy** command:

```
RTA-1# copy running-config tftp:
Address or name of remote host []? 172.16.1.2
Destination filename [RTA-1-confg]? <cr>
```

d. Issue the command to display the files in flash.

e. Copy the IOS in flash to the **TFTP Server** using the following command:

```
RTA-1# copy flash tftp:
Source filename []? c1900-universalk9-mz.SPA.151-4.M4.bin
Address or name of remote host []? 172.16.1.2
Destination filename [c1900-universalk9-mz.SPA.151-4.M4.bin]? <cr>
```

10.3.1.9 Lab–Managing Router Configuration Files with Terminal Emulation Software

Topology

Addressing Table

Device	Interface	IP Address	Subnet Mask	Default Gateway
R1	G0/1	192.168.1.1	255.255.255.0	N/A
S1	VLAN 1	192.168.1.11	255.255.255.0	192.168.1.1
PC-A	NIC	192.168.1.3	255.255.255.0	192.168.1.1

Objectives

Part 1: Configure Basic Device Settings

Part 2: Use Terminal Emulation Software to Create a Backup Configuration File

Part 3: Use a Backup Configuration File to Restore a Router

Background/Scenario

It is a recommended best practice to maintain backup configuration files for routers and switches in the event that they need to be restored to a previous configuration. Terminal emulation software can be used to easily back up or restore a router or switch configuration file.

In this lab, you will use Tera Term to back up a router running configuration file, erase the router startup configuration file, reload the router, and then restore the missing router configuration from the backup configuration file.

Note: The routers used with CCNA hands-on labs are Cisco 1941 Integrated Services Routers (ISRs) with Cisco IOS Release 15.2(4)M3 (universalk9 image). The switches used are Cisco Catalyst 2960s with Cisco IOS Release 15.0(2) (lanbasek9 image). Other routers, switches, and Cisco IOS versions can be used. Depending on the model and Cisco IOS version, the commands available and output produced might vary from what is shown in the labs. Refer to the Router Interface Summary Table at the end of this lab for the correct interface identifiers.

Note: Make sure that the routers and switches have been erased and have no startup configurations. If you are unsure, contact your instructor.

Required Resources

- 1 Router (Cisco 1941 with Cisco IOS Release 15.2(4)M3 universal image or comparable)
- 1 Switch (Cisco 2960 with Cisco IOS Release 15.0(2) lanbasek9 image or comparable)

- 1 PC (Windows 7, Vista, or XP with terminal emulation program, such as Tera Term)
- Console cables to configure the Cisco IOS devices via the console ports
- Ethernet cables as shown in the topology

Part 1: Configure Basic Device Settings

In Part 1, you will set up the network topology and configure basic settings, such as the interface IP addresses, device access, and passwords on the router.

Step 1:   Cable the network as shown in the topology.

Attach the devices as shown in the topology and cable as necessary.

Step 2:   Configure the PC-A network settings according to the Addressing Table.

Step 3:   Initialize and reload the router and switch.

Step 4:   Configure the router.

   a.   Console into the router and enter global configuration mode.

   b.   Copy the following basic configuration and paste it to the running-configuration on R1.

```
no ip domain-lookup
hostname R1
service password-encryption
enable secret class
banner motd #
Unauthorized access is strictly prohibited. #
Line con 0
password cisco
login
logging synchronous
line vty 0 4
password cisco
login
```

   c.   Configure and activate the G0/1 interface on the router using the information contained in the Addressing Table.

   d.   Save the running configuration to the startup configuration file.

Step 5:   Configure the switch.

   a.   Console into the switch and enter into global configuration mode.

   b.   Copy the following basic configuration and paste it to the running-configuration on S1.

```
no ip domain-lookup
hostname S1
service password-encryption
enable secret class
banner motd #
Unauthorized access is strictly prohibited. #
Line con 0
password cisco
login
logging synchronous
```

```
line vty 0 15
password cisco
login
exit
```

c. Configure the default SVI management interface with the IP address information contained in the Addressing Table.

d. Configure the switch default gateway.

e. Save the running configuration to the startup configuration file.

Part 2: Use Terminal Emulation Software to Create a Backup Configuration File

Step 1:   Establish a Tera Term console session to the router.

Launch the Tera Term Program, and in the New Connection window, select the **Serial** radio button and the appropriate communications port for your PC (i.e., COM1).

Note: If Tera Term is not installed, you can download the latest version from a number of Internet sites. Simply search for a Tera Term download.

---

a. In Tera Term, press Enter to connect to the router.

b. From the **File** menu, choose **Log...**, and save the **teraterm.log** file to the Desktop. Ensure that the **Append** and **Plain text** check boxes are enabled (checked).

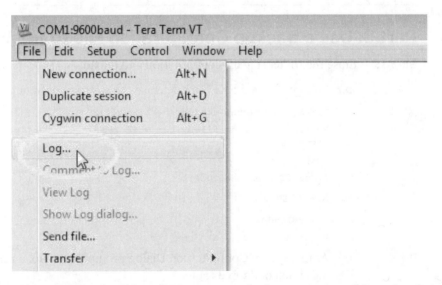

c. The Tera Term log file will create a record of every command issued and every output displayed.

Note: You can use this feature to capture the output from several commands in sequence and use it for network documentation purposes. For example, you could issue the **show version**, **show ip interface brief**, and **show running-config** commands to capture information about the router.

Step 2: Display the router running-configuration.

    a. Use the console password to log in to the router.

    b. Enter privileged EXEC mode.

    c. Enter the **show running-config** command.

    d. Continue pressing the space bar when **--More--** is displayed until you see the router R1# prompt return.

    e. Click the **Tera Term: Log** icon on the Task bar. Click **Close** to end log session.

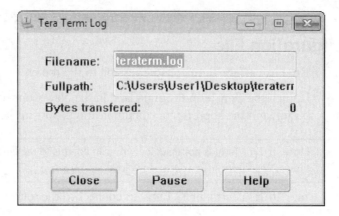

Note: You can also copy and paste the text from the Tera Term window directly into a text editor.

Part 3: Use a Backup Configuration File to Restore a Router

Step 1: Erase the router startup-configuration and reload.

    a. From privileged EXEC mode erase the startup configuration.

```
R1# erase startup-config
Erasing the nvram filesystem will remove all configuration files! Continue?
[confirm]
[OK]
Erase of nvram: complete
```

    b. Reload the router.

```
R1# reload
Proceed with reload? [confirm]
```

    c. At the System Configuration Dialog prompt, type **no**; a router prompt displays, indicating an unconfigured router.

```
        --- System Configuration Dialog ---


Would you like to enter the initial configuration dialog? [yes/no]:

Press RETURN to get started!
<output omitted>
Router>
```

    d. Enter privileged EXEC mode and enter a **show running-config** command to verify that all of the previous configurations were erased.

Step 2:   Edit the saved configuration backup file to prepare it for restoring the router configuration.

To restore the router configuration from a saved running configuration backup file, you must edit the text.

    a.   Open the **teraterm.log** text file.

    b.   Remove each instance of **--More--** in the text file.

Note: The --More-- was generated by pressing the Spacebar when displaying the running configuration.

    c.   Delete the initial lines of the backup configuration file, so that the first line starts with the first configuration command as shown below.

    d.   In the lines for interface GigabitEthernet0/1, insert a new line to enable the interface.

```
interface GigabitEthernet0/1
 ip address 192.168.1.1 255.255.255.0
 duplex auto
 speed auto
```

Change to:

```
interface GigabitEthernet0/1
 ip address 192.168.1.1 255.255.255.0
 duplex auto
 speed auto
 no shutdown
```

    e.   After you have made all of the edits to the backup configuration file, save your changes to filename **R1-config-backup**.

Note: When saving the file, an extension such as **.txt**, may be added to the filename automatically.

Step 3:   Restore the router configuration.

You can restore the edited running configuration directly to the console terminal in router global configuration mode, and the configurations are entered as if they were commands entered individually at the command prompt.

    a.   From the Tera Term console connection to the router, enter global configuration mode.

    b.   From the **File** menu, select **Send file....**

    c.   Locate **R1-config-backup** and select **Open**.

    d.   Save the running configuration to the startup configuration file.

```
R1# copy running-config startup-config
```

    e.   Verify the new running configuration.

Step 4:   Back up and restore the switch.

Go back to the beginning of Part 2 and follow the same steps to backup and restore the switch configuration.

Reflection

Why do you think it is important to use a text editor instead of a word processor to copy and save your command configurations?

_____

_____

_____

Router Interface Summary Table

Router Interface Summary				
Router Model	Ethernet Interface #1	Ethernet Interface #2	Serial Interface #1	Serial Interface #2
1800	Fast Ethernet 0/0 (F0/0)	Fast Ethernet 0/1 (F0/1)	Serial 0/0/0 (S0/0/0)	Serial 0/0/1 (S0/0/1)
1900	Gigabit Ethernet 0/0 (G0/0)	Gigabit Ethernet 0/1 (G0/1)	Serial 0/0/0 (S0/0/0)	Serial 0/0/1 (S0/0/1)
2801	Fast Ethernet 0/0 (F0/0)	Fast Ethernet 0/1 (F0/1)	Serial 0/1/0 (S0/1/0)	Serial 0/1/1 (S0/1/1)
2811	Fast Ethernet 0/0 (F0/0)	Fast Ethernet 0/1 (F0/1)	Serial 0/0/0 (S0/0/0)	Serial 0/0/1 (S0/0/1)
2900	Gigabit Ethernet 0/0 (G0/0)	Gigabit Ethernet 0/1 (G0/1)	Serial 0/0/0 (S0/0/0)	Serial 0/0/1 (S0/0/1)

Note: To find out how the router is configured, look at the interfaces to identify the type of router and how many interfaces the router has. There is no way to effectively list all the combinations of configurations for each router class. This table includes identifiers for the possible combinations of Ethernet and Serial interfaces in the device. The table does not include any other type of interface, even though a specific router may contain one. An example of this might be an ISDN BRI interface. The string in parentheses is the legal abbreviation that can be used in Cisco IOS commands to represent the interface.

10.3.1.10 Lab–Managing Device Configuration Files Using TFTP, Flash, and USB

Topology

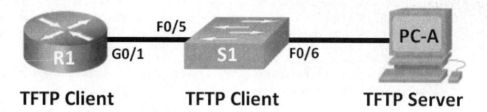

TFTP Client   TFTP Client   TFTP Server

Addressing Table

Device	Interface	IP Address	Subnet Mask	Default Gateway
R1	G0/1	192.168.1.1	255.255.255.0	N/A
S1	VLAN 1	192.168.1.11	255.255.255.0	192.168.1.1
PC-A	NIC	192.168.1.3	255.255.255.0	192.168.1.1

Objectives

Part 1: Build the Network and Configure Basic Device Settings

Part 2: (Optional) Download TFTP Server Software

Part 3: Use TFTP to Back Up and Restore the Switch Running Configuration

Part 4: Use TFTP to Back Up and Restore the Router Running Configuration

Part 5: Back Up and Restore Running Configurations Using Router Flash Memory

Part 6: (Optional) Use a USB Drive to Back Up and Restore the Running Configuration

Background/Scenario

Cisco networking devices are often upgraded or swapped out for a number of reasons. It is important to maintain backups of the latest device configurations, as well as a history of configuration changes. A TFTP server is often used to backup configuration files and IOS images in production networks. A TFTP server is a centralized and secure method used to store the backup copies of the files and restore them as necessary. Using a centralized TFTP server, you can back up files from many different Cisco devices.

In addition to a TFTP server, most of the current Cisco routers can back up and restore files locally from CompactFlash (CF) memory or a USB flash drive. The CF is a removable memory module that has replaced the limited internal flash memory of earlier router models. The IOS image for the router resides in the CF memory, and the router uses this IOS Image for the boot process. With the larger size of the CF memory, additional files can be stored for backup purposes. A removable USB flash drive can also be used for backup purposes.

In this lab, you will use TFTP server software to back up the Cisco device running configuration to the TFTP server or flash memory. You can edit the file using a text editor and copy the new configuration back to a Cisco device.

Note: The routers used with CCNA hands-on labs are Cisco 1941 Integrated Services Routers (ISRs) with Cisco IOS Release 15.2(4)M3 (universalk9 image). The switches used are Cisco Catalyst 2960s with Cisco IOS Release 15.0(2) (lanbasek9 image). Other routers, switches, and Cisco IOS versions can be used. Depending on the model and Cisco IOS version, the commands available and output produced might vary from what is shown in the labs. Refer to the Router Interface Summary Table at the end of this lab for the correct interface identifiers.

Note: Make sure that the routers and switches have been erased and have no startup configurations. If you are unsure, contact your instructor.

Required Resources

- 1 Router (Cisco 1941 with Cisco IOS Release 15.2(4)M3 universal image or comparable)

- 1 Switch (Cisco 2960 with Cisco IOS Release 15.0(2) lanbasek9 image or comparable)

- 1 PC (Windows 7, Vista, or XP with terminal emulation program, such as Tera Term, and a TFTP server)

- Console cables to configure the Cisco IOS devices via the console ports

- Ethernet cables as shown in the topology

- USB flash drive (Optional)

Part 1: Build the Network and Configure Basic Device Settings

In Part 1, you will set up the network topology and configure basic settings, such as the interface IP addresses for router R1, switch S1, and PC-A.

Step 1: Cable the network as shown in the topology.

Attach the devices as shown in the topology diagram, and cable as necessary.

Step 2: Initialize and reload the router and switch.

Step 3: Configure basic settings for each device.

    a. Configure basic device parameters as shown in the Addressing Table.

    b. To prevent the router and switch from attempting to translate incorrectly entered commands as though they were host names, disable DNS lookup.

    c. Assign **class** as the privileged EXEC encrypted password.

    d. Configure the passwords and allow login for console and vty lines using the **cisco** as the password.

    e. Configure the default gateway for the switch.

    f. Encrypt the clear text passwords.

    g. Configure the IP address, subnet mask, and default gateway for PC-A.

Step 4:   Verify connectivity from PC-A.

  a.   Ping from PC-A to S1.

  b.   Ping from PC-A to R1.

  If the pings are not successful, troubleshoot the basic device configurations before continuing.

Part 2: (Optional) Download TFTP Server Software

A number of free TFTP servers are available on the Internet for download. The Tftpd32 server is used with this lab.

Note: Downloading a TFTP server from a website requires Internet access.

Step 1:   Verify availability of a TFTP server on PC-A.

  a.   Click the **Start** menu and select **All Programs**.

  b.   Search for a TFTP server on PC-A.

  c.   If a TFTP server is not found, a TFTP server can be downloaded from the Internet.

Step 2:   Download a TFTP server.

  a.   Tftpd32 is used in this lab. This server can be downloaded from the following link:

  http://tftpd32.jounin.net/tftpd32_download.html

  b.   Choose the appropriate version for your system and install the server.

Part 3: Use TFTP to Back Up and Restore the Switch Running Configuration

Step 1:   Verify connectivity to switch S1 from PC-A.

  The TFTP application uses the UDP Layer 4 transport protocol, which is encapsulated in an IP packet. For TFTP file transfers to function, there must be Layer 1 and 2 (Ethernet, in this case) and Layer 3 (IP) connectivity between the TFTP client and the TFTP server. The LAN topology in this lab uses only Ethernet at Layers 1 and 2. However, TFTP transfers can also be accomplished over WAN links that use other Layer 1 physical links and Layer 2 protocols. As long as there is IP connectivity between the client and server, as demonstrated by ping, the TFTP transfer can take place. If the pings are not successful, troubleshoot the basic device configurations before continuing.

Note: A common misconception is that you can TFTP a file over the console connection. This is not the case because the console connection does not use IP. The TFTP transfer can be initiated from the client device (router or switch) using the console connection, but there must be IP connectivity between the client and server for the file transfer to take place.

Step 2:   Start the TFTP server.

  a.   Click the **Start** menu and select **All Programs**.

  b.   Find and select **Tftpd32** or **Tftpd64**. The following window displays that the TFTP server is ready.

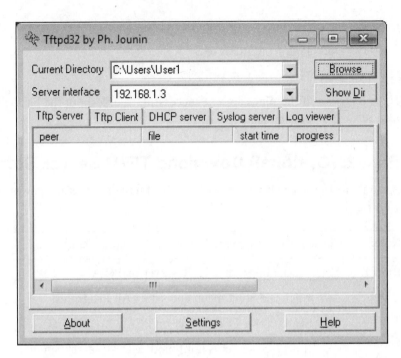

c. Click **Browse** to choose a directory where you have write permission, such as C:\Users\ User1, or the Desktop.

Step 3: Explore the **copy** command on a Cisco device.

a. Console into switch S1 and, from the privileged EXEC mode prompt, enter **copy ?** to display the options for source or "from" location and other available copy options. You can specify **flash:** or **flash0:** as the source; however, if you simply provide a filename as the source, **flash0:** is assumed and is the default. Note that **running-config** is also an option for the source location.

```
S1# copy ?
  /erase           Erase destination file system.
  /error           Allow to copy error file.
  /noverify        Don't verify image signature before reload.
  /verify          Verify image signature before reload.
  archive:         Copy from archive: file system
  cns:             Copy from cns: file system
  flash0:          Copy from flash0: file system
  flash1:          Copy from flash1: file system
  flash:           Copy from flash: file system
  ftp:             Copy from ftp: file system
  http:            Copy from http: file system
  https:           Copy from https: file system
  null:            Copy from null: file system
  nvram:           Copy from nvram: file system
  rcp:             Copy from rcp: file system
  running-config   Copy from current system configuration
  scp:             Copy from scp: file system
  startup-config   Copy from startup configuration
  system:          Copy from system: file system
  tar:             Copy from tar: file system
  tftp:            Copy from tftp: file system
```

```
tmpsys:          Copy from tmpsys: file system
xmodem:          Copy from xmodem: file system
ymodem:          Copy from ymodem: file system
```

    b. Use the **?** to display the destination options after a source file location is chosen. The **flash:** file system for S1 is the source file system in this example.

```
S1# copy flash: ?
  archive:          Copy to archive: file system
  flash0:           Copy to flash0: file system
  flash1:           Copy to flash1: file system
  flash:            Copy to flash: file system
  ftp:              Copy to ftp: file system
  http:             Copy to http: file system
  https:            Copy to https: file system
  idconf            Load an IDConf configuration file
  null:             Copy to null: file system
  nvram:            Copy to nvram: file system
  rcp:              Copy to rcp: file system
  running-config    Update (merge with) current system configuration
  scp:              Copy to scp: file system
  startup-config    Copy to startup configuration
  syslog:           Copy to syslog: file system
  system:           Copy to system: file system
  tftp:             Copy to tftp: file system
  tmpsys:           Copy to tmpsys: file system
  xmodem:           Copy to xmodem: file system
  ymodem:           Copy to ymodem: file system
```

Step 4:   Transfer the running-config file from switch S1 to TFTP server on PC-A.

    a. From the privileged EXEC mode on the switch, enter the **copy running-config tftp:** command. Provide the remote host address of the TFTP server (PC-A), 192.168.1.3. Press Enter to accept default destination filename (**s1-confg**) or provide your own filename. The exclamation marks (**!!**) indicate the transfer process is in progress and is successful.

```
S1# copy running-config tftp:
Address or name of remote host []? 192.168.1.3
Destination filename [s1-confg]?
!!
1465 bytes copied in 0.663 secs (2210 bytes/sec)
S1#
```

The TFTP server also displays the progress during the transfer.

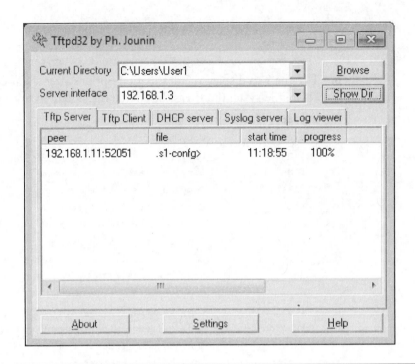

Note: If you do not have permission to write to the current directory that is used by the TFTP server, the following error message displays:

```
S1# copy running-config tftp:
Address or name of remote host []? 192.168.1.3
Destination filename [s1-confg]?
%Error opening tftp://192.168.1.3/s1-confg (Permission denied)
```

You can change the current directory in TFTP server by clicking **Browse** and choosing a different folder.

Note: Other issues, such as a firewall blocking TFTP traffic, can prevent the TFTP transfer. Please check with your instructor for further assistance.

    b. In the Tftpd32 server window, click **Show Dir** to verify that the **s1-confg** file has been transferred to your current directory. Click **Close** when finished.

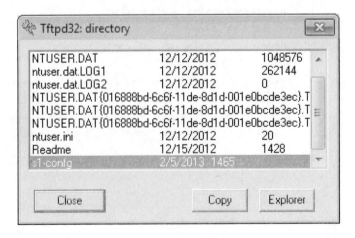

Step 5:   Create a modified switch running configuration file.

The saved running configuration file, **s1-confg**, can also be restored to the switch by using the **copy** command from the switch. The original or a modified version of the file can be copied to the flash file system of the switch.

a.   Navigate to the TFTP directory on PC-A by using the file system of PC-A, and then locate the **s1-confg** file. Open this file using a text editor program, such as WordPad.

b.   With the file open, locate the **hostname S1** line. Replace **S1** with **Switch1**. Delete all the self-generated crypto keys, as necessary. A sample of the keys is displayed below. These keys are not exportable and can cause errors while updating the running configuration.

```
crypto pki trustpoint TP-self-signed-1566151040
 enrollment selfsigned
 subject-name cn=IOS-Self-Signed-Certificate-1566151040
 revocation-check none
 rsakeypair TP-self-signed-1566151040
!
!
crypto pki certificate chain TP-self-signed-1566151040
 certificate self-signed 01
  3082022B 30820194 A0030201 02020101 300D0609 2A864886 F70D0101 05050030
  31312F30 2D060355 04031326 494F532D 53656C66 2D536967 6E65642D 43657274
<output omitted>
  E99574A6 D945014F B6FE22F3 642EE29A 767EABF7 403930CA D2C59E23 102EC12E
  02F9C933 B3296D9E 095EBDAF 343D17F6 AF2831C7 6DA6DFE3 35B38D90 E6F07CD4
  40D96970 A0D12080 07A1C169 30B9D889 A6E2189C 75B988B9 0AF27EDC 6D6FA0E5
  CCFA6B29 729C1E0B 9DADACD0 3D7381
        quit
```

c.   Save this file as a plain text file with a new filename, **Switch1-confg.txt**, in this example.

Note: When saving the file, an extension, such as .txt, may be added to the filename automatically.

---

d.   In the Tftpd32 server window, click **Show Dir** to verify that the **Switch1-confg.txt** file is located in the current directory.

Step 6:   Upload the running configuration file from TFTP server to switch S1.

a.   From the privileged EXEC mode on the switch, enter the **copy tftp running-config** command. Provide the remote host address of the TFTP server, 192.168.1.3. Enter the new filename, **Switch1-confg.txt**. The exclamation mark (!) indicates the transfer process is in progress and is successful.

```
S1# copy tftp: running-config
Address or name of remote host []? 192.168.1.3
Source filename []? Switch1-confg.txt
Destination filename [running-config]?
Accessing tftp://192.168.1.3/Switch1-confg.txt...
Loading Switch1-confg.txt from 192.168.1.3 (via Vlan1): !
[OK - 1580 bytes]
[OK]
1580 bytes copied in 9.118 secs (173 bytes/sec)
*Mar  1 00:21:16.242: %PKI-4-NOAUTOSAVE: Configuration was modified.  Issue
"write memory" to save new certificate
```

```
*Mar  1 00:21:16.251: %SYS-5-CONFIG_I: Configured from tftp://192.168.1.3/
Switch1-config.txt by console
Switch1#
```

After the transfer has completed, the prompt has changed from S1 to Switch1, because the running configuration is updated with the **hostname Switch1** command in the modified running configuration.

b. Enter the **show running-config** command to examine the running configuration file.

```
Switch1# show running-config
Building configuration...

Current configuration : 3062 bytes
!
! Last configuration change at 00:09:34 UTC Mon Mar 1 1993
!
version 15.0
no service pad
service timestamps debug datetime msec
service timestamps log datetime msec
no service password-encryption
!
hostname Switch1
!
boot-start-marker
boot-end-marker
<output omitted>
```

Note: This procedure merges the running-config from the TFTP server with the current running-config in the switch or router. If changes were made to the current running-config, the commands in the TFTP copy are added. Alternatively, if the same command is issued, it updates the corresponding command in the switch or router current running-config.

If you want to completely replace the current running-config with the one from the TFTP server, you must erase the switch startup-config and reload the device. You will then need to configure the VLAN 1 management address, so there is IP connectivity between the TFTP server and the switch.

Part 4: Use TFTP to Back Up and Restore the Router Running Configuration

The backup and restore procedure from Part 3 can also be performed with a router. In Part 4, the running configuration file will be backed up and restored using a TFTP server.

Step 1:   Verify connectivity to router R1 from PC-A.

If the pings are not successful, troubleshoot the basic device configurations before continuing.

Step 2:   Transfer the running configuration from router R1 to TFTP server on PC-A.

    a.   From the privileged EXEC mode on R1, enter the **copy running-config tftp** command. Provide the remote host address of the TFTP server, 192.168.1.3, and accept the default filename.

    b.   Verify that the file has been transferred to the TFTP server.

Step 3:   Restore the running configuration file to the router.

    a.   Erase the startup-config file on the router.

    b.   Reload the router.

    c.   Configure the G0/1 interface on the router with an IP address 192.168.1.1.

    d.   Verify connectivity between the router and PC-A.

    e.   Use the **copy** command to transfer the running-config file from the TFTP server to the router. Use **running-config** as the destination.

    f.   Verify the router has updated the running-config.

Part 5: Back Up and Restore Configurations Using Router Flash Memory

For the 1941 and other newer Cisco routers, there is no internal flash memory. The flash memory for these routers uses CompactFlash (CF) memory. The use of CF memory allows for more available flash memory and easier upgrades without the need to open the router case. Besides storing the necessary files, such as IOS images, the CF memory can store other files, such as a copy of the running configuration. In Part 5, you will create a backup copy of the running configuration file and save it on the CF memory on the router.

Note: If the router does not use CF, the router may not have enough flash memory for storing the backup copy of the running configuration file. You should still read through the instructions and become familiar with the commands.

Step 1:   Display the router file systems.

The **show file systems** command displays the available file systems on the router. The **flash0:** file system is the default file system on this router as indicated by the asterisk (*) symbol (at the beginning of the line). The hash (#) sign (at the end of the highlighted line) indicates that it is a bootable disk. The **flash0:** file system can also be referenced using the name **flash:**. The total size of the **flash0:** is 256 MB with 62 MB available. Currently the **flash1:** slot is empty as indicated by the — under the headings, Size (b) and Free (b). Currently **flash0:** and **nvram:** are the only available file systems.

```
R1# show file systems
File Systems:
```

Size(b)	Free(b)	Type	Flags	Prefixes
—	—	opaque	rw	archive:
—	—	opaque	rw	system:
—	—	opaque	rw	tmpsys:
—	—	opaque	rw	null:
—	—	network	rw	tftp:
* 260153344	64499712	disk	rw	flash0: flash:#
—	—	disk	rw	flash1:

```
   262136        242776      nvram    rw    nvram:
        -             -      opaque   wo    syslog:
        -             -      opaque   rw    xmodem:
        -             -      opaque   rw    ymodem:
        -             -      network  rw    rcp:
        -             -      network  rw    http:
        -             -      network  rw    ftp:
        -             -      network  rw    scp:
        -             -      opaque   ro    tar:
        -             -      network  rw    https:
        -             -      opaque   ro    cns:
```

Where is the startup-config file located?

_____

_____

Note: Verify there is at least 1 MB (1,048,576 bytes) of free space. If there is not enough space in the flash memory, please contact your instructor for further instructions. You can determine the size of flash memory and space available using the **show flash** or **dir flash:** command at the privileged EXEC prompt.

Step 2: Copy the router running configuration to flash.

A file can be copied to flash by using the **copy** command at the privileged EXEC prompt. In this example, the file is copied into **flash0:**, because there is only one flash drive available as displayed in the previous step, and it is also the default file system. The **R1-running-config-backup** file is used as the filename for the backup running configuration file.

Note: Remember that filenames are case-sensitive in the IOS file system.

a. Copy the running configuration to flash memory.

```
R1# copy running-config flash:
Destination filename [running-config]? R1-running-config-backup
2169 bytes copied in 0.968 secs (2241 bytes/sec)
```

b. Use **dir** command to verify the running-config has been copied to flash.

```
R1# dir flash:
Directory of flash0:/

    1  drw-           0  Nov 15 2011 14:59:04 +00:00  ipsdir
<output omitted>
   20  -rw-    67998028  Aug 7 2012 17:39:16 +00:00   c1900-universalk9-mz.
SPA.152-4.M3.bin
   22  -rw-        2169  Feb 4 2013 23:57:54 +00:00   R1-running-config-backup
   24  -rw-        5865  Jul 10 2012 14:46:22 +00:00  lpnat
   25  -rw-        6458  Jul 17 2012 00:12:40 +00:00  lpIPSec

260153344 bytes total (64503808 bytes free)
```

c. Use the **more** command to view the running-config file in flash memory. Examine the file output and scroll to the Interface section. Notice the **no shutdown** command is not included with the GigabitEthernet0/1. The interface is shut down when this file is used to update the running configuration on the router.

```
R1# more flash:R1-running-config-backup
<output omitted>
```

```
interface GigabitEthernet0/1
 ip address 192.168.1.1 255.255.255.0
 duplex auto
 speed auto
<output omitted>
```

Step 3:   Erase the startup configuration and reload the router.

Step 4:   Restore the running configuration from flash.

   a.   Verify the router has the default initial configuration.

   b.   Copy the saved running-config file from flash to update the running-config.

   Router# **copy flash:R1-running-config-backup running-config**

   c.   Use the **show ip interface brief** command to view the status of the interfaces. The interface GigabitEthernet0/1 was not enabled when the running configuration was updated, because it is administratively down.

   R1# **show ip interface brief**

Interface	IP-Address	OK?	Method	Status	Protocol
Embedded-Service-Engine0/0	unassigned	YES	unset	administratively down	down
GigabitEthernet0/0	unassigned	YES	unset	administratively down	down
GigabitEthernet0/1	192.168.1.1	YES	TFTP	administratively down	down
Serial0/0/0	unassigned	YES	unset	administratively down	down
Serial0/0/1	unassigned	YES	unset	administratively down	down

   The interface can be enabled using the **no shutdown** command in the interface configuration mode on the router.

   Another option is to add the **no shutdown** command for the GigabitEthernet0/1 interface to the saved file before updating the router running configuration file. This will be done in Part 6 using a saved file on a USB flash drive.

Note: Because the IP address was configured by using a file transfer, TFTP is listed under the Method heading in the **show ip interface brief** output.

Part 6: (Optional) Use a USB Drive to Back Up and Restore the Running Configuration

A USB flash drive can be used to back up and restore files on a router with an available USB port. Two USB ports are available on the 1941 routers.

Note: USB ports are not available on all routers, but you should still become familiar with the commands.

Note: Because some ISR G1 routers (1841, 2801, or 2811) use File Allocation Table (FAT) file systems, there is a maximum size limit for the USB flash drives that can be used in this part of the lab. The recommended maximum size for an ISR G1 is 4 GB. If you receive the following message, the file system on the USB flash drive may be incompatible with the router or the capacity of the USB flash drive may have exceed maximum size of the FAT file system on the router.

```
*Feb  8 13:51:34.831: %USBFLASH-4-FORMAT: usbflash0 contains unexpected values in partition
table or boot sector.  Device needs formatting before use!
```

Step 1:   Insert a USB flash drive into a USB port on the router.

Notice the message on the terminal when inserting the USB flash drive.

```
R1#
* *Feb  5 20:38:04.678: %USBFLASH-5-CHANGE: usbflash0 has been inserted!
```

Step 2:   Verify that the USB flash file system is available.

```
R1# show file systems
File Systems:

        Size(b)       Free(b)      Type   Flags   Prefixes
              -             -     opaque      rw   archive:
              -             -     opaque      rw   system:
              -             -     opaque      rw   tmpsys:
              -             -     opaque      rw   null:
              -             -    network      rw   tftp:
*     260153344      64512000       disk      rw   flash0: flash:#
              -             -       disk      rw   flash1:
         262136        244676      nvram      rw   nvram:
              -             -     opaque      wo   syslog:
              -             -     opaque      rw   xmodem:
              -             -     opaque      rw   ymodem:
              -             -    network      rw   rcp:
              -             -    network      rw   http:
              -             -    network      rw   ftp:
              -             -    network      rw   scp:
              -             -     opaque      ro   tar:
              -             -    network      rw   https:
              -             -     opaque      ro   cns:
     7728881664    7703973888   usbflash      rw   usbflash0:
```

Step 3:   Copy the running configuration file to the USB flash drive.

Use the **copy** command to copy the running configuration file to the USB flash drive.

```
R1# copy running-config usbflash0:
Destination filename [running-config]? R1-running-config-backup.txt
2198 bytes copied in 0.708 secs (3105 bytes/sec)
```

Step 4:   List the file on the USB flash drive.

Use the **dir** command (or **show** command) on the router to list the files on the USB flash drive. In this sample, a flash drive was inserted into USB port 0 on the router.

```
R1# dir usbflash0:
Directory of usbflash0:/

    1  -rw-        16216   Nov 15 2006 09:34:04 +00:00  ConditionsFR.txt
    2  -rw-         2462   May 26 2006 21:33:40 +00:00  Nlm.ico
    3  -rw-     24810439   Apr 16 2010 10:28:00 +00:00  Twice.exe
    4  -rw-           71   Jun  4 2010 11:23:06 +00:00  AUTORUN.INF
    5  -rw-        65327   Mar 11 2008 10:54:26 +00:00  ConditionsEN.txt
    6  -rw-         2198   Feb  5 2013 21:36:40 +00:00  R1-running-config-backup.txt

7728881664 bytes total (7703973888 bytes free)
```

Step 5: Erase the startup-config and reload the router.

Step 6: Modify the saved file.

    a. Remove the USB drive from the router.

```
Router#
*Feb  5 21:41:51.134: %USBFLASH-5-CHANGE: usbflash0 has been removed!
```

    b. Insert the USB drive into the USB port of a PC.

    c. Modify the file using a text editor. The **no shutdown** command is added to the GigabitEthernet0/1 interface. Save the file as a plain text file on to the USB flash drive.

```
!
interface GigabitEthernet0/1
 ip address 192.168.1.1 255.255.255.0
 no shutdown
 duplex auto
 speed auto
!
```

    d. Remove the USB flash drive from the PC safely.

Step 7: Restore the running configuration file to the router.

    a. Insert the USB flash drive into a USB port on the router. Notice the port number where the USB drive has been inserted if there is more than one USB port available on the router.

```
*Feb  5 21:52:00.214: %USBFLASH-5-CHANGE: usbflash1 has been inserted!
```

    b. List the files on the USB flash drive.

```
Router# dir usbflash1:
Directory of usbflash1:/

    1  -rw-      16216  Nov 15 2006 09:34:04 +00:00  ConditionsFR.txt
    2  -rw-       2462  May 26 2006 21:33:40 +00:00  Nlm.ico
    3  -rw-   24810439  Apr 16 2010 10:28:00 +00:00  Twice.exe
    4  -rw-         71  Jun 4 2010 11:23:06 +00:00  AUTORUN.INF
    5  -rw-      65327  Mar 11 2008 10:54:26 +00:00  ConditionsEN.txt
    6  -rw-       2344  Feb 6 2013 14:42:30 +00:00  R1-running-config-backup.
txt

7728881664 bytes total (7703965696 bytes free)
```

    c. Copy the running configuration file to the router.

```
Router# copy usbflash1:R1-running-config-backup.txt running-config
Destination filename [running-config]?
2344 bytes copied in 0.184 secs (12739 bytes/sec)
R1#
```

    d. Verify that the GigabitEthernet0/1 interface is enabled.

```
R1# show ip interface brief
Interface                  IP-Address      OK? Method Status                Protocol
Embedded-Service-Engine0/0 unassigned      YES unset  administratively down down
GigabitEthernet0/0         unassigned      YES unset  administratively down down
GigabitEthernet0/1         192.168.1.1 YES TFTP    up                    up
```

```
Serial0/0/0                 unassigned  YES unset  administratively down down
Serial0/0/1                 unassigned  YES unset  administratively down down
```

The G0/1 interface is enabled because the modified running configuration included the no shutdown command.

Reflection

1. What command do you use to copy a file from the flash to a USB drive?

_____

2. What command do you use to copy a file from the USB flash drive to a TFTP server?

_____

Router Interface Summary Table

Router Interface Summary				
Router Model	Ethernet Interface #1	Ethernet Interface #2	Serial Interface #1	Serial Interface #2
1800	Fast Ethernet 0/0 (F0/0)	Fast Ethernet 0/1 (F0/1)	Serial 0/0/0 (S0/0/0)	Serial 0/0/1 (S0/0/1)
1900	Gigabit Ethernet 0/0 (G0/0)	Gigabit Ethernet 0/1 (G0/1)	Serial 0/0/0 (S0/0/0)	Serial 0/0/1 (S0/0/1)
2801	Fast Ethernet 0/0 (F0/0)	Fast Ethernet 0/1 (F0/1)	Serial 0/1/0 (S0/1/0)	Serial 0/1/1 (S0/1/1)
2811	Fast Ethernet 0/0 (F0/0)	Fast Ethernet 0/1 (F0/1)	Serial 0/0/0 (S0/0/0)	Serial 0/0/1 (S0/0/1)
2900	Gigabit Ethernet 0/0 (G0/0)	Gigabit Ethernet 0/1 (G0/1)	Serial 0/0/0 (S0/0/0)	Serial 0/0/1 (S0/0/1)

Note: To find out how the router is configured, look at the interfaces to identify the type of router and how many interfaces the router has. There is no way to effectively list all the combinations of configurations for each router class. This table includes identifiers for the possible combinations of Ethernet and Serial interfaces in the device. The table does not include any other type of interface, even though a specific router may contain one. An example of this might be an ISDN BRI interface. The string in parentheses is the legal abbreviation that can be used in Cisco IOS commands to represent the interface.

10.3.1.11 Lab–Configure and Verify Password Recovery

Topology

Objectives

Part 1: Configure Basic Device Settings

Part 2: Reboot Router and Enter ROMMON

Part 3: Reset Password and Save New Configuration

Part 4: Verify the Router is Loading Correctly

Background/Scenario

The purpose of this lab is to reset the enable password on a specific Cisco router. The enable password protects access to privileged EXEC and configuration mode on Cisco devices. The enable password can be recovered, but the enable secret password is encrypted and will need to be replaced with a new password.

In order to bypass a password, a user must be familiar with the ROM monitor (ROMMON) mode, as well as the configuration register setting for Cisco routers. ROMMON is basic CLI software stored in ROM that can be used to troubleshoot boot errors and recover a router when an IOS is not found.

In this lab, you will change the configuration register in order to reset the enable password on a Cisco router.

Required Resources

- 1 Router (Cisco 1941 with Cisco IOS Release 15.2(4)M3 universal image or comparable)
- 1 PC (Windows 7, Vista, or XP with terminal emulation program, such as Tera Term)
- Console cable to connect to the Cisco IOS device via the console port

Part 1: Configure Basic Device Settings

In Part 1, you will set up the network topology and copy the basic configuration into R1. The password is encrypted to set up the scenario of needing to recover from an unknown enabled password.

Step 1:   Cable the network as shown in the topology.

Step 2:   Initialize and reload the routers as necessary.

Step 3: Configure basic settings on the router.

    a. Console into the router and enter global configuration mode.

    b. Copy the following basic configuration and paste it to the running-configuration on the router.

```
no ip domain-lookup
service password-encryption
hostname R1
enable secret 5 $1$SBb4$n.EuL28kPTzxMLFiyML15/
banner motd #
Unauthorized access is strictly prohibited. #
line con 0
logging sync
end
write
exit
```

    c. Press **Enter** and try to enable Privileged Exec mode.

       As you can see, access to a Cisco IOS device is very limited if the enable password is unknown. It is important for a network engineer to be able to recover from an unknown enable password issue on a Cisco IOS device.

Part 2: Reboot Router and Enter ROMMON

Step 1: Reboot the router.

    a. While still consoled into R1, remove the power cord from the back of R1.

Note: If you are working in a NETLAB pod, ask your instructor how to power cycle the router.

---

    b. From the console session on PC-A, issue a hard break to interrupt the router's normal boot process and enter ROMMON mode.

Note: To issue a hard break in Tera Term, vpress the Alt and the B keys simultaneously.

Step 2: Reset the configuration register.

    a. From the ROMMON prompt, type a **?**, then press **Enter**. This will display a list of available ROMMON commands. Look for the **confreg** command in this list.

```
rommon 1 > ?
alias            set and display aliases command
boot             boot up an external process
break            set/show/clear the breakpoint
confreg          configuration register utility
cont             continue executing a downloaded image
context          display the context of a loaded image
cookie           display contents of motherboard cookie PROM in hex
dev              list the device table
dir              list files in file system
frame            print out a selected stack frame
help             monitor builtin command help
history          monitor command history
```

```
iomemset            set IO memory percent
meminfo             main memory information
repeat              repeat a monitor command
reset               system reset
rommon-pref         Select ROMMON
set                 display the monitor variables
showmon             display currently selected ROM monitor
stack               produce a stack trace
sync                write monitor environment to NVRAM
sysret              print out info from last system return
tftpdnld            tftp image download
unalias             unset an alias
unset               unset a monitor variable
hwpart              Read HW resources partition
rommon 2 >
```

Note: The number at the end of the ROMMON prompt will increment by one each time a command is entered.

b. Type **confreg 0x2142** and press **Enter.** Changing the register to Hex 2142 tells the router not to automatically load the startup configuration when booting. The router will need to be rebooted for the configuration register change to take effect.

```
rommon 2 > confreg 0x2142


You must reset or power cycle for new config to take effect
rommon 3 >
```

c. Issue the **reset** ROMON command to reboot the router.

```
rommon 3 > reset

System Bootstrap, Version 15.0(1r)M15, RELEASE SOFTWARE (fc1)
Technical Support: http://www.cisco.com/techsupport
Copyright (c) 2011 by cisco Systems, Inc.

Total memory size = 512 MB - On-board = 512 MB, DIMM0 = 0 MB
CISCO1941/K9 platform with 524288 Kbytes of main memory
Main memory is configured to 64/-1(On-board/DIMM0) bit mode with ECC disabled


Readonly ROMMON initialized
program load complete, entry point: 0x80803000, size: 0x1b340
program load complete, entry point: 0x80803000, size: 0x1b340


IOS Image Load Test

_____

Digitally Signed Release Software
program load complete, entry point: 0x81000000, size: 0x480ce0c
```

```
Self decompressing the image : ############################################
######################################################################
######################################################################
######################################################################
######################################################################
######################################################################
######################################################################
######################################################################
######################################################################
############################################################ [OK]
```

d. When asked if you would like to enter the initial configuration dialog, type **no** and press **Enter.**

```
Would you like to enter the initial configuration dialog? [yes/no]: no
```

e. The router will complete its boot process and display the User Exec prompt. Enter Privileged Exec mode.

```
Router> enable
Router#
```

Part 3: Reset Password and Save New Configuration

a. While in Privileged Exec mode, copy the startup configuration to the running configuration.

```
Router# copy startup-config running-config
Destination filename [running-config]?
1478 bytes copied in 0.272 secs (5434 bytes/sec)

R1#
```

b. Enter global configuration mode.

c. Reset the enable secret password to **cisco.**

```
R1(config)# enable secret cisco
```

d. Reset the configuration register back to 0x2102 to allow the startup configuration to automatically load the next time the router is rebooted.

```
R1(config)# config-register 0x2102
```

e. Exit global configuration mode.

f. Copy the running configuration to the startup configuration.

```
R1# copy running-config startup-config
Destination filename [startup-config]?
Building configuration...
[OK]
R1#
```

You have successfully reset the enable password on a router.

Part 4: Verify the Router is Loading Correctly

Step 1:   Reboot R1.

Step 2:   Verify that the startup configuration loaded automatically.

Step 3:   Enter Privileged Exec mode.

The new enable secret password should be cisco. If you are able to enter Privileged Exec mode, then you have successfully completed this lab.

Reflection

Why is it of critical importance that a router be physically secured to prevent unauthorized access?

_____

_____

_____

10.3.3.5 Packet Tracer–Using a TFTP Server to Upgrade a Cisco IOS Image

Topology

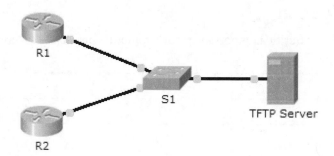

Addressing Table

Device	Interface	IP Address	Subnet Mask	Default Gateway
R1	F0/0	192.168.2.1	255.255.255.0	N/A
R2	G0/0	192.168.2.2	255.255.255.0	N/A
S1	VLAN 1	192.168.2.3	255.255.255.0	192.168.2.1
TFTP Server	NIC	192.168.2.254	255.255.255.0	192.168.2.1

Objectives

Part 1: Upgrade an IOS Image on a Cisco Device

Part 2: Back Up an IOS Image on a TFTP Server

Scenario

A TFTP server can help manage the storage of IOS images and revisions to IOS images. For any network, it is good practice to keep a backup copy of the Cisco IOS Software image in case the system image in the router becomes corrupted or accidentally erased. A TFTP server can also be used to store new upgrades to the IOS and then deployed throughout the network where it is needed. In this activity, you will upgrade the IOS images on Cisco devices by using a TFTP server. You will also back up an IOS image with the use of a TFTP server.

Part 1: Upgrade an IOS Image on a Cisco Device

Step 1:   Upgrade an IOS image on a router.

   a.   Access the TFTP server and enable the TFTP service.

   b.   Note the IOS images that are available on the TFTP server.

   Which IOS images stored on the server are compatible with 1841?

   _____

   _____

c. From **R1**, issue the **show flash:** command and record the available flash memory.

_____

d. Copy the IPBase with strong encryption IOS image (ipbasek9) for the 1841 router from the TFTP Server to **R1**.

```
R1# copy tftp: flash:
Address or name of remote host []? 192.168.2.254
Source filename []? c1841-ipbasek9-mz.124-12.bin
Destination filename [c1841-ipbasek9-mz.124-12.bin]?

Accessing tftp://192.168.2.254/c1841-ipbasek9-mz.124-12.bin....
Loading c1841-ipbasek9-mz.124-12.bin from 192.168.2.254: !!!!!!!!!!!!!!!!!!!!!!
!!!!!!!!!!!!!!!!!!!!!!!!!!!!!!!!!!!!!!!!!!!!!!!!!!!!!!!!!!!!!!!!!!!!!!!!!!!!!!!!!!
!!!!!!!!!!!!!!!!!!!!!!!!!!!!!!!!!!!!!!!!!!!!!!!!!!!!!!!!!!!!!!!!!!!!!!!!!!!!!!!!!!
!!!!!!!!!!!!!!!!!!!!!!!!!!!!!!!!!!!!!!!!!!!!!!!!!!!!!!!!!!!!!!!!!!!!!!!!!!!!!!!!!!
!!!!!!!!!!!!!!!!!!!!!!!!!!!!!!!!!!!!!!!!!!!!!!!!!!!!!!!!!!!!!!!!!!
[OK - 16599160 bytes]

16599160 bytes copied in 3.44 secs (1079726 bytes/sec)
```

e. Verify that the IOS image has been copied to flash. How many IOS images are located in the flash:? _____

f. Use the **boot system** command to load the IPBase image on the next reload.

```
R1(config)# boot system flash c1841-ipbasek9-mz.124-12.bin
```

g. Save the configuration and reload **R1**.

h. Verify the upgraded IOS image is loaded after **R1** reboots.

Step 2:   Upgrade an IOS image on a switch.

a. Access the TFTP server and copy the c2960-lanbase-mz.122-25.FX.bin image to **S1**.

_____

b. Verify that this new image is listed first in the **show flash:** output.

_____

Note: The first image listed in the **show flash:** output is loaded by default.

_____

c. Reload S1 and verify the new image has been loaded into memory.

Part 2: Back Up an IOS Image to a TFTP Server

a. On R2, display the contents of flash and record the IOS image.

_____

_____

b. Use the **copy** command to back up the IOS image in flash memory on **R2** to a TFTP server.

_____

c. Access the TFTP server and verify that the IOS image has been copied to the TFTP server.

10.4.1.1 Packet Tracer—Skills Integration Challenge

Topology

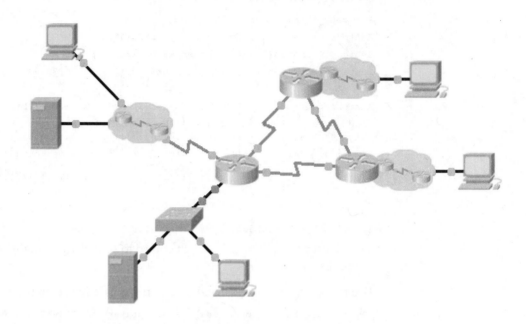

Addressing Table

Device	Interface	IP Address	Subnet Mask	Default Gateway
	G0/0.15			N/A
	G0/0.30			N/A
	G0/0.45			N/A
	G0/0.60			N/A
	S0/0/0		255.255.255.252	N/A
	S0/0/1		255.255.255.252	N/A
	S0/1/0		255.255.255.252	N/A
	G0/0			N/A
	S0/0/0		255.255.255.252	N/A
	S0/0/1		255.255.255.252	N/A
	G0/0			N/A
	S0/0/0		255.255.255.252	N/A
	S0/0/1		255.255.255.252	N/A
	VLAN 60			
	NIC	DHCP Assigned		DHCP Assigned

VLANs and Port Assignments Table

VLAN Number - Name	Port Assignment	Network
15 - Servers	F0/11 - F0/20	
30 - PCs	F0/1 - F0/10	
45 - Native	G0/1	
60 - Management	VLAN 60	

Scenario

This culminating activity includes many of the skills that you have acquired during this course. First, you will complete the documentation for the network. So, make sure you have a printed version of the instructions. During implementation, you will configure VLANs, trunking, port security, and SSH remote access on a switch. Then, you will implement inter-VLAN routing, DHCP, RIPv2, default routing, and NAT on a router. Finally, you will use your documentation to verify your implementation by testing end-to-end connectivity.

Documentation

You are required to fully document the network. You will need a print out of this instruction set, which will include an unlabeled topology diagram:

- Label all the device names, network addresses, and other important information that Packet Tracer generated.

- Complete the **Addressing Table** and **VLANs and Port Assignments Table**.

- Fill in any blanks in the **Implementation** and **Verification** steps. The information is supplied when you launch the Packet Tracer activity.

Implementation

Note: All devices in the topology except _____, _____, and _____ are fully configured. You do not have access to the other routers. You can access all the servers and PCs for testing purposes.

Implement to following requirements using your documentation:

_____

- Configure remote management access including IP addressing and SSH:
  - Domain is cisco.com
  - User _____ with password _____
  - Crypto key length of 1024
  - SSH version 2, limited to 2 authentication attempts and a 60 second timeout
  - Clear text passwords should be encrypted
- Configure, name, and assign VLANs. Ports should be manually configured as access ports.
- Configure trunking.

- Implement port security:

    - On F0/1, allow 2 MAC addresses that are automatically added to the configuration file when detected. The port should not be disabled, but a syslog message should be captured if a violation occurs.

    - Disable all other unused ports.

- Configure VTY lines to be accessible via SSH only

_____

- Configure inter-VLAN routing.

- Configure DHCP services for VLAN 30. Use **LAN** as the case-sensitive name for the pool.

- Implement routing:

    - Use RIP version 2

    - Disable automatic summarization

    - Configure one network statement for the entire _____ address space

    - Configure a default route to the Internet

- Implement NAT:

    - Configure a standard, one statement ACL number 1. All IP addresses belonging to the _____ address space are allowed.

    - Refer to your documentation and configure static NAT for the File Server.

    - Configure dynamic NAT with PAT using a pool name of your choice, a /30 mask, and these two public addresses:

        _____

    - Bind the NAT pool to ACL 1 and configure PAT. Packet Tracer does not grade this command.

    - Activate NAT on all appropriate interfaces.

_____

    Verify _____ has received full addressing information from _____

Verification

All devices should now be able to ping all other devices. If not, troubleshoot your configurations to isolate and solve problems. A few tests include:

- Verify remote access to _____ by using SSH from a PC.

- Verify VLANs are assigned to appropriate ports and port security is in force.

- Verify OSPF neighbors and a complete routing table.

- Verify NAT translations and statics.

    - **Outside Host** should be able to access **File Server** at the public address.

    - Inside PCs should be able to access **Web Server**.

Suggested Scoring Rubric

Packet Tracer scores 70 points. Documentation is worth 30 points.

REGISTER YOUR PRODUCT at CiscoPress.com/register

Access Additional Benefits and SAVE 35% on Your Next Purchase

- Download available product updates.
- Access bonus material when applicable.
- Receive exclusive offers on new editions and related products.
  (Just check the box to hear from us when setting up your account.)
- Get a coupon for 35% for your next purchase, valid for 30 days.
  Your code will be available in your Cisco Press cart. (You will also find
  it in the Manage Codes section of your account page.)

Registration benefits vary by product. Benefits will be listed on your account page under Registered Products.

CiscoPress.com – Learning Solutions for Self-Paced Study, Enterprise, and the Classroom
Cisco Press is the Cisco Systems authorized book publisher of Cisco networking technology, Cisco certification self-study, and Cisco Networking Academy Program materials.

At CiscoPress.com you can
- Shop our books, eBooks, software, and video training.
- Take advantage of our special offers and promotions (ciscopress.com/promotions).
- Sign up for special offers and content newsletters (ciscopress.com/newsletters).
- Read free articles, exam profiles, and blogs by information technology experts.
- Access thousands of free chapters and video lessons.

Connect with Cisco Press – Visit CiscoPress.com/community
Learn about Cisco Press community events and programs.

Cisco Press